Matthias Fischer
Fintech Business Models

I0034918

Reviews of the book

Fintech is not the next 'big thing.' It is the big thing now! Fintech is the new business model for the global financial sector, offering clear and enormous potential for vast economies of scale and scope, massive cost savings and efficiency gains, significant risk reduction, and opening the door to banking for literally billions of currently unbanked people. Professor Fischer has done a masterful job of expertly and informatively taking us through all aspects of the revolutionary new fintech business models. Using state-of-the-art research techniques, he insightfully shows us how fintech firms are financed and how they aspire to create value. His in-depth case studies unlock the keys to success in the fintech sector. His fascinating book is a 'must read' for all financial professionals.

Professor Dr. Stephen Morrell, Professor of Economics and Finance, Andreas School of Business, Barry University, Miami, USA

Matthias Fischer's latest book offers a comprehensive overview of fintech business models around the world. With a very pedagogical approach, and in a particularly fluid style, the author takes us into the strategic logics of these new entrants to finance, who are carriers of innovation and sometimes of disruption, and whose strategies are focused on the need to always meet the emerging expectations of their customers. This precise and well-documented analysis should enable banks to reposition themselves in their ecosystem by studying these new business models, which will enable them to boost their growth.

Professor Dr. Nadine Tournois, Dean of IAE Nice Graduate School of Management, Université Côte d'Azur, France, Chevalier de la Légion d'honneur

Fintech Business Models is a must-have book to understand the rapid and intense changes occurring in the financial sector. New technologies have allowed the birth of new financial species, such as fintech, more adapted to the new digital economy. The content dedicated to the application of blockchain technology helps to understand its opportunities in the financial sector, not only in the means of payment and cryptoactives, but also in how blockchain can make multiple internal processes improve, allowing to optimize the management, efficiency and even security of operations. Without any doubt, this book offers an extraordinary vision of how the fintech sector has become a catalyst for change in banking in the context of the current Digital Society.

Phd. Ricardo Palomo, Full Professor of Finance, Deputy Chancellor for Digital Transformation at Universidad CEU San Pablo, Madrid, Spain and member of the Board of Alastria Blockchain Ecosytem

This book provides a detailed and original overview of the most important fintech business models in the major global markets. Through a savvy use of the well-known

Business Model Canvas methodology, the author explores the unique ecosystem, business model's components, and sources of competitive advantage of successful fintech firms. The book, in particular, offers an insightful and comprehensive analysis of the winning and losing strategies and performances of fintech firms by segment of activity such as, instant digital payments, crowd-funding, robo-advisory, alternative finance, credit & factoring, social trading, personal finance management, blockchain and cryptocurrencies. It is indeed a very unique and valuable study on the fintech industry, its trends, and its emerging business models.

Prof. Dr. Ivo Pezzuto, The International School of Management, Paris, France and Adjunct Professor of International Business and Strategic Management Università Cattolica del Sacro Cuore, Department of Business Management, Milan, Italy

The emergence of fintechs is one of the most relevant drivers of change in the financial services industry. The book presented here delivers an impressing overview of fintechs' activity areas, business models and funding patterns. The book reflects the state of the art of the current fintech world.

Prof. Dr. Jürgen Moormann, Professor of Bank and Process Management at Frankfurt School of Finance & Management, Germany

Matthias Fischer

Fintech Business Models

—

Applied Canvas Method and
Analysis of Venture Capital Rounds

DE GRUYTER

ISBN 978-3-11-070450-1
e-ISBN (PDF) 978-3-11-070490-7
e-ISBN (EPUB) 978-3-11-070493-8

Library of Congress Control Number: 2020946366

Bibliographic information published by the Deutsche Nationalbibliothek
The Deutsche Nationalbibliothek lists this publication in the Deutsche Nationalbibliografie;
detailed bibliographic data are available on the Internet at http://dnb.dnb.de.

© 2021 Walter de Gruyter GmbH, Berlin/Boston
Cover image: olaser/E+/Getty Images
Typesetting: Integra Software Services Pvt. Ltd.
Printing and binding: CPI books GmbH, Leck

www.degruyter.com

Preface

This book gives an insight to the DNA of the most important fintech business models and their funding with venture capital (VC). Fintech examples from Europe, the U.S. and China illustrate the development of important players and the changing consumer behavior in financial services. Fintechs including alternative payments systems, robo-advisors, crowdfunding, credit & factoring, social trading, personal finance management (PFM), blockchain, cryptocurrencies, big data and artificial intelligence are analyzed regarding their relevant value drivers.

Some fintechs will replace the services of banks and others will not succeed in seizing a notable market share. Time will tell which banks will disappear and which fintechs will continue to be successful. But since banks have been trying to create their own fintechs, to acquire fintechs or to collaborate with fintechs, there is no doubt that fintechs have already changed the management strategies in traditional banks.

Tech companies are expanding into the field of banking and of course Google, Apple, Facebook and Amazon (GAFA) are active in financial services, too. Google Pay users can pay in stores or in apps or on websites. Amazon has built and launched tools and services mostly focused on payments, cash deposits and lending. Facebook is active in digital payments and has successfully integrated its Messenger app with American Express, Mastercard, MoneyGram and PayPal. Apple currently offers Apple Pay and is expanding into finance and banking. When we talk about the future of the fintech market we should concentrate not only on the U.S. or the European market; we must look at China as well. Alipay is a relatively young company but with more than one billion users it is the world's leading payment platform.

Overview

One of the main objectives of this book is to systematically explain fintech business models around the world, as well as their financing with venture capital. Readers will get to know the business DNA of fintechs as they are all analyzed with the help of the Business Model Canvas. Each specific fintech business model is structured according to the canvas logic to better understand and compare the new financial industry sector.

The Business Model Canvas shows the key partners of the fintechs with the respective resources, activities, specialization, advantages and the size of their user base. Also covered are the key activities with platforms used for services, sales channels, innovations and applications. And we answer the following questions: What is the value proposition; what value is delivered to the customer? How is the service offered – for example, mobile, internet, platforms? Which of the customer's

https://doi.org/10.1515/9783110704907-202

problems are solved? In addition, the customer relationships are analyzed to answer the questions: For whom is value created? Who are the most important customers? What fees are charged? The customer segments are shown for business-to-consumer (B2C) and business-to-business (B2B) and how they are integrated with the rest of the business model as well as the benefits for the customers. Finally, the channels to reach the customer segments are analyzed and for every business model the significant costs and revenue streams are illustrated. The Business Model Canvas is applied as a common format to compare the many different fintech business models.

Fintechs raised more than $102 billion worldwide in venture capital from April 1992 until April 2020 and this book includes analysis for relevant locations, business segments and financing rounds for this enormous amount of money. Most fintechs are financed with venture capital and very few fintechs have made an initial public offering (IPO), a first offer of shares to the public. This book shows the results of several venture capital financing rounds for different fintech business models. More than 2,000 financing rounds have been analyzed in an empirical study and the book shows for more than 1,000 financing rounds the detailed funding pattern for fintechs in payments, crowdfunding, robo-advisory, social trading, blockchain, credit & factoring, personal finance management and artificial intelligence. The results show which fintech business models get the highest valuations and financings. Our empirical data of venture capital rounds for different fintech sectors delivers findings for more and less successful venture capital financings. The data analysis on the financing rounds could give us important hints for winner and loser fintech segments. It therefore gives investors and entrepreneurs in fintechs relevant information to confirm or change their decisions.

Finally, as the book illustrates developments for the various fintech segments, it also shows possible changes in consumer behavior for financial services or banking needs. Examples of fintech applications are shown that will replace traditional services provided by banks, and which could lead to disruptive changes in the banking environment. But we also learn of limitations in growth for some business models and the problems encountered in the effort to replace banks.

We also added some extra material to the book which is available online. This will allow the readers of the book to have access to additional training material regarding fintechs. The digital supplement provides multiple choice tests where readers can check their knowledge on specific aspects of fintechs covered by the book. We have also added extra material for some features of fintechs for those who would like to take a more detailed look. Check out. *https://www.degruyter.com/view/title/579910* to learn more.

Acknowledgments

Thanks go to many people, particularly those who worked on my Fintech Research Project at the Institute of Technology Nuremberg Georg Simon Ohm and who assisted in preparing this book: Thomas Neuhofer, Toni Oed, Martina Fesenmayr, Nico Wellm, Ferdinand Ehrenberger and Daniel Pirner. I thank Thorsten Lonishen for proofreading and Denise Pangia for copyediting. I also thank the Staedtler Foundation in Nuremberg, Germany, as they financially supported the empirical part of the Fintech Research project. I also want to express my appreciation to those professionals in the financial sector who offered insightful suggestions, for example, Stefan Stalmann. Finally, I would like to thank all those at De Gruyter who worked on this book and Stefan Giesen for supporting the publication.

Matthias Fischer

Contents

1 Fintech markets and players

1.1 The fintech market segments

Fintechs are financial technology companies that are replacing traditional banking services. They offer services in the areas of payments, investment, crowdfunding, credit, factoring, blockchain, cryptocurrencies or personal finance management. The history of fintechs is very new, as most of the fintechs did not exist before 2007. Of course, digital banking services have already been offered for quite a while, especially by direct or internet banks. From April 1992 until April 2020 more than $102 billion in venture capital worldwide have been invested in 8,448 financing rounds.[1] But the bulk of venture capital investments in innovative fintech start-ups just began after the sub-prime crisis and drastically increased during 2014 and 2015. Thousands of small and young companies are trying to take over parts of the value chain in banking with the help of digital business models. Scalability plays an important role in all fintech companies. In many cases the most important user interface is the mobile phone, rather than – as in traditional banking – the bank branch or the desktop browser platform. The new business models put a strong emphasis on customer-focused services and usability, and users are invited to be an active part of the financial service, for example, in crowdfunding or in social trading.

Figure 1.1 categorizes fintech business models according to the services typically provided by banks, insurance companies or financial services providers. Different fintech classifications exist in the academic literature.[2] A primary service offered by banks is the management of client accounts and client payments. Since payments constitute a transaction-oriented business in banks, fintechs started to penetrate this field early on, for example, with alternative payment methods. PayPal, Adyen and Alipay are prominent fintechs in the field of payments. Cryptocurrencies like Bitcoin (BTC), Ethereum (ETH) and Crypto Wallet Services belong to the field of accounts and payments because not only are they an instrument for speculation, but they also aim to eventually replace traditional payment services. Finally, the field of personal financial management (PFM) tools belongs to the traditional banking field of account and payment services. PFM tools from Mint by Intuit, for example, analyze the payment streams of users, categorize the cash-flows and sometimes even derive recommendations for the saving, investment and financing behavior of users.

The fintech segment of financing includes crowdfunding, factoring and credit. Crowdfunding platforms like Kickstarter ask the individual users to finance the needs of other users on the platform. Factoring fintechs offer services along the factoring value chain to retail and corporate clients. In a factoring transaction, receivables are

---

1 Data as of April 30, 2020 from Crunchbase 2020e.
2 See, for example, Allayannis and Becker 2019 or Allayannis and Cartwright 2017.

https://doi.org/10.1515/9783110704907-001

```
                                    ┌──────────┐
                                    │ Fintech  │
                                    └──────────┘
```

Payment & Account	Financing	Investment	Services & Tools	Insurtech	Proptech
Alternative Payment Methods	Credit	Robo-Advice	Comparison Sites	Marketplace	Sales and Rental
Crypto-currencies	Crowdfunding/-investing/-lending	Savings	Infrastructure & IT	Product Focus	Market Places
Personal Finance Management	Factoring	Social Trading	Blockchain	P2P	Real Estate Management
		Pension Scheme	Big Data & AI	Insurance Data	3D/VR Data Rooms

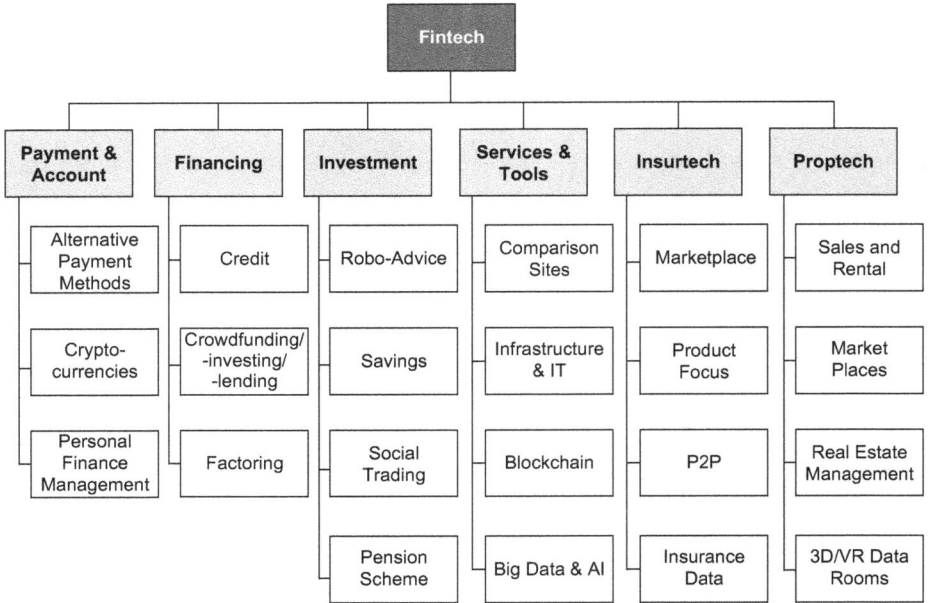

Figure 1.1: Classification of fintech business models.
(Source: own illustration adapted from Fischer 2017, p. 184)

sold to a third party after deducting a discount in order to convert the receivables into cash quickly. And fintechs in the credit business facilitate loans of all sizes, sometimes for businesses, via a mobile phone app.

In the investment sector we can find fintechs that are active in robo-advisory, social trading, savings and pension plans. Betterment and Wealthfront, based in the U.S., are among the first fully automated asset managers or so-called robo-advisors. Vanguard's robo-advisor has one of the highest volumes worldwide in assets under management, with a total of $161 billion as of April 2020.[3] Raisin, based in Berlin, Germany, started in savings but has expanded to other areas of financial investments. And eToro and wikifolio are among the social trading fintechs that provide the option of automatically following other retail investors or so-called signal providers.

Many fintechs also developed as service providers for banks or other fintechs; they provide the infrastructure for various financial services and products.[4] Fintechs like IDnow enable identification and authentication services for banks and insurance companies via video identification. Other infrastructure fintechs offer blockchain services to enable banks to issue obligations or bonds. As the internet

---

3 Friedberg 2020.
4 Fischer 2020.

permits users to easily compare the prices and services of financial products, some fintechs simply specialize in the comparison of financial services. They have become particularly powerful since they have first contact with the client and determine the gateway for the digital sales channels of banks and insurance companies. Examples are wallethub.com, comparexpress.com, check24.de and scout.de. A new fintech segment offers Big Data & AI services.

Insurtechs such as Ethos Life offer services around the value chain of insurance companies in the form of marketplaces, online product offerings, Peer-to-Peer (P2P) services or data providers on customers and potential customers. Another area with close ties to the business fields of banks and insurance companies is the segment of proptechs. Proptechs such as U.S.-based Opendoor or Compass are active in real estate brokerage, real estate financing and real estate insurance. Proptechs offer comparison services as marketplaces, support online sales, collect and analyze the data of target groups or try to position themselves as gatekeepers for all the needs of homeowners.

The application of the Business Model Canvas—one conceptual format for all fintechs

In the following chapters several fintech sectors of Figure 1.1 will be analyzed in detail with their key players, the logic of the business model, case studies and financing history with venture capital financing rounds. The systematic understanding of the fintech ecosystem requires a holistic and comprehensible analysis of the respective business models. This book applies the Business Model Canvas according to Osterwalder and Pigneur to provide a common format for the analysis. The Canvas model helps to highlight the opportunities and challenges of fintech business models and consists of nine building blocks covering the four most important areas of business activity: customers, value proposition, required infrastructure and financial viability:[5]

- *Key partners*: Minimize the risks of the operating activities and help to achieve economies of scale and scope as well as to enable access to the necessary resources.
- *Key activities*: Create the value proposition that reaches customers through the chosen channels, build up the customer relationships and generate revenue.
- *Key resources*: Tangible or intangible resources necessary to deliver the value proposition to the customers.
- *Value proposition*: Product or service for the respective customer segments, either as an innovation or an existing basic product with more and improved features.

---

5 Osterwalder and Pigneur 2013, pp. 14–44.

- *Customer relationships*: The set-up of communication channels and intertwining distribution channels strongly influences the subsequent customer experience.
- *Channels*: Drawing attention to products and services, communication of the value proposition, points of sale and description of customer support after the purchase.
- *Customer segments*: Segmentation of customers according to their needs, behavior or other characteristics to create a customer-tailored value proposition.
- *Cost structure*: Identification of the costs of the value proposition, of the distribution process as well as of the value-adding activities.
- *Revenue streams*: Income, for example, from fixed prices or subscription models.

Figure 1.2 illustrates the interconnected modules of the Business Model Canvas in a compact and clear form. The nine blocks in the model are applied for the final assessment of the respective fintech business models.

Key partners	Key activities	Value proposition	Customer relationships	Customer segments
	Key resources		Channels	
Cost structure			Revenue streams	

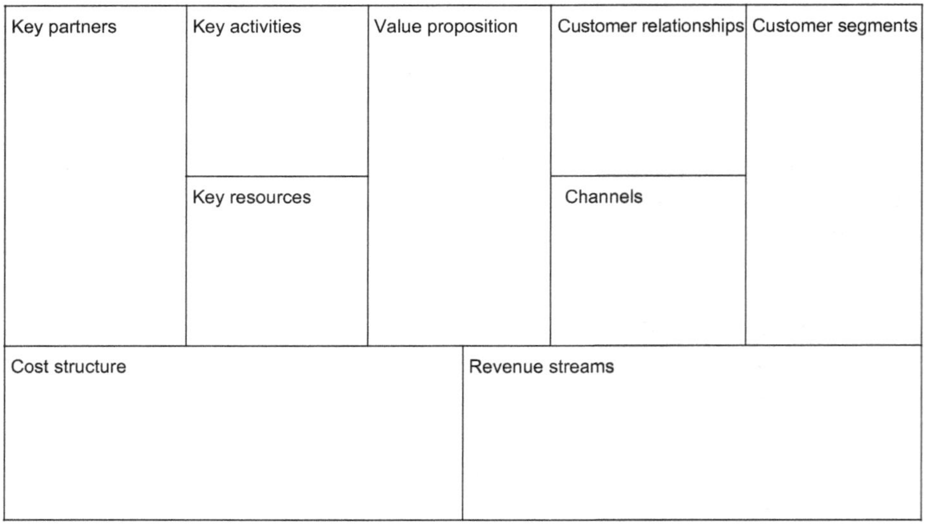

Figure 1.2: The Business Model Canvas.
(Source: own illustration adapted from Osterwalder and Pigneur 2013, p. 44)

Analysis of venture capital financing and data collection

It is important to look at the development of company valuations to get a better understanding of the growth perspectives of different fintech business models. Venture capital investors analyze each business model and the chances of raising money for the fintech depend on the company evaluation by the investors. The evolution of financing amounts of fintechs reflects the growth perspectives in the business models seen by investors. This book analyzes two different financing periods for fintech venture capital financing: April 2000 until June 2017 with a focus on Europe and the U.S., and the period January 2017 until April 2020 with a global view and a comparison of Europe, the U.S. and China.

Three hundred seventy-nine fintechs in Europe and the U.S. were identified in our empirical study with relevant data on financing rounds and valuation between April 2000 and June 2017.[6] Of course there were more than 379 fintechs in the European and the U.S. market. But then they had not been financed with venture capital in the analyzed time or there was no public data on financing rounds available. Existing databases differ in methodologies and due to the relative lack of disclosure surrounding venture capital it is difficult to paint in definitive terms the volume of financing amounts.[7] Therefore, we can conclude that the 379 fintechs in our analysis depict a representative picture of the fintech financing market. The underlying data on fintechs has been gathered from company research including CB Insights, Financial Technology Partners, Mercer Capital, Mergermarket, Pitchbook, Raymond James, Refinitiv, crunchbase.com, empirica-software.com, fintechranking.com, letstalkpayments.com, app.dealroom.co and tech.eu.

A total of more than 2,000 financing rounds have been analyzed and 1,096 financing rounds have been compiled in detail for the period April 2000 until June 2017, comprising 486 European and 610 U.S. deals. The financing rounds show systematic differences in venture capital financing for fintechs in Europe, the U.S. and China. Not enough relevant public data on fintech venture capital financing was available for the period early 2000 until mid-2017 for China. But the financing rounds in China have been included in our study in the sample period January 2017 until April 2020 based on data from Crunchbase. Compared to Europe and the U.S., the venture capital rounds for fintechs in China started several years later, but with very high amounts of money raised and high company valuations. Figure 1.3 summarizes the conceptual model of fintech analysis in this book.

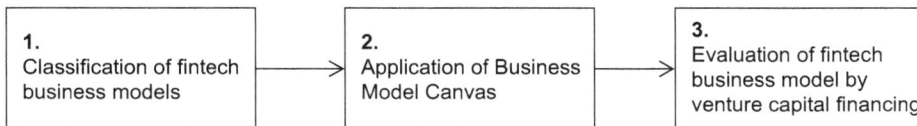

1. Classification of fintech business models	2. Application of Business Model Canvas	3. Evaluation of fintech business model by venture capital financing

Figure 1.3: Conceptual Model of Fintech Analysis.
(Source: own illustration)

---

6 See Appendix A for list of fintechs in research sample.
7 Kaplan and Lerner 2016.

1.2 GAFA versus Alibaba and Co

The fintech market has created many new companies around the world, ranging in employee numbers from a handful to several thousand. Most of these young companies are financed with venture capital. But some tech companies – such as GAFA and their Chinese counterparts, Alibaba, Baidoo and Tencent – have successfully expanded into financial services. So we may come to the conclusion that sooner or later it is all not about fintechs – it is just tech. GAFA and Alibaba, Baidoo or Tencent own the interface to the client and the client data; they can use their platforms to offer all kinds of banking services. They all start with payment services but eventually add more and more financial products and end up posing a real threat to traditional banks.

Google Pay allows users to pay using their phone in stores or for transit, in apps or on websites. Apple Pay is a mobile payment and digital wallet service. It works with Apple devices and accepts credit and debit cards. In the Apple Card – supported by Mastercard and Goldman Sachs – users have a payment tool they can use when Apple Pay is not accepted. Facebook uses its Messenger, with the support of American Express, Mastercard, MoneyGram and PayPal, to enable digital payments. Users can connect their Visa or Mastercard debit card to Messenger to send money to friends on iOS, Android and desktop platforms with zero fees.

Facebook also promotes the development of its cryptocurrency project, Libra. Mass-market usage of the blockchain-based Libra requires strong trust in the new currency (see Figure 1.4). Libra is therefore backed by a reserve of real assets, such as short-term securities from central banks, to guarantee a stable value in the currency. The Libra blockchain will be open-source and is intended to facilitate peer-to-peer payments. The founding members of the Libra association include Facebook/Calibra, Mastercard, Visa, PayPal, Mercado Pago, Stripe, eBay, Lyft, Uber, Spotify AB, Vodafone Group, Coinbase, Anchorage, Xapo and many more. The ambitious Libra project started as an association of the incompatible pairing up of disruptors and traditional payment providers. Due to regulatory pressure from the U.S. and the threat of a ban on Libra in France and Germany, large founding members like Visa, Mastercard, Stripe, eBay and Mercado Pago reconsidered their involvement and have left the association.[8]

Amazon Pay is a digital wallet for customers as well as a payment network for both online and brick-and-mortar merchants or shoppers. The key priority is making payments more efficient for Amazon and easier for customers with a focus on biometric and contactless transactions by means of computer vision, sensor fusion and advanced machine learning. The goal of Amazon Cash – launched in 2017 – is to bridge the gap between online and offline commerce. It allows customers to

---

8 Libra Association 2019; Barber 2019.

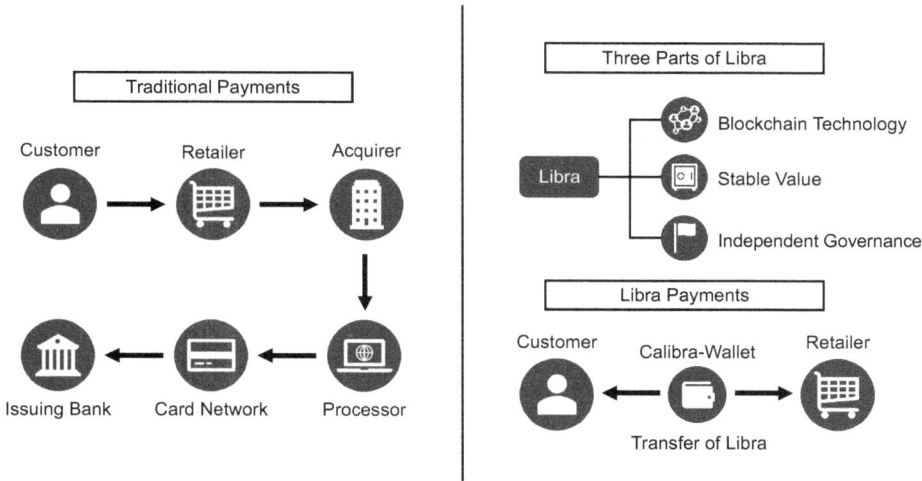

Figure 1.4: Traditional payments versus Libra payments.
(Source: own illustration adapted from Libra Association 2019)

deposit cash via barcode scan or mobile phone, without fees, in a digital account at a partner brick-and-mortar retailer. Customers do not need a bank account or a phone to open an account. Amazon Allowance was launched in 2015 and enables kids, with parental consent, to set up their own Amazon accounts and make purchases. Amazon launched Amazon Lending as early as 2011 to help small and medium businesses (SMBs) and to sell more goods on Amazon. Amazon has partnered with Bank of America (BoA) Merrill Lynch to provide loans to merchants. The loans offered have a maximum payback period of 12 months and, because merchants can provide a lot of information to Amazon, it just takes a few clicks to get approval for a loan. In fact, Amazon seems to want to make loan applications for small businesses as convenient as the shopping experience on Amazon: with only three clicks the loan should be available. In the long run this approach poses a real threat to the short-term credit business of traditional banks.[9]

One could also argue that Amazon only distributes BoA loans and that they do not carry out the lending themselves. And one could critically say that lending is a low return on equity (ROE) business while Amazon is a high ROE business and therefore GAFAs have very little incentive to go into the regulated bank lending business directly. But will the focus on loan distribution be for the long run and will GAFAs never come out of that niche? What happens if ROE becomes more attractive for lending businesses in the future or GAFAs gain experience in that field and own the client

---

9 Amazon Payments Inc online 2019; Friedman 2017; Inside Amazon Videos 2014.

relationship? Then GAFAs could decide to replace more phases in the value chain of bank lending and for example offer homemade GAFA loans to take over profitable products.

China's tech giants, Alibaba, Tencent and Baidoo, have successfully expanded into financial services, especially in the payments area with Alipay and WeChat. Ant Financial is the finance arm of Alibaba and was founded in October 2014. It originated from Alipay (see Figure 1.5). Ant Financial wants to create an open, shared credit system and a financial services platform. The goal is to build a financial ecosystem that provides consumers and small businesses with safe and convenient financial services around the world.[10]

Figure 1.5: Alibaba Group companies.
(Source: own illustration adapted from Alibaba Group 2019)

Alipay is a leading payment platform. It was launched in 2004 and evolved from a digital wallet to a so-called lifestyle enabler. It is Ant Financials' main business. Users book a taxi, a hotel room, buy movie tickets, pay utility bills, make appointments with doctors, or purchase wealth management products directly within the Alipay app. It has more than one billion users and completed more than $8 trillion in transactions in 2017. Alipay is expanding to in-store offline payments, both inside and outside of China. Three characteristics of the financial conditions in China have contributed to the rapid growth of Alipay: low credit card penetration, weaknesses in

---

10 Ant Financial is analyzed in a three-part case study by Zhu et al. 2019.

China's banking system, state-owned enterprises, and China's transition to a consumption-driven economy.[11]

In addition to Alipay, Ant Financial also operates the following platforms: Ant Fortune, a wealth management app; MYbank, a direct bank; Zhima Credit, a credit scoring service; and Ant Financial Cloud, an open platform providing cloud services to financial companies. In 2013 Ant acquired 51% of a small fund manager, called Tianhong Asset Management. Alipay users were leaving leftover money in their Alipay wallets so Ant Financial launched Yu'E Bao – a digital money market fund platform – to allow Alipay users to invest the leftover money in their wallets. Yu'E Bao, which translates as "leftover treasure", allows users to make payments directly from the funds using Alipay and offers on-demand redemption into the user's bank account. Tianhong Yu'E Bao quickly became the world's largest money market mutual fund with more than 500 million users and more than $250 billion of assets under management at the end of March 2018. The Yu'E Bao platform also offers 13 other money market funds from outside fund managers that are not managed by Tianhong but are fully integrated into Ant's online payments service, Alipay.[12]

With Ant Fortune, Ant Financial operates a wealth management app that pairs China's asset management companies with consumers. Ant Financial offers financial newsfeeds, updates on stock movements, an investor community and personalized investment recommendations.[13] Zhima (also known as Sesame) Credit provides a private credit-scoring and loyalty programs. Zhima is a private alternative credit service from Ant Financial and uses data from Alibaba's services to compile its score. The aim is to bridge the "trust gap" between consumers and businesses by assessing individuals' willingness and ability to fulfil a commercial contract. It is powered by Big Data and AI technologies. The scoring algorithms include shopping transactions, bill payment and credit loan repayment history. Ant's JieBei is a consumer credit loan service for Ant users with high Zhima scores. Ant Financial established MYbank in 2015 to provide financial services to small and micro enterprises, as well as individual entrepreneurs.[14]

Ant Financial holds many world records. Up to April 2020 it had the highest pre-money valuation of all fintechs in the world with $136 billion and so far also had the biggest amount of new venture capital in one financing round with $14 billion.[15] Ant Financial has built up services for retail clients and small businesses in payments, financing and investments. Of course, Ant Financial also has to follow the same regulation as banks as soon as they act like a bank and therefore will be regulated in the respective businesses. But thanks to the technological advantage, the experience with

---

11 CBInsights 2018b; Ant Financial 2019.
12 Wildau and Jia 2019.
13 Ant Financial 2019.
14 Ant Financial 2019, 11/6/2018.
15 Data as of April 30, 2020 from Crunchbase 2020e.

big data, the connectivity of finance tools with other consumer habits and the advantage of low data protection barriers in China, the market penetration in many banking fields could be profitable.

1.3 Strong worldwide growth of venture capital-financed fintechs

The money invested in venture capital financing rounds for fintechs has strongly increased. Figure 1.6 shows the total money raised worldwide for different fintech segments from January 2017 until April 2020. More than $22 billion were invested in the area of payments fintechs, more than $5.7 billion in personal finance fintechs and already $1.4 billion in fintechs with a focus on artificial intelligence (AI). The fintech segments can not always be separated clearly and therefore one should assume overlaps between the data of the various fintech segments. But the overall size of money raised shows us systematic trends and differences between the business models. For example, crowdfunding has already existed for a long time, but the amount of money raised from January 2017 until April 2020 is far lower than the volume of blockchain or cryptocurrency fintechs.

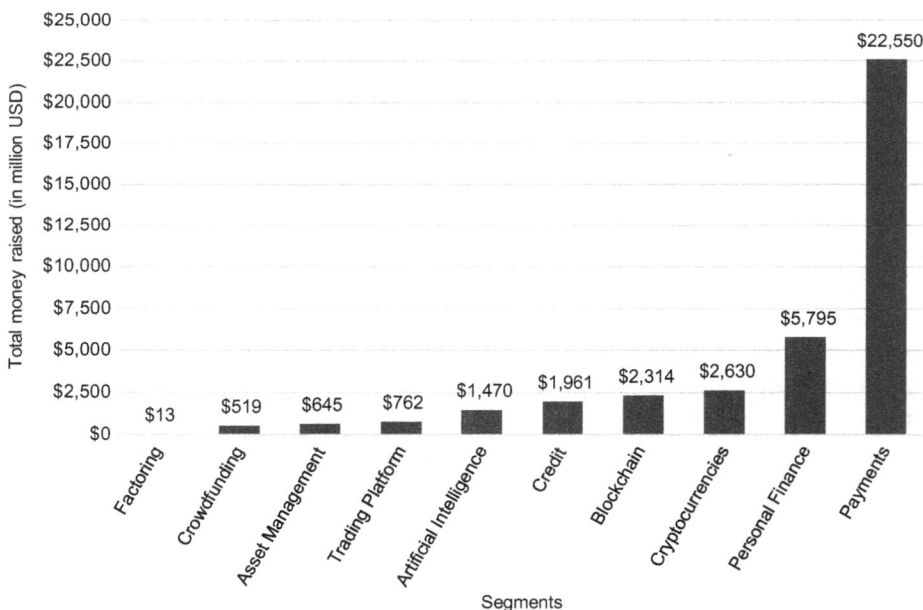

Figure 1.6: Money raised worldwide per segment for sample January 2017–April 2020 (in USD m). (Source: own illustration with data from Crunchbase 2020e)

According to our own empirical analysis based on several databases, in Europe and the U.S. about 379 fintechs were financed with venture capital between 1999 and 2016; 52% or 197 fintechs were founded in Europe and the remaining 182 that is 48%, originated in the U.S.

Figure 1.7 visualizes the split of fintechs founded in Europe and the U.S. each year from 1999 to 2016.

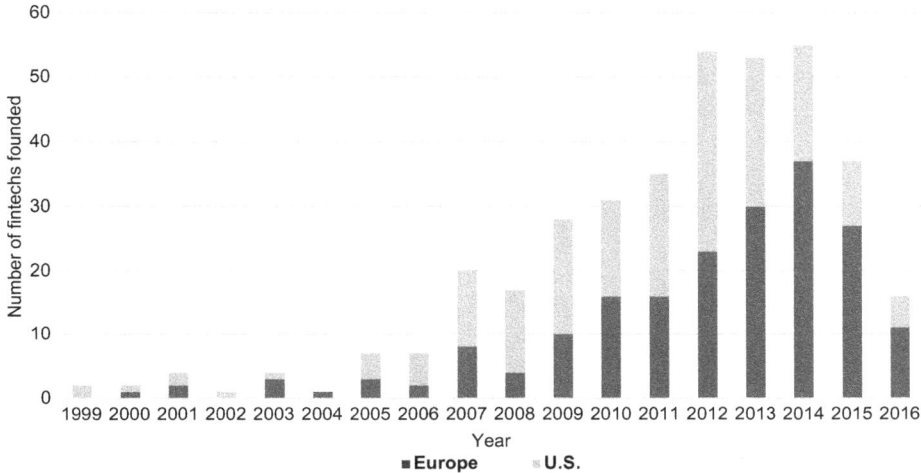

Figure 1.7: Number of fintechs founded in Europe and the U.S. from 1999–2016 for sample April 2000–June 2017.
(Source: own illustration)

No more than seven fintechs were established each year until 2006, the majority of these in the U.S. From 2006 to 2007, the number of fintechs founded almost tripled with eight financial services start-ups founded in Europe and 12 in the U.S. A dip in the following year was more than compensated for in the following years, as more and more fintechs were founded each year until 2012. From 2011 to 2012 the number rose especially dramatically. Between 2012 and 2014, the total of newly founded fintechs stagnated at around 54 fintechs per year and reached its peak of 55 fintechs founded in 2014. Since then, the number of new fintechs has declined significantly, reaching pre-financial crisis levels of 16 newly established start-ups in 2016. One reason for the increase in fintechs founded between 2009 and 2014 can be explained by the strong increase in regulation in the aftermath of the financial crisis, allowing fintechs to enter a market where traditional players struggled to comply with the new requirements.

Of course the post crisis regulatory backlash strongly affected capital market businesses, but retail banking areas also suffered from stronger regulation. For example, traditional investment advisory services in European banks faced new reporting requirements due to Markets in Financial Instruments Directive (MiFID) regulations and therefore the scalable business model of a fully automated asset manager of robo-advisors became more attractive. Another reason for the increase in fintech foundations, especially in the payments area, is technological innovation and positive user experience. Mobile payments and internet payments therefore provide business opportunities for new innovative market entrants. The payments area did not see a post crisis regulatory backlash creating new opportunities for fintechs. But the regulatory environment for payments provides greater opportunities for profitable businesses by tech companies than does the banking regulation for loans and retail investments. That is why the strong market entrance of fintechs and GAFAs in the payments sector is no surprise. What is perhaps surprising, however, is that the amount of venture capital financed fintech foundations in Europe was slightly higher than in the U.S. during the time horizon of the study.

Foundations and innovation potential strongly differentiate the fintech business models

From January 2017 until April 2020 the average amount per financing round was the highest for payment fintechs followed by personal finance fintechs. Figure 1.8 shows that fintechs in blockchain, cryptocurrency and AI had relatively many financing

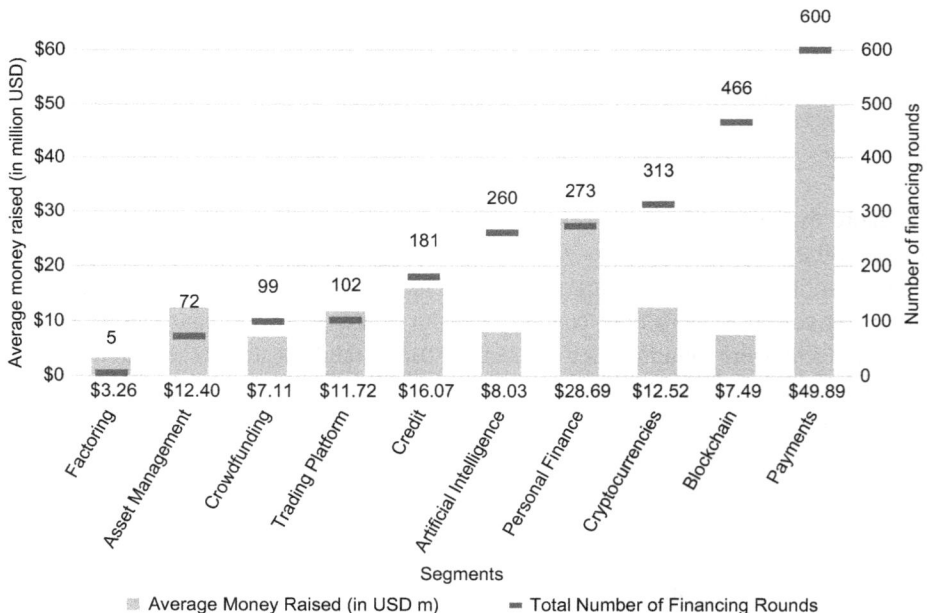

Figure 1.8: Average money raised worldwide per round and total number of financing rounds per segment for sample January 2017–April 2020.
(Source: own illustration with data from Crunchbase 2020e)

rounds, but the money invested per round was relatively small. One reason may be that the later business models started several years behind fintech business models in payments or personal finance. Payments had 600 financing rounds, blockchain had 466 and crowdfunding only 99 rounds from January 2017 until April 2020.

The drop in new fintech start-ups since 2015 is probably explained by the difficulty fintechs experience in finding a suitable niche with a viable business model. Table 1.1 provides an overview of the foundations of fintechs, split into 14 segments each, analyzing different fintech business models.

Until 2004 most deals were focused on infrastructure & IT and alternative payment systems. Between 2005 and 2010 fintechs active in payments or infrastructure & IT still dominated the start-up scene. Fintechs in crowdlending, PFM and robo-advice started to emerge. From 2011 until 2014, 35 fintechs were founded in credit & factoring, 30 in alternative payment systems, 25 in IT infrastructure, 19 in blockchain and cryptocurrencies, 17 in PFM and 17 in robo-advice. Additionally, 13 insurtechs have been founded since 2013. The study sample shows that most innovation potential is in alternative payment systems, representing 18.5% of all fintechs founded, in infrastructure & IT with 15.8%, and in credit & factoring with 14.0%.

On the one hand, the development of the number of venture capital-financed fintechs in various segments suggests attractive business areas. On the other hand, some fintech segments struggle to find suitable niches. One can conclude that some areas in banking will possibly be replaced by fintechs in the medium term whereas others will not. Some of the incumbent fintechs are already so dominant that small fintechs will get squeezed out. And some other small fintechs will not get the chance to succeed as soon as GAFAs enter the market.

Table 1.1: Number of venture capital financed fintechs founded in Europe and the U.S. split into segments of yearly fintech foundations for sample April 2000–June 2017.

Segment	1999	2000	2001	2002	2003	2004	2005	2006	2007	2008	2009	2010	2011	2012	2013	2014	2015	2016
Crowdfunding	0	0	0	0	0	0	0	0	1	0	2	2	1	5	2	5	0	0
Crowdlending	0	0	0	0	0	0	3	1	3	0	0	3	0	1	4	2	1	0
Credit & Factoring	0	1	1	0	0	0	0	1	1	2	4	0	7	11	10	7	4	3
Social Trading	0	0	0	0	0	0	1	0	1	2	0	0	1	0	0	0	1	0
Robo-Advice	0	0	0	0	0	0	0	0	1	3	4	3	2	2	3	10	1	2
Personal Finance Management	0	1	0	0	0	0	1	0	3	1	6	2	4	5	5	3	6	3
Savings	0	0	0	0	0	0	0	0	0	0	0	0	2	3	3	5	1	0
Alternative Payment Methods	1	0	1	0	1	0	2	3	4	6	7	10	5	12	7	6	4	1
Blockchain & Cryptocurrencies	0	0	0	0	0	0	0	0	0	0	0	0	2	2	8	7	4	0
Comparison Sites & Search Engines	0	0	0	0	0	0	0	0	0	0	0	2	0	2	1	0	0	0
Infrastructure & IT	1	0	2	1	2	1	0	1	4	3	4	6	7	10	3	5	6	3
Insurtech	0	0	0	0	0	0	0	0	1	0	0	2	1	2	4	4	7	3
Healthtech	0	0	0	0	0	0	0	1	1	0	0	1	0	0	2	1	0	1
Others	0	0	0	0	1	0	0	0	0	0	1	0	3	2	1	0	2	0
Total	**2**	**2**	**4**	**1**	**4**	**1**	**7**	**7**	**20**	**17**	**28**	**31**	**35**	**54**	**53**	**55**	**37**	**16**

(Source: own illustration)

2 More convenience with alternative payment methods

Online payment systems play a very important role in completing transactions in e-commerce. In addition to the payment systems of banks and credit card providers, alternative payment methods (APMs) are becoming increasingly popular as they enable consumers to manage digital wallets and use mobile devices with biometrics for payment. According to the World Payment Report, by 2021 about half of all payment transactions will be handled through APMs.[16] Figure 2.1 shows an example of a POS terminal for mobile payments in a coffee shop in Zurich.

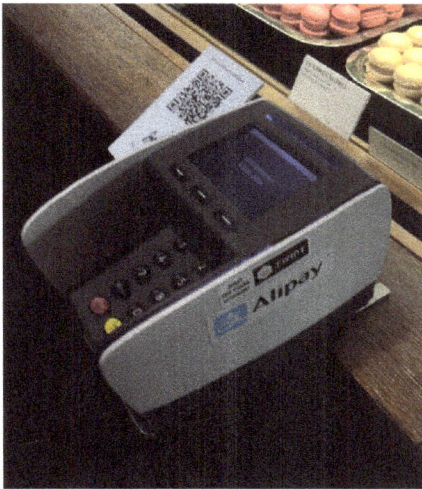

Figure 2.1: POS terminal for mobile payments in coffee shop in Zurich.
(Source: own illustration; own photo)

APMs enable two payment options via a wallet solution – in-person transactions using a smartphone or paying online per digital wallet. When paying by mobile device, the smartphone or smartwatch essentially becomes a wallet. eWallets can be funded in a variety of ways, such as linking it to a bank account, topping it up by credit card or via bank transfer.[17] As digital wallets are fed by bank accounts, some bank payment services will get replaced. However, that can not be said for the entire client relationship with the bank.

---

16 WorldPay 2017, p. 6.
17 Dragt 2018.

https://doi.org/10.1515/9783110704907-002

Figure 2.2 shows a full purchase flow using the Barcode/QR code payment method with the Alipay application on smartphones. A barcode/QR code payment is an offline instant payment solution for the in-store checkout. This payment method allows merchants to collect money by scanning the barcode/QR code displayed in a customer's Alipay Wallet app. The process starts with the customer opening the Alipay app generating a barcode/QR code. This Alipay barcode or QR code is then shown at the checkout. The cashier scans the customer's Alipay barcode or QR code to initiate a payment request. By scanning the barcode/QR code, a payment request is sent to the merchant's backend system and then transmitted to Alipay for further processing. In the last step, Alipay processes the payment request in real time and sends a payment notification to the customer and merchant that the payment is complete or incomplete.[18]

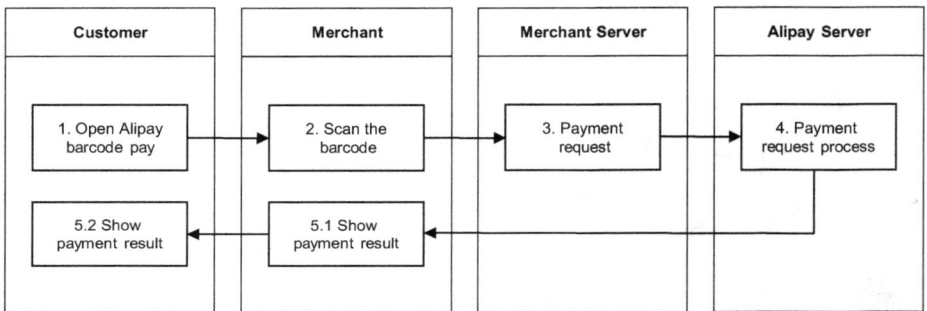

Customer	Merchant	Merchant Server	Alipay Server
1. Open Alipay barcode pay	2. Scan the barcode	3. Payment request	4. Payment request process
5.2 Show payment result	5.1 Show payment result		

Figure 2.2: Alipay payment process flow.
(Source: own illustration adapted from Alipay 2019a)

2.1 The competitors in the payments market

A huge market for mobile payments has developed in China, dominated by the two largest national technology giants Tencent and Alibaba. Their competing apps – WeChat Pay by Tencent and Alibaba's Alipay – are used by almost everyone in the country (see Table 2.1).[19]

Tencent is a Chinese internet service portal founded in November 1998, which went public in 2004 with a valuation of $11 billion. The company released WeChat as a chat service for smartphones in 2011 and enhanced the application with numerous features, including a mobile payment system. Tencent offers value-added

---

18 Alipay 2019b.
19 Jacobs 2018.

Table 2.1: Market overview of alternative payment fintechs.

Company / Payment System	Founding Year / Market Launch	Country	Valuation	Users Payment System
Tencent / WeChat Pay	1998 / 2011	CHN	$670B	600M
Ant Financial / Alipay	2014	CHN	$136B (Alibaba: $680B)	400M
PayPal	1998	U.S.	$230B	210M
Apple / Apple Pay	1976 / 2014	U.S.	$1,645B	87M
Skrill	2001	U.K.	–	36M
Samsung / Samsung Pay	1938 / 2015	KOR	$393B	34M
Amazon / Amazon Pay	1994 / 2007	U.S.	$1,500B	33M
Alphabet (Google) / Google Pay	1997 / 2015	U.S.	$1,000B	24M
Revolut	2015	U.K.	$5.5B	1.5M
Adyen	2006	NL	$42B	0.35M
Klarna	2005	SWE	$5.5B	85M

(Source: Data from Crunchbase company profiles, Company websites, Bary (2020), Coresight Research (2017) and valuation for public companies as of July 30, 2020 from Yahoo Finance (2020a, 2020g, 2020b, 2020e, 2020d, 2020f, 2020c))

services (VAS) for the internet, mobile communications, telecommunications and online advertising. With the goal of meeting the various needs of its online customers, it operates several internet platforms including WeChat, QQ Instant Messenger, QQ.com, QQ Games, Qzone, 3g.QQ.com, PaiPai, SoSo and Tenpay.[20]

Ant Financial Services Group is an online payment service provider founded in October 2014 by the Alibaba group. Ant Financial raised a total of $22 billion in funding over four rounds. With a pre-money valuation of $136 billion Ant Financial is above the threshold of $1.0 billion for start-ups and therefore described as a so-called "unicorn". Its popular platform Alipay allows individuals and companies to execute payments online. Ant Financial also operates Ant Fortune, Zhima Credit, MYbank and Ant Financial Cloud, which offer services in payments, wealth management, independent credit scoring and reporting, private banking and cloud computing.[21]

PayPal offers its users online payment solutions and has quickly become one of the world's leading providers. The PayPal platform operates the subsidiaries

20 Crunchbase 2019g; Millward 2018b.
21 KPMG and H2 Ventures 2017, p. 12; Crunchbase 2019b.

Braintree, Venmo and Xoom, which are available in more than 200 markets worldwide. Consumers and merchants can receive money in more than 100 currencies, withdraw money in 56 currencies and hold funds in their PayPal account in 25 currencies. In 2017 the total payment volume transferred via PayPal amounted to more than $451 billion, with mobile payments accounting for $155 billion.[22] The payment market is still very attractive for new fintechs penetrating the market. For example, in April 2020 $600 million of venture capital was invested in U.S.-based Stripe in one single financing round and the valuation of the company has already reached a multi-billion US Dollar (USD) level.[23]

Well-known companies such as Apple, Samsung and Google have also entered the APM market and provide mobile payment solutions for their in-house mobile devices. All the systems virtually serve the same functionality. They offer contactless payment with a smartphone or a smartwatch at POS systems, which support near field communication (NFC) transactions. So far, Apple Pay has recorded the highest overall usage, with 13% of smartphone users stating that they have accessed the mobile payment solution at least once. Usage rates for Android Pay and Samsung have reached 7% and 5%, respectively.[24]

Amazon Pay allows Amazon customers to use their accounts in online stores that do not belong to Amazon itself. Users can shop on third-party websites without registering, as Amazon Pay forwards them to their Amazon account where they can set the payment details. Skrill (former Moneybookers) has provided international payment solutions for business and personal use since 2001. Its worldwide payment network offers access to more than 100 payment options, with 41 currencies covering 200 countries. Skrill was acquired by Paysafe in 2015. Revolut is a digital alternative to banks that offers free international money transfers and global fee-free spending. Its service includes a prepaid debit card, currency exchange, cryptocurrency exchange, commission-free stock trading and peer-to-peer payments. Revolut raised a total of $336.4 million in funding over 10 rounds.[25]

The Swedish company Klarna offers flexible payment solutions to enhance e-commerce. It supports consumers as they can buy now online and pay later. The fintech Adyen from the Netherlands supports companies in the acceptance of electronic payments from all sales channels. For this purpose, a global multi-channel platform bundles international payment acceptance and procedures with fraud prevention solutions. Other examples of start-up companies in the payments area that have reached unicorn valuation status are Berlin-based bank N26, which has grown primarily with mobile account and payment services, and London-based Revolut.

---

22 PayPal 2019c, 2018c, p. 2.
23 Crunchbase 2020f.
24 Uzialo 2018.
25 Uzialo 2018; Amazon Pay 2019; Crunchbase 2019f; Revolut 2019; Crunchbase 2019e.

2.2 PayPal – important partnerships made it great

PayPal was originally founded as a money transfer service by Confinity in 1999 and became part of X.com due to the merger between X.com and its Confinity in 2000. The merger created a human talent pool including X.com founder Elon Musk, Confinity founder Peter Thiel, Roelof Botha of Sequoia Capital and their teams. This group of people made PayPal a world market leader in online payments.[26]

The most important partner of PayPal is probably eBay. Initially, PayPal was a direct competitor of eBay's online payment system eBay Payments, which was limited to eBay auctions. Due to that disadvantage, PayPal slowly but surely gained ground. When eBay acquired the company for $1.5 billion in 2002, it preserved the target's brand identity since, at that time, PayPal had already positioned itself as the most popular payment method on the eBay platform.[27]

From 2015, the businesses were listed as two separate companies. The spin-off reduced the eBay share by about 50% until eventually PayPal replaced it in the S&P 100. eBay announced in early 2018 that the partnership and current contracts with PayPal would expire at the end of 2020. Adyen, an Amsterdam-based payment company focused on providing back-end payment services such as corporate credit card processing, will replace PayPal. However, there will be no visible Adyen payment button on eBay and PayPal will continue to be offered as a payment option, however, not as well presented as it is today.[28]

Today, PayPal is probably the most popular online payment system in the world. In order to extend its market leadership to mobile transactions, the company acquired Braintree and its subsidiary Venmo for $800 million in 2013. Braintree specializes in mobile and web payment systems for e-commerce companies.[29] Venmo functions as a mobile payment platform and processed more than $40 billion in Total Payment Volume (TPV) in 2017. In the first quarter of 2018, Venmo achieved over $12 billion in TPV, which is an 80% increase compared to the same period in the previous year.[30]

In 2015 PayPal purchased Xoom, an electronic money transfer service, for $890 million. With that acquisition, PayPal secured access to 1.5 million active U.S. customers who sent a volume of $7.1 billion to people in 40 countries according to Q3 2015 results. Sixty percent of Xoom's active users access its service via mobile devices and approximately 97% of the payment volume stems from repeated users.[31]

---

26 Bharath 2017.
27 Bharath 2017.
28 Seetharaman and Mukherjee 2014; S&P Dow Jones Indices 7/14/2015, pp. 1–2; PYMNTS 2018; Rey 2018.
29 Rao et al. 2013.
30 PayPal 2018d.
31 PYMNTS 2015.

Three steps to global leadership

The success of PayPal was based on a three-step strategy described by former eBay CEO Meg Whiteman: "First, PayPal focused on expanding its service among eBay users in the U.S. Second, we began expanding PayPal to eBay's international sites. And third, we started to build PayPal's business off eBay."[32]

In the first phase, customers and payment volumes mainly resulted from the eBay website. The system was very attractive to auction sellers, most of whom were private individuals or small businesses that did not accept credit cards. The service also appealed to auction buyers as they could fund PayPal accounts with credit cards or bank accounts without providing private data to unknown vendors. PayPal offered new users $10 for their registration and rewarded referrals to friends with a commission. The service soon became the most popular payment system on eBay.[33]

In August 2000, PayPal expanded its product range with accounts for residential and business customers, the features and benefits of which were the same. Customers were so eager for the services that X.com had to install security tools against fake accounts. This move led to the buyer and seller protection that PayPal uses today. In September 2002, the PayPal service became even more user-friendly as it gave international customers the possibility to pay in foreign currencies including British pound, Euro, Canadian Dollar and Yen. PayPal executes the currency conversion.[34]

PayPal raised $217 million in five financing rounds between 1999 and 2001, including investors such as eBank, ING Group and Credit Agricole. One year later, in February 2002, PayPal received another $70 million through its IPO, which generated fresh capital for the expansion of its businesses. At the end of Q1 2002, PayPal increased its profit to $1.2 million, compared to a loss of $29.3 million in Q1 2001. Revenues grew by 248% from $14 million in 2001 to $48.8 million in 2002.[35]

Adding value for customers with buyer protection

PayPal uses an encryption software to carry out financial transfers between computers. Users who wish to receive a money transfer via PayPal must have a PayPal account with the e-mail address to which the money was sent. Simple PayPal accounts as well as many financial transactions, including all purchases from merchants who accept PayPal payments, are free.[36]

---

32 Whitman 2006.
33 Grabianowski et al. 2019.
34 Konakanchi 2004, pp. 4–5.
35 Crunchbase 2019d; Konakanchi 2004, pp. 4–5.
36 PayPal 2018e.

Payment recipient

P PayPal   🛒 14,95 EUR

     Hello User!   **Log out**

Pay with

    Credit Union   14,95 EUR
🏛   Bank account •••0000

+ Add payment option

Pay Now

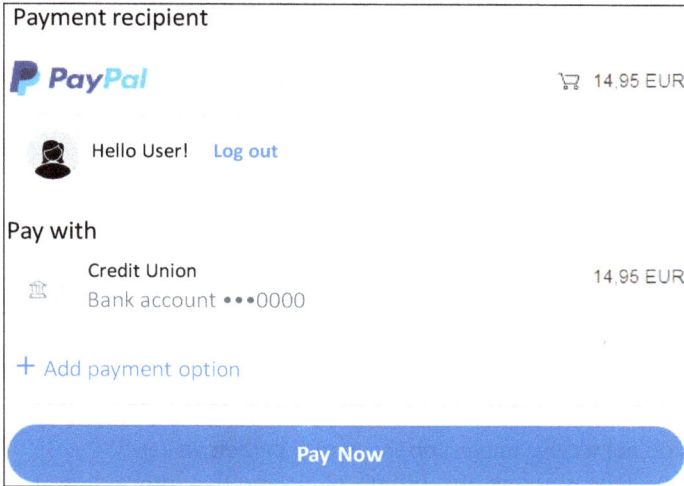

Figure 2.3: PayPal invoice example.
(Source: own illustration adapted from PayPal DE 2020)

Money can be added to or withdrawn from a PayPal account in many ways. For example, users can link their wallet with their bank account or credit cards for direct transactions (see Figure 2.3). Other payout options include the use of a PayPal debit card for purchases or money withdrawals from an ATM.[37]

PayPal also provides protection for its customers. These can claim buyer protection if a purchased item has not been delivered or if the delivered item differs significantly from the merchant's item description. If the request for PayPal buyer protection is successful, the buyer is refunded the amount paid including shipping costs. Seller protection is aimed at certain types of payment default and only applies if the refund or chargeback has been made for specific reasons.[38]

PayPal categorizes its accounts according to the types of users: private customers, business customers, as well as partners and developers. The three account types can use the basic PayPal features and in addition to the standard functions, also share certain characteristics and limitations.[39]

PayPal relies on a mix of online videos, visibility in e-commerce, social media and television commercials. In the U.S., the brand cooperates with Facebook, which allows customers to send and request money via Facebook Messenger using

---

37 PayPal 2018e.
38 PayPal 2017.
39 PayPal 2019b.

PayPal. The peer-to-peer payment system is available in the U.S., where PayPal has connected more than 2.5 million accounts to Facebook.[40]

Two main revenues streams

PayPal acts as an intermediary for financial transactions between buyer and seller. Both parties provide their bank account or credit card information to PayPal, which handles all transactions with various banks and credit card companies. As a result, PayPal generates revenues in two ways. The first stream is the fee charged to the recipients of a payment. Although most transactions are free for the average user, merchants pay a transaction fee. Furthermore, PayPal collects interest on the money remaining in PayPal accounts as it places these funds on one or more interest-bearing bank accounts. The PayPal account holders do not receive interest on the money in their wallet.[41]

PayPal generates revenue through the billing of transaction processing and other payment-related services, which primarily depend on the level of activity handled through the payment platform. PayPal does not charge private accounts but generates revenue from foreign exchange and by offering value-added solutions such as credit and gateway services to consumers and merchants. These pay a variable fee depending on their transaction volume, for example, 2.49% through their PayPal account if the TPV is less than $2,000, and only 1.49% if the TPV is more than $100,000. Revenues for PayPal exceeded $17.8 billion in 2019, growing by 19% at a constant operating margin.[42]

Operating expenses for 2019 reached $15 billion, with 45% being transaction costs. Marketing, customer service, Research and Development (R&D), general administrative expenses and wages account for about 45% of total operating expenses. In 2019 PayPal acquired 37 million new active accounts, resulting in a total of 305 million accounts worldwide. The company executed more than 12.4 billion transactions with a TPV of approximately $712 billion, an increase of 23% compared to the previous year.[43]

2.3 Ant Financial with Alipay – connecting payments and lifestyle

In 2018 Alibaba acquired a 33% equity stake in Ant Financial to strengthen the strategic partnership. According to Alibaba's filing, Ant Financial paid approximately

---

40 Zaveri 2017.
41 Grabianowski et al. 2019.
42 PayPal 2018a, 2019a, 2018b, p. 32, 2020, pp. 4, 12.
43 PayPal 2020, pp. 11–12, 144, 147.

RMB3.4 billion[44] in license and technology fees to the e-commerce giant in fiscal year (FY) 2018. The Alibaba Group is looking to advance the acceptance of mobile payments in the retail sector in order to acquire new users and retain existing clients for the long-term use of Alipay's digital wallet. The partnership intends to facilitate international expansion. In addition, the investment in Ant Financial allows Alibaba to participate in the future growth of the financial technology sector.[45]

The Alipay payment system has been integrated into millions of online sites that allow online shoppers to purchase goods and services through the Alipay application. These include Alibaba's Taobao consumer-to-consumer and Tmall business-to-consumer (B2C) platforms, which are very popular in China. Alipay works with more than 200 domestic finance companies and with more than 250 overseas financial institutions and payment solution providers in its effort to expand globally.[46]

Ant Financial has raised $18.5 billion in five rounds of financing. In the last round (Series C, June 8, 2018), investors funded $14 billion based on a $150 billion post-money valuation. This capital injection was the largest private equity funding round in history paving the way for a possible IPO. It helped Ant Financial to expand its business model from payments to wealth management, with 870 million active users per year worldwide.[47]

Simple and cheap solutions for customers

Just as PayPal processes payments for eBay, Alipay processes transactions on Alibaba's Taobao and Tmall e-commerce platforms. However, Alipay has expanded to mobile payments, which is a growing trend that is reducing the need for cash in China. Alipay offered a simple and cheap solution since most Chinese merchants could not afford expensive POS equipment for bank and credit card processing and only accepted cash. More than half of the 1.37 billion people in the Chinese population have access to the internet, for which more than 99% use mobile phones. Alipay took the opportunity and provided its diverse services on a single smartphone application: Alipay Wallet. Chinese small and medium enterprises (SMEs) print the individual QR-code including the key to their e-wallet on a paper to show it to customers. All payments from customers and SMEs are executed as P2P with zero percent commission.[48]

As Alipay's user numbers increased, many customer accounts showed excess balances. In 2013 Ant Financial introduced its investment product Yu'e Bao, which

---

44 USD–RMB: 7.0959 RMB. Retrieved April 1, 2020 from: OnVista 2020a.
45 Alibaba Group 2018a, p. 1, 2018b, pp. 6, 26; Chen 2018.
46 Ant Financial 2019; Alexa 2018c.
47 Crunchbase 2019b; Chen 2018.
48 Cheng 2018; China Internet Network Information Center 2019, p. 13; Kuzmina 2018.

has become the largest money market fund in the world with a total of $165 billion as of May 2017. Yu'e Bao means "leftover treasure." Accordingly, the idea of the fund is to invest small amounts, which remain in the app when Alipay processes an online payment. The fund has no minimum investment amount and withdrawals and deposits are made through Alipay accounts. Yu'e Bao has more than 260 million investors and according to the company, 70% of individual accounts have a balance of less than RMB1,000 ($145).[49]

Due to its extensive consumer databases, Ant Financial can tap into another important area of financial technology: data analysis. Since results derived from data analysis help to innovate new products and expand the business, not only Ant Financial is growing but the entire Alibaba Group.

More than payments – lifestyle

Founded in 2004, Alipay claims to be the world's largest mobile and online payment platform. By the end of 2018 it had more than 520 million active users and cooperated with more than 200 domestic finance companies.[50]

Alipay is much more than just a digital wallet. It has actually become a lifestyle app. Users can call a taxi, book a hotel room, buy movie tickets, pay utility bills, arrange a doctor's appointment or manage their assets with the app (see Figure 2.4). Millions of merchants accept Alipay throughout China and the in-store payment service covers more than 40 countries and regions around the world. Alipay works with more than 250 overseas financial institutions and payment solution providers to facilitate cross-border payments for Chinese traveling abroad.[51]

Strong customer base by connecting with e-commerce

One reason for the widespread adoption of Alipay is the popularity of the Alibaba e-commerce platforms Taobao and Tmall. The two subsidiaries are the third and fourth most popular websites in China and globally rank eighth and ninth. In the Chinese market, only the Baidu site, a Chinese search engine, and Qq.com, a Tencent platform, are visited more frequently. In general, Alipay has two alternative means of payment: indirect payment with escrow service set by default and instant payment, which is less secure but simple. For indirect payments Alipay does not immediately transfer the money to the seller but keeps it as escrow. When buyers receive the

---

49 Guo 2017.
50 Ant Financial 2019.
51 Ant Financial 2019.

Financial services   **Merchant resources**

Zhima Credit   Restaurants
Ant Check Later   Travel & Leisure
Yu'e Bao   Entertainment
Zhao Cai Bao   Shopping

Social platforms   **Life services**

Love Pay   Mobile Top-Up
Lucky Money   Transfer
Friends   Utilities
                                                          City Services

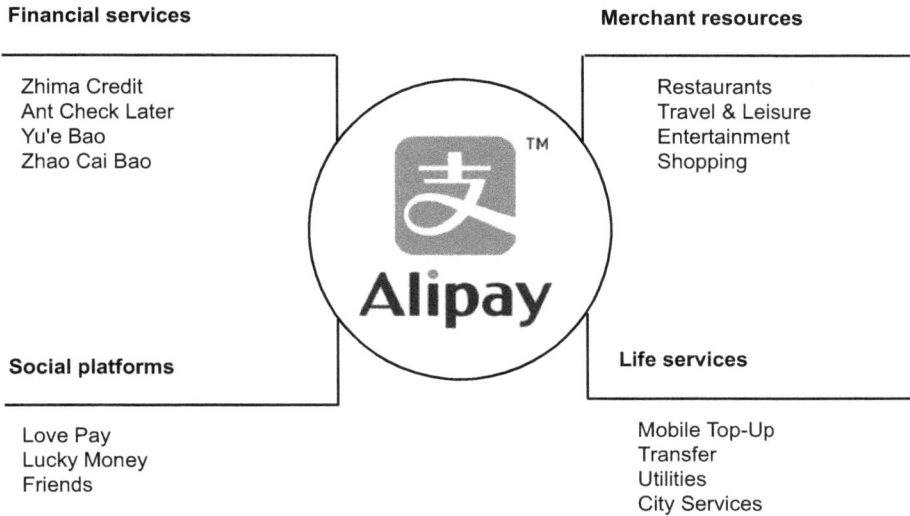

Figure 2.4: Lifestyle App Alipay.
(Source: own illustration adapted from Ant Financial 2019)

goods and are satisfied with the transaction, they send a confirmation to Alipay, which passes the retained money to the respective sellers. The escrow procedure guarantees buyer protection, intensifying the trust of customers in Alipay services.[52]

Ant Financial, along with Alipay and the other platforms, targets the broader Chinese population rather than a special customer base. Alibaba's extensive customer and dealer network is based on a low-cost, low-margin business model. Businesses are not charged any setup fees or transaction fees on Taobao.com. Consumers do not have to pay to shop at Taobao.com and benefit from individual promotions on the website. Instead, revenues are generated through advertising and other trading services. The number of customers is decisive for the company as its low margin model only becomes profitable with a broad user base. Finally, individuals and smaller businesses with limited access to financial services account for a large proportion of users.[53] Due to the large number of customers, the various Ant Financial Platforms generate massive customer information, which creates cross-selling potential within the group.

In addition, Alipay is trying to expand to Europe and the U.S. The company is banking on local transaction processing services that enable both foreign individuals and companies to do business with Chinese consumers in different currencies. Alipay's

---

52 Ant Financial 2019; Alexa 2018a, 2018c; Wang 2011.
53 Lee and Teo 2015, pp. 5–9; Hua 2018.

presence on popular trading platforms, such as the previously described Alibaba subsidiaries Taobao and Tmall, probably serves as its most important distribution channel.[54]

Undisclosed costs and revenues

The cost structures of Ant Financial or Alipay are not publicly available. However, due to the high level of innovation, they probably face high R&D costs. Further important expenses result from international expansion as well as from wages and salaries. Barclays analysts estimate that online payments in 2017 accounted for approximately 55% of Alipay´s total revenue of $8.9 billion. They expect revenues to fall to one-third by 2021 as the company focuses on providing services to its more than 600 million higher-margin customers. Furthermore, due to increased regulatory frameworks, Ant Financial is shifting its focus from payments and consumer credit to technology services, including online risk management and fraud prevention software for banks and other institutions. By 2021, technology services will likely account for approximately 65% of Ant Financial's revenues, compared to approximately 34% in 2017. According to forecasts, total revenue is predicted to increase by 40% annually from 2017 to 2021.[55]

Ant Financial and Alibaba might also shift away from payments and consumer credit to technology services in case of regulatory pressure. This could be a common theme among fintechs; they grow rapidly and have fun as long as the business is small and not regulated as a bank. Once the fintechs have reached a certain scale in lending and deposit taking, regulation, compliance and consumer protection become a huge issue. In case ROE drops to 10%, fintechs like Ant Financial will then rather expand into technology services to explore more profitable markets.

2.4 WeChat Pay – red envelope campaign

The most important key partners for WeChat are other Tencent platforms such as the QQ web portals that provide online social games, music, shopping and more. Tencent controls hundreds of subsidiaries and associates in various business areas, which provide access to large amounts of customer data. For example, the strategic partnership with JD.com, the largest online retailer in China, includes access to more than 300 million customers.[56]

---

54 Adyen 2019; Alexa 2018c.
55 Wu and Zhu 2018; Zhang and Ruwitch 2018.
56 JD.com 2018; Crunchbase 2019g.

Innovative mobile usage and data generation for Tencent

WeChat, or Weixin as it is known in China, was launched in October 2010 at the Tencent Guangzhou Research and Project Center. With about 780 million active users at the beginning of 2011 on its QQ instant messenger and accompanying Qzone social network, Tencent was China's social media giant. Its social networks are rooted in the PC era and the online gaming empire. Although the development of a pure mobile messaging app meant a big break for the company, it recognized the game-changing potential of the smartphone. WeChat has become the most popular mobile app in China with more than 1 billion active users per month chatting, playing games, shopping, reading news, paying for meals and posting their thoughts and pictures. The goal is to address every aspect of their users' lives. In August 2013 the app began offering mobile and cashless payments, which are still challenging e-commerce titan Alibaba.[57]

In many Chinese regions, users access the internet via smartphones instead of laptops or desktops. In contrast to many other social media platforms, WeChat was designed for smartphone usability and has consistently maintained that focus. WeChat applies an "app within an app" model using mini programs. It acts as a platform on which external providers can integrate their applications and does not develop and manage the programs itself. Unlike native apps, mini programs do not need to be downloaded and installed but can immediately be used in the WeChat ecosystem. Consequently, users do not have to leave WeChat to switch between different apps but benefit from a smooth and uncomplicated user experience. One example is the mini app called Bus Steward, which was introduced in 13 cities to enable users to buy bus tickets. By the end of 2017, it had been used 11 million times.[58] Due to the large number of users, WeChat obtains large amounts of information and data. This data can be used by the parent company Tencent or by WeChat itself to improve targeted advertising and analysis of customer preferences.

One app for everyday situations

WeChat combines instant messenger, e-commerce, banking, dating, gaming and marketing on a single platform, where users can shop, order food, book doctors' appointments, book hotels, hire babysitters, hail taxis and much more.[59] With the payment feature, its users can complete mobile payments by linking a bank or credit card to their account. WeChat Pay offers quick pay, QR code payment, in-app

---

57 Deng and Chen 2018; Millward 2018a.
58 China Internet Network Information Center 2019, pp. 7–8; Spöde 2018; Graziani 2018.
59 Chen 2016.

web-based payment and native in-app payment to meet the needs of customers in all types of payment situations and supports the following currencies: GBP, HKD, USD, JPY, CAD, AUD, EUR, NZD, KRW.[60]

WeChat Pay usage almost doubled between 2016 and 2017 due to growing subscriptions to WeChat official accounts and mini programs. This increase was based primarily on daily expenses such as supermarket payments, food payments and online payments. In 2017 transactions in supermarkets and convenience stores were the most popular forms of use with 76.3% of overall usage, with a year-over-year (YOY) growth of 56%. The same year, 45.2% of users used WeChat Pay for online shopping, compared to only 26% in the previous year.[61] As an important step toward marketing and promoting a brand in China, official accounts provide companies with a variety of ways in which to interact with customers on the WeChat platform.[62]

WeChat Pay has a broad customer base, both B2B and B2C. For companies, official accounts are an important feature to interact with their customers; private users appreciate mini programs that provide innovative and user-friendly solutions. The penetration of WeChat Pay is impressive, particularly for users below 18 years of age where the penetration was 97.3% in 2017. For users above the age of 60, WeChat Pay penetration reached 46.7% in the same year.[63]

WeChat is not just an equivalent of popular messaging services like WhatsApp. For many Chinese people, WeChat is an indispensable part of their everyday lives, on which they spend about a third of their entire mobile phone time.[64] To exploit this opportunity, Tencent integrated extra features into its services on top of the basic messaging function. With many of these new features, it entered the market at exactly the right time, supporting WeChat in becoming a giant.[65]

A Chinese tradition for marketing

In 2014 WeChat launched the new feature of giving red envelopes. The concept is based on the old Chinese tradition hangbao, where money is given to relatives in a red envelope during Chinese New Year. Users who wanted to hand over WeChat envelopes were required to connect a bank account to their WeChat Wallet. The red envelope campaign was a huge success, with over one billion WeChat envelopes exchanging hands digitally (see Figure 2.5).[66]

---

60 Weixin 2018.
61 Graziani 2018.
62 Chen 2016.
63 Graziani 2018.
64 Deng and Chen 2018.
65 Brennan 2018.
66 Qian 2015.

Prepare Red Packet	Send Red Packet	Receive Packets

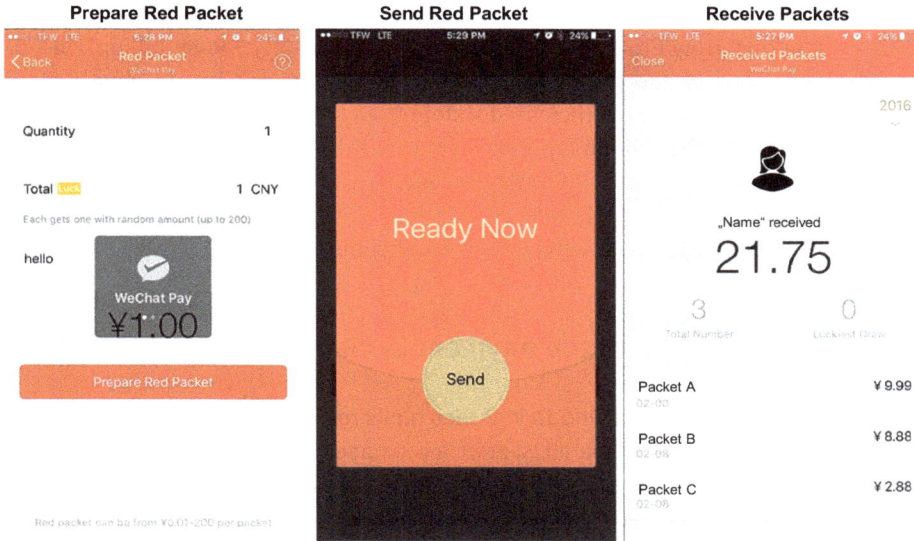

Figure 2.5: WeChat Red Envelopes exchange.
(Source: own illustration adapted from Chen 2016)

WeChat Red Envelope Shake is a giveaway introduced for the most-watched Chinese event of the year, the Spring Festival Gala. During the event, users shake their smartphones to win red envelopes, which consist of cash and coupons and are sponsored by various brands. A total of 1.2 billion red envelopes worth over half a billion RMB ($83 million) were processed during the 2015 gala.[67]

7200% revenue growth in 10 years

Value-added services (VAS) generate fee-based revenue through social networks with digital media subscriptions, membership privileges and virtual article sales. Further sources of revenues are online games such as mobile or PC games. The online advertising segment achieves traffic-based revenues with media and social ads. The last segment earns transaction-based revenues through online payments such as WeChat Pay and Cloud Services.[68] Overall, in 2019 Tencent generated revenues of RMB377.3 billion and net income after tax of RMB95,888 million – representing a YOY growth of 21% and 20%, respectively. VAS contributed 53% of revenue, fintech and Business Services contributed 27%, while online advertising contributed 18% and others 2%.[69]

---

67 Qian 2015.
68 Tencent 2018, p. 8.
69 Tencent 2020, p. 136.

In 2005 revenue amounted to RMB1.47 billion (approximately $206 million).[70] By 2015 revenue had grown to RMB102.86 billion (approximately $14.89 billion), meaning that the company had grown by 7200% in just 10 years.[71] In the same period, Tencent´s net income after tax increased sixfold from RMB485 million (approximately $70 million) to RMB29.11 billion (approximately $4.22 billion).[72]

At the end of 2019, cost of revenues increased by 23% on a YOY basis to RMB209.8 billion, which equals 56% of revenues. This increase reflects higher content costs, costs of payment-related services and channel costs.[73]

2.5 Adyen – disrupting the payment back-end

Customers of online and brick-and-mortar merchants rely on a range of payment methods across the different sales channels. From a consumer perspective, the payment process for products and services by credit card or digital wallet services like Apple Pay seems to be relatively simple. However, several steps are required within a few seconds to perform a standard payment transaction. For example, the process starts at the POS terminal of a retailer; then the payment passes through a payment processing and risk management system to avoid fraud; afterwards the credit card network is used; and finally the transaction arrives at the customer's bank. If the payment is verified, a confirmation is sent back to the POS terminal through the various stages. This patchwork of interconnected process steps has historically grown from old technologies and different providers. To ensure that a payment is processed correctly all parts of this process must function smoothly.[74] The fraud case of the German company Wirecard shows how complex payment transactions are and how difficult it is for external persons to understand the processes. Even the regulatory supervisors and auditors of Wirecard did not completely understand the processes and discovered the fraud in the business processes much too late in the year 2020.

One-stop payment platform versus traditional patchwork

Adyen—Surinamese for "Start over again"[75]—a Dutch payment fintech that went public in 2018, wants to disrupt the traditionally grown patchwork of payment service providers. Adyen operates a single, global payment platform consisting of a

---

70 USD–RMB: 6,9052 RMB. Retrieved April 1, 2020 from: OnVista 2020a.
71 Tencent 2016, p. 3.
72 Tencent 2016, p. 3.
73 Tencent 2020, pp. 136, 197.
74 Adyen 2018, 2020f, p. 4.
75 Adyen 2020e.

plug-and-play package for payments. Its one-stop payment platform provides the following services: the gateway for merchants to initiate payments for a wide range of payment methods, risk management to prevent fraudulent transactions, payment processing to communicate the transaction between the merchant and the customer banks, the bearing of transaction risks and the authorization of the payment to merchants, and finally the payment settlement. Adyen is focused on large and mid-sized international online as well as brick-and-mortar merchants with its customizable payment platform. Adyen offers integration at the POS, as well as online and mobile payments across different channels and markets. By providing a one-stop solution for the processing of payments, Adyen can use the generated payment data to offer value-added services (VAS) such as cross-channel and cross-location analysis of sales and end-customer behavior.[76]

Figure 2.6 depicts the value chain of the Adyen payment platform.

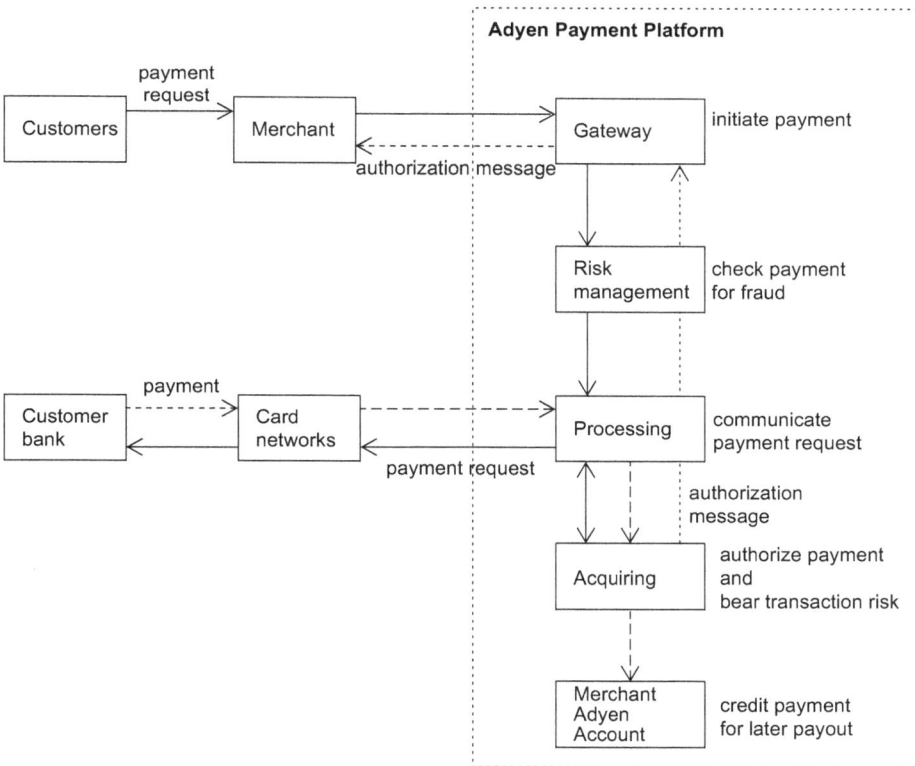

Figure 2.6: Adyen payment value chain.
(Source: own illustration adapted from Adyen 2020c)

---

76 Adyen 2020g, pp. 9–12, 2020d.

Growing with the customer

Europe is Adyen's core market but it also offers its services in the U.S., Brazil, Canada, Hong Kong, Malaysia, Australia, Singapore and New Zealand. Adyen cooperates with system integrators or platforms such as Microsoft Dynamics 365 to provide the payment platform for large international customers in other regions.[77] The company recognizes that its long-term business success and competitiveness is strongly driven by its customers. For this reason, the fintech is organized around customer-centric, interdisciplinary "workflows" that integrate product development with technical and sales staff. The customer centric business organization helps Adyen to continuously enhance its platform and to expand the business through complementary services.[78]

Expenses and revenues

Adyen's main expenses consist of fees for settlement, interchange, payment networks and other costs incurred from financial institutions amounting to €2.1 billion, or 80% of revenues in 2019. Wages and salaries in the same year amounted to €100 million, or approximately 4% of revenues. In 2019 the processed payment volume increased by 51% YOY to €240 billion and net revenues by 42% YOY to €497 million. EBITDA climbed to €279.3 million, which represents a 54% YOY growth.[79]

2.6 Klarna – buy now and pay later in e-commerce

Klarna was founded in Stockholm, Sweden, in 2005 and focuses on payment solutions for online shops. Klarna's "buy now, pay later" service has made it popular with online shoppers and e-commerce merchants alike. The company provides payment solutions for 85 million consumers of 200,000 merchants across 17 countries. Klarna's core markets are Sweden, Germany, Austria and Switzerland with the U.K. and the U.S. considered growth markets.[80]

---

77 Adyen 2020b, 2020g, p. 96, 2020a.
78 Adyen 2020g, p. 10.
79 Adyen 2020g, pp. 7, 87, 94.
80 Klarna Inc. 2020b; Klarna Bank AB 2020e, pp. 3–8, 51.

Country-adapted flexible payment options

Klarna provides different payment solutions for merchants and consumers adapted to local markets. For example in the U.S. consumers have the option to pay for on-line purchases in four interest-free installments debited from their credit card every two weeks or to pay the full amount within 30 days or to finance the purchases free of interest for six months or up to 36 months at an annual percentage rate (APR) of 19.99%. Klarna circumvents the role of a creditor while complying with regulatory requirements through a partnership with WebBank to originate loans to consumers in the U.S.[81]

In Germany, one of Klarnas core markets, consumers have the option of paying the full amount within 14 days. This payment period can be extended up to 60 days for a small fee. Consumers in Germany can also finance the invoice amount inter-est-free for a period of six months and up to a maximum of 24 months at an APR of 14.79%. Klarna additionally enables the payment of invoices by direct debit. The direct debit option was made available by the acquisition of the company SOFORT GmbH in 2014, a fintech that has developed a software solution for instant bank transfers.[82]

Enhanced usability in online shopping

Klarna does not charge the consumer interest or fees for the offered standard pay-ment options and several of the installment purchase options. Instead, only the merchant pays the transaction fee with a fixed and variable component. Despite the loss of revenue for merchants from payment processing fees, Klarna's service model remains attractive for merchants helping to increase their overall revenues. The conversion rate from online shop visitors to buyers increases by 30% if the mer-chant uses Klarna's payment services. Furthermore, Klarna offers merchants several tools to further enhance sales. The tools include the Insight Dashboard to analyze key data like the number of orders or weekly sales and personalized notifications for online shop visitors to make them aware of Klara's flexible payment options available through the merchant even before the checkout process.[83]

The strategy of Klarna also integrates services to improve the shopping experi-ence for consumers and to simultaneously increase the revenues for merchants. The Klarna Card in combination with the Klarna app provides the advantages of Klarna's "buy now, pay later" online payment options for all online and offline

---

81 Klarna Inc. 2020a, 2020e, 2020d, 2018, p. 1.
82 Klarna Bank AB 2020a, 2020b, p. 1, 2020d.
83 Klarna Inc. 2020f, 2020c; Klarna Bank AB 2020c.

purchases made by a consumer. The Klarna Card enables the integration into digital wallets like Google Pay.[84] And with Klarna Boost, merchants benefit from fast and transparent loans. SMEs can borrow money at a flat fee; the repayment of the loan is handled by the deduction of a fixed percentage of the online shop's daily payment settlements. This flexibility allows the merchant to preserve liquidity even in phases of temporarily stagnating sales.[85]

Impressive revenue growth

In 2019 Klarna reported net operating income of SEK7.1 billion[86] growing at an annual compound growth rate (CAGR) of 29.5% from 2011 to 2019. The main drivers of net operating income are commissions with fixed and variable components, for example, from consumers for handling the various long-term financing options or from merchants for consumer transactions. Commissions contribute SEK4.7 billion to the net operating income, up 30% YoY. Net interest income from, for example, consumer and merchant loans grew 34.7% YoY amounting to SEK2.4 billion in 2019.[87]

Klarna has succeeded in reporting a positive net profit since 2011. Due to high investments in a technology hub in Berlin and a focus on growth in the U.K. and U.S. markets this trend was broken with a negative net income of SEK900 million in 2019.[88] Klarna has raised a total of $2.1 billion in venture capital from investors such as BlackRock and Ant Financial, as per the latest financing round announced in October 2020.[89]

2.7 Venture Capital financing of payment fintechs

Between January 2017 and April 2020 the number of venture capital-based financing rounds in the area of payments fintechs amounted to 600 transactions. Table 2.2 shows that the median amount of money raised per round in Europe was $2 million and $3.3 million in the U.S. Not much data on financing rounds for payment fintechs is available for China. Only 14 rounds have been registered in publicly available data bases. And as the total money raised as well as the total premoney valuation falls back almost entirely on Ant Financial, no more conclusions can be made for China.

---

84 Klarna Bank AB 2020e, pp. 7, 12.
85 Klarna Bank AB 11/19/2018.
86 USD–SEK: 9.1758 SEK. Retrieved July 9, 2020 from: OnVista 2020b.
87 Klarna Bank AB 2020e, pp. 6, 22, 32–33, 73.
88 Klarna Bank AB 2020e, pp. 6, 10, 21, 2016, p. 5.
89 Crunchbase 2020i.

Table 2.2: Payment fintechs overview of venture capital financing statistics for sample January 2017–April 2020.

Location	Number Financing Rounds	Median Money Raised	Total Money Raised	Total Pre-Money Valuation
China	14	$11,201,155	$14,151,776,551	$136,000,000,000
Europe	179	$2,000,000	$2,740,426,233	$20,032,102,787
U.S.	199	$3,350,073	$3,113,114,381	$19,483,049,000
World	600	$2,913,682	$22,550,323,492	$199,902,905,780

(Source: own illustration with data from Crunchbase 2020e)

For investors and fintech managers it is important to know the financing patterns of venture capital from early financing rounds until later stage financing rounds. The payment fintech segment was therefore analyzed regarding all publicly available financing rounds. As there was only very limited venture capital funding data available for Chinese fintechs, the funding analysis concentrated on Europe and the U.S. Fintechs in alternative payment methods were initially founded in the U.S. In 2003 the first payment fintech was then established in Europe. Alternative payment methods were one of the first segments in which fintechs were founded – even though the name fintech did not exist at the time. From 2005 onwards, the segment saw a rising number of new fintechs every year until 2010. The majority of the first payment fintechs was founded in the U.S., as 19 fintechs started business there, while only 13 fintechs were founded in Europe. However, since 2010, each year more alternative payment method fintechs have been founded in Europe than in the U.S. After a decrease in founding activity by 50% in 2011 to a total of only five new fintechs, 2012 saw founding efforts reach an all-time high of 12 new start-ups. Ever since that, less and less fintechs have been founded in the payments segment (see Figure 2.7).

In line with the number of fintechs founded, very limited deal activity can be seen until 2005 (see Figure 2.8). No financing rounds were recorded in 2006 despite five fintechs being founded in 2005 and 2006. One explanation could be that deal terms were not publicly disclosed. Between 2007 and 2013, the number of deals constantly rose each year, with the bulk of transactions accounted for by the U.S. This situation changed in 2013 when 21 financing rounds were closed in Europe and 16 in the U.S. In recent years, Europe has also accounted for the larger part of the total amount of deals, even though the number of financing rounds itself has slightly decreased. It can be concluded that alternative payment method fintechs in Europe are less mature than in the U.S. as Europe sees more foundations, which could be a hint that Europe still has more chances for new market entrants.

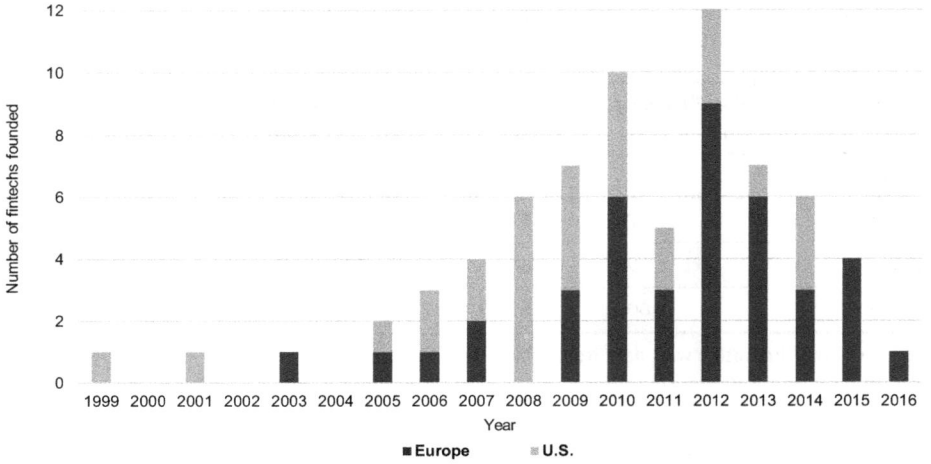

Figure 2.7: Number of fintechs founded in alternative payment methods in Europe and the U.S. from 1999–2016 for sample April 2000–June 2017.
(Source: own illustration)

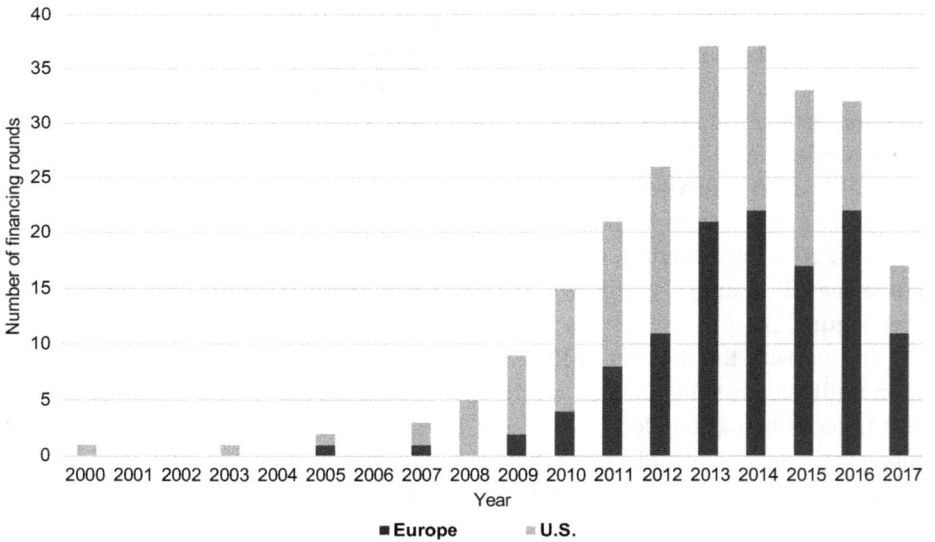

Figure 2.8: Number of financing rounds in alternative payment methods in Europe and the U.S. for sample April 2000–June 2017.
(Source: own illustration)

Figure 2.9 illustrates the development of the annual amount raised in the alternative payments segment. The amount raised increased from €25.1 million in 2008 to €379.4 million in 2012, implying a CAGR of more than 97%. After a drop of more than 48% in the 2013, funding not only recovered in the following three years but rather jumped to new hights of funding as approximately €1,530 million were raised in 2016. The U.S. market was much more successful in raising capital in the payments segment than Europe. However, this changed in 2016. Hence, it may be inferred that alternative payment methods are slowly reaching maturity. This development appears to be substantially further advanced in the U.S. as the average amount raised has been constantly increasing since the number of deals is declining disproportionally to the capital raised. The augmenting average amount raised suggests an increasing trend toward growth financing, which is usually the case when markets mature.

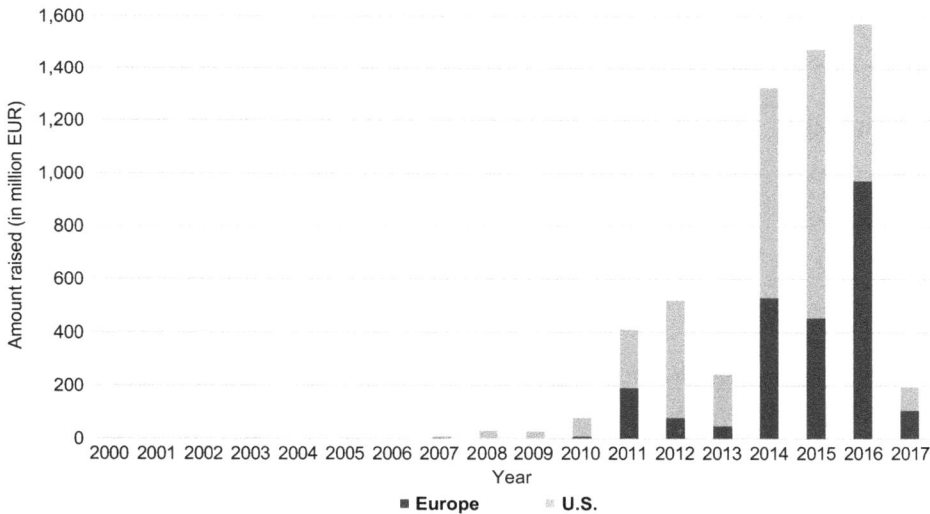

Figure 2.9: Annual overview of amount raised in alternative payment methods in Europe and the U.S. for sample April 2000–June 2017 (in € m).
(Source: own illustration)

Of course, the amounts raised by fintechs are still tiny compared to the multi-billion technology budgets of large banks. Theoretically, large banks could try to copy fintechs, buy them or destroy them competitively. But in practice we can see fintechs that took on an innovative lead position and where banks were too late with their own solutions or where fintechs simply became too expensive to be taken over. PayPal is a good example!

Table 2.3 focuses on a comparison of the median amount raised in each stage of financing. Seed funding in Europe and the U.S. for alternative payment method fintechs is very similar and generally amounts to approximately €1.3 million. In the subsequent financing round A, European payment fintechs manage to raise roughly €1.3 million or approximately 20% more in capital than their counterparts in the U.S. In contrast, U.S. payment fintechs accomplish a 10% higher median funding in round B, before the median amounts raised in both regions in financing round C are pretty much the same. In financing round D, U.S. payment fintechs manage to outperform European start-ups by around 15% as they raise €26.6 million. Due to the lack of data on European alternative payment method fintechs for the financing rounds E and F, no comparison can be made. Out of the three IPOs in this segment, the two public offerings in the U.S. only raised 22% of the one IPO taking place in Europe. The findings do not show any trends or patterns in terms of early or late stage financing.

Table 2.3: Median amount raised in alternative payment methods in Europe and the U.S. for sample April 2000–June 2017 (in € m).

	Seed	A	B	C	D	E	F	IPO
Overall Median	1.3	5.5	12.1	15.9	23.3	32.2	60.4	228.5
Median Europe	1.2	6.2	13.0	15.9	23.2	n/a	n/a	739.7
Median U.S.	1.4	4.9	12.0	15.9	26.6	32.2	60.4	159.2
Sample size *n*	29	50	35	23	17	6	2	3

(Source: own illustration)

Figure 2.10 presents the median increase in amount raised between two successive financing rounds. The sample size is as follows: Seed/A $n = 22$; A/B $n = 32$; B/C $n = 19$; C/D $n = 15$; D/E $n = 6$; and E/F $n = 2$. The median increase in capital raised between seed investment and financing round A in Europe is almost double the increase in the U.S. as it amounts to 457% while it stands at 223% in the U.S. The gap between the U.S. and Europe then decreases to approximately 50% for financing rounds A and B as the median increase in Europe is 142% and 93% in the U.S. In the subsequent round B/C increase, the U.S. produces a 37% higher median amount raised (U.S. 191% vs. Europe 154%). For the round C/D comparison, the increases in amount raised are almost identical, with fintechs in Europe receiving 16% higher funding in financing round D than in round C, while U.S. fintechs receive 14% more.

With regard to the median change in percent between two successive financing rounds, it can be observed that Europe achieves significantly higher early stage funding in alternative payment methods, while there is no valid conclusion for later stage financing. The comparison between financing rounds B and C is dominated by U.S. fintechs and the round C/D comparison sees both regions with marginal

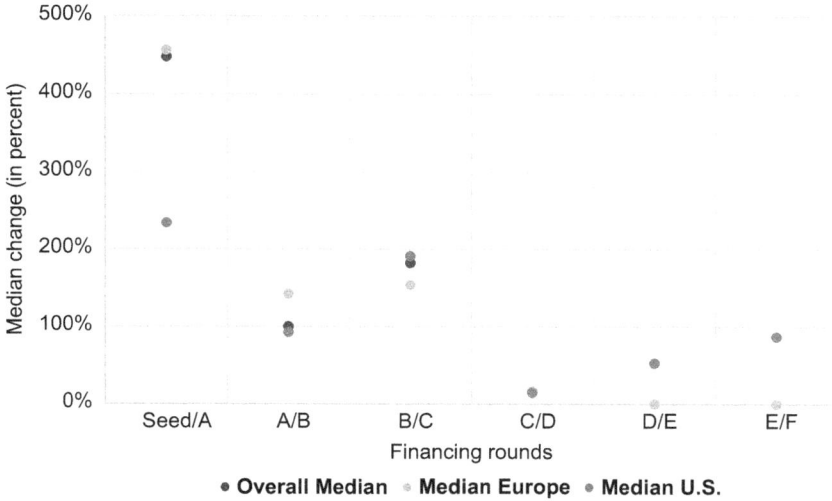

Figure 2.10: Median change in amounts raised between two successive financing rounds in alternative payment methods for sample April 2000–June 2017 (in percent). (Source: own illustration)

differences. In addition, no decisive insights can be gained for the financing rounds E and F due to the lack of publicly available data, especially for Europe.

There is a marginal difference in the time between seed investment and financing round A in the payments segment (see Figure 2.11). Alternative payment method fintechs in Europe and the U.S. need roughly 1.5 years to close their round A after having raised the seed capital. The same can be seen for the period between round A and B, where fintechs in both regions need around 15 months to secure the next funding. However, one should note that European fintechs operating in this segment achieve an increase of 50% more in capital raised than their U.S. counterparts in the same period (Europe 149% vs. U.S. 93%). In order to close round C, it again takes around 15 months from the closing of round B for fintechs in Europe, whereas it takes around three months longer for fintechs in the U.S. Yet, the crucial factor is the aspect that funding in the U.S. also increases by 191% from financing round B to financing round C, while it only increases by 154% in Europe. Hence, the disparities in timing could possibly be explained by the considerably higher increase in amount raised in the U.S. In terms of the time required to secure round D funding, both regions require approximately 1.4 years. Since the median increase in amount raised is also very similar, no substantial differences can be observed. No patterns can be identified for the subsequent financing rounds, mainly due to the lack of information on European alternative payment method transactions. Regarding the patterns in the time between financing rounds it can be concluded that it generally takes around 15 to 18 months for fintechs to secure their following financing.

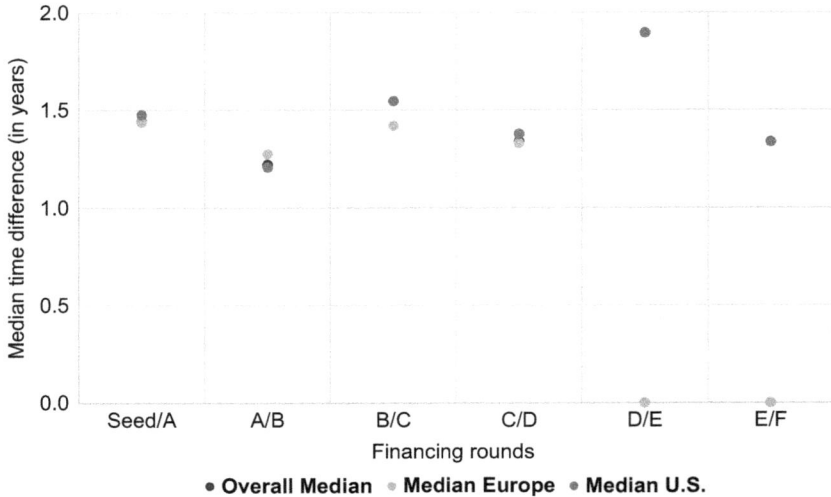

Figure 2.11: Median time difference in years between two successive financing rounds in alternative payment methods for sample April 2000–June 2017.
(Source: own illustration)

Summary

More than half of all payments will be processed via APMs. APMs, especially the three giants PayPal, Alipay and WeChat Pay, are on the rise. PayPal is most popular in Western countries, while Alipay and WeChat Pay dominate the Chinese market. The European players Adyen and Klarna are expanding worldwide and will benefit from digitalization in the financial sector and the outsourcing of payment systems by merchants.[90]

PayPal, Alipay and WeChat Pay have one thing in common. They all founded companies that offer their payment methods on the largest online marketplaces, which soon made them the biggest cash cows in their groups. Online marketplaces like eBay, Alibaba and QQ started small, but their presence on popular internet platforms made them extremely scalable without increasing costs. Due to rising internet and mobile usage, they can reach a particularly large number of users and achieve profitability through low margins and high demand.

Successful payment providers must also be innovative, in terms of products and operations. Alipay was introduced to address the issue of online trust between buyers and sellers and therefore provides payment and escrow services. PayPal is easy and quick to use. All that users must do is download an app to their mobile

---

90 WorldPay 2017, pp. 6, 36–104.

Key partners	Key activities	Value propositions	Customer relationships	Customer segments
Online marketplaces: e.g., eBay, Taobao, Amazon Mobile operating system providers: e.g., Apple, Google Financial services providers to outsource payment options	B2B marketing: Service offerings on popular marketplaces, platforms UX design: Great onboarding and user-friendly service Expand business into complementary services	Requisition-driven payments via NFC, QR code, web-based payment, in-app payments Service offerings beyond payment options; provision of a lifestyle app Worldwide availability and offering of payments in alternative or foreign currencies	Cheap, user-friendly solution Central hub for customer's daily life and expenses Buyer protection or escrow services	Targeting according to the type of user: e.g., private customers, business customers and platform, marketplace developers Targeting of broad mass rather than individual customer solutions
	Key resources Customer access via marketplaces, platforms		**Channels** Regional, culturally specific marketing activities: e.g., Chinese red envelope campaign	
Cost structure Charges from the credit card-issuing bank Fees to credit card companies Transaction costs and transaction-related charges to third-party providers		**Revenue streams** Low cost, low margin business model based on extensive customer and dealer network Free transactions for average users; merchants pay a transaction fee Cross-selling e.g., investment products		

Figure 2.12: Business Model Canvas – payment fintechs.
(Source: own illustration)

device or sign up with an e-mail. Tencent saw its opportunity in the increasing use of mobile phones to develop more than a payment service – the lifestyle app. All big APM providers generate massive data about consumer behavior. In the next step, they can transform this information into smart data and offer their users new features, such as a personal finance management tool or a robo-advisor to invest the remaining capital from the eWallet. Alipay and Yu'e Bao are an innovative combination of mobile payment and finance. Figure 2.12 summarizes the key components for the business model of alternative payment providers.

3 Why robo-advisory will replace many human investment advisors

Banks as well as asset managers have invested heavily in digital investment advisory and automated asset management. On the one hand, the costs of documentation requirements are rising due to the increasing regulation in investment advisory. On the other hand, margins and revenues are diminishing due to cost-effective exchange-traded fund (ETF) products and the need for more transparency of fees as well as the prohibition of kickbacks due to stronger regulation. Retail investors with relatively small investment amounts of between €1,000 and €50,000 are in a difficult situation. They will not get neutral and qualified individual advice from bank advisors as the fee for a bank's advisory service is not sufficient to cover the respective expenses. Therefore, online solutions also present very important alternatives to guarantee neutral and cost-effective advice for customers in the future. Automation can make small-scale business profitable for banks and asset managers.[91]

In 2017 global assets under management of robo-advisory grew above $200 billion. Expectations for worldwide growth of assets under management vary greatly and did range from at least $500 billion to even $8,000 billion in 2020. But the forecasts have been too optimistic and a realistic number should be below $1,000 billion in assets at the end of 2020. The U.S. market, with an expected CAGR of 68% for the period from 2016 to 2020, is leading the market in terms of assets under management (AUM) compared to its European counterpart. However, the European market is likely to accelerate its growth. While in 2020 the forecasted share of American digital advisors is approximately 50% of total global assets managed by robos, the share taken by e.g., the German digital advisors is predicted to reach only 4% to 6%. Distinction of assets under management between online platforms, traditional asset managers and banks will become difficult in the future since more or less everyone will provide digital offers. The growth of robo-advice also depends on the general performance of stock markets. Robo-advisors benefit from a positive capital market development and will experience slowed growth in a stock market downturn. The algorithmic investment strategies of robo-advisors still must prove how successful they are in difficult capital market conditions.[92]

91 Fischer 2017, pp. 187–188, 192–193.
92 Eule 2018; Dapp 2016, p. 2; Kocianski 2016; Deloitte GmbH Wirtschaftsprüfungsgesellschaft 2016; ATKearney 2015, p. 26; Fischer 2017, pp. 187–188.

https://doi.org/10.1515/9783110704907-003

3.1 Key differences in business models of the robos

Robo-advice or robo-advisory is offered by banks, asset managers and fintechs in the field of investments. The term robo-advice comprises the digital service of investment advisory and automated asset management for private clients. The offer mainly aims at private individuals and not at institutional clients. Several different business models can be found in the retail investment area besides robo-advisory, for example, savings fintechs with a focus on the brokerage of high-yield savings accounts rather than on advice for capital market products. Another fintech segment for investments is social trading, with players such as eToro or wikifolio. They support clients with investment tools and information just like robo-advisors do. However, the social trading platforms do not offer asset management contracts for the clients but provide the opportunity to track the trades in capital market products by other members of the respective platform transparently and automatically. Next to traditional asset management, three different business models exist in the area of investment advice for private clients: fully automated asset management, hybrid offerings and self-decision-making platforms (see Figure 3.1).[93]

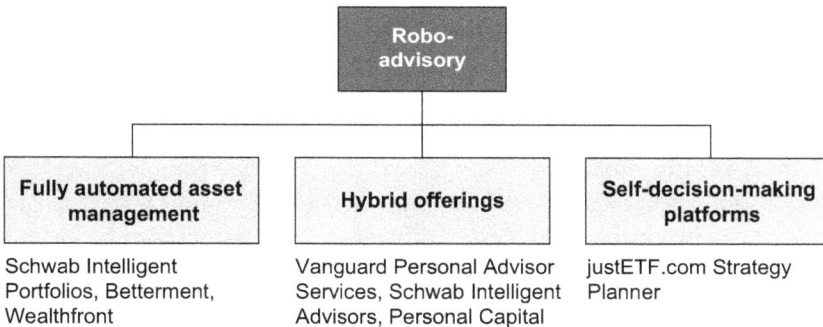

```
                          ┌──────────────┐
                          │    Robo-     │
                          │   advisory   │
                          └──────┬───────┘
         ┌───────────────────────┼───────────────────────┐
┌─────────────────────┐ ┌─────────────────────┐ ┌─────────────────────┐
│ Fully automated asset│ │                     │ │ Self-decision-making │
│     management        │ │  Hybrid offerings   │ │      platforms       │
└─────────────────────┘ └─────────────────────┘ └─────────────────────┘
```

Fully automated asset management	Hybrid offerings	Self-decision-making platforms
Schwab Intelligent Portfolios, Betterment, Wealthfront	Vanguard Personal Advisor Services, Schwab Intelligent Advisors, Personal Capital	justETF.com Strategy Planner

Figure 3.1: Classification of robo-advisors.
(Source: own illustration)

Traditional asset managers

In traditional asset management, the face-to-face contact with clients presents an important part of investment advisory. The target groups are wealthy individuals with normally at least €500,000 to €1 million of liquid assets available for investments. Traditional asset managers offer all available financial products and the fees for clients are relatively high. Typical traditional providers of wealth management

---

93 Fischer 2017, pp. 184–186.

services include UBS or Deutsche Bank. Advisors discuss and determine the individual investment strategy in personal meetings with the clients, and the asset managers execute the rebalancing of the asset classes.[94]

Fully automated robo-advisors

Most new, fully automated robo-advisors have positioned themselves as counterparts to traditional asset management. Investment advisory relies on algorithms and on fully automated processes. A personal meeting with an investor is not emphasized as the query of investment objectives and risk preference takes place online via the website. The target group tends to include price-sensitive investors who are open to technological solutions. The product focus is on cost-effective ETFs to decrease relative administrative costs for the customers of robo-advisors. The investment strategy results from online queries via the website of the providers. The robo-advisor executes the automated rebalancing of the deposits. Typical new start-up providers in the area of robo-advice are Betterment and Wealthfront in the U.S. or Scalable Capital in Germany.[95]

Hybrid offerings

Some asset managers take a market position between traditional investment advisory and fully automated online offers as a hybrid solution. For example, Blackrock in the U.S. linked the traditional business with the online world by purchasing FutureAdvisor. Following the example of Betterment, Wealthfront also examined the adjustment of its pricing model in order to win wealthy individuals with the need for personal meetings or telephone calls as additional customers. The advisor-assisted digital business model links the digital platform with telephone consultation and enables a significant expansion of the target group as it also includes new customers with little affinity for technology and capital market products. Thanks to personal advice, the offer is not limited to ETFs alone, and customers are willing to pay extra for the additional service. The investment strategy can be determined in consultation with the advisor or automatically on the website. The asset manager automatically executes the rebalancing of the asset classes.[96]

---

94 Fischer 2017, p. 185.
95 Fischer 2017, p. 185.
96 Fischer 2017, p. 186.

Self-service robos only for self-decision-makers

The fourth alternative of asset management or investment advisory are robo-advisor platforms for self-decision-makers, which can be referred to as recommendation platforms or self-service platforms. There are normally no contracts for asset management or investment advisory between users and self-decision robos. Such offers, which are often free of charge, can be found on specialized websites or on the websites of banks. The investors receive structured and systematic support for their investment decision. The users answer online questions on investment objective and risk preference and are then presented with an investment proposal broken down according to asset classes. However, the final decision for a specific product, for example an ETF, and the respective execution of an order are the responsibility of the investors themselves, as the recommendation of specific ETFs would result in investment advisor liability of the platform.[97]

The target group consists of financially educated self-decision-makers who refuse to delegate the investment to an asset manager but instead wish to inform themselves about financial products. No personal conversation with the investor takes place, as the user receives the investment proposals exclusively online through an algorithm on the website of the robo-advisor. These offers are either free of charge for the customers or part of payable so-called premium services in which customers are given access to special analytical tools or information on rebalancing. The responsibility for executing the rebalancing of asset classes remains with the client or investor. Due to large gaps in knowledge regarding investing, especially in capital market products, the target group of self-decision-makers with financial interest is relatively small, since most investors require a personal explanation on financial products.[98]

The innovators: Betterment and Wealthfront

The two start-up robo-advisors Betterment and Wealthfront are fierce competitors. Similar to most other robo-advisors, Betterment relies on a questionnaire for risk assessment but also identifies the risk tolerance, which is necessary to set an investment goal. Betterment's Digital Plan is available without a required minimum account balance and charges a fee of 0.25% regardless of the assets in the portfolio up to an overall amount of $2 million. With the Premium Plan, in addition to the service provided by the Digital Plan clients are granted access to a base of certified

---

97 Fischer 2017, p. 186.
98 Fischer 2017, p. 186; Fischer and Wagner 2016.

financial advisors, but investors have to invest at least $100,000 and are charged 0.40% of assets under management.[99]

Wealthfront offers its clients tax-effective, passive investments without any access to financial advisors. Following the approach to make asset management attractive for lower net worth customers, the opening of an account requires a relatively low minimum investment of $500 with an annual fee of 0.25% on the investor's assets under management. Wealtfront's ultimate service, advanced indexing, is an option for investment amounts starting at $500,000 and provides tax optimization services.[100]

Once a client has decided to invest with Wealthfront, the robo starts the risk assessment based on insights of behavioral economics, which allows narrowing the query down to only a few questions. This process results in a portfolio of ETFs, which is regularly monitored and rebalanced. Furthermore, Wealthfront has also developed a mobile financial planner called Path, which helps users to ensure their desired lifestyle at the age of retirement by setting savings targets.[101]

Personal Capital

Personal Capital's business model provides a free analytics tool, which helps customers to manage their entire financial lives. Clients can link all financial accounts, ranging from credit cards to loans, to the software and can develop a long-term financial strategy, while keeping up to date with their net worth at all times. Further services, such as the Investment Checkup tool for investment optimization complement the free offer. Moreover, Personal Capital provides a fee-based package with integrated full-time access to financial advisors. The fees range from 0.49% to 0.89% and decline with a rising investment amount while the available service components increase with higher investible assets.[102]

Scalable Capital

Although Scalable Capital is a relatively small business compared to the U.S. players presented above, the company is one of the largest players in the European robo-advisory market. Scalable Capital was founded in 2014 in Munich, Germany, and is today one of the most promising and fastest growing digital investment managers. It collected more than €1 billion of assets under management during the first

---

99 Benke 2017; Betterment Holdings Inc 2014.
100 Wealthfront Inc. 2019b, 2019c.
101 Wealthfront Inc. 2019a; Carroll 2017.
102 Personal Capital Corporation 2019a, 2019b; Meola 2017b; Personal Capital Corporation 2019c.

28 months of existence. For example, Wealthfront took 2.5 years until it reached €1 billion AUM while Betterment took 4 years to reach that level. Moreover, venture capital presented a decisive factor for its growth. In 2017 the world's largest asset manager Blackrock led a funding round amounting to €30 million alongside existing investors and acquired a significant minority equity stake.[103]

In a Series C financing round, Scalable Capital received further equity capital of €25 million. The investors are BlackRock, HV Holtzbrinck Ventures and Tengelmann Ventures. All investors already had stakes from prior financing rounds in Scalable Capital. The new capital is used in the R&D department to develop new services for retail customers and white label solutions for institutional customers like banks, insurance companies or asset managers. In July 2020, Scalable Capital raised $58 million in a Series D funding (see Figure 3.2). The fintech is investing the funds in Prime Broker, its flat-rate trading service targeting Millenials.[104]

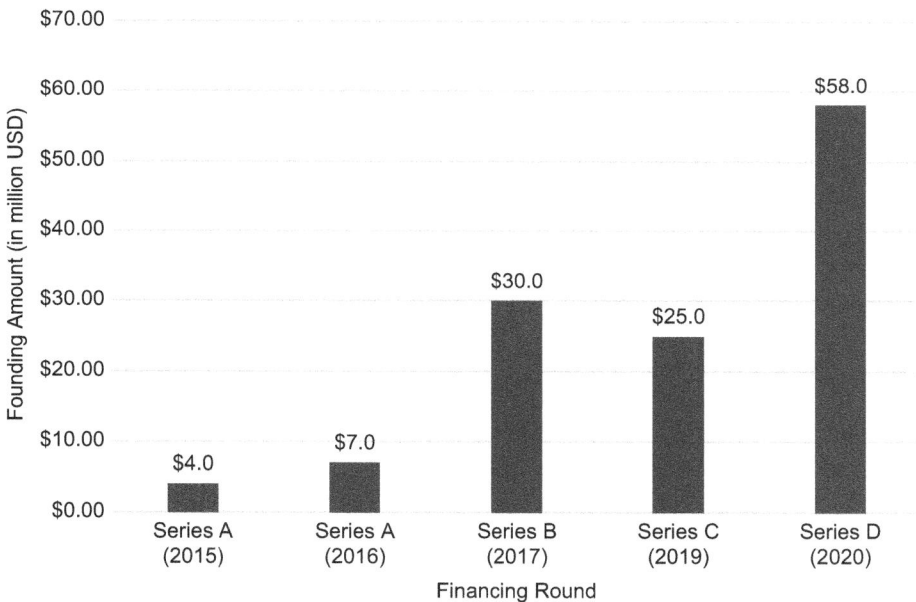

Figure 3.2: Venture Capital Investments in Scalable Capital (in € m).
(Source: own illustration with data from Crunchbase 2020g)

---

103 Scalable Capital Limited 5/29/2018; Meola 2017c; Scalable Capital Limited 6/20/2017.
104 Scalable Capital Limited 8/2/2019; Lunden 2020.

The market leader – Vanguard Personal Advisor Services

Many traditional asset management companies have also developed own fully automated robo-advisors or have bought and integrated fintech robo-advisors. As a consequence, the robo-advisors with the largest volumes in assets under management in the U.S. are Vanguard Personal Advisor Services with $118.5 billion and Schwab Intelligent Portfolios with $43 billion. Vanguard, as an asset manager, has more than 30 million clients. Low cost is also an important feature of Vanguard's traditional asset management services. It is therefore no surprise that the annual cost for Vanguard Personal Advisor Services is only 0.30% of the assets under management.[105]

Vanguard's robo-advice integrates human assistance as a central element. Certified financial advisors create a tax-efficient portfolio tailored to the client's financial situation and with automatic portfolio rebalancing. As an additional feature, investors with an account balance of at least $500,000 receive consultation from a single advisor, while those with a lower balance interact with different employees. Vanguard's service requires a relatively high minimum investment amount of $50,000 along with a relatively low annual fee.[106]

The cost leader – Schwab Intelligent Portfolios robo-advisory

Charles Schwab provides a cost-free package with questionnaire-based risk assessment, recommendation of a goal-based, diversified investment portfolio and portfolio rebalancing as well as continuous monitoring of the customized asset allocation. As there are no fixed fees, Charles Schwab primarily generates its profit from the operating expense ratio charged on its own ETFs and from service fees payed by third party ETF providers that participate in Charles Schwab's ETF investing platform. Just as if investors were to invest on their own, the diversified portfolio consists of low-cost ETFs and a cash allocation. Investors only pay the operating expenses on the ETFs in their portfolios, which include Schwab ETFs. Based on a client's risk profile, a cash portion of the portfolio is placed in a Federal Insurance Corporation (FDIC)-insured deposit at Schwab Bank even if some cash alternatives outside of the program might pay a higher yield.[107]

Schwab Intelligent Portfolios invests in own Schwab ETFs to create revenue for Charles Schwab Investment Management, Inc., a Schwab affiliate that receives management fees on those ETFs. Schwab Intelligent Portfolios also invests in third-party ETFs, and Schwab also receives compensation for providing shareholder

---

105 Friedberg 2020; The Vanguard Group Inc. 2020a, 2020b, p. 7; Business Insider Intelligence 2020.
106 The Vanguard Group Inc. 2014, 2018; Meola 2017a.
107 Charles Schwab & Co Inc. 2019c, 2019b.

services to those third-party ETFs. Schwab also receives brokerage revenue from the execution of ETF trade orders. Clients do not pay for the rebalancing service or the tax-loss harvesting service, as Schwab's robo-advisor has automated these tasks. Tax-loss harvesting is available for taxable portfolios with a balance of $50,000 or more.[108]

Schwab Intelligent Portfolios have up to 20 asset classes in a single portfolio with automated rebalancing, tax-loss harvesting and goal tracking. Schwab's robo-advisor recommends a diversified portfolio in line with the respective risk profiles and financial goals of clients. Based on the answers to a short set of questions on Schwab's website, the robo-advisor selects from among 53 low-cost ETFs. Schwab also offers the possibility to harvest the investment losses to offset the taxes on any investment gains. The portfolio of ETFs covers the following asset classes: gold and other precious metals, U.S. Treasuries, emerging markets bonds, securitized bonds, investment-grade corporate bonds, high-yield bonds, U.S. real estate investment trusts (REITs), emerging markets stocks, international large cap stocks, U.S. large cap stocks, international small cap stocks and U.S. small cap stocks. The clients get 24/7 live support from U.S.-based service professionals and can start with a minimum of $5,000.[109]

Next to this fully automated approach, Schwab Intelligent Advisors also provides access to hybrid asset management and employs certified financial advisors to assist customers with any finance-related issues. However, this more complex and detailed consultancy service entails a fee of 0.28% on a minimum investment amount of $25,000. For invested assets beyond $1.4 million the quarterly charge is capped at $900.[110]

How efficient is the investment strategy of a robo-advisor?

Most investment strategies in robo-advisory rely on modern portfolio theory (MPT) to allocate the amount of investment across different asset classes. The MPT supports building diversified portfolios to maximize the expected return for a given level of market risk and risk aversion of the investor. In this aspect, there is no difference to traditional asset managers. The new feature is the online query to assess the risk tolerance of the investor. However, the systematic problem might be that retail investors give an answer to a question that most unexperienced investors do not even understand. Automated risk classification is very difficult and not a new insight. Robo-advisory research has yet to prove the validity of answers to online questionnaires. Robos also must examine the sustainable causality between risk classification and the automated allocation to an appropriate portfolio of asset classes with matching products.[111]

---

108 Charles Schwab & Co Inc. 2019a.
109 Charles Schwab & Co Inc. 2019a.
110 Charles Schwab & Co Inc. 2019d.
111 Bouchey 2004; Fischer 2017, pp. 192–193.

For example, Wealthfront is one of the largest pure robo-advisors worldwide. Its questionnaire consists of only seven questions on the assessment of risk tolerance and uses a combination of the mean-variance method, the Capital Asset Pricing Model (CAPM) and the Black Litterman model as an investment strategy. The CAPM provides the equilibrium returns for each asset class. After that, the imputed equilibrium returns are adjusted by Wealthfront's individual assessment of long-term returns derived from the Black Litterman model.[112] Although Betterment, the largest start-up robo-advisor in the U.S., also employs the Black Litterman model, the two leading robo-advisors' approaches differ in important details. Wealthfront defines minimum and maximum restrictions for each asset class between 5% and 35%. Betterment does not adjust the investment strategy by own expert assessments but instead fully relies on the model results. Theoretically, both portfolio management approaches are efficient and the results must be evaluated in the long run with empirical studies.[113]

The vast majority of robo-advisors gets exposure to asset classes by investments in ETFs. While about 4 in 10 European robos integrate other actively managed funds as an addition to passive funds, the majority relies exclusively on the use of ETFs. In the U.S., the picture delivers an even clearer trend toward ETFs as unique investment vehicles. This excessive use of index tracking through ETFs is due to obvious advantages such as cost-efficiency and diversification. However, the universe of investible ETFs is sheer infinite and thus robos must set certain criteria to select from the entirety of options. The selection of ETFs usually follows a top-down approach, which results in a remainder of about 3% to 6% of available ETFs.[114]

Wealthfront sets four selection criteria: fee, tracking error, liquidity and securities lending. It keeps the amounts of expense ratios as well as tracking errors at a minimum level. To account for concerns of insufficient liquidity, it disregards newly issued ETFs, which do not yet provide a solid history. Lastly, securities lending in ETFs must remain at a minimum level and is only acceptable if the fund passes related profits through to investors. Betterment approaches the ETF selection similarly and analyzes the total cost of ownership, called TACO, which captures liquidity concerns and cost-driven aspects. This assessment comprises bid-ask spreads, liquidity in terms of trading volume, expense ratio and tracking difference.[115]

---

112 Pirner and Fischer 2018.
113 Fischer 2017, p. 192.
114 Orçun 2017, pp. 4–5, 8.
115 Wealthfront Inc. 2019a, Betterment Holdings Inc.

3.2 Business Model Canvas for robo-advisory

Robo-advisors characterize their value propositions by low cost and largely automated all-in-one investment services to which clients can add a human element in return for a fee. These unique selling propositions (USPs) help to differentiate robo-advisors from their traditional competitors. Moreover, some digital advisors have expanded their offer with add-ons such as assistance in retirement planning to support their clients in organizing the remaining part of their lives. Ultimately, clients can obtain all these services either online or via a smartphone app at any time.

The provision of these values requires certain key activities. Robos onboard their customers online and usually also query their risk tolerance based on a questionnaire on their website. Robo-advisors carry out their main activities – provision of investment advice, realization of the asset allocation through cost-efficient ETFs and portfolio management – with the help of algorithms or automation. The algorithms and automated processes as well as the overall software employed are the key resources. Given that some digital advisors enrich their offered services with the contact to human consultants, certified financial advisors also represent vital resources (see Figure 3.3).

A significant number of robo-advisors has been founded as start-ups financed with venture capital. Venture capitalists and other investors function as key partners. The most important aspect for running a digital advisory business is the integrated partnership with ETF providers and custodian banks, as investment processes, account openings and reporting must be online and automated. Lastly, regulatory authorities are particularly important for robo-advisory. Regulatory authorities can decide whether the specific business model even gets the chance to become successful, irrespective of a possible high demand from clients or retail investors. The robo-advisory business models must comply with the respective regulations or they will be closed.

The different business models of robo-advice enable clients with heterogeneous levels of financial literacy to be served in different customer segments. Initially coming from primarily appealing young and lower net worth investors in the private segment, robo-advisors are additionally shifting their target group toward middle-aged customers as well as corporate clients. Robos address potential investors with higher available assets through a multichannel strategy including traditional phone calls and modern ways of communication via online devices or the usage of artificial intelligence-enabled (AI) methods like chatbots. Robo-advisors can create customer relations with an emphasis on convenient service for investors and cost-effectiveness thanks to a high degree of automation.

The new automated asset managers exert immense cost pressure on their traditional counterparts. Heavy reliance on non-face-to-face communication reduces personnel costs to those for back-office employees and minimizes other operating expenses such as the investment in office buildings. Consequently, the cost structure in robo-advisory is dominated by the development and maintenance of its central elements, that is, the online platform and software. Since the major advantage over

Key partners	Key activities	Value propositions	Customer relationships	Customer segments
ETF providers Custodian banks and wealth managers Venture capitalists and investors Regulatory authorities Banks or insurance companies with large client base	Online on-boarding and risk assessment Algorithm-based portfolio advice and automated adjustments Investment implementation via cost-efficient ETFs Online platform **Key resources** Algorithms, software, and automated processes Certified financial advisors Regulatory permission for portfolio management Access to retail investors	Customized investment advice Low-cost, diversified, and tax-efficient investment solutions Automated rebalancing and monitoring Full-time access to accounts via online platform or smartphones Fee-based access to certified financial advisors Telephone-based advice Support in further finance-related topics, such as retirement savings Management of all financial needs	Personalized, automated communication, e.g., chatbots Transparent, convenient user experience without physical restrictions On-demand contact to human advisor **Channels** Online Mobile apps Telephone Social media TV commercials	Private customers and corporate customers Fully automated robos: tech-savvy and price-sensitive investors Hybrid robos: mass and mass affluent market Self-decision platforms: financially literate self-decision-makers

Cost structure	Revenue streams
Maintenance of online platform	Management fee for assets under management
R&D spending for software and AI development	Income from software licensing
Personnel cost and operating expenses	Product fee for incumbents
Marketing and client acquisition	Fee for premium offers
Reporting to regulatory authorities	Rebalancing fees
Brokerage fees	Profit participation
ETF product cost	Securities lending

Figure 3.3: Business Model Canvas – robo-advisory.
(Source: own illustration)

traditional asset managers is the lower fees, the question is how robos can generate revenues to transform their business into a profitable operation. The management fee on assets under management presents the primary revenue stream charged by robo-advisors. The robos of incumbents like Blackrock additionally receive fees on their own ETFs offered to investors. Some robos complete the product portfolio with a fee-based premium for extra services or participate in the profits of their investors.

3.3 Strategic challenges

Cooperation with a robo-advisor, acquisition or even in-house development?

Before 2014 there was almost no investing activity of banks in robos. But that position has changed. Incumbents are increasingly becoming aware of the new landscape shaped by digital advice. According to a study by PwC, incumbent market participants estimate that their clients have already used fintechs in various product fields: 84% for payment services, 68% for fund transfers and 60% for personal finance management (PFM) services. In digital wealth management, consumers are more prudent with an estimated fintech involvement of only 38%.[116] As of 2017, globally about 45% of traditional financial institutions have partnerships with fintechs and 82% expect to increase such cooperations over the next few years.[117] Considerable benefits for both sides support the positive attitude to cooperation. Robo-advisors make use of the knowledge and the experience of established financial players in regulatory or compliance-related topics in order to overcome barriers to entry easier. For example, robo-advisors with own portfolio management and securities trading need a banking or portfolio manager license to legally participate in this area. Furthermore, the existing customer base of banks facilities and accelerates the market entry of robos and the massive amount of data in banks provides an ideal opportunity to "test" their solutions. At the same time, cooperation also provides opportunities for the counterparties, that is, traditional banks, investment advisors and asset managers. Banks in particular can take advantage of the innovative power of fintechs which is driven by their dynamic and flexible environment.[118]

Furthermore, the cooperation with fintechs enables banks to outsource parts of their Research and Development (R&D) and to accelerate the market launch of their products. A good example is the successful cooperation of ING bank in Germany with the robo-advisor Scalable Capital, while other banks in Germany have tried to set up their own robo-advisors but even after years of development have not managed to gain a significant market share. Ultimately, the success of a fruitful cooperation crucially depends on the awareness of the partially heterogeneous characteristics of the two partners and the creation of an appropriate environment to maintain the innovative character of the fintechs.

Banks can of course also develop their own robo-advisors. But this bears the risk that a prolonged development period may lead to a delayed market entry. In order to prevent customers from migrating to competitors, the acquisition of or cooperation with an existing robo-advisor is therefore a valid important strategic option. Banks

---

116 PwC 2017, p. 5.
117 PwC 2017, pp. 1, 7.
118 Accenture 2016, p. 6; PwC 2017, pp. 5, 7, 9; Juengerkes 2016, pp. 179–182.

spend billions of USD or Euro (EUR) for IT projects every year. The vast majority of software budgets is spent on in-house development while buying external solutions is the exception. In 2015 and 2016 numerous banks and asset managers engaged in fintechs in the area of robo-advice: Ally Financial acquired Tradeking, Goldman Sachs acquired Honest Dollar, Invesco acquired Yemstep, Blackrock acquired FutureAdvisor, John Hancock acquired Guide Financial, Interactive Brokers acquired Covestor, Northwestern Mutual acquired Learnvest, CBOE acquired VEST, TIAA acquired My Vest and Envestnet acquired Upside.[119]

In 2017 BNP Paribas conducted its first fintech investment by acquiring the robo-advisor Gambit, and BlackRock injected a substantial amount of capital into German-based Scalable Capital. All these acquisitions share the feature of established companies buying innovative online investment platforms to assure a rapid market entry into online investment advisory or fully automated asset management. The acquisition of robo-advisors depicts a very commonly applied strategy as the time-consuming in-house development of technology can entail too much uncertainty for established asset managers. However, a strategic acquisition also comes with certain risks. If the integration of the acquired product portfolio into the existing offer does not occur quickly enough, the synergetic potential of the entire transaction might not be exploited fully. To prevent this drawback from happening, the robo might continue its operations outside the scope of the existing company structures.[120]

Investment advisory regulation as chance and limitation

Another challenge to exploit the full market potential of robo-advice is regulation. Robo-advisors must prove that they meet the requirements for transparency and independence from conflicts of interest that traditional asset managers must comply with. The implementation of MiFID II in Europe provides opportunities to strengthen the business models of robo-advice as the new regulatory world requires traditional asset management companies to change their business model. For example, the German Securities Trading Act § 64 (7) regulates the prohibition of benefit in connection with investment services for financial portfolio management. The term "benefit" is defined in § 70 (2) Securities Trading Act and refers to monetary and non-monetary benefits or countervailing benefits. All existing asset management contracts have had to be examined critically regarding the prohibition of benefits. Mixed calculations with relatively low and thus attractive management fees for the customer on the one hand and income from stock commissions or kickbacks for the asset manager on the other

---

119 Fischer 2017, pp. 186–187; Financial Technology Partners 2017, p. 37.
120 CB Insights 2018a; Jessop and Hunnicutt 2017; Everling and Lempka 2016.

hand are no longer allowed. Conflicts of interest must be clearly disclosed to the clients. Robo-advisors can ideally use the required customization of traditional business models to increase their own market potential due to their transparent fees and scalable processes.[121]

In Germany, robo-advisors assess the suitability of asset management for the customer in accordance with § 64 (3) Securities Trading Act. Like traditional asset managers, robo-advisors are required to ask the client about existing knowledge and experience in certain types of financial instruments and investment services. The robo-advisors must clarify the financial circumstances, in particular the loss capacity of the client, to identify the investment objectives and the risk appetite of the customer. Furthermore, the periodic reports of the asset management companies directed to the clients must show how the investment is developing in comparison to the customer's investment objectives and preferences according to § 63 (12), 64 (8) Securities Trading Act.[122]

On the one hand, robo-advisors provide the benefit of automation, but on the other hand, there is a lack of historical experience as to whether the algorithms on the website always properly and sustainably perform the suitability tests required by the regulator. As robo-advisors are in an initial stage of development, robust studies on suitability tests are not available. In particular, it needs to be analyzed to what extent robo-advisors are able to evaluate customers' risk classification with only a few online queries. Initial empirical studies on robo-advice in Germany show that the scoring of risk preferences of private investors by evaluating their input values still has significant room for improvement since the algorithms do not sufficiently take into account all the inputs of the customer.[123] But we also have to take into consideration that financial supervisory authorities around the world react very differently. In some countries the supervisor does not accept any sandbox regime where new innovative solutions can be tested, for example, Germany. In other countries, like the Baltic states or Great Britain, a sandbox regime is allowed, and in countries like China restrictions regarding individual data collection barely exist, which is why new digital business models can develop very fast.

Artificial Intelligence and robo-advice

There is an important difference between the application of AI and automation in robo-advisory. Automation relies on algorithms to avoid manual process steps in wealth management. AI tries to copy and learn human behavior with the goal to act

---

121 Fischer 2017, pp. 187–188.
122 Fischer 2017, pp. 187–188.
123 Fischer 2017, pp. 188, 192; Tertilt and Scholz 2018.

humanlike when carrying out certain tasks. As asset and wealth management traditionally emphasizes the relationship between client and human advisor, AI offers great potential to close the gap left by fully automated robo-advisors in this area. As a result, the customer enjoys a convenient service at low cost while being served by a human-like machine, which continuously learns from experience to self-improve over the course of time.[124]

There are several subsets of AI, but the areas of machine learning and natural language are of particular interest in asset and wealth management. In machine learning, the computer repeatedly connects input in a large set of data with the desired output. This trial and error learning process ultimately results in the ability to predict outcomes from data which per-se seem uncorrelated or unstructured. Robo-advisors can either give the signals resulting from the trial and error analysis to the clients or can use the analysis in their portfolio management. In this context, a neural network or deep learning presents a sophisticated approach in which artificial neurons go through machine learning, get stronger by frequent use or get removed if proven to be unnecessary. This process is repeated with the goal of creating a functioning and intelligent network, which can link input and output based on its own logic without the need for human support.[125]

Robo-advisors can also use neural networks to analyze a massive amount of input parameters about an individual client to assess risk appetite or the suitability of different investment recommendations for the investor. Processing big data on a real-time basis creates a further advantage since it allows robos to offer the execution of rebalancing as well as the adjustment of the tailored investment strategy better than human competitors.[126]

The second important subset, natural language, provides machines with the ability to interpret spoken or written language in the form of human data requests (natural language processing) and allows them to generate language answering these requests (natural language generation). Robo-advisors can use chatbots to manage the interaction with investors more efficiently. The chatbots are trained by machine learning and equipped with the ability to respond to client queries in a text-based and real-time interaction. Yet they have already surpassed a pure Questions and Answers (Q&A) nature and are on the way to developing emotional intelligence. Chatbots can perform several tasks ranging from client onboarding to investment and product recommendations. On the one hand, the application of chatbots significantly enhances customer engagement as clients quickly and conveniently obtain information or support without being restricted to certain office hours or service times. On the other hand, robo-advisors integrating chatbots can benefit, since this type of

---

124 Knezevic and Teelucksingh 2017, pp. 4, 8.
125 Rosov 2017.
126 Rosov 2017; Knezevic and Teelucksingh 2017, pp. 4, 8.

AI presents a very cost-efficient tool for customer service. Moreover, chatbots can be embedded into social media platforms and other messaging applications in order to connect with customers and therefore take customer service to the next level.[127]

In the future retail investors will ask Google Assistant, Siri – Apple's voice-controlled personal assistant – or Amazon's Alexa for investment advice. Pure service answers will not create problems but if it comes to individual investment advisory the virtual assistant AI providers could be made liable for investors' losses that come about due to the answers of the machine. Therefore Google, Apple or Amazon will rather tend to avoid their virtual assistants answering financial questions with high regulatory risks.

A start-up operating with AI is the Canada-based robo-advisor Responsive in which human portfolio managers decide on asset allocation in ETFs and execute rebalancing based on market events. Responsive applies AI in the form of machine learning to signals, which emerge from historical macroeconomic data going back to the 1960s. The company claims to adjust clients' portfolios as an optimal response to such AI-based signals and uses the signals in optimistic markets as well as during turbulent market times. However, like any other robo-advisor, the company still must prove if it can keep its ambitious promises in an economic downturn and in the long run.

Potential pitfalls of AI raise regulatory concerns. The main issue is the fact that neither investors themselves nor regulators can know exactly what hides behind the neural networks and other AI mechanisms. The criticism already arose with the emergence of robo-advisors and automation. However, when it comes to AI, regulators are worried even more, as neural networks learn and develop themselves. Evaluation and monitoring of the dynamic and uncontrollable characteristic of AI are opaque factors. Another disadvantage of AI is that in asset management, a human backbone must be created to build trust in the client relationship, since in turbulent market phases investors do not trust AI 100%. But trust is essential to avoid purely emotional decisions by customers. Ultimately, opinions greatly vary as to whether these drawbacks will affect traditional asset and wealth management negatively or if AI will create an additional boost for robo-advisors.[128]

The price clients pay for robo-advisory – a case study in Germany

According to own empirical analysis of 27 German robo-advisors, about 37% of the analyzed companies operate with the license to manage financial portfolios according to § 32 of the German Banking Act, followed by 26% with a full banking license.

---

127 Thrasher 2018; Adarlo 2018; Borysowich and Bansal 2017, p. 5; Morgan 2017.
128 Doyle 2016; Responsive Capital Management 2019; Schlesinger 2017; Rosov 2017; Berman 2017; Yuen 2017.

In the remaining cases, the robo-advisors serve as pure financial intermediaries or do not own any type of license.

Figure 3.4 shows yearly total costs for investors from 27 providers. Total cost indications are provided in ranges in order to take into account the minimum and maximum Total Expense Ratio (TER) of ETFs and to consider the upper and lower bounds of administration fees (% of investment amount) which usually decline with an increasing investment sum.

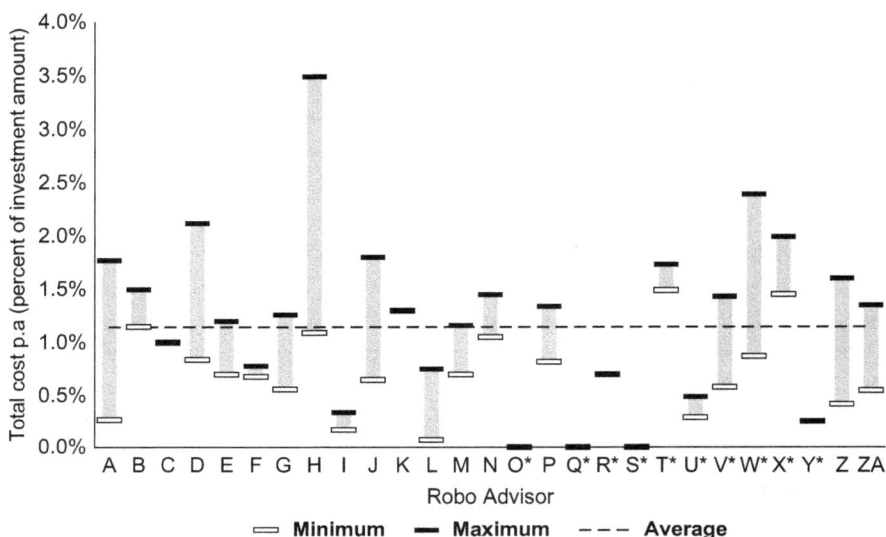

* = total cost information either only for administration fee or product cost available
data as of January 31, 2018

Figure 3.4: Total cost per year of German robo-advisors (in percent).
(Source: own illustration)

The resulting average total costs amount to 1.15% of which 52 basis points can be attributed to product cost and 63 basis points to administration. A clear message from the diagram is the fluctuation of cost ratios from provider to provider. Actively managed products naturally entail higher TERs compared to their passive counterparts and entail elevated expenses to pursue a special investment focus, for example sustainable and responsible investments. However, administrative fees require cautious interpretation. Obviously, a higher degree of freedom in decision left to the investor along with a lower level of service provided by the robo-advisor implies less administrative effort for the robo-advisory platform, which in turn results in reduced cost. Zero administration cost does not mean that the entire service is for free, as the provider might have outsourced some activities to another bank charging a fee or might have integrated fee-based premium offers.

Except for one, all companies rely on questionnaire-based assessment, which on average comprises 11 questions. Whereas the questions raised during the assessment process mostly cover similar risk and loss tolerance-related matters as well as aspects concerning the financial situation, large differences can be seen in the total number of questions and in two cases the query design is particularly short.

3.4 Venture capital financing of robo-advice

Robo-advice or automated asset management is only one business model in the broad area of personal finance fintechs. Table 3.1 shows the global venture capital investments for all personal finance fintechs including robos from January 2017 until April 2020. Overall, more than $5.7 billion were invested in fintechs in the category of personal finance between January 2017 and April 2020 in 273 financing rounds. The median amount raised per fintech financing round was $5.5 million in the U.S. and $2.6 million in Europe. The data available for China is not significant for the analysis of the robo-advice sector. Therefore, the analysis of financing rounds specifically for the robo segment focuses on the U.S. and Europe.

Table 3.1: Personal finance fintechs overview of venture capital financing statistics for sample January 2017–April 2020.

Location	Number Financing Rounds	Median Money Raised	Total Money Raised	Total Pre-Money Valuation
China	2	n/a	$1,511,000	n/a
Europe	59	$2,614,188	$245,370,445	$170,516,084
U.S.	122	$5,500,000	$3,974,230,349	$42,326,073,000
World	273	$4,350,000	$5,795,060,025	$46,308,209,084

(Source: own illustration with data from Crunchbase 2020e)

We have seen significant increases in the number of fintech start-ups in the U.S. and in Europe since 2012. The number of start-ups pursuing a business model specialized in robo-advice grew from 6 companies in 2010 to 17 in 2012 and to 101 in 2015. In contrast, only 63 robo-advisors were newly founded in 2016. While the first fintech in the U.S. launched its operations in 2007, the foundation of new robo-advisors in Europe started two years later and reached its peak in 2014. Since then, activities seem to have slowed down in recent years, which is also reflected in the lower number of start-ups in the U.S. The development shows that the euphoric phase of start-ups with robo-advice business models is losing steam. First, robo-advisors, which already exist on the market, must prove that they can operate profitably with their business models. The venture capital investment in robo-advisors is a longer-term commitment as the high initial investment needed to build the business model and to acquire customers will take at least 3–5 years to be profitable.[129]

Most of the start-ups in robo-advice focus on developing a fully automated investment platform. The number of start-ups for advisor-assisted investment platforms and hybrid platforms is significantly lower. In addition, a relatively low number of pure recommendation platforms or white label platforms have been founded. In 2014, 83% of robo-advisor start-ups focused on fully automated investment platforms, compared to nearly 97% in 2015. This development highlights a trend toward fully automated investment platforms for fintech start-ups, but it does not automatically mean that the advisor-assisted investment platforms or white-label platforms will disappear from the market. Instead, particularly established asset managers and banks will provide hybrid solutions with advisor support as they employ personal advisors anyway.[130]

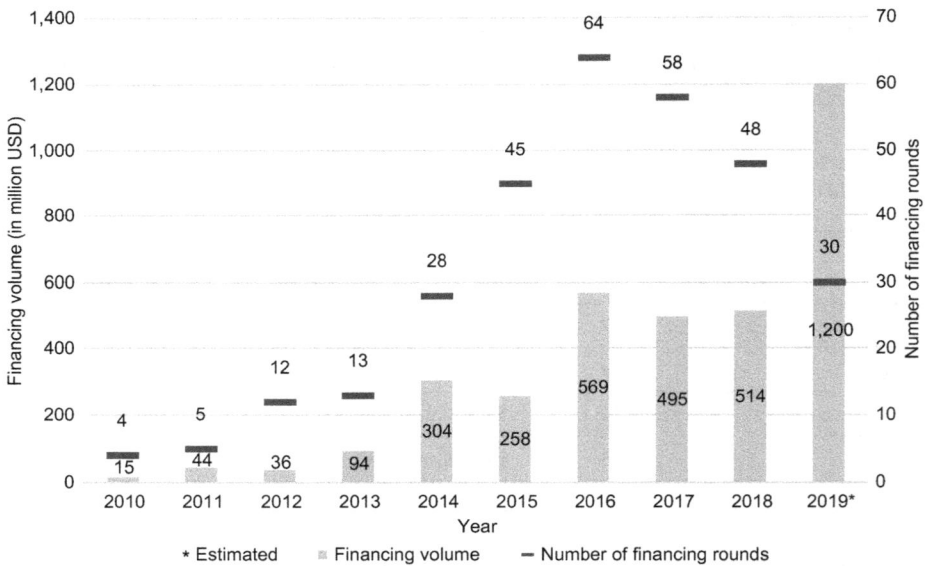

Figure 3.5: Financing volumes and rounds of financing in robo-advisory worldwide 2010–2019. (Source: own illustration with data from Kothari and Bansal 2017, p. 10; Kumar and Bansal 2020, p. 5)

Figure 3.5 shows that worldwide there were only four rounds of financing for robo-advice in 2010 at a total of $15 million in venture capital. Despite an increase in the

---

129 Kothari and Bansal 2017, pp. 6, 10; Fischer 2017, p. 190.
130 Fischer 2017, p. 190; Kothari and Bansal 2017, pp. 6, 10.

following year, the amount of financing dropped again from 2011 to 2012, whereas the number of financing rounds continuously rose. Therefore, the amount of raised funds declined on average. From 2012 onward funding amounts returned to their previous trend and reached $304 million in 2014, which equals a CAGR of 191% for this period. In 2015 the financing volume experienced another decline along with a simultaneous rise in the number of deals. This observation might stem from the high financing requirements of the substantially high number of start-ups in 2014, leaving less capacity for financing activities in the following year. However, the number of financing rounds developed in a rather constant manner. The level of 12 rounds of financing in 2012 followed a steadily positive trend to reach 45 rounds in 2015. Despite the decreasing development in the number of start-ups in 2016 compared to the previous year, the financing rounds amounted to 64 worldwide, and the volume grew to $569 million.[131] In 2017 and 2018, the financing volume remained at a stable level of $495 million and $514 million respectively. However, the number of financing rounds fell from 58 in 2017 to 48 in 2018. This trend accelerated in the first quarter of 2019. By April 2019, robo-advisors raised $414 million in only ten financing rounds.[132]

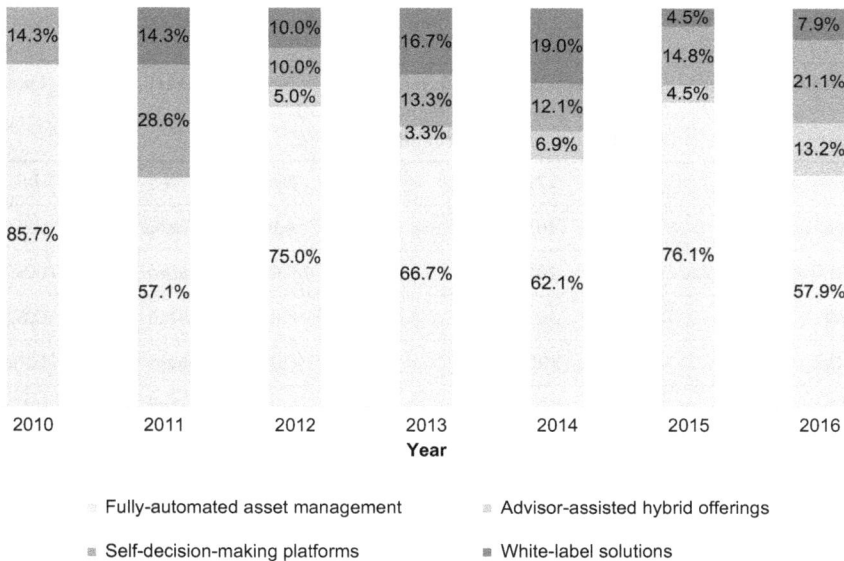

Figure 3.6: Distribution of the financing volume in the area of robo-advisory worldwide from January 2010–November 2016 by sub-area (in percent).
(Source: own illustration with data from Tracxn 2016, pp. 10–38)

---

131 Kothari and Bansal 2017, pp. 6, 10.
132 Kumar and Bansal 2020, p. 5.

Figure 3.6 shows that fully automated investment platforms attract most of the equity financing for robo-advice and the financing volumes for hybrid investment platforms or recommendation platforms are significantly lower. However, the latter are slowly catching up, as their share has increased from 0% in 2010 to 16.6% in 2013 and to 34.3% in 2016.

Table 3.2 provides an overview of the highest financing volumes for robo-advisors in Europe and North America. For example, Betterment, as a fully automated robo-advisor in the U.S., has received $275 million in equity through seven rounds of financing. Personal Capital operates with an advisor-assisted business model and has raised $265 million in equity through nine rounds of financing. In Germany, Blackrock became a lead investor in the fully automated asset manager Scalable Capital in 2017; the total financing volume in Scalable Capital after five rounds amounts to $116 million. The high volume of financing shows that the 2020 forecast of $1 trillion and more in AUM for robo-advisory will be absolutely necessary in the medium term to make the new robo business models profitable.[133]

Table 3.2: Robo-advisors in Europe and North America by amount of invested external equity.

Company	Invested equity (published; in million USD)	Number of financing rounds	Business Model	Country
Betterment	275	7	Fully-automated	U.S.
Personal Capital	265	9	Advisor-assisted	U.S.
Wealthfront	205	6	Fully-automated	U.S.
Acorns	207	10	Fully-automated	U.S.
WealthSimple	200*	6	Fully-automated	Canada
Motif Investing	127	6	Fully-automated	U.S.
Nutmeg	154	7	Fully-automated	U.K.
SigFig	120	6	Fully-automated	U.S.
Scalable Capital	116	5	Fully-automated	Germany

* CAD267 million converted by prevailing exchange rate USD – CAD: 1,3214 CAD. Retrieved August 10, 2020 from: OnVista 2020c.
(Source: own illustration based on own research and data from Fischer 2017, p. 191 and crunchbase.com)

---

133 Fischer 2017; Crunchbase 2020h, 2020g.

Financing in the U.S. and in Europe

Figure 3.7 shows the annual number of fintechs founded in the robo-advice segment since 1999 in the U.S. and in Europe. In 2007 the first robo-advisor was founded in the U.S. according to the data in our sample April 2000 to June 2017. Ever since, each year between one and three fintechs have been founded in the U.S., except for 2016 where none were newly established. In 2009 the first European robo-advisor launched operations. Unlike in the U.S., robo-advisors in Europe were rarely a part of the fintech landscape until 2014, when 7 out of the total of 10 fintechs were founded in Europe. Since the robo-advisory start-up hype in 2014, only three more fintechs were founded in 2015 and 2016 – one in the U.S. and two in Europe.

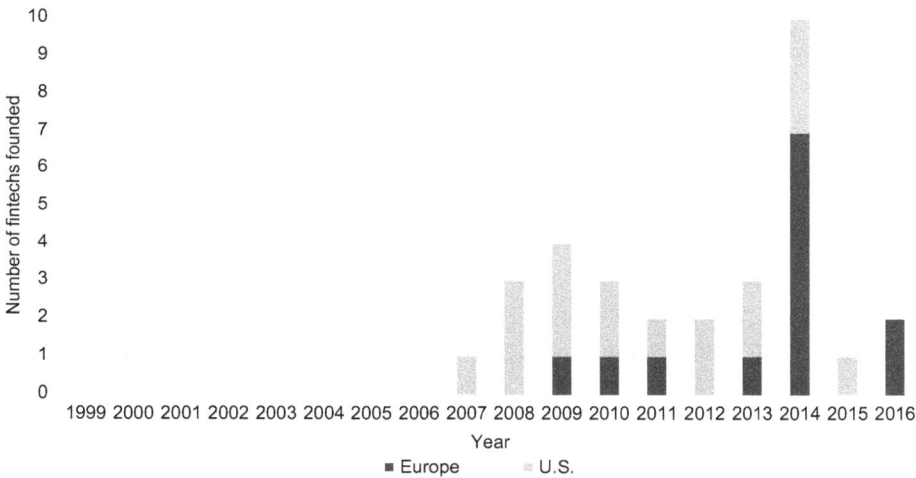

Figure 3.7: Number of fintechs founded in robo-advice in Europe and the U.S. from 1999–2016 for sample April 2000–June 2017.[134]
(Source: own illustration)

Deal activity within the robo-advisory segment started in 2008 with three financing rounds closing in the U.S. In Europe the first financing round was recorded in 2009. Deal activity then started to pick up pace in 2011 and has permanently increased each year. For example, deal count amounted to 4 financing rounds in 2011, while it stood at 19 in 2016 (see Figure 3.8). Europe has seen a growing number of financing rounds, which leads to the conclusion that the market is not mature yet. On the other hand, the U.S. market appears to offer little possibilities for new players, as

---

134 Please note that the year of foundation of one fintech operating in this segment is not known and hence excluded in the graph.

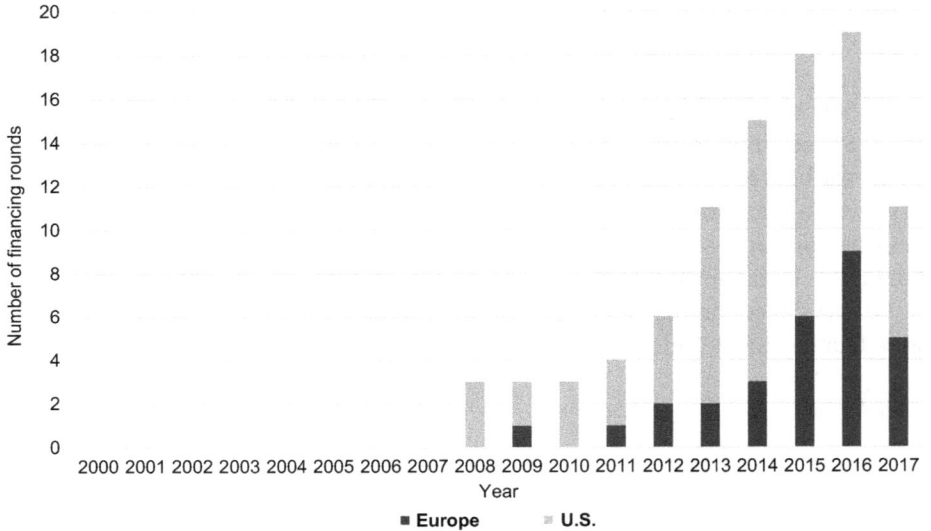

Figure 3.8: Number of financing rounds in robo-advice in Europe and the U.S. for sample April 2000–June 2017.
(Source: own illustration)

the number of new robo-advisory fintechs is very low. Additionally, deal count is stagnating or slightly declining lately, which could mean that the U.S. market for robo-advice is moving to the next stage of maturity.

In 2008 fintech funding for robo-advisors amounted to €5.4 million and increased until 2011, but dropped by roughly 19% from 2011 to 2012 (see Figure 3.9). This is remarkable as the number of financing rounds rose over the same period, implicating a decline in average amount raised. Funding recovered and jumped to €251.3 million in 2014. In 2015 the annual amount raised once again declined, even though deal count increased. A possible explanation could be the large number of new fintechs founded in the prior year requiring financing and hence diminishing the average amount raised, as seed investments are typically smaller than subsequent financing amounts. In 2016 the amount raised reached €355.5 million, mainly driven by larger financing rounds in the U.S. as the number of deals in that region accounted for 52.6% of all deals and almost 80% of capital was raised in the U.S. in that year. Robo-advice in the U.S. required much more capital, possibly explained by growth investments to survive in a maturing market environment. This trend can not be observed in Europe, suggesting that the market is not as evolved as in the U.S.

After having compared the two regions irrespective of the financing round series, the focus is now shifted toward specific financing rounds and the median amount raised. In Table 3.3 large differences in median amount raised can be

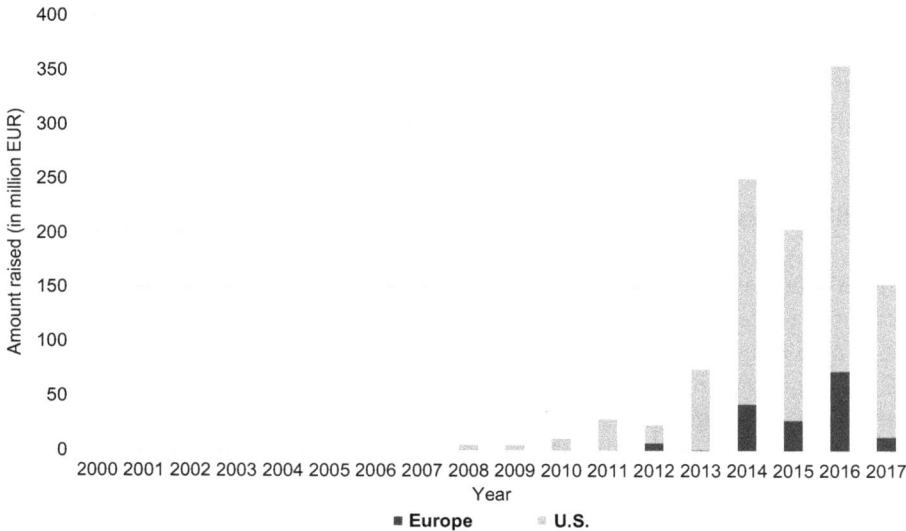

Figure 3.9: Annual overview of amount raised in robo-advice in Europe and the U.S. for sample April 2000–June 2017 (in € m).
(Source: own illustration)

Table 3.3: Median amount raised in robo-advice in Europe and the U.S. for sample April 2000–June 2017 (in € m).

	Seed	A	B	C	D	E	F	IPO
Overall Median	2.0	4.2	11.8	22.4	29.4	72.3	n/a	n/a
Median Europe	2.3	3.5	23.5	34.9	14.1	n/a	n/a	n/a
Median U.S.	1.5	6.5	11.8	21.6	34.3	72.3	n/a	n/a
Sample size *n*	20	20	12	8	7	3	0	0

(Source: own illustration)

observed for the different robo-advisory financing rounds. For instance, the median seed investment in Europe amounts to €2.3 million, whereas it only amounts to €1.5 million in the U.S., implying a difference of close to 34%. In strong contrast to that, the median capital of €6.5 million raised in financing round A in the U.S. is much higher than in Europe where funding stands at €3.5 million. For financing rounds B and C, the median amount raised in Europe is significantly higher than in the U.S. In financing round D, precisely the opposite is true, as €34.3 million in the U.S. outweigh €14.3 million in Europe. Consequently, it can neither be said that early stage financing for robo-advisory is higher in any of the two regions by rule nor can it be confirmed for later stage financing rounds. The only conclusion that can be drawn concerns the maturity of the markets. Although only three financing rounds E have been identified, all of them were closed in the U.S., slightly hinting at the growing maturity in this market in contrast to the European market.

Large differences in amounts raised between two successive financing rounds

Another robo-advice comparison between Europe and the U.S. illustrates the differences in changes of amounts raised from one financing round to another in percent. The sample is made up as follows: Seed/A n = 10; A/B n = 11; B/C n = 8; C/D n = 7; D/E n = 3; and E/F n = 0 (see Figure 3.10). The change in amounts raised from the seed round to financing round A in Europe amounts to 367% and 475% in the U.S. This outperformance of the U.S. compared to Europe is reversed when taking into consideration financing rounds A and B. For instance, the median growth in amount raised from the A-round to the B-round is 460% in Europe and 204% in the U.S. The median decline from financing round B to C of 13% after the previous median result of 460% shows that the amounts raised after round B never surpass round B. But doubts about the significance of this value can be raised. In the U.S. the evolution of growth from financing rounds A to B of 204% as well as the growth of 77% from B to C appear more logical. The results for the following

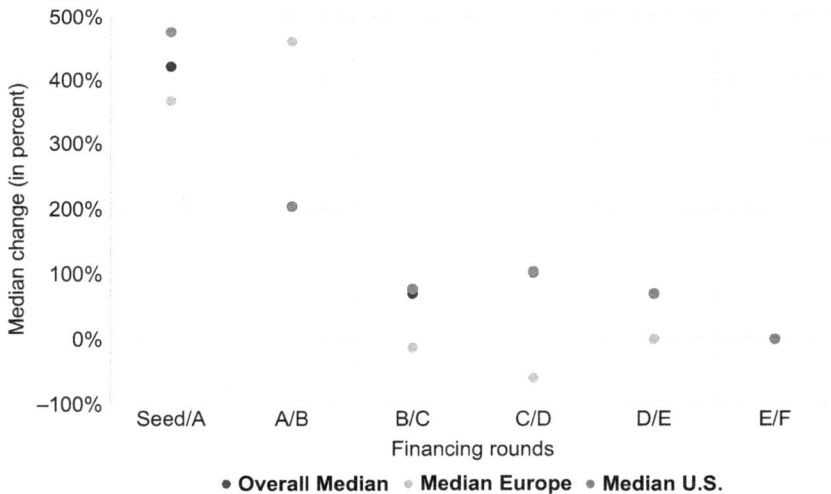

Figure 3.10: Median change in amounts raised between two successive financing rounds in robo-advice for sample April 2000–June 2017 (in percent).
(Source: own illustration)

comparison of round C and round D illustrate a median decrease of 60% in Europe and an increase of 104% in the U.S. In this context the calculation approach of the median does not appear to be suitable for the European figures as the subsample for Europe only consists of two data sets, resulting in the undesired outcome of the outlier influencing the median. Therefore, no further conclusions can be made for the comparison of financing rounds and their median change in amounts raised.

Shorter financing gaps between funding rounds in the U.S. than in Europe

Figure 3.11 illustrates the median time difference between years. Although the sample is the same as for Figure 3.10, it is helpful to take a closer look at the findings due to the observation that the problem of an outlier having too much influence only affects the median change in amounts raised and not the date difference.

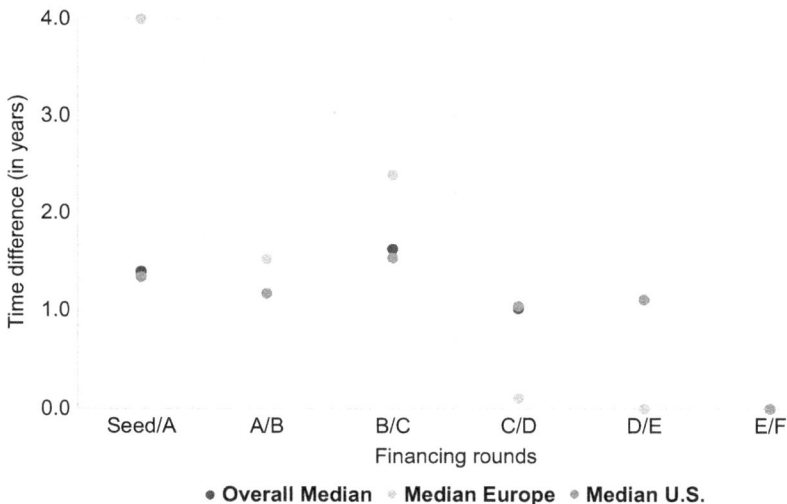

Figure 3.11: Median time difference in years between two successive financing rounds in robo-advice for sample April 2000–June 2017.
(Source: own illustration)

The median time difference between seed investment and round A clearly shows that significantly less time passes in the U.S. than in Europe (1.3 years vs. 4.0 years). This difference between Europe and the U.S. with regard to time required to close successive financing rounds narrows from 2.7 years to four months for financing rounds A and B as the median for these rounds is 1.5 years in Europe and 1.2 years in the U.S. It takes U.S. robo-advisors around 1.5 years to close financing round C after having raised capital in round B, whereas it takes the European counterparts approximately 2.4 years to accomplish the same. The gap in time to fund two following rounds increases in Europe. Further comparisons between the regions are not possible as European data is only available for the C/D-round comparison and this data includes one very late add-on financing to a C-round, shortly before actually closing the financing round D. Nevertheless, it can be stated that follow-on financing in this segment is achieved much faster in the U.S. than in Europe, suggesting that the timing and success of robo-advisors is much more critical in the U.S.

3.5 Insights into valuation of robo-advisor business models

Company valuation in the context of fintechs entails a substantial challenge in data availability since the financial history of such companies is either short term or does not exist yet due to their early development stage. Furthermore, challenges such as high uncertainty regarding future growth rates as well as potentially negative cash flows hinder the application of most traditional valuation models. For example, the result of a discounted cash flow (DCF) valuation might be distorted as the forecasting of cash flows of early-stage companies is fraught with a substantial degree of uncertainty. At the same time, reliance on book values and accounting-based methods might be critical as especially in the short-term external factors can influence some items of a financial statement. Thus, three general approaches remain as reasonable and viable choices with regard to fintechs and robo-advisors: the valuation based on certain multiples, the venture capital approach and the Scorecard method. Negative cash flows may be an obstacle in DCF-valuation but can be overcome. The key problems for the evaluator will probably be the forecast of growth, the estimation of the sustainable level of profit and the calculation of the cost of capital.

The application of multiples fits particularly well for the valuation of fintechs and the multiple enterprise-value-to-revenues (EV/revenues) is frequently applied. In regard to robo-advisory, the multiple enterprise-value-to-assets-under-management (EV/AUM) delivers some valuable insights. Nevertheless, this metric must be interpreted with caution since the exponential growth that robos are experiencing lately will drop significantly in the future and thus influence the EV/AUM metric negatively (see Table 3.4).

Table 3.4: EV/AUM multiple of Betterment.

Date	Company	Financing Round	EV (in million EUR)	AuM (in million EUR)	EV/AuM
Feb-15	Betterment	D	450.0	1,400.3	0.32x
Mar-16	Betterment	E	700.0	4,037.1	0.17x

(Source: own illustration)

Betterment's EV/AUM multiple tends to decrease the later the stage of financing gets. Although the absolute Enterprise Value grows by €250 million from the date of round D financing to round E, the corresponding EV/AUM valuation drops to a figure of 0.17x compared to a previous valuation of 0.32x. The reason is the immense boost of assets under management, which almost triples its level within this period. Another drawback commonly seen when using multiples is a potential reflection of a prevailing over- or undervaluation of the entire sector.[135]

The second alternative, the VC approach, combines DCF modelling with multiple valuation and assumes that at a certain point of time the investor will exit the project. The key figures calculated in the VC method are the terminal value derived by using a multiple such as EV/Revenues and the Internal Rate of Return, which serves as the discount rate applied to the terminal value in order to arrive at the corresponding present value. This approach is often used in start-up valuation.[136]

Lastly, the Scorecard method compares the start-up to the average valuation of an appropriate peer group at the same stage of development by assessing its relative strength as well as its overall performance. This assessment is usually broken down to six differently weighted criteria chosen in a way to reflect the importance of the criterion for the company. For example, the criterion "Competitive Environment" might be assigned the maximum value of the scale, if the business is characterized by strong competition as well as high barriers to entry. In the next step, the weights are multiplied by comparison factors derived from qualitative and quantitative questions. These factors reflect the individual characteristics of the target company. Lastly, the values resulting from the previous multiplication are summed up and multiplied by the average valuation of the peer group. However, two important drawbacks lie in the importance of the quality of the peer group and the high degree of subjectivity involved during the entire valuation process.[137]

The question remains which of the presented methods is most appropriate for the valuation of robo-advisors. Own empirical analysis based on more than 200 fintechs has shown that prices of robo-advisors resulting from the Venture Capital method and

---

135 Riethdorf 2017.
136 Sahlman and Scherlis 1987 (Revised 2009).
137 Kowlessar 2016.

the Scorecard approach tend to be significantly higher than valuations obtained from the assessment by multiples. According to the comparison of actual acquisition prices of precedent transactions with the valuations obtained in the study, next to the VC method the EV/AUM multiple also delivers a significantly higher price than actually observed, which deviates by a factor of more than 14 from the actual price. This extreme fluctuation might have its roots in restricted data availability and a sample size of only 6 companies compared to 13 to 14 robos, which are assessed in the course of other valuation methods. The multiple EV/Revenues and the Scorecard assessment estimate the price most accurately – for robo-advisors as well as for the other fintech segments.

Summary

The global robo-advisory market has grown significantly since 2012 – in terms of the number of start-ups, financing volumes and assets under management. Only with very high growth in assets under management can robos meet the return expectations of VC investors. The year 2020 has seen a strong but short stock market crash due to the coronavirus crisis. However, robo-advisors have not yet had to cope with a long-term strong slump on the capital market and automated investment models have not been tested in several economic crises. During the 2020 coronavirus crisis some robo advisors had to learn that e.g., simple automated processes based on the value-at-risk model are not sufficient to successfully manage a stock crisis. Regulation has created benefits for the scalable business models of fully automated asset management due to the pressure for transparency and cost reduction. But robo-advisors have yet to prove themselves to the regulators in the future. Robo-advisors aim to grant retail clients access to asset management, but their business models must prove profitable in this regard, too.

Overall, automation of investment processes can provide a great benefit to investors. The costs of asset management will be very transparent on the one hand and significantly reduced by automation on the other hand. In addition, automation of investment advisory and asset management provides the opportunity for banks to maintain the quality of advice for customers with smaller investment volumes. Otherwise, without digitalization and automation, a client with small investment volume will not receive qualified investment advice since the resulting income would not be sufficient to cover the expense of personal consultation by a human advisor.

Our empirical research shows that round E financing has been focused on the U.S., which demonstrates a higher degree of maturity in the U.S. compared to Europe. The median time that passes between seed investment and round A financing in Europe amounts to 4.0 years compared to only 1.3 years in the U.S. Although this time gap declines to only 4 months to move from round A to round B, the difference is again greater for the accomplishment of round C financing. Overall, the findings show that U.S. robos obtain financing after seed investment faster than their European competitors do. Therefore, timing tends to be a more crucial factor in the mature U.S. market.

4 The need for social trading

Social trading builds on one aspect that is vital for its activity: the social web. The social web can be defined as "the sum of all web-based applications which support the exchange of information, relationship building and maintaining, communication as well as collaboration in a social or shared context."[138] The most prominent examples of social web applications are online lexica like Wikipedia, social sharing platforms such as YouTube or social networks of which the leading representative is Facebook. Social networks enable a vast number of individuals to effortlessly get in touch, so they can exchange and collaborate online. Users can get information from interaction on social platforms as an alternative to opinions they would otherwise obtain from experts and professionals. Initially, social networks also served as the channel for sharing investment ideas. However, in the meantime specialized online forums have emerged, combined with direct interfaces to users' brokerage accounts.[139] These specialized networks are so-called social trading platforms. Social trading is a rather young concept, which is why no uniform definition exists. In the context of this book however, we will use the following definition: Social trading is security trading on a digital platform where investors derive their investment decisions from information or signals provided by other traders in the community.

The basic idea underlying social trading is based on the provision of access to financial information and investments, which were otherwise primarily available to professional investors. This access is achieved through so-called signal providers who share their investment strategies or portfolios with the online community and provide signal followers the opportunity to observe their ideas and to discuss, comment or even copy them. Due to its nature, social trading is an innovative form of delegated portfolio management.[140]

The trend of social trading started when ZuluTrade launched its operations as the first social trading platform in 2007 and became more and more popular as other start-ups including eToro or wikifolio entered the business area in the following years. While in the beginning such platforms often primarily served as information tools, they reached their break-through in financial trading when they achieved control over the entire value chain. The value chain comprises the generation of a trade signal, its transformation into an order and the execution of the order in a cost-efficient way with a broker.[141]

---

138 Braun 2013, p. 16.
139 Braun 2013, p. 16; Lochmaier 2014; Doering et al. 2015, p. 1.
140 Lochmaier 2014; Doering et al. 2015, p. 1; BaFin 2017a.
141 Dorfleitner et al. 2018, p. 2; Brylewski and Lempka 2016, p. 140.

https://doi.org/10.1515/9783110704907-004

4.1 Disrupting the investment landscape

How social trading works

The concept of social trading combines the investment ideas of traders with the leader-follower-principle known from social networks. Consequently, there are two stakeholders involved on social trading platforms. On the one side, signal providers share their investment ideas with the online community. They execute their strategies and portfolios in a real-money account or in a virtual portfolio where no real funds are at risk. On the other side, signal followers screen the published investment ideas for the strategies and portfolios that best fit their investment needs and preferences. The social trading platform provides live data; followers monitor the activities of the respective trader and discuss these activities with other users or address the signal provider directly with their questions.[142] Investors select one or more traders to follow; then the copying of signals usually happens in an automated way.

Although the process differs from provider to provider, most commonly the platform forwards the trading signal to the investor's brokerage firm, which transforms the signal into an executable order – without any further intervention by the client. Depending on the specific arrangement, the platform might receive a commission for transmitting the order to the respective broker. Signal providers get rewards from the social trading platform. The use of the platforms is usually free, so investors only incur the usual charges for the orders they place.[143]

In social trading users can choose between two alternatives: mirror trading and copy trading. In mirror trading, investors copy the trades of auto-trading services and signal services, usually with large investment sums. In copy trading, investors also copy trading signals but choose one specific trader or a small number of individual traders. Thus, they allocate a smaller-scaled proportion of their own funds to the replication of a certain trader. Next to the adaptation of the entire strategy, investors can also decide to replicate only certain individual signals and thus customize their investment. Regardless of the preferred approach, copy trading requires a certain degree of active involvement and financial knowledge since investors at least must select the traders they wish to follow.[144]

Wisdom of the online community

In the area of automated asset management and investment, there are two segments that seem to provide similar services to their clients: robo-advisory and social

---

142 Doering et al. 2015, p. 1; Financial Conduct Authority 2016; Kern 2017, p. 190.
143 Financial Conduct Authority 2016; BaFin 2017a; Doering et al. 2015, p. 1.
144 Financial Conduct Authority 2016; Global Banking & Finance Review 2011.

trading. In both areas, investment tools as well as investment-related information support customers; however, robo-advisors do not bring their users together as a community. In social trading, however, the online community is the most valuable element. Its users publicly comment and discuss signal providers' activities. The platform functions as a forum, which gives its members space to inform and support each other. Among other things, this interaction also improves the financial knowledge of individual investors and new entrants can benefit from the provision of comprehensive basic knowledge.[145]

The idea underlying the concept of an active online community is to benefit from collective intelligence, which states that a group can arrive at better decisions than single individuals can, even if the latter are experts. However, it is important to note that this applies to the average of a group rather than each one of its individuals. The concept in its simplest form is based on the natural phenomenon of swarm intelligence. Individual animals, such as ants, do not have a particularly high intelligence, but as an organized swarm these insects manage to optimize the search for food in an "intelligent" way. Nowadays, the digital age and specifically social media apply this concept to various areas such as financial markets.[146] Ideally the information and decisions derived by collective capital market intelligence are superior to information and decisions of individual traders. Collective market intelligence in theory should have better access to relevant information due to a network of decentralized, independent actors with different views.[147]

The definition implies that collective intelligence is not necessarily present in every context or situation, as the crowd must meet certain criteria to be wiser than the individual. In line with this finding, the following four requirements are indispensable for collective intelligence to prevail. The first condition is "diversity of opinion," which refers to the heterogeneity of investors' private information and the individual interpretation of publicly available facts. The second and third conditions are the "independence" of own opinions from other users and the "decentralization" referring to the ability to specialize and draw on local knowledge. The final condition is that the "aggregation" of private information into the consensus of the collective must also function.[148]

Research on the Austrian platform wikifolio clearly negates the existence of the wisdom of the crowd in respect of signal followers. Although the authors admit that the amount invested in single portfolios might be a result of the aggregation of opinions, empirical analysis finds that, in fact, the portfolio performance of the recent past as well as the overall sum attracted by an investment strategy influence

---

145 Kern 2017, p. 190; BaFin 2017a; Doering et al. 2015, p. 1.
146 Lochner 2014; Defren et al. 2017, p. 202.
147 Öynhausen 2015, p. 110.
148 Surowiecki 2005, p. 10.

the amount of investment. For this reason, rather than collective intelligence, herd behavior might drive signal followers' investments.[149]

In contrast, signal providers fulfill the four conditions as firstly, they meet "diversity of opinions" by the fact that traders follow a great variety of strategies and retrieve information from different sources. Since the vast majority of users engages in social trading without being employed by institutional asset management firms and has different private or professional backgrounds, wikifolio traders also satisfy the requirements for "independence" and "decentralization," respectively. Lastly, the average composition of all wikifolio portfolios is evidence for a functioning information aggregation mechanism.[150] Although the paper proves that from a theoretical point of view collective intelligence is present on the platform wikifolio, research has not yet found a consensus on its general existence in social trading.[151]

Can you trust signal providers?

Social trading platforms act as an intermediary between signal providers and signal followers. The platforms try to mitigate potential agency problems, which are a general risk in any form of asset management. Consequently, an important task of these service providers lies in the elimination of ex-ante existing information asymmetries and undesirable ex-post behavior of signal providers to protect the interest of signal followers. Information asymmetry refers to the disadvantageous position of signal followers who face uncertainty about the financial skills and quality of signal providers. As a countermeasure, social trading platforms usually integrate screening tools into their dashboards, which support investors in filtering traders according to risk and performance-related criteria. Detailed track records help users to assess the trading history of signal providers. Moreover, platforms commonly claim to set high prerequisites for traders to be approved or to even sign-up to a platform.[152] However, it remains doubtful to which extent platforms achieve an improvement of traders' quality through these requirements. The previously mentioned measures certainly provide a higher degree of transparency, but investors are still well advised to carefully decide whom to follow.

By focusing on the mitigation of ex-post moral hazard, that is, preventing signal providers from actions that are harmful or undesirable for signal followers, platforms can reduce the probability of such behavior through their respective compensation scheme. Social trading is a rather young business model and no compensation model has yet evolved that optimally incentivizes the effort made by signal providers while

---

149 Defren et al. 2017.
150 Defren et al. 2017, pp. 206–207.
151 See, for example, Defren et al. 2017 or Oehler et al. 2016.
152 Doering et al. 2015, p. 3.

controlling the risks they assume. However, three different forms of compensation schemes are currently applied in existing social trading networks: follower-based models, profit-based models and volume-based models.[153]

Follower-based compensation rewards the signal provider with a fixed amount per user subscription and thus sets an incentive to increase the number of followers. This model is comparable to asset-based management fees, which have established themselves as the common approach among mutual funds and which, being linear fees, theoretically reward gains and punish losses to the same extent. However, empirical studies show that the liability of portfolio managers for losses is somewhat restricted and thus risk-taking behavior might be supported.[154]

Another compensation scheme known from traditional asset management or hedge funds is the profit-based approach, which charges performance fees from signal followers. These fees are convex in the sense that they reward positive performance without penalizing losses in a similar way. Therefore, investors cover full losses while their participation in the upside potential is limited. Compared to linear fees, the profit-based system entails an incentive for traders to take excessive risks. That is why performance fees often follow a High Watermark (HWM) through which signal providers only receive compensation when they reach a new maximum. Thus, traders must make up for previous losses first.[155]

The third alternative, compensation based on volume, is an innovative method that has developed along with social trading and pays signal providers in terms of a participation in the bid-ask spreads generated by followers who copy their trading signals. However, if the social trading platform does not distinguish between profitable and loss-making signals, signal providers might be likely to increase the execution of trades to drive up the number of spread-generating copy trades.[156]

Social trading and contracts for differences

The universe of products offered on social trading platforms differs from provider to provider. However, investors very often like to use Contracts for Differences (CFDs). In a CFD, the buyer and the seller agree to exchange the difference amount between the price of the underlying asset as of the date of settlement and the initial price fixed in the contract.[157] If the value of the asset depreciates, the buyer pays to the seller and vice versa. Consequently, investors enter a short position to bet on

---

153 Doering et al. 2015, p. 4.
154 Doering et al. 2015, p. 5.
155 Doering et al. 2015, p. 5; Swedroe 2014.
156 Doering et al. 2015, pp. 5–6.
157 Doering et al. 2015, p. 6.

decreasing prices and go long, if they expect prices to rise.[158] Since the development of the asset value serves as a basis for the instrument's value, the contract does not require ownership of the underlying asset itself.[159]

Even though CFDs present highly speculative derivatives, they are very popular among investors on social trading platforms. An advantage lies in the margin account that CFD traders must post. Since the margin only amounts to a fraction of the value of the underlying asset, CFDs allow for a substantial degree of leverage. Consequently, investors benefit disproportionally strongly from upside movements of the underlying asset compared to a similarly high but direct investment in the asset itself.[160] However, the lower the margin posted in relation to the value of the underlying, the higher the leverage and the more extreme the participation in upsides – and in downsides. Therefore, leverage not only provides great opportunities for profit generation but at the same time bears an enormous risk, which can lead to the total loss of the invested capital.[161] Despite the transparent and simple pricing of CFDs, the construction of some contracts asymmetrically favors the seller.[162]

CFDs offer flexibility since they do not have a pre-defined maturity. Due to their trading over the counter (OTC), CFDs are available in a variety of different contract sizes.[163] High cost efficiency as well as low trading cost and simple structure make CFDs an instrument that can be easily traded online. That is why their great popularity in social trading is no surprise.[164] The risk that investors take with CFDs is generally very high, as they accept losing the full investment amount or even more in case the investment strategy is not successful. That is why unexperienced investors should not invest in CFDs. When CFDs come into play, some people might also say that this is not about investing, but gambling.

4.2 Three business models of social trading

Online brokers can simply add social trading and generate revenues from the spread earned on the execution of the copied signals. In general, such platforms can fall back on three different types of business models: broker-only revenues, network only revenues or a combination of both.[165]

---

158 Beck 2015, p. 232.
159 Meyer zu Schwabedissen and Prager 2016, p. 236.
160 Doering et al. 2015, p. 6.
161 Meyer zu Schwabedissen and Prager 2016, p. 236.
162 Beck 2015, p. 234; Meyer zu Schwabedissen and Prager 2016, p. 237.
163 Meyer zu Schwabedissen and Prager 2016.
164 Brylewski and Lempka 2016, p. 138; Meyer zu Schwabedissen and Prager 2016, pp. 240–241, 244.
165 Social Trading Guru 2018.

In a broker-only business model, no other brokerage firm is involved, and the social trading provider earns the full spread on all trades executed by the signal followers. In contrast, in a network only social trading model the provider does not actually appear as a broker but takes the role of an introducing broker. The introducing broker acts as an "organization that solicits or accepts orders to buy or sell futures contracts, Forex, commodity options, or swaps but does not accept money or other assets from customers to support these orders."[166] Consequently, the signal followers still copy trades from signal providers on the social trading platform itself. However, the broker of the follower or a supporting brokerage firm ultimately executes the trade. Finally, as illustrated in Figure 4.1, a combination of both revenue streams can also be implemented.[167]

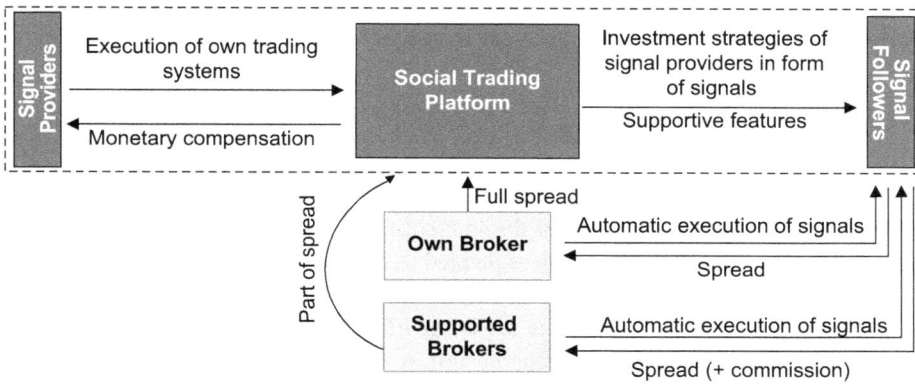

Figure 4.1: Social trading business model based on a combination of broker and network revenues. (Source: own illustration)

Pure social trading providers apply a fourth, innovative alternative with a connection of signal followers and signal providers through certificates. This is where the social trading platform does not interact at all with any executing broker. Instead, an issuing entity and a marketplace are involved in its operations as shown in Figure 4.2.

Social trading does not copy trade in the narrow sense. In fact, it copies social investing. Signal providers still construct and share their portfolios on the platform, but a notional index and a certificate substitute the copying approach. The signal provider portfolios form the notional reference for an index on which a partnering entity issues a certificate. In order to participate in signal providers' ideas and strategies, signal followers can invest in these certificates through the partnering exchange or OTC with the issuing entity itself.

---

166 National Futures Association 2018b.
167 Social Trading Guru 2018.

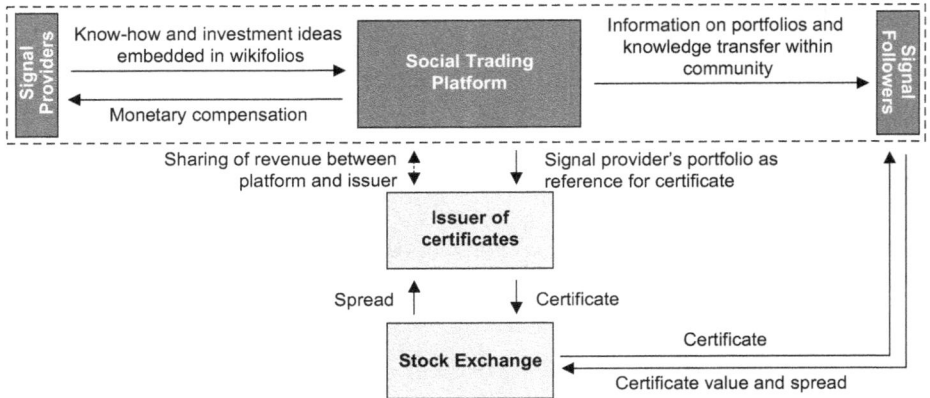

Figure 4.2: Social trading business model based on certificates.
(Source: own illustration)

eToro – a leader in social trading

The Israeli fintech eToro was founded in 2007 with the aim of giving users access to online trading. In 2010 eToro added the first social trading platform on their website, named OpenBook. In 2015 both services merged to the new eToro where users can trade with CFDs on indices, commodities, currencies and stocks, as well as cryptocurrencies and ETFs.[168] Customers in Europe are served by eToro Europe, which is registered as a Cypriot investment firm by the Cyprus Securities and Exchange Commission (CySEC), while in the U.K. eToro is authorized by the Financial Conduct Authority (FCA). eToro Europe and eToro UK both comply with MiFID requirements. Furthermore, eToro in Australia acts as a licensed intermediary for eToro Europe. As of today, due to tight regulatory restrictions in relation to trading with CFDs in the U.S., the platform does not accept U.S. clients anymore.[169]

eToro has become one of the most popular and well-established providers of social trading. Figure 4.3 provides detailed insights into the building blocks that helped the fintech to get to where it is today.

Users of eToro start with a virtual account that allows them to get familiar with all the tools on the platform and get training with a virtual investment of up to $100,000 without having any real money at risk.[170] eToro supports its users with a value-at-risk based scoring that provides an indication about the maximum portfolio volatility of a signal provider and assigns a weekly score ranging from 1 to 10. Scores between 1 and 6 approve investors to be followed, while a value from 8 to 10 automatically

---

168 Crunchbase 2019c; eToro 2018c.
169 eToro 2018f.
170 eToro 2019b.

Key partners	Key activities	Value propositions	Customer relationships	Customer segments
Affiliates Brokers CopyFund partners Tipranks WeSave Meitav Dash Product providers	Online onboarding & authentication of signal providers Review of signal providers' risk score and blocking if necessary Online platform	Free access to platform Manual as well as copy trading at the same spreads Risk assessment of traders Professional trading tools Unlimited virtual account with $100,000 to practice without risking real money	Online Direct communi-cation between signal providers and followers User experience and convenience Trading tools and courses Customer service via live chat or a ticket available 24/7	Private signal providers Private signal followers Corporate signal followers
	Key resources Innovative signal providers Active online community Online platform CopyFunds based on machine learning Venture capital	CopyFunds: access to aggregate knowledge of top traders and various market strategies Customer promotion program ($20 per promoted customer) Knowledge transfer within the online community Signal providers: Implementation of own trading systems and monetary compensation	**Channels** Online platform Mobile app Webpage of affiliates Channels of introducing brokers Social media	

Cost structure	Revenue streams
Development and maintenance of online platform Fixed and personnel cost Compensation paid to signal providers dependent on Popular Investor level Commission paid within the framework of eToro Partners Program: Affiliates: 25% of monthly net revenues and $400 DCPA Introducing brokers: no disclosure of commission amounts	Bid-Ask spread earned on every trade dependent on type of product

Figure 4.3: Business Model Canvas – eToro.
(Source: own illustration)

blocks the signal provider from being copied. Signal providers who score 7 can be followed but will not receive compensation for the respective month.[171] A customer promotion program entices with $20 per promoted sign-up.[172]

In 2016 eToro added CopyPortfolios to its portfolio; the former name was CopyFunds. For a minimum investment of $5,000 investors get exposure to one of three different alternatives: Market CopyPortfolios, Top Trader CopyPortfolios and Partner CopyPortfolios. Market CopyPortfolios essentially implement a pre-defined market strategy and provide access to a selected combination of CFDs on stocks, commodities or ETFs. The second option, CopyPortfolios on Top Traders, bundles the best performers selected by machine learning, a type of AI, who follow a pre-defined strategy. eToro's investment management committee rebalances both fund types at no additional fees. Finally, one of eToro's investment management partners can create Partner CopyPortfolios.[173]

Since the total funding of the fintech amounted to about $223 million in July 2018, venture capitalists and investors obviously play an important role in its growth.[174] Additionally, the platform set up the eToro Partners Program in order to expand its customer base through the marketing of affiliates and introducing brokers.[175] eToro is a financial broker and generates income from spreads earned on every signal provider's trade and every copied signal. Affiliates receive a compensation of 25% of net revenues generated from the affiliate's customers during a month.[176]

eToro calls signal providers popular investors and requires them to undergo a 4-tier program during their online trading career. Once a popular investor has a trading history of more than 2 months, has managed to attract at least one copier with AUM of more than $200 and fulfills a set of further mandatory criteria, the investor has reached the "Cadet" level. However, eToro does not provide any compensation for cadets. The next popular investor levels are "Rising Star," "Champion" and ultimately "Elite." The achievement of each level brings certain requirements with it but also offers a more attractive compensation scheme. Having become a "Rising Star," withdrawal fees are no longer due, and traders receive a fixed monthly payment of $500 as "Rising Star" and $1,000 as "Champion" and "Elite," respectively. Once popular investors reach the ultimate level of "Elite," they receive an additional variable, asset-based compensation amounting to 2% of the annual average AUM.[177]

---

171 eToro 2014, 2018h.
172 eToro 2018a.
173 eToro 2018b, 2018g.
174 Crunchbase 2019c.
175 eToro 2018e.
176 eToro 2017, p. 18.
177 eToro 2019a, 2018d.

ZuluTrade – networking pays off

ZuluTrade was founded in 2007 in the U.S. Ten years later, the company became part of the financial services provider Formax Group.[178] As of July 2018, ZuluTrade has attracted signal providers from 192 different countries and its users have executed a trading volume of above $1 trillion.[179] The rejection of U.S. customers by eToro partly explains this success, as ZuluTrade does not have such a restriction. Due to regulatory reasons, the Greek investment services firm Triple A Experts (AAAfx), which has an EU investment license, operates the platform's European business. Furthermore, European investors face some specialties when using ZuluTrade, one of which most importantly is the range of signal providers they can choose to follow. The universe of approved traders is limited to the best 1,000 traders who comply with certain criteria for drawdown, trading history and profit per trade.[180]

ZuluTrade applies the concept of combined broker and network revenues (see Figure 4.1). Thus, next to its own integrated broker Triple A Experts (AAAfx), it also enables its users to open new accounts or to link existing accounts with a variety of supported brokerage firms.[181] Figure 4.4 shows the Business Model Canvas for ZuluTrade.

At ZuluTrade, users can invest in the foreign exchange market (Forex), CFDs and cryptocurrencies, either exclusively through copy trading with a profit-sharing account or with a classic account, which also enables manual trading. Before ultimately opening a real account, investors can get started with a free demo account, which provides all the features that are available in a live account.[182] However, this service also comes with a disadvantage since signal providers are not limited to sending signals from live accounts. Instead, they can also execute trades with a risk-free demo account, which is why their trades are likely to bear higher risks. ZuluTrade grants users access to the complete record of historical trades of each signal provider and ranks signal providers by a proprietary algorithm considering parameters such as maturity, exposure and drawdown.[183] Risk-mitigating features such as the "Automator" are available to serve clients as a personal assistant who monitors, reports or automatically executes actions based on an "if . . . then" logic that can be configured by the account users themselves.[184]

---

178 Crunchbase 2019i.
179 ZuluTrade 2019e.
180 ZuluTrade 2019b.
181 ZuluTrade 2019e.
182 ZuluTrade 2019e.
183 ZuluTrade 2019d.
184 ZuluTrade 2019a.

Key partners	Key activities	Value propositions	Customer relationships	Customer segments
Owner FORMAX Group	Online onboarding and authentication of signal providers	Free use of platform	Online	Private signal providers
Own brokerage firm Triple A Experts (AAAfx)	Algorithm-based ranking and monitoring of signal providers	Manual as well as copy trading	Direct communication between signal providers and followers	Private signal followers
Other supported brokers	Online platform	Ranking of traders and sophisticated analysis tools	User experience and convenience	Institutional signal providers
Affiliates		Knowledge transfer within the online community	Online education	Institutional signal followers
Providers of offered products		Free and fully-featured demo account	On-demand support via telephone, mail, or live chat available 24/7	
		Choice between several different brokers		
	Key resources	Automated trading based on "if-then" conditions via Automator	**Channels**	
	Innovative signal providers		Online platform	
	Active online community	Risk mitigation via ZuluGuard	Mobile app	
	Online platform	Signal providers: Realization of own trading systems and monetary compensation	Webpage of affiliates	
	Network of supported brokers		Social media (e.g., linkage of ZuluTrade account to Facebook or Twitter)	

Cost structure	Revenue streams
Development and maintenance of online platform	Bid-Ask spread earned on trades through accounts with AAAfx
Fixed and personnel cost	Part of Bid-Ask spread for initiation of a trade through accounts with other brokers
Performance/membership fee paid to signal providers	
Commission paid to affiliates of 0.4 pips per traded lot of clients who signed up through their URL	

Figure 4.4: Business Model Canvas – ZuluTrade.
(Source: own illustration)

ZuluTrade requires a functioning and active community as well as successful signal providers. Moreover, the role of the network of supported brokerage firms is essential for its business since it provides flexibility. Communication with customers happens almost purely online. Additionally, clients can get personal, on-demand support via phone, mail or live chat.[185] In addition to the desktop browser platform, users can access their accounts via a mobile app and link their ZuluTrade accounts to social media networks like Facebook or Twitter to share trades with their private followers.[186]

Due to the combined business model of broker and network revenues, ZuluTrade's revenue streams comprise both the full spread earned on trades with the integrated broker AAAfx and the participation in spreads on trades initiated as the introducing broker. Next to unavoidable expenses such as cost of maintenance and development of the platform, ZuluTrade shares 0.4 pips per lot traded by clients who have signed up through the URL of an affiliate with the corresponding marketing partner.[187] Moreover, European signal providers earn a fixed, volume-based compensation of 0.5 pips per lot copied by clients with a classic account and are paid a monthly performance-based fee of 20% according to the High Watermark (HWM) principle for profit sharing accounts. In contrast, U.S. traders receive a variable, monthly membership fee that is primarily determined by the total capital invested in the strategy and the number of signals generated per month.[188]

Wikifolio – following traders with certificates

Wikifolio was founded in 2008 and the company received about €6 million in funding until 2019. The platform's operator wikifolio Financial Technologies GmbH serves clients in Austria, Germany and Switzerland, and provides an investment universe including shares, exchange-traded products (ETPs) and structured products.[189] Wikifolio is a pure social trading provider that operates under the certificate-based business model. On wikifolio's platform, private signal providers as well as professional asset management firms and media companies embed their know-how and investment ideas in "wikifolios" in which signal followers can participate through certificates issued by the service provider's partner Lang & Schwarz. The certificates can be acquired either on the cooperating exchange in Stuttgart or OTC from the issuing entity itself.[190] Consequently, signal followers are not limited to certain brokers but can open an account with a brokerage firm of their own choice.

As in the previous examples, Figure 4.5 provides a Business Model Canvas for wikifolio. It offers a cost-free platform where investors can find an online community,

185 ZuluTrade 2019c.
186 ZuluTrade 2019e, 2020.
187 ZuluTrade 2014.
188 ZuluTrade 2018.
189 Wikifolio 2019f; Crunchbase 2019h.
190 Wikifolio 2019i.

Key partners	Key activities	Value propositions	Customer relationships	Customer segments
Lang & Schwarz AG as issuer of investment certificates	Online onboarding & authentication of signal providers	Free use of platform	Online	Private signal followers
		Access to rated portfolios	Indirect communication between signal providers and followers	Private signal providers
Stuttgart Stock Exchange as trading platform	Approval of wikifolio as basis for the reference index for an investment certificate	Knowledge transfer within the online community		Professional signal providers, i.e., asset managers and media companies
Providers of shares, funds, ETPs, and structured products	Scoring & ranking of wikifolios	Transparent pricing of certificates on the exchange	User experience and convenience	
	Online platform	Transparent cost structure	Online tutorials	
Brokerage firms		Performance-driven motivation of signal providers	On-demand support via telephone or mail available 24/7	
Professional signal providers	**Key resources**		**Channels**	
Advertising partners	Innovative signal providers	Collateralized certificates	Online platform	
Venture capitalists	Active online community	Use of broker of own choice	Internet	
	Online platform		Social media	
	wikifolio certificates	Signal providers: Realization of own investment ideas at no transaction cost and performance fee		

Cost structure	Revenue streams
Payments between Wikifolio and Lang & Schwarz	Payments between Wikifolio and Lang & Schwarz
Development and maintenance of online platform	Fee on structured investment product wikifolio-certificate of 0.95% per year
Fixed and personnel cost	Performance fee of up to 30%, which is based on HWM principle and partly shared with the signal provider
Proportion of performance fee paid to signal providers	
Issuing cost for the structured investment product wikifolio-certificate	

Figure 4.5: Business Model Canvas – wikifolio.
(Source: own illustration)

which interacts through comments and forum discussions. When it comes to the vehicle of copying, that is, certificates, wikifolio has some unique advantages for investors. Firstly, trading on the exchange provides transparent pricing. Secondly, Lang & Schwarz completely hedges the positions.[191] However, investors must be aware that

---

191 Wikifolio 2019g.

the issuer risk remains due to the nature of the certificate product. Moreover, the fees entailed in the investment consist of two components already considered in the price of the certificate. Therefore, the investors pay the charges indirectly. The certificate value as well as its return are net of fees, resulting in a transparent cost structure. No transaction fees occur as the trading in wikifolios exclusively takes place on a virtual basis.[192]

In order to provide the values described in Figure 4.5, wikifolio has to authenticate signal providers and approve their wikifolios to assure a certain quality for investors. Thus, the platform requires its users to legitimize their identity before they offer an "investible" wikifolio.[193] In order to be "investible," the portfolio has to comply with certain criteria such as a minimum lifetime of 21 days and at least 10 unbinding reservations by other wikifolio users with an aggregate potential investment amount of 2,500 EUR or CHF.[194] After a consultation call held to clarify title, trading idea, as well as compliance-related aspects, the wikifolio receives approval and the certificate can be issued.[195] To further assist signal followers to distinguish between reasonable investment ideas and unsuitable portfolios, wikifolio scores and ranks the portfolios according to the trader's performance, activity, popularity, etc.[196]

It is vital for the business of wikifolio that ideas of signal providers are innovative as well as profitable and that the online community engages in brisk interaction. Moreover, the business model crucially relies on key partners such as Lang & Schwarz and Stuttgart Stock Exchange. wikifolio also communicates actively on social media.

Wikifolio users have to pay two different fees: a certificate fee and a performance fee, implying a profit-based approach for the compensation of signal providers. The certificate fee amounts to 0.95% per annum and is calculated daily based on the market value of the wikifolio. The performance fee follows the HWM principle and ranges from 5% to 30% per annum; the signal provider and the platform fix the exact level. The percentage share that is attributed to the signal provider depends on the capital invested in the certificates of the respective portfolio and can amount to up to 50%. The exact sharing of fee income between wikifolio, Lang & Schwarz and other involved parties is not transparent from an external perspective. This opacity also holds for the cost incurred on the platform due to the emission of certificates.[197]

---

192 Wikifolio 2019a.
193 Wikifolio 2019b.
194 Wikifolio 2019e.
195 Wikifolio 2019c.
196 Wikifolio 2019h.
197 Wikifolio 2019a, 2019d.

4.3 Prospects of social trading

Benefits for traders

Ultimately, the question remains how successful social trading turns out to be for the different stakeholders on the platform. On the one side, the providers of signals usually receive compensation payment, whether it be a performance fee or another form of participation. On the other side, it is straight forward that the success of signal followers is equivalent to the net performance of copied signal providers. The average trader in social trading is a male investor between the ages of 31 and 60 who has previous experience in financial markets. In his portfolio, social trading investments present only a minor share of invested capital and serve for diversification or for reasons of self-education.

Simple strategies, that is, simply following the signal providers who offer the highest cumulative returns, yield extremely negative results on some platforms. A simulation of this naive strategy on the until the year 2019 in Frankfurt existing social trading platform ayondo, for example, led to an investment loss of 92.3%. In contrast, a more advanced strategy, which selects traders based on the Sharpe ratio, can achieve a better performance. And does high trading activity translate into elevated returns? Empirical results show that increased trading activity exerts a negative impact on performance. And what about the wisdom of the crowd? Empirical findings on portfolios with the highest capital invested and the highest number of followers could not confirm that the wisdom of the crowd produces higher yields.[198]

Pan, Altshuler and Oentland investigated how well the crowd of Israeli social trading platform eToro performs in selecting signal providers. Since the crowd likely sees traders of portfolios with the most followers as top picks, the authors applied this strategy to mimic collective intelligence. They compared the obtained Sharpe ratio to the corresponding metric resulting from a second strategy, which simply copied the best traders according to accumulated continuously compounded return. For the top 5 and top 10 signal providers, the community's selection outperforms the second strategy, presumably as the crowd is less inclined to take risks. However, when going beyond the top 10, the performance of the crowd deteriorates. This observation contradicts the assumption of a rational crowd whose preference would be in line with traders' performance.[199]

Signal followers are well advised to not blindly delegate portfolio management to signal providers. Instead, investing on such platforms makes the assessment of traders' qualities and skills as well as thorough analysis of their strategies indispensable. By implementing reasonable criteria for the approval of traders to the community, social trading platforms can assure a minimum quality of signal providers and support

---

198 Dorfleitner et al. 2018, pp. 7–8, 15, 21, 24–26, 28.
199 Pan et al. 2012, pp. 203, 205–206.

followers with identifying the most talented picks among the mass of traders through the provision of efficient screening tools as well as extensive trading records. Moreover, not only platform providers but also social traders themselves should understand the consequences of compensation schemes since an appropriate setting of incentives could help to align the trading behavior of signal providers with the interest of their followers. Given that platform providers understand their role in providing help to users, rational social traders can well make money in social trading if they understand the need for active involvement in the copying decision as well as for performance monitoring in order to adjust the copied universe if necessary.

Market potential

In Europe, first deals in social trading fintechs took place in 2009. In the U.S., deal activity happened slightly earlier in 2007, but financing rounds almost ceased again in the years after 2008. In Germany, social trading started to pick up speed in 2012 and its AUM grew at a CAGR of 213% from 2008 to 2015. By the end of 2015, users in Germany transferred about €190 million on social trading platforms.[200]

As the social trading community relies heavily on the use of CFDs, the CFD market serves as a potential proxy of market volume in this segment. In Germany, the CFDs Association commissioned a study in the attempt to assess the German CFD market and, among other things, also classified the different methods and tools CFD investors use as a basis of investment decision (see Figure 4.6).

Among other things, the study revealed that the most influential factors that triggered traders' investment decisions in 2017 were chart analysis and economic or financial news. However, information based on social trading influences 6.8% of decisions. Since the recommendations of other traders and automated trading signals are closely associated with social trading, additional 12.7% and 9.9%, respectively, add to the CFD volume available to social trading. Lastly, as social trading may be "the next generation of market letters,"[201] a further 13.6% are included. The analysis shows a target group for social trading of 43% of investors in CFD trading in Germany.

According to a study by Research and Markets the global CFD market is expected to grow at a CAGR of about 9% from 2018 to 2022.[202] But other more critical market participants only look at CFDs as a certain form of betting; it can be a short-term hype and the potential in the overall market could be very limited. One example of a social trading platform which failed to meet the expectations was the Singapore and Frankfurt based company ayondo. It filed for insolvency in August 2019.

---

200 Dorfleitner and Hornuf 2016, pp. 37–39.
201 Brylewski and Lempka 2016, p. 149.
202 Research and Markets 2018.

Chart technique and tools	83.30%
Economic and financial news	51.40%
Fundamental data	36.40%
"Gut feeling"	22.00%
Market letters	13.60%
Recommendations of other traders	12.70%
Automated trading signals	9.90%
Social trading	6.80%

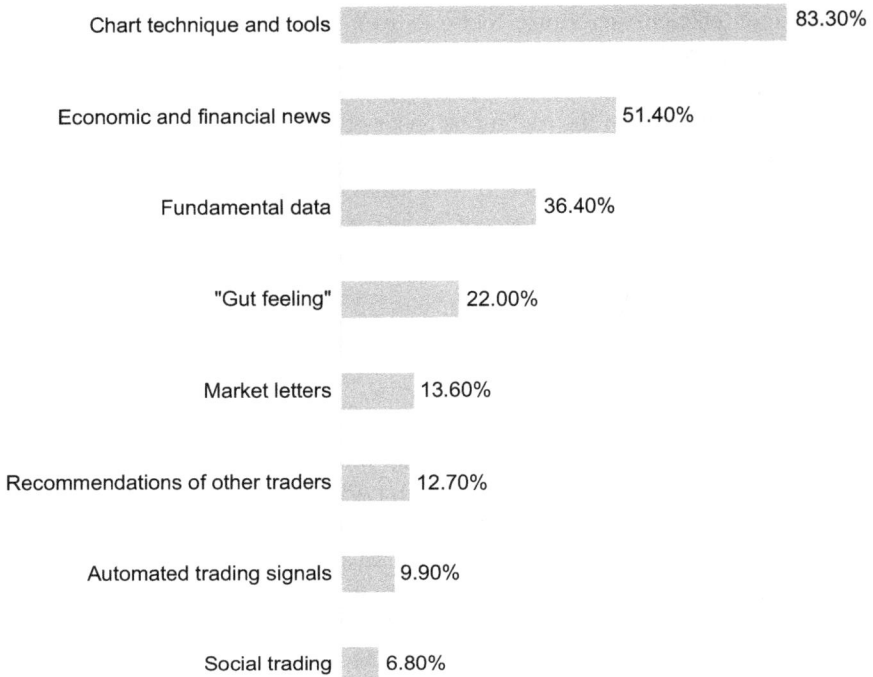

Figure 4.6: Decision factors impacting German CFD investments in 2017.
(own illustration with data from Contracts for Difference Verband e.V. 2017, p. 12)

The regulatory challenge

The regulatory perspective may trigger further dynamics. In 2012 the European Securities and Markets Authority (ESMA) stated that it considers mirror and copy trading as an automated execution of trade signals, which functions without any intervention by the client but allows the service provider to act on behalf of the client after giving a mandate. Therefore, this service falls within Article 4(1)(9) of the MiFID regulation, which defines portfolio management as "managing portfolios in accordance with mandates given by clients on a discretionary client-by-client basis where such portfolios include one or more financial instruments."[203] Therefore, ESMA requires social trading platforms to comply with the MiFID regulation.

Further national regulations, which are relevant for social trading, exist on a European country level. For example, in the U.K. the regulatory entity Financial

---

203 ESMA 2012, p. 15.

Conduct Authority (FCA) agrees with the view of ESMA and requires providers of such activities to own FCA portfolio management authorization in addition to European guidelines.[204] The relevant institution in Germany is the German Federal Financial Supervisory Authority (BaFiN), which similarly concentrates on the mandate given to the platform as a focal point. It concludes that social trading platforms provide financial portfolio management according to §1 Banking Act, which is why such providers are required to own the respective license in line with §32 Banking Act.[205]

In the U.S., regulation in terms of social trading is less straightforward. Depending on the business model, a platform can be classified as Commodities Trading Advisor (CTA), which is "an individual or organization that, for compensation or profit, advises others, directly or indirectly, as to the value of or the advisability of trading futures contracts, options on futures, retail off-exchange Forex contracts or swaps."[206] Furthermore, all registered CTAs who manage or exercise discretion over customer accounts have to be a National Futures Association (NFA) member. Therefore, all social trading networks that offer one of these instruments and provide specific investment advice to clients and/or have authority over a client's account, require corresponding authorization. Although there are some exemptions that might apply in individual cases, the majority of social trading providers in the U.S. fall within this regulation.[207]

In the U.S. there is further regulation that imposes restrictions on the business of social trading and that leads several platforms to refuse U.S. citizens. Especially the trading of OTC products like CFDs is subject to heavy regulation by the Securities and Exchange Commission (SEC).[208] Also, in Germany laws have become more stringent and since 2017 CFDs with an additional payment obligation offered to private investors are forbidden. Before this regulation was enforced, investors potentially had to face losses exceeding the invested capital.[209]

Undoubtedly, strict regulation might deter entrepreneurs from starting a social trading business and present a threat to this fintech segment. However, the regulatory framework will at the same time lead to a growing need for innovative solutions and create the opportunity for adopters of new business models to position themselves successfully in the market.

---

204 Financial Conduct Authority 2016.
205 BaFin 2016.
206 National Futures Association 2018a.
207 National Futures Association 2018a.
208 Matonis 2012.
209 BaFin 2017b.

4.4 Venture capital financing of social trading fintechs

Social trading belongs to the broader area of trading platforms but also to the area of personal finance. Table 4.1 illustrates the global venture capital investments for the broad area of trading systems from January 2017 until April 2020. The number of financing rounds in these three years was 102 globally with a total of $761 million raised. With nearly $4 billion, the pre-money valuations in the U.S. are significantly higher than in Europe. The median amount of money raised in 32 financing rounds in the U.S. was $2.2 million while in Europe the median amount of money raised in 34 financing rounds was $1.5 million. The data available for China is not significant for further analysis. Therefore, the detailed analysis of financing rounds for social trading focuses on the U.S. and Europe.

Table 4.1: Trading platform fintechs overview of venture capital financing statistics for sample January 2017–April 2020.

Location	Number Financing Rounds	Median Money Raised	Total Money Raised	Total Pre-Money Valuation
China	1	n/a	$28,951,730	n/a
Europe	34	$1,574,430	$201,766,409	$768,417,115
U.S.	32	$2,250,000	$357,881,000	$3,917,000,000
World	102	$3,000,000	$761,865,362	$5,090,937,855

(Source: own illustration with data from Crunchbase 2020e)

Six venture capital financed fintechs are attributed to the social trading segment in the data sample April 2000 to June 2017. The split of fintechs founded each year in Europe and the U.S. is shown in Figure 4.7.

The first social trading fintech with venture capital financing was founded in the U.S. in 2005. However, this milestone did not yet result in a wave of new social trading start-ups. New social trading fintechs were established in both Europe and the U.S. only sporadically in the following 10 years (see Figure 4.8). Correspondingly, it can be stated that no real trend can be determined based on the new foundations. This could mean that founders do not see a lot of potential in this segment as there are only a few players in the market so far.

Deal activity in social trading in Europe and the U.S. started in 2007 when the first deal in this segment was publicly recorded. In the subsequent six years only one financing round was closed each year, before the peak of four deals in one year was reached in 2014 (see Figure 4.9). After that, deal activity cooled down again to one deal per year. It is apparent that deal activity in Europe was much higher than

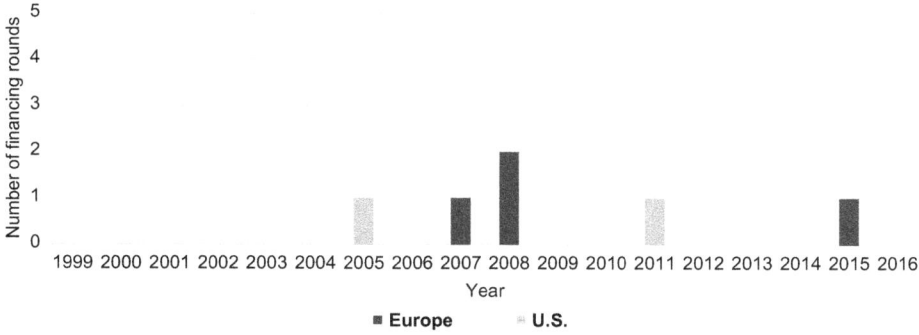

Figure 4.7: Number of fintechs founded in social trading in Europe and the U.S. from 1999–2016 for sample April 2000–June 2017.
(Source: own illustration)

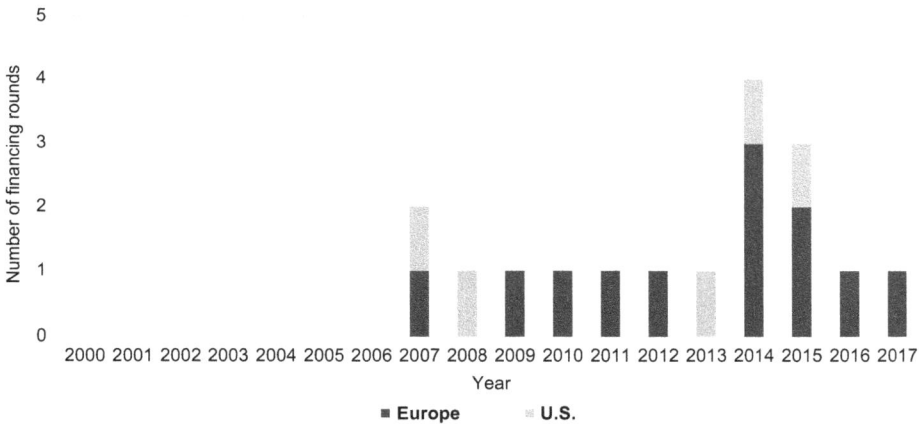

Figure 4.8: Number of financing rounds in social trading in Europe and the U.S. for sample April 2000–June 2017.
(Source: own illustration)

in the U.S., which is mainly explained by the fact that the U.S. had only two fintechs, whereas Europe had four social trading start-ups.

Figure 4.9 shows the annual amount raised in the social trading segment. Social trading is a segment with small funding amounts because the total raised amount of €100 million represents only 0.4% of the amount raised across all segments within the sample. Nevertheless, it is apparent that funding fluctuates quite strongly, given the low scale of the graph. The amounts raised only surpassed the €10 million mark in four years (2012, 2014, 2015, 2017), predominantly driven by Europe. In general, social trading seems to attract more funding in Europe than in the U.S.

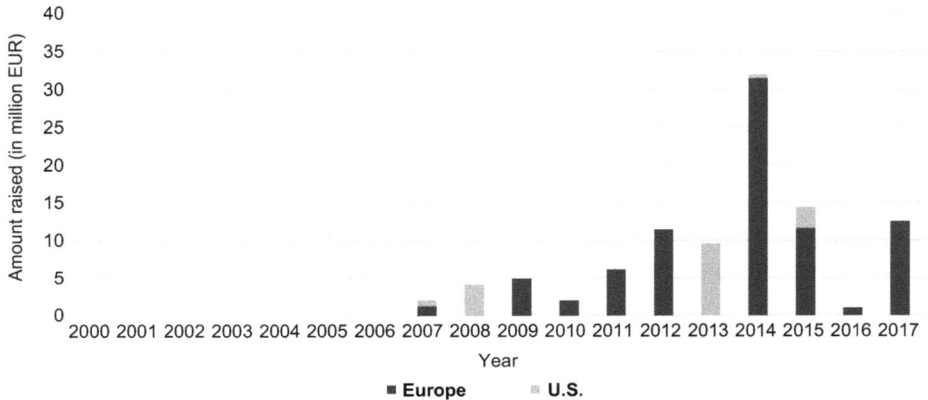

Figure 4.9: Annual overview of amount raised in social trading in Europe and the U.S. for sample April 2000–June 2017 (in € m).
(Source: own illustration)

In Table 4.2, the median amount raised for each financing round is compared for Europe and the U.S. It should be noted that the sample size is very low and hence only permits indications to be made rather than profound conclusions.

Table 4.2: Median amount raised in social trading in Europe and the U.S. for sample April 2000–June 2017 (in € m).

	Seed	A	B	C	D	E	F	IPO
Overall Median	0.5	3.4	10.0	2.9	21.6	n/a	n/a	n/a
Median Europe	n/a	3.6	4.9	2.9	21.6	n/a	n/a	n/a
Median U.S.	0.5	3.4	15.0	n/a	n/a	n/a	n/a	n/a
Sample size *n*	1	4	2	2	1	0	0	0

(Source: own illustration)

In the Seed Round, U.S. social trading fintechs secure €0.5 million of funding, which then increases to €3.4 million in round A. This is broadly in line with the European median of €3.6 million. In the subsequent financing round B, U.S. start-ups in this field manage to raise 95% more funds than their European counterparts (€9.6 million vs. €4.9 million). One European fintech collected €21.6 million of funding in its financing round D.

In line with the analysis of other segments, the median change in amounts raised between two financing rounds was analyzed. However, based on the extremely low sample size (Seed/A n = 1; A/B n = 2; B/C n = 1; C/D n = 1; D/E n = 0; E/F n = 0), only a comparison between rounds A and B can be conducted (see Figure 4.10).

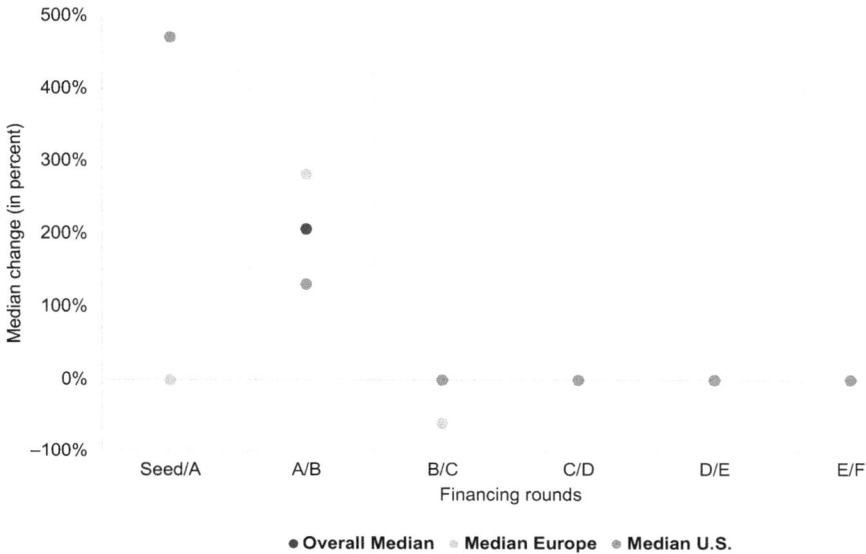

Figure 4.10: Median change in amounts raised between two successive financing rounds in social trading (in percent).

The median time difference between two successive financing rounds usually allows conclusions to be drawn about the difficulty of raising funds in conjunction with the median change in amounts raised. However, as mentioned before, the sample size (Seed/A n = 1; A/B n = 2; B/C n = 1; C/D n = 1; D/E n = 0; E/F n = 0) is not sufficient enough to draw any conclusions (see Figure 4.11).

U.S. social trading fintechs take roughly 1.5 years to close financing round A after the Seed round. This period then jumps to more than five years, which is an exceptionally high value across all segments, and compares to a little over two years for European fintechs in that space. The median increase in amount raised is significantly lower in the U.S., despite requiring approximately 2.5 times as long as their European counterparts to close the next financing round. Due to the limited availability of data for the social trading segment, the explanatory power of the analysis is minimal for this segment.

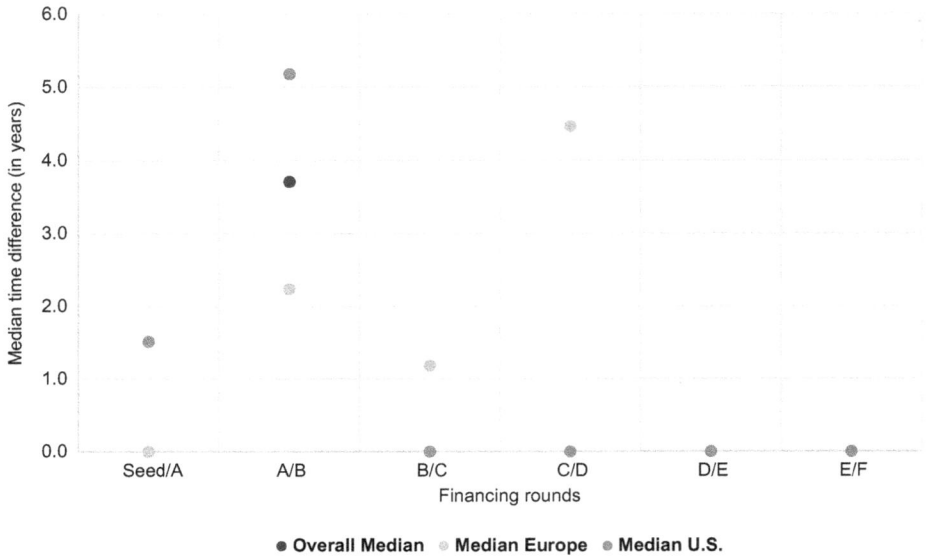

Figure 4.11: Median time difference in years between two successive financing rounds in social trading.

Summary

The fintech segment of social trading enables experienced retail investors to build up their own trading business as they can participate in the assets under management of their followers. The signal providers are therefore competitors of professional fund managers. But so far, the volumes traded over social trading platforms are quite small compared to the traditional investment fund industry and do not pose a real threat. Also, the venture capital volumes invested in the social trading fintech segment are far lower than in other fintech areas like payments or crowdfunding. Social trading platforms must comply with MiFID regulations just like robo-advisors or investment fund managers – there are no exceptions. For retail investors it can be exciting to transparently follow the signal providers. However, to date there are no empirical studies that clearly indicate that followers have performance advantages through the support of social trading. When CFDs are used on platforms, the risk for the investor can be very high as it becomes less about investing and more about gambling. CFDs are leverage products with the potential to produce significant losses in a very short time if the trade moves against an investor without an adequate risk management. Social trading platforms are therefore recommended only for experienced investors.

5 Will crowdfunding replace the bank loan?

5.1 When they mobilized the crowd

Crowdfunding is able to replace the traditional concept of a single big investor by mobilizing the crowd.[210] Thus, in its basic setting, a large number of individual investors contribute with relatively small amounts of money to provide funding for private and business purposes.[211]

In 2003, ArtistShare launched the first designated crowdfunding platform with the goal of supporting creative music artists.[212] In 2014, 3,000 crowdfunders sponsored the production of the German movie "Stromberg" with a total of €1 million. In return, the supporters participated in the revenues from the sale of tickets.[213] Another successful campaign was the new name of a soccer stadium in Nuremberg, Germany. The soccer fans wanted the stadium to bear the name of one of the former players and funded the stadium name change in cooperation with a bank.[214] We can see that the funding power of the crowd is not restricted to certain target areas but can be an appealing solution to almost any project.

Social media has supported the successful development of crowdfunding. The functional expansion of the internet has encouraged users to network online and to not only follow projects but rather to contribute to them. In addition to that, social media have become the primary channel of communication, which has enabled campaigns to be easily generated and spread to a wide audience.[215] Since this new coverage also provides the opportunity of introducing new ideas to the market and assessing their adoption, crowdfunding is no longer limited to financing purposes and actually serves as a mixture of funding, market research and marketing tool.[216]

No uniform definition has yet emerged for crowdfunding. Since crowdfunding represents a sub-segment of crowdsourcing, the participation of the crowd has become a common feature of definitions of crowdfunding. Investors can receive different forms of return for their financial contribution, which is why it is possible to attract almost any type of investor.

---

210 Wenzlaff and Philipps 2015, p. 1.
211 Belleflamme et al. 2012, p. 2.
212 ArtistShare 2018.
213 WELT 2014.
214 Consorsbank 2017.
215 Sixt 2014, pp. 8–9.
216 Dorfleitner and Hornuf 2016, p. 23; Wenzlaff and Philipps 2015, p. 1.

https://doi.org/10.1515/9783110704907-005

An answer to every demand

The idea of crowdfunding is to coordinate project initiators and investors to match supply and demand. In this regard, a crowdfunding platform provides an online market, which serves as the technical solution for fundraisers to spread their ideas and to introduce their projects to a wide base of backers.[217] Furthermore, the online platform provides mechanisms to implement required pledge levels or minimum investible pledge amounts. In many cases, a pre-defined minimum funding amount entails the "all-or-nothing principle" according to which the collected pledge amount is only paid out if the minimum funding goal has been reached. The concept assumes that project initiators are only able to set up the project successfully and to achieve the required returns in case they raise the minimum funding. The platform acts as an instance, which reduces information asymmetries and thus the risk for both parties.[218]

Crowdfunding has emerged in five different forms in terms of the returns offered to investors or backers. In crowdinvesting, crowdlending and real estate crowdfunding the project initiator pays a monetary compensation, while supporters in crowdrewarding and crowddonating receive a non-monetary reward in return for their financial pledge.[219]

The crowdfunding market landscape

The worldwide crowdfunding market has grown significantly in recent years. For example, in Europe overall crowdfunding volume grew from €408 million in 2013 to more than €6.5 billion in 2018 (see Figure 5.1). From 2013 to 2018, lending-based crowdfunding in the European Union (excl. U.K.) always accounted for the highest share in terms of volume, with 83% in 2018. Crowdinvesting had a share between 3% and 21%, while crowddonating was the smallest segment (see Figure 5.2).

Within the European Union, Germany took the leading position in donation-based crowdfunding ($28.0 million), real estate crowdfunding ($313.9 million) and P2P consumer lending ($651.3 million) in 2018. Within Germany, the crowdfunding market volume mainly consisted of P2P consumer lending, followed by real estate crowdfunding and P2P business lending.[220]

---

217 Bank for International Settlements and Financial Stability Board 2017, p. 11; Gierczak et al. 2016, p. 12.
218 Gierczak et al. 2016, p. 12.
219 Sixt 2014, pp. 56–57.
220 Ziegler et al. 2020, p. 82.

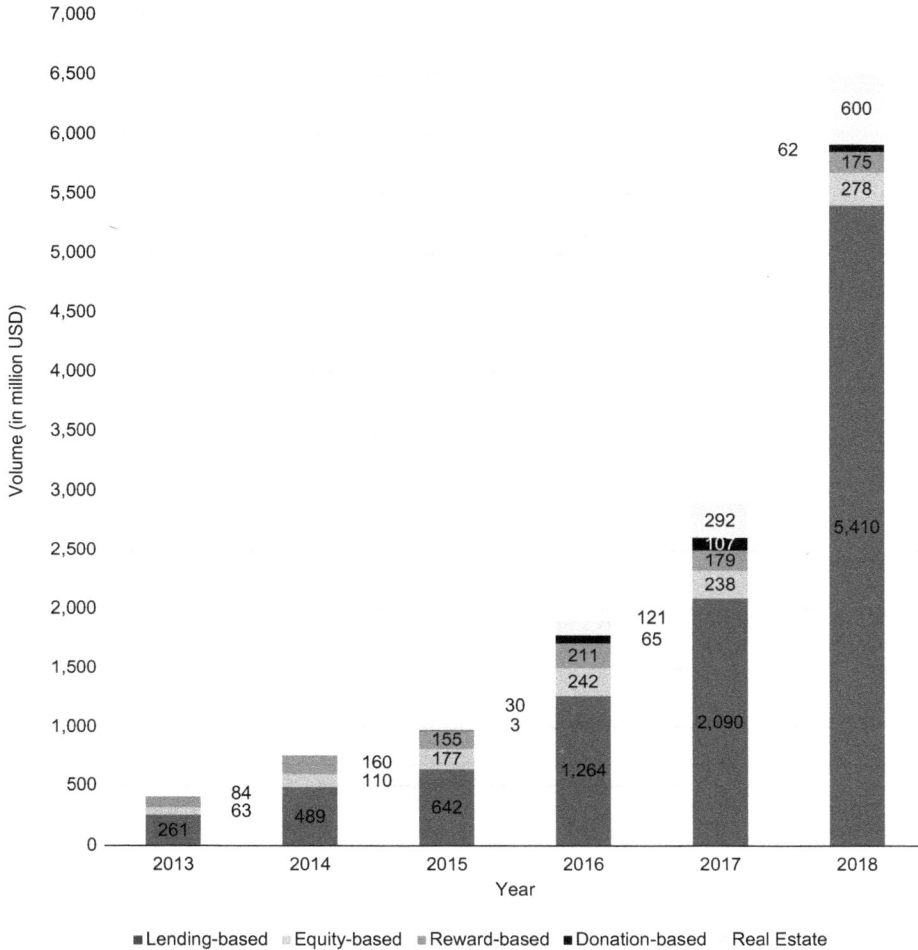

Figure 5.1: Crowdfunding market volume by type in million USD from 2013–2018 in the EU (excl. U.K.).
(Source: own illustration with data from Ziegler et al. 2020, p. 78)

Table 5.1 shows the amount of collected capital per segment, the number of successful projects and backers and the corresponding funding amounts. In 2016 reward-based crowdfunding in Germany collected the smallest amount of capital, but showed a higher financing sum per successful project when compared to the leading segment of crowdlending. However, while in 2013 the success rate of crowd-rewarding projects amounted to an impressive 72%, this number decreased to only 54% in 2016 – although the funding sum continued to rise during these four years. A lower number of realized projects can be observed, which attract relatively high average amounts.

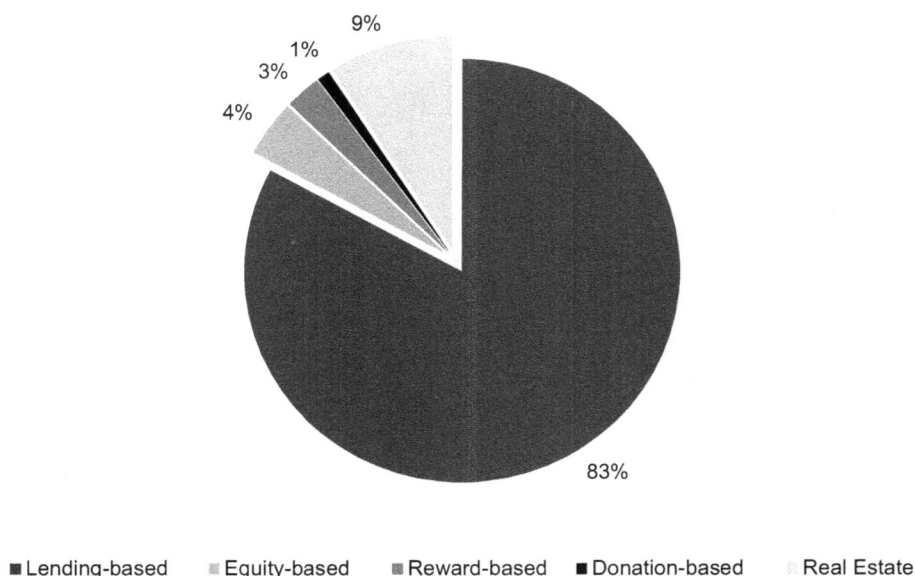

Figure 5.2: Percentage share in overall crowdfunding volume by type in 2018 in the EU (excl. U.K.). (Source: own illustration with data from Ziegler et al. 2020, p. 78)

Table 5.1: German crowdfunding market by segment in 2016.

	Reward-based	Donation-based	Equity-based	Lending-based
Collected capital	€9,700,00	€13,142,000	€63,843,198	€242,000,000
Number of successful projects	1,158	n/a	n/a	34,000
Amount per project	€8,377	n/a	n/a	€7,118
Number of backers	n/a	100,400	n/a	n/a
Amount per backer	n/a	€111	n/a	n/a

(Source: own illustration)

Regulatory barriers slow down growth

The rise of crowdfunding is impressive. However, the size of the alternative finance market can diverge between regions. In China alternative finance market volumes reached $216.55 billion in 2018 dwarfing Europe with $9.15 billion and the Americas with $64.05 billion. Segment-specific expectations are primarily available for crowd-lending. The dominance of the Chinese market has been possible mostly due to the lack of regulation for peer-to-peer lending which accounts for 99,7% of market share.[221]

In 2015 Morgan Stanley was very positive about the future development and estimated global marketplace lending to grow annually by 51% from 2014 to 2020. This trend would have resulted in a loan volume of $150 to $490 billion by the end of 2020.[222] Furthermore, Morgan Stanley expected online marketplaces to execute about 10% of financing granted to private borrowers and individuals.[223] This high market share was too optimistic.

Regulatory pressure and a crackdown on high-risk financing in China resulted in a drop of crowdlending platforms from 2,595 in 2015 to 1,021 at the end of 2018, dampening future growth estimates of the industry. Due to the regulatory development in China worldwide growth is estimated to be a CAGR of 17% p.a. in the period from 2018 to 2022.[224]

In contrast to China, the European market lags. To some part, this might be attributable to the regulatory framework as suggested by the European Alternative Finance Industry Report. According to this analysis, 43% of equity-based crowdfunding platforms indicate that there is excessive regulation in place, while only 5% actually see a need for further expansion of the regulatory framework.[225] In crowddonating and rewarding, queried platforms consider existing regulation to be adequate. However, since no specific regulation is in place for these segments, that result is not surprising.[226]

In the U.S. regulation concentrates on equity-based crowdfunding implemented through Pillar III of the JOBS Act, which is referred to as Regulation Crowdfunding. Platforms registered with the SEC can raise a total amount of $1,070,000 with crowdfunding offerings during a 12-month period. Furthermore, the Act sets rules for yearly investment amounts of individuals and defines disclosure requirements.[227]

In March 2018 the European Commission presented a legislative proposal for equity- and lending-based crowdfunding. Following the goal of lower hurdles to growth, the proposal aims at easing cross-border provision of crowdfunding services within the EU to improve access to this type of financing, in particular for start-ups.[228]

221 Ziegler et al. 2020, pp. 34–35; P2PMarketData 2019a.
222 Morgan Stanley 2015.
223 Steinkühler 2017, p. 39.
224 P2PMarketData 2019b; TechNavio 2018.
225 Ziegler et al. 2018, p. 51.
226 Ziegler et al. 2018, pp. 52, 64.
227 U.S. Securities and Exchange Commission 2017.
228 European Commission 2018.

On a national level, for example, in Germany, crowdfunding operations are regulated by the German Capital Investment Act (Vermögensanlagengesetz, VermAnlG), applying to investments publicly offered in Germany. The German Capital Investment Act requires a prospectus for funding projects beyond €100,000 according to § 2 (1) sentence 3 VermAnlG. Since the creation of such documents entails considerable complexity and cost, equity-based platforms generally shift their financing method toward subordinate loans, which have been exempted from the prospectus requirement since 2015.[229] Furthermore, loan brokerage does not require crowdlending platforms to hold a banking license but a commercial license according to §34c or §34f Trade Regulation (GewO). Therefore, in such cases BaFin is no longer the supervising authority.

However, individual contracts might fall within the scope of the Payment Services Supervisory Act or German Banking Act. Individuals who invest their money with the goal of profit realization are subject to supervision, which automatically applies equally to the platform due to its interaction with these customers (§ 37 (1) sentence 4 Banking Act). Consequently, crowdlending platforms usually cooperate with a partner with a banking license.[230]

5.2 Equity-based crowdfunding

Start-ups often apply equity-based crowdfunding, also called crowdinvesting, because they can not successfully raise venture capital or public funding, but hope to obtain financing from a number of private investors. The investors either obtain a participation in equity and mezzanine capital or participate in the financial performance of the project.[231] In a profit participating loan, for example, the capital provider receives a revenue or earnings-based component in addition to fixed interest rate payments, but carries no loss participation. Another option, participating rights, entitles the capital provider to benefit from future earnings and, in the case of qualified participating rights, from the liquidation of the company.[232] The options presented above all share one characteristic: there is no participation in an increase in value of the funded company.[233]

As presented in Figure 5.1, a major value proposed by crowdinvesting platforms is that entrepreneurs can easily approach a broad base of potential private and institutional financiers, which for their part are attracted by the opportunity to invest in attractive projects and ideas at an early stage. However, these online marketplaces

---

229 Ziegler et al. 2018, p. 64.
230 BaFin 2007, 2018.
231 Beck 2014, pp. 13, 90.
232 Sixt 2014, pp. 17–19.
233 Beck 2014, p. 91.

not only act as a means of communication, but also induce an exchange of information and set certain framework conditions for the legal relationship between both
parties.[234]

Key partners	Key activities	Value propositions	Customer relationships	Customer segments
Investors	Development and maintenance of platform	Free use of platform	Online	Private and institutional investors
Borrowers		Access to capital and a wide investor base for borrowers	Self-service	
Regulatory authorities	Online onboarding		On-demand customer support	Borrowers
Venture capitalists	Thorough assessment of projects	Access to attractive projects at an early stage	Community	
Affiliates	Due diligence		Blog	
Custodian to manage invested capital	Marketing and user acquisition	Available for small investment and financing amounts		
	Key resources		**Channels**	
	Platform		Website	
	Software		Social networks	
	Community		TV commercials	
	Regulatory approval and licenses		Affiliates' webpages	
	Venture capital		Mobile app	

Cost structure	Revenue streams
Development and maintenance of platform	Origination fee as a percentage of total invested capital charged from borrower
Marketing expense	Yearly handling fee
Fixed and personnel expenses	
Cost for approval of projects and support	

Figure 5.3: Business Model Canvas – equity-based crowdfunding.
(Source: own illustration)

Equity-based crowdfunding platforms must onboard their users online (see Figure 5.3).
Assessing the projects in depth to guarantee qualitatively high investment opportunities for the investors is crucial for success. Therefore, platforms require potential entrepreneurs to present elaborated business plans with all relevant data and carry out
sophisticated assessments, where the individual steps differ from provider to provider.[235] An online portal might, for example, measure potential on the basis of the

---

234 Beck 2014, p. 115.
235 Ronsdorf 2014, pp. 33–34.

number of participants who express their interest in a project in the form of likes.[236] Such an innovative approach might be considered superficial and lacking the sophisticated assessment otherwise carried out by venture capitalists, business angels and banks. Professional investors, banks or insurance companies usually try to reduce information asymmetries through a deep fundamental analysis of the business model.

During the vetting phase, the companies also set a minimum funding amount as well as an upper limit and elaborate a valuation with the platform, which later serves as a basis for the derivation of investors' profit participation.[237] Once the platform approves the project and the project has reached the required financing volume, investor and initiator enter into a legal agreement and the project receives the collected amount.[238] If the investor can not collect the minimum amount, financiers are refunded their capital.[239]

As is usual in the fintech sector, the interaction with customers primarily takes place online, with the addition of mobile apps in some cases. The platforms usually provide customer service via different channels such as phone or live chat. Most marketing measures involve social media or TV commercials, and in many cases affiliates support providers with the expansion of their user base. Next to affiliate partners, the business model of an equity-based crowdfunding platform builds on a number of additional partnerships. For example, the involvement of a custodian bank is normally required for the management of invested capital. Crowdinvesting is subject to supervision, which makes interaction with regulatory authorities indispensable. In most cases, revenues come from the commission charged on the total financing sum. Some platforms also collect secondary charges such as a yearly handling fee or listing fees. On the expense side, some of the most influential items include marketing and staff expenses as well as costs related to the technological platform.[240]

AngelList – with zero management fees

A well-known player in the field of equity-based crowdfunding is U.S.-based AngelList, which funded the impressive sum of $1.2 billion for 4,115 start-ups since its establishment in 2010 until January 2020.[241] Its founders started their business with a website called VentureHacks, which they launched with the intention to provide a place where the start-up community could gather and reduce the opacity of the venture capital market. Following their users' wish to get in touch with angel investors, the founders

—————
236 Hahn and Naumann 2014, p. 179.
237 Beck 2014, pp. 20–21; Ronsdorf 2014, p. 35.
238 Hahn and Naumann 2014, p. 180.
239 Beck 2014, p. 19.
240 Beck 2014, pp. 117–119, 120.
241 AngelList 2020.

listed the entrepreneurs and started to share interesting investment opportunities with them.[242] This step formed the cornerstone of today's AngelList platform.

"At AngelList, we fundamentally believe in startups. We're building the definitive platform for startups – where they raise money [...], build teams [...], and launch their products."[243] This holistic concept presents one of the reasons for the success of AngelList. Next to crosslinking start-ups and financiers, the platform also serves as a recruiting marketplace for job seekers searching for employment in a start-up company and offers a website to share and discover new products with an acquired company called Product Hunt.[244] The participation on AngelList is restricted to SEC-accredited investors who, among other things, have to have had an individual annual income of at least $200,000 for the last two years.[245]

AngelList investors have different options to invest in start-ups. For affluent individuals or institutions, the platform provides a professional investor program for funding amounts starting at $1 million. On a more affordable scale, backers can also choose to participate in a diversified start-up fund managed by AngelList. As a third option, the crowdinvesting provider has developed a unique business model based on single-deal funds created to invest in single start-ups that it calls syndicates. Syndicate leads are experienced angel investors who not only vet the target investment but also confirm their trust in the project through their own capital injection to the fund. They bring syndicates to the online market. Backers can follow the contribution of the syndicate lead at minimum amounts of between $1,000 and $10,000 per deal.[246] Each syndicate investment entails a one-time cost component for third-party services of about $8,000, which is split among all investors on a pro-rata basis. There is no management fee involved.[247]

For its syndication business model, AngelList received a non-action letter by the SEC, which allows the platform to carry out its activities without registration as a broker-dealer under federal securities law. Instead, the company acts as an investment advisor charging carried interest and receives a cut of positive returns of usually 20% in total.[248]

Low fixed cost and scalable business model

The uniqueness of AngelList's business model becomes clear when comparing it with the economics of a traditional VC fund. In a traditional VC setting as illustrated in

---

242 Levy 2015.
243 AngelList 2018a.
244 Crunchbase 2019a; Wagner 2016.
245 AngelList 2020.
246 AngelList 2018b.
247 AngelList 2015.
248 Roderick 2013; AngelList 2018b.

Figure 5.4, limited partners invest almost the entire investment volume and delegate the management of the fund to general partners, who in return charge a fee of about 2% for their services and receive 20% carried interest. In an AngelList syndicate, syndicate leads provide on average 16% of the fund volume (see Figure 5.5). As mentioned above, there is no management fee and the average deal carry is approximately 20%, which the platform claims to be equivalent to about 25% in terms of fund carry.[249]

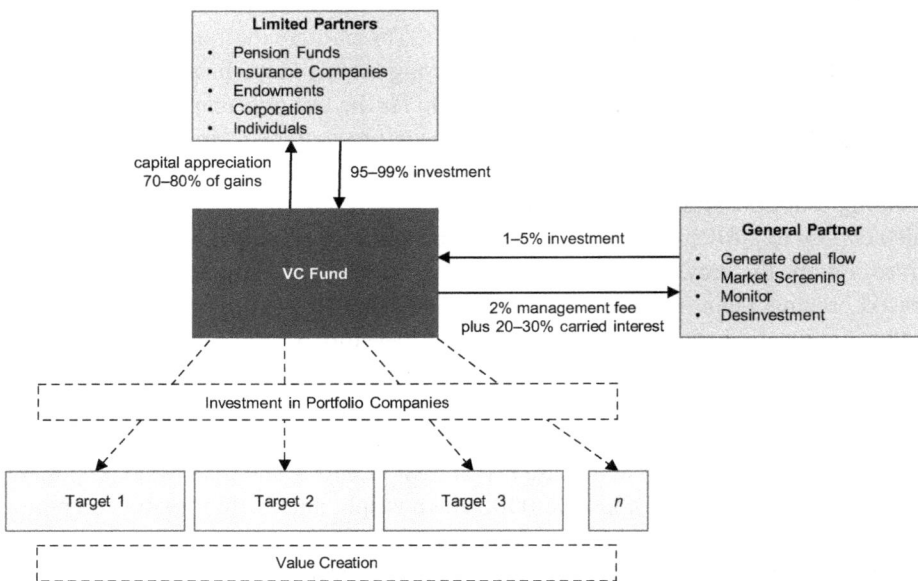

Figure 5.4: Structure of a classical Venture Capital fund.
(Source: own illustration)

AngelList keeps 5% of deal carry – and that is the aspect where the scalability of its business model steps in.[250] Given that the number of start-ups on AngelList will continue its upward trend, a considerable proportion of businesses will naturally fail. Since AngelList's operations rely predominantly on software, it only incurs very low variable costs. Moreover, failing projects do not significantly harm it. Instead, the crowdinvesting platform receives its carry for every successful project and even if only few projects turn out to be extremely profitable, the carry on these deals represents considerable income.[251]

---

249 Hackerbay 2015; AngelList 2015.
250 AngelList 2018c.
251 Hackerbay 2015.

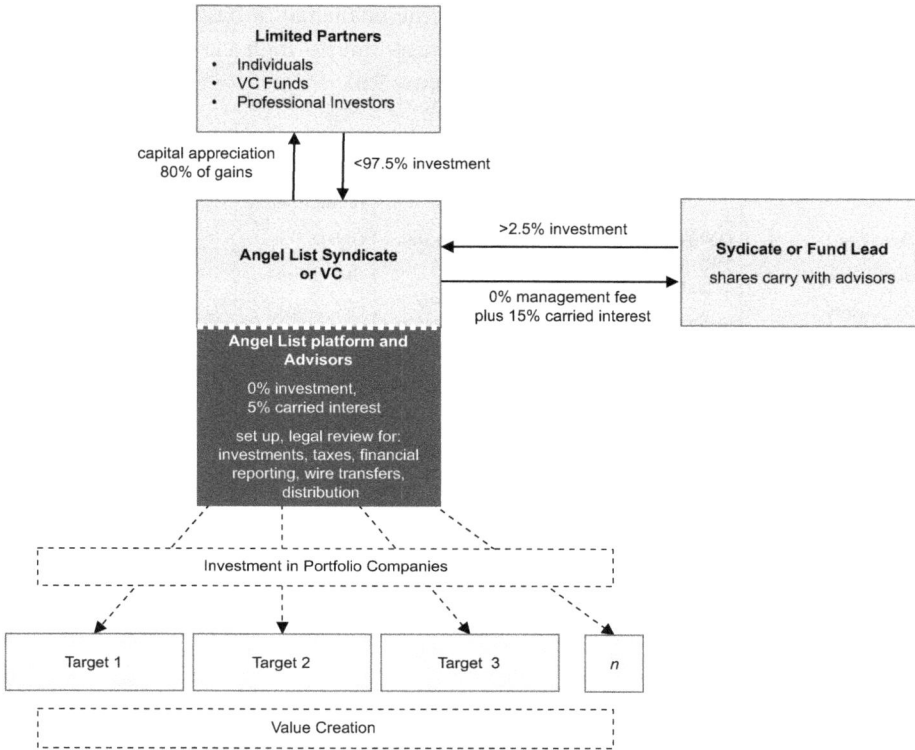

Figure 5.5: Structure of an AngelList Venture Capital fund.
(Source: own illustration)

5.3 Lending-based crowdfunding and LendingClub

Crowdlending or peer-to-peer lending platforms function as digital marketplaces and match the offers of funders with the requests of borrowers, without assuming ownership of the loans.[252] The basic idea is that crowdlending platforms enable the exclusion of an intermediary – the bank – in the loan process. The service platforms try to benefit from a reduced risk in case they do not hold the loans in the balance sheet. And theoretically, digital platforms could have huge cost savings compared to traditional lenders. According to the U.S. Federal Reserve, this advantage could make a cost difference of about 4% compared to traditional banks, which largely results from relatively fewer branches and higher process automation.[253]

---

252 Morgenthaler 2016, pp. 206–207; Ziegler et al. 2018, p. 28; Bank for International Settlements and Financial Stability Board 2017, p. 11.
253 Morgenthaler 2016, p. 206.

However, such crowdfunding providers face the challenge of balancing supply and demand, and might face negative gross returns due to high customer acquisition costs – particularly in the early stages (see Figure 5.6).

Key partners	Key activities	Value propositions	Customer relationships	Customer segments
Investors	Development and maintenance of platform	Efficient financial intermediation	Online	Private borrowers
Borrowers			Self-service	
Regulatory authorities	Online onboarding	Less complexity and faster settlement compared to traditional bank lending	On-demand customer support	Corporate borrowers
Venture capitalists	Online credit assessment of borrowers		Community	Credit card clients
Affiliates	Assessment of loan requests	Easier access to credit	Blog	Consumers with poor credit ratings
Partnering banks (in case no bank license is owned by fintech)	Loan performance statistics	Access for consumers with poor credit ratings		Consumers in areas with bad access to traditional banking offers
Software developers	Marketing and user acquisition	Solid returns for investors		
	Key resources		**Channels**	
External credit bureaus	Venture capital	Available at small investment/ financing amounts	Website	Investors
	Platform		Social networks	
	Software	Replacement of more expensive loans, e.g., from credit card companies	TV commercials	
	Community		Affiliates' webpages	
	Regulatory approval and licenses		Mobile app	
Cost structure		**Revenue streams**		
Development and maintenance of platform		Origination fee/commission charged from borrowers (often only if funding goal is reached)		
Marketing expense				
Fixed and personnel expenses		Service fee charged from investors		
Cost of credit assessment				

Figure 5.6: Business Model Canvas – lending-based crowdfunding. (Source: own illustration)

Lending-based crowdfunding involves pure debt financing. In comparison to a traditional bank loan, this alternative approach theoretically entails interest rates, which are more attractive to both the creditor as well as the borrower.[254] In practice, however, the interest rates for borrowers may also be quite high in comparison to attractive offers from traditional banks. Crowdfunding should also know to convince through relatively fast settlement and low complexity. These advantages could be the result of efficient financial intermediation due to the renouncement of a bank. However, platforms usually still partner with an institution owning a banking license for regulatory reasons, which is referred to as a notary crowdlending model.[255] It can be stated that although theoretical advantages for crowdlending platforms do exist, the important obstacles for future growth are regulation and experienced, sophisticated credit scoring systems in banks. Therefore, for most customers bank loans are still cheaper and easier to get than lending from crowdlending platforms.

In its most basic form, a prospective borrower applies for a loan and the platform decides if it approves the user or not on the basis of credit information provided by the borrower and external credit bureaus. In many cases, external software providers develop algorithms to create credit scores or to rate users. The leading provider of lending-based crowdfunding is U.S.-based LendingClub, which offers fixed-rate consumer loans at amounts ranging from $1,000 to $40,000.[256] LendingClub charges borrowers origination fees of 1% to 6%, which it directly deducts from the loan volume. The individual interest rates range from 6.46% to 28.80% depending on the credit score.[257] For borrowers with a very good rating these interest rates would be very high. However, especially in the U.S., they can still be beneficial for some borrowers as many borrowers use the loans to refinance even more expensive loans from credit card debt. As the interest rates are very high, most of the borrowers in Europe, for example, would never accept the high interest rates from LendingClub, but would prefer a consumer loan from their house bank.

Businesses can obtain loans with a maximum volume of $500,000 and incur origination fees of 1.99% to 8.99% and interest rates ranging from 5.99% to 29.99%.[258] Investors face a service charge of 1% on any payment and a collection fee in case a borrower's payment is delayed.[259] Moreover, LendingClub's fully-owned subsidiary LendingClub Asset Management, formerly LC Advisors, provides high-net-worth clients with efficient access to its marketplace consumer loans through customized investment services and strategies.[260] As a marketplace lender operating a notary business model, the platform circumvents the role of a creditor

---

254 Morgenthaler 2016, p. 206.
255 Bank for International Settlements and Financial Stability Board 2017, p. 13.
256 LendingClub 2019c.
257 LendingClub 2018b, 2019d.
258 LendingClub 2019a, 2018c.
259 LendingClub 2019d.
260 LendingClub Asset Management, LLC 2018.

while complying with regulatory requirements through its partnership with WebBank, which owns a banking license. With this approach, LendingClub does not assume default risk, but instead provides market transparency and price discovery.[261]

However, there is a more sophisticated idea behind the way LendingClub's cooperation works. First, WebBank originates a loan and immediately sells it to LendingClub, which in turn resells the loan backed by WebBank in small portions to its users.[262] These loan increments, which are referred to as notes, each have a value of $25 and are registered as securities with the SEC. Since the minimum initial contribution amounts to $1,000, users can split their investment to up to 40 loans and therefore diversify their capital across different terms, grades and interest rates – either on their own or by delegating the investment to the "automated investing" feature.[263] Registered investors can additionally trade their LendingClub notes with other users on an official secondary market, the note trading platform operated by Folio Investing. Transactions on this platform may not only be attractive for liquidity reasons, but also enable investment at other terms than the standardized 36- or 60-month period and, if identified by the user, with the possibility of taking advantage of underpricing.[264]

Crowdlending may have better future growth potentials once the important questions regarding regulation obstacles are solved and the big tech companies enter the market. But so far, important issues have not yet been solved: How can the platform have superior credit scoring and risk-adjusted pricing compared to the banks, given the vast scale difference? How can the economic results of the crowdfunding platforms, after loan losses, become better than the results of banks? How could the platforms solve the problem of adverse selection? How can users decide what to fund based on low levels of loan losses and highly sophisticated scoring systems? The goal must be that the scoring systems of the crowdlending platforms become more sophisticated than the scoring systems of the banks and that consumers get cheaper loans than offered by banks. Actual market observations show that there is still a long way do go.

5.4 Donation-based crowdfunding

Donation-based crowdfunding provides donations, which is why supporters receive no financial or material compensation.[265] Instead, beneficiaries often acknowledge

261 O'Connor 2016; Young 2019.
262 Young 2019.
263 LendingClub 2018d, 2018e.
264 LendingClub 2018a.
265 Sixt 2014, p. 57.

the investment through a letter of thanks, the public announcement of the donator's name on the webpage or another form of appreciation. Projects in this crowdfunding area often have a social and non-profit background and require a tight emotional relationship between the two protagonists. Donation-based crowdfunding is sometimes also referred to as fan-funding.[266]

To cover expenses, donation-based crowdfunding platforms charge a relatively small fee on pledges (see Figure 5.7). On top of that, investors are free to donate to the platform itself to support its operations and its growth. For example, betterplace.org founded in Germany in 2010, finances itself through cooperation with businesses and other supporters, private donations and a transaction fee of 2.5% charged on the donated amount.[267]

Key partners	Key activities	Value propositions	Customer relationships	Customer segments
Donors	Development and maintenance of platform	Access to a wide supporter base for fundraisers	Online	Donors
Fundraisers			Self-service	Fundraisers
Venture capitalists	Online onboarding	Comfortable access to projects for donors	On-demand customer support	
NGOs, non-profit organizations	Payment processing		Community	
Payment gateway	Marketing	International access for donors and fundraisers		
		Possibility of doing good at small amounts for donors		
	Key resources		**Channels**	
	Platform		Website	
	Community		Social networks	
	Network		Mobile app	
			NGOs' webpage	

Cost structure	Revenue streams
Development and maintenance of platform	Origination fee as a percentage charged on project donations
Marketing expenses	Donations to the platform
Fixed and personnel expenses	Payment processing fee (if processing is done by fintech)

Figure 5.7: Business Model Canvas – donation-based crowdfunding.
(Source: own illustration)

---

266 Beck 2014, pp. 25–26.
267 betterplace.org 2018.

Betterplace.org focuses on social projects carried out by acknowledged non-profit organizations in Germany and Austria and is designed to collect recurring donations over a longer period of time.[268] So far, the platform has crowdfunded roughly €90 million for more than 33,000 projects.[269]

The value added by the involvement of a donation platform such as betterplace.org surely lies in a huge expansion of the audience to which initiators can communicate their projects. Furthermore, a well-known stakeholder might increase the credibility of fundraisers and back the trust of potential donators. That is why non-governmental organizations as well as non-profit organizations often enter co-operations with crowd-donation businesses.

5.5 Reward-based crowdfunding and Kickstarter

Backers of crowdrewarding projects receive material and/or non-material compensation in return for their financial support. The material value of the reward is not necessarily equal to the amount of the investment, but the non-material value of the return usually is or even exceeds it. In general, the reward has a connection to the funded project and often consists of a discount on the developed product or in the privilege of getting a special variation of it. Pre-sales campaigns in which supporters provide advance payment for technical gadgets are an additional form of reward-based crowdfunding.[270]

Entrepreneurs see the greatest advantage of crowdrewarding platforms in the opportunity to implement their ideas or projects from scratch and to discover potential drawbacks in time, as they might pop up in the course of pre-sales. Moreover, the ideal value of non-material rewards often increases with the sponsored sum so that project initiators are given an indication of the willingness of potential future customers to pay for the product. On the other side, reward-based platforms give sponsors the opportunity to search for new talents and promising projects that they may want to support (see Figure 5.8).

U.S.-American Kickstarter is well established in crowdfunding and committed to enabling the realization of creative projects by bringing together creators and supporters.[271] Its focus on art and culture-related ideas gives it a competitive advantage in that niche but also enables Kickstarter to successfully expand in other project areas like technology. Since Kickstarter's foundation in 2009, its creators have collected almost $5 billion for more than 175,000 successfully financed projects

---

268 Kinzel 2018.
269 betterplace.org 2020.
270 Sixt 2014, p. 57.
271 Kickstarter, PBC 2020b.

Key partners	Key activities	Value propositions	Customer relationships	Customer segments
Sponsors Creators Venture capitalists Payment gateway provider	Development and maintenance of platform Online onboarding Qualitative assessment of projects Support in campaign management Marketing	Realization of ideas and projects from scratch Support of new talents and access to innovative projects for sponsors Rewards, e.g., in the form of prototypes, promotion material, T-shirts, stickers, sponsored products Available at small investment/ financing amounts Generation of presales	Online Self-service On-demand customer support Community	Entrepreneurs and artists Start-up businesses Sponsors
	Key resources Platform Community Quality of projects		**Channels** Website Social networks Mobile app Events	
Cost structure Development and maintenance of platform Marketing expenses Fixed and personnel expenses			**Revenue streams** Origination fee on funding amount (often only if funding goal is reached)	

Figure 5.8: Business Model Canvas – reward-based crowdfunding. (Source: own illustration)

until January 2020, which is equivalent to a success rate of about 37%.[272] In order to underline its philosophy, the company changed into the legal form of a Public Benefit Cooperation (PBC) in 2015, thus promising that it would not launch an IPO or be sold. Furthermore, as a PBC its board is bound to Kickstarter's charter while pursuing profits in a responsible manner.[273]

While use of the Kickstarter platform is free, Kickstarter charges a service fee of 5% on the funding amount if the project reaches its financing target.[274] It is important for Kickstarter to grow its network and assure top-quality projects, since both factors will increase the number of successful projects and boost the absolute

---

272 Kickstarter, PBC 2020c.
273 Kickstarter, PBC 2018; Thomas 2017.
274 Kickstarter, PBC 2020b.

amount of commissions. The strict all-or-nothing principle is one reason for the success of the platform, as it assures backers that initiators will only realize the respective idea if it reaches its monetary goal. As a positive side effect, it also significantly reduces marketing expenses, as users themselves share projects and consequently promote the platform.

Kickstarter has also entered a partnership with the payment gateway Stripe. In addition to the existing service fee of 5%, investors now face a further payment of 5% per financing amount plus €0.05 for amounts below €10. For amounts exceeding €10, Stripe charges 3% per financing amount plus €0.20.[275] Regarding the quality of its projects, Kickstarter has gone through challenging times, and even faced a major scandal with the company CST. CST had successfully collected its minimum funding sum of $1 million but then realized that without another huge capital injection, the project would be unviable. The company ultimately filed for bankruptcy.[276] Although Kickstarter clearly stated that it only acted as a service provider and does not vouch for creators, it reacted with the implementation of a thorough assessment process, in which it screens projects for suitability in line with the rules and its 15 main categories. Consequently, Kickstarter now claims that it approves only 80% of applications to the platform.[277]

After successful assessment, a submitted project is published in one of the project categories. Each of the approved projects is presented to potential backers with a video and its story. The creator introduces his team and similar work they have already completed. Drafts, examples and prototypes of the project give potential backers an insight into the project's current state of development. A clear schedule and breakdown of project costs helps to increase the trust of potential backers regarding the serious planning and the feasibility of the project. The project page is an information interface between the creator and the backers. The creator publishes regular updates on the progress of the project while backers can share their opinions, give feedback and ask questions about the project. Convinced backers can fund the project from a minimum contribution of $1.00. Depending on the amount of the contribution, backers can access different levels of rewards. Reward levels can be freely set by the creators. The higher the contribution of the backer, the higher the reward from products or services developed within the project. The financing period of a project can be between 1 and 60 days. The most successful Kickstarter projects are those with a financing period of 30 days or less. Once the project is published, the financing target can not be changed. However, after successful financing, creators can set extended financing goals to expand the features of the product or services with the additional funds. If the project is successfully

---

275 Kickstarter, PBC 2020b.
276 McAlone 2016.
277 Benovic 2016.

Project	Sector	Year	Funding (in million USD)	
Pebble Time - Awesome Smartwatch, No Compromises	Technology	2015		20.34
COOLEST COOLER: 21st Century Cooler that's Actually Cooler	Technology	2014		13.29
Pebble 2, Time 2 + All-New Pebble Core	Technology	2016		12.78
Kingdom Death: Monster 1.5	Games	2016		12.39
Travel Tripodby Peak Design	Technology	2019		12.14
Critical Role: The Legend of Vox Machina Animated Special	Film	2019		11.39
Pebble: E-Paper Watch for iPhone and Android	Technology	2012		10.27
TRAVEL JACKETS with 15 Features by BAUBAX	Fashion	2015		9.19
Exploding Kittens	Games	2015		8.78

Figure 5.9: Most backed projects on Kickstarter.
(Source: own illustration with data from Kickstarter, PBC 2020d)

funded, the creator sends the rewards to the backers.[278] Figure 5.9 depicts the most successful Kickstarter projects.

5.6 Real estate crowdfunding with high growth rates

In real estate financing, senior debt covers about 50% to 70% of required capital. For the remaining percentage, other sources of funding such as subordinate debt, mezzanine capital or equity are used.[279] Crowdfunding constitutes an alternative as it allows individuals and institutional funders to provide financing for real estate projects.[280] However, regardless of the type of source, investors usually do not obtain ownership of the object since a Special Purpose Vehicle (SPV), established by a parent company to meet narrow, specific or temporary objectives, is pooling their investments and acts as the real estate owner. Investors thus own a participation in or a claim against the SPV.[281]

Opening the real estate market to the crowd significantly reduced entry barriers for private investors since an investment in this asset class via crowdfunding comes at lower minimum amounts and higher transparency compared to alternatives such as REITs or private equity funds. The crowdfunding volume allocated to real estate

278 Kickstarter, PBC 2020a.
279 Matthiesen and Steininger 2017, p. 5.
280 Ziegler et al. 2018, p. 28.
281 Kotas 2018, pp. 6, 9.

still presents a rather small percentage. However, from 2015 to 2016 the share in the European market grew by an impressive 306%.[282] For example, the equity-based platform Bergfürst collected capital for the property Middendorf Haus Hamburg, and companisto – which raised €7.5 million for a project named Weissenhaus – even achieved the highest crowdfunding volume for real estate in Germany as of 2016.[283]

Generally, crowdinvesting platforms can either operate as brokers for other real estate sponsors or raise capital for their own property investments.[284] The real estate crowdfunding platforms coordinate sponsors and investors while applying individual screening criteria to select credible, high-quality project initiators for their investors. Therefore, they often look for sponsors that have previously collected capital from private syndicates or successfully complemented prior projects on the platform. It is important to apply due diligence not only to the party behind the project, but also to the project itself.[285]

If a project completes the verification process successfully, the platform creates tender documents and lists the project on the website. SEC guidelines oblige the crowdfunding platform to transparently report to its investors. Real estate platforms cut traditional intermediaries such as real estate brokers and try to achieve significant cost savings.[286]

Fundrise, a popular example of such crowdfunding platforms, carries out a thorough vetting process and claims that it accepted only 2% out of more than 2,000 applications that it received in 2015.[287] In order to catch the attention of potential investors, the platform has created a marketing strategy around its offering, which it calls Modern Portfolio Theory 2.0. The idea is to grant individual investors access to direct private market investments, which have been largely reserved for institutional investors. Thus, Fundrise takes advantage of the structural inefficiencies between the public and the higher-return private market and allocates 30% to 40% of its portfolios to private real estate. The platform gave this approach its catchy name because Fundrise's asset allocation deviates from the traditional portfolio school of thought of 70% investment in stocks and 30% in bonds.[288]

The company accepts non-accredited investors with investment amounts of only $500 in its starter plan. The users choose from a range of SEC-regulated eDirect offers, which invest in private real estate assets located in the U.S., which can be either eREITs or eFunds. The difference between the two vehicles is that

---

282 Athwal 2014; Kaufman 2018; Rashid 2017; Ziegler et al. 2018, pp. 28–29.
283 Beck 2015, p. 219; Dorfleitner and Hornuf 2016, p. 28.
284 Cohen 2016, p. 20.
285 Crowdcircus 2018; Vogel Jr. and Moll 2014, p. 7.
286 Cohen 2016, pp. 19–22.
287 Fundrise, LLC 2018f.
288 Fundrise, LLC 2018a, 2018d.

the former concentrates on commercial real estate, while eFunds target residential objects.[289]

Investors acquire eDirect products with a starter plan or one of three advanced investment plans managed by Fundrise that are geared toward different investment goals. Advanced Fundrise plans have a minimum investment amount of $1,000 and hold a mix of eREITs and eFunds depending on the plan's objective. Both eDirect products charge 0.85% as an annual fee for asset management but investors might also be subject to further charges such as up-front costs or fees for investment advisory.[290]

The success factor of the business model of Fundrise is the choice of real estate objects. Large private equity funds and REITs usually concentrate on large assets and overlook smaller investment opportunities due to aspects such as elevated administrative costs. Fundrise focuses entirely on deals located in the lower million-dollar range, where they face little competition, and connects the smaller projects with short-term investment horizons. Consequently, it achieves higher returns for both the platform and its investors.[291]

5.7 Venture capital financing rounds for crowdfunding

Crowdfunding is one of the relatively old fintech segments in comparison to robo-advice or social trading platforms. But the growth in venture capital financing volume and financing rounds has been much higher in the segment of payments. Table 5.2 shows 99 financing rounds globally with more than half a billion USD of total money raised between January 2017 and April 2020. The median amount per

Table 5.2: Crowdfunding fintechs overview of venture capital financing statistics for sample January 2017–April 2020.

Location	Number Financing Rounds	Median Money Raised	Total Money Raised	Total Pre-Money Valuation
China	1	n/a	n/a	n/a
Europe	43	$1,584,189	$176,313,598	$17,183,315
U.S.	28	$5,000,000	$207,007,798	$505,525,000
World	99	$2,000,000	$519,391,810	$549,118,478

(Source: own illustration with data from Crunchbase 2020e)

---

289 Fundrise, LLC 2018b, 2018c.
290 Fundrise, LLC 2018c, 2018b, 2018e.
291 Fiebert 2018; Greenberg 2015.

financing round was $5 million in the U.S. and $1.5 million in Europe. Further analysis of financing rounds will focus on the U.S. and Europe as the data available for China is not significant.

Figure 5.10 shows that in the crowdfunding segment, a total of 19 venture capital-backed fintechs were established from 1999 to 2016 in Europe and the U.S. Crowdfunding fintechs in Europe started in 2007 and in 2012 in the U.S. The number of foundations in Europe fluctuated between zero and two fintechs per year, and the development peaked in 2014 with four newly established crowdfunding fintechs. For the U.S. a total of six fintechs could be identified in the crowdfunding segment, all launched between 2012 and 2014.

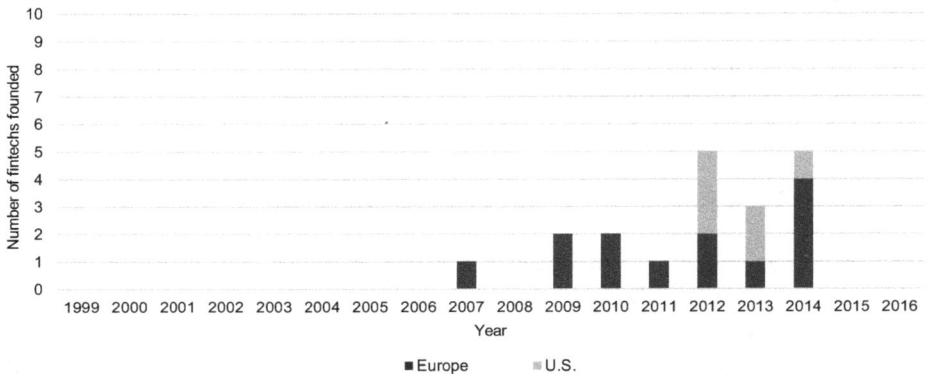

Figure 5.10: Number of venture capital financed crowdfunding fintechs founded in Europe and the U.S. from 1999–2016 for sample April 2000–June 2017.
(Source: own illustration)

Figure 5.11 depicts financing rounds in crowdfunding fintechs, which began in 2010. In subsequent years, a still limited level of deal activity with no more than two financing rounds per year can be observed in both Europe and the U.S. In 2014 deal activity jumped significantly to eight deals and even reached 10 in the following two years.

Figure 5.12 illustrates the annual amount raised in crowdfunding in Europe and the U.S. The amounts raised before 2014 in crowdfunding do not even exceed €5.0 million. From 2013 to 2014 the funding amount increased from €0.9 million to €34.4 million. In the U.S. €30.3 million were raised in three deals, while in Europe only €4.2 million were collected in five deals. In the two years after that, the overall amounts raised rose dramatically to roughly €114.0 million.

The levels of funding in the U.S. and Europe differ significantly, as the average amount raised in 2017 was €4.3 million in Europe and €40.0 million in the U.S. One possible explanation could be that the U.S. market is not as segmented as the

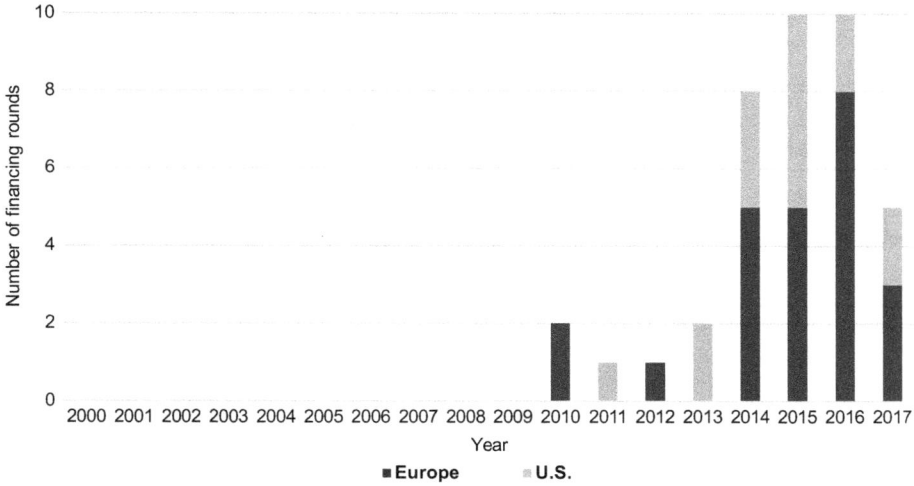

Figure 5.11: Number of financing rounds in crowdfunding in Europe and the U.S. for sample April 2000–June 2017.
(Source: own illustration)

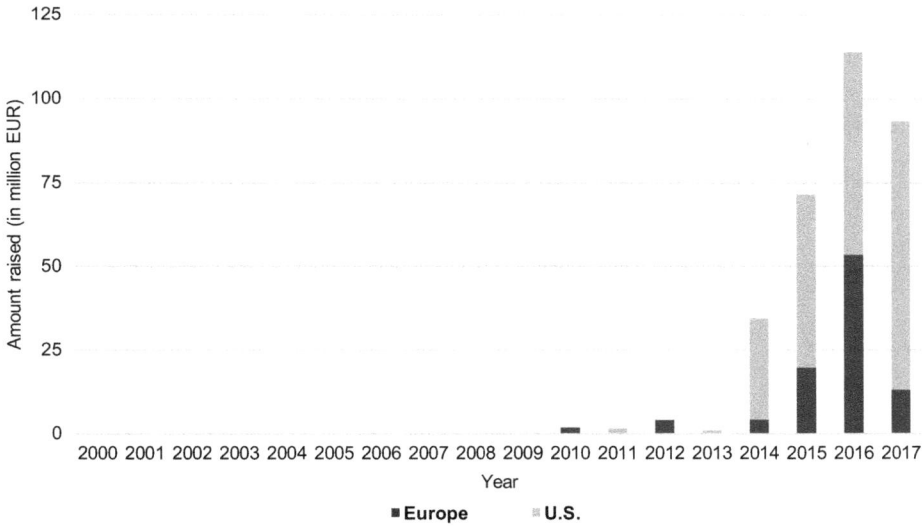

Figure 5.12: Annual overview of amount raised in crowdfunding in Europe and the U.S. for sample April 2000–June 2017 (in € m).
(Source: own illustration)

European market, where funding is possibly restricted by national regulations and borders. The median amount raised in each financing round is analyzed in Table 5.3.

Table 5.3: Median amount raised in crowdfunding in Europe and the U.S. (in € m) for sample April 2000–June 2017.

	Seed	A	B	C	D	E	F	IPO
Overall Median	0.9	7.7	7.3	57.7	n/a	n/a	n/a	n/a
Median Europe	0.7	3.8	7.3	n/a	n/a	n/a	n/a	n/a
Median U.S.	1.5	19.3	24.6	57.7	n/a	n/a	n/a	n/a
Sample size *n*	9	12	5	1	0	0	0	0

(Source: own illustration)

Crowdfunding in the U.S. is defined by considerably higher funding than in Europe across all stages of financing. In the seed stage, crowdfunding fintechs in the U.S. manage to collect more than twice the amount of their European counterparts. This gap even widens to more than five times in financing round A, before declining to approximately 3.5 times in financing round B. As only one C round and no later stage financing rounds were identified, no further comparisons can be made.

Figure 5.13 analyzes the median change as well as the increase or decrease in amounts raised between two successive financing rounds. The sample size differs from Table 5.3 due to the fact that only fintechs are included where data for two

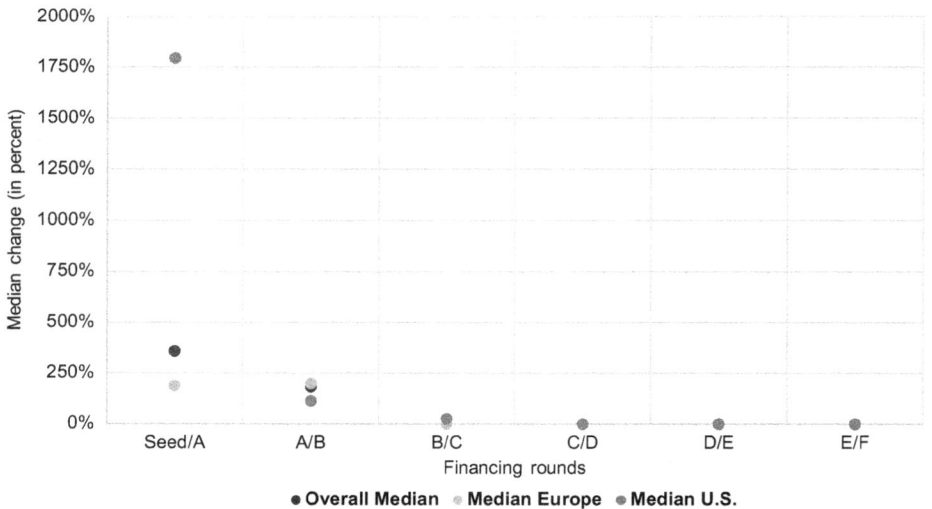

Figure 5.13: Median change in amounts raised between two successive financing rounds in crowdfunding for sample April 2000–June 2017 (in percent).
(Source: own illustration)

consecutive financing rounds was available. The analysis is based on the sample size as follows: Seed/A n = 8; A/B n = 4; B/C n = 1; C/D n = 0; D/E n = 0; E/F n = 0.

The median increase from the seed round to financing round A in the U.S. is 1,794% versus 186% in Europe. The value for the U.S. is considered to be biased due to the low sample size but is nevertheless expected to be above the European figure. The comparison for financing rounds A and B actually suggests that the increase in Europe is 84% higher than in the U.S. (197% vs. 113%). The explanation could be that round A in the U.S. is already that well-funded (median of € 19.3 m) as shown in Table 5.3 so that the increase is not as impressive in percent as for the European counterparts.

U.S. crowdfunding start-ups with higher financing amounts

Figure 5.14 shows the time passed between two successive financing rounds. The median percentage change allows conclusions to be drawn about whether funding in later stages becomes more or less difficult for fintechs. The sample size corresponds to the one for Figure 5.14 (Seed/A n = 8; A/B n = 4; B/C n = 1; C/D n = 0; D/E n = 0; E/F n = 0).

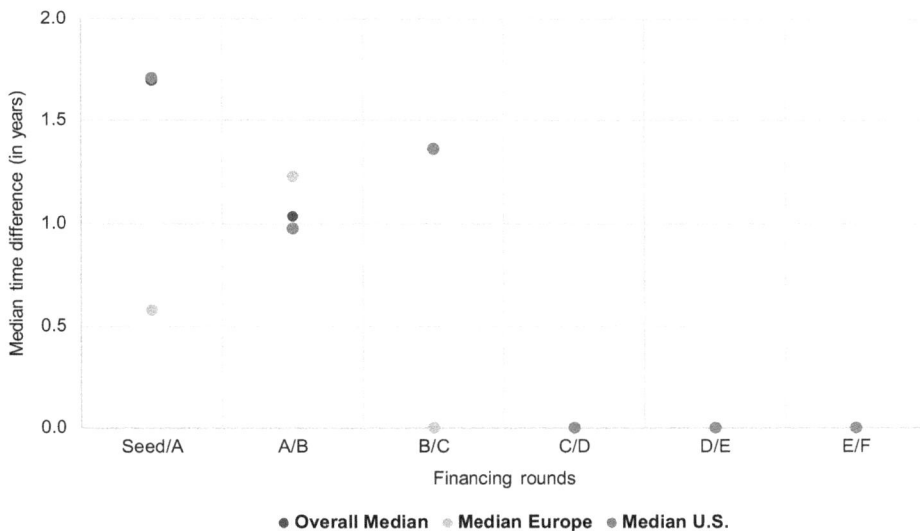

● Overall Median ◦ Median Europe ● Median U.S.

Figure 5.14: Median time difference in years between two successive financing rounds in crowdfunding for sample April 2000–June 2017.
(Source: own illustration)

Financing round A is concluded much faster after the seed investment in Europe than in the U.S. (0.6 years vs. 1.7 years). This observation explains why U.S. crowdfunding fintechs achieve a higher median amount raised in round A: they almost have three times as much time to find investors. However, in financing round B, U.S. crowdfunding fintechs manage to achieve higher funding despite closing round B roughly three months faster than European fintechs operating in this segment (1 year vs. 1.2 years). But the sample size is too small to provide clear indications of reasons. The crowdfunding market in the U.S. requires higher capital input compared to the European market, which is shown by the median amount raised for the various financing rounds. The explanation is that in comparison to the situation in the U.S., borders and different regulations in Europe might hinder crowdfunding platforms from attracting investors.

Crowdlending with only few start-ups in the U.S.

As shown in Figure 5.15 in the crowdlending segment 18 fintechs were established from 1999 to 2016.

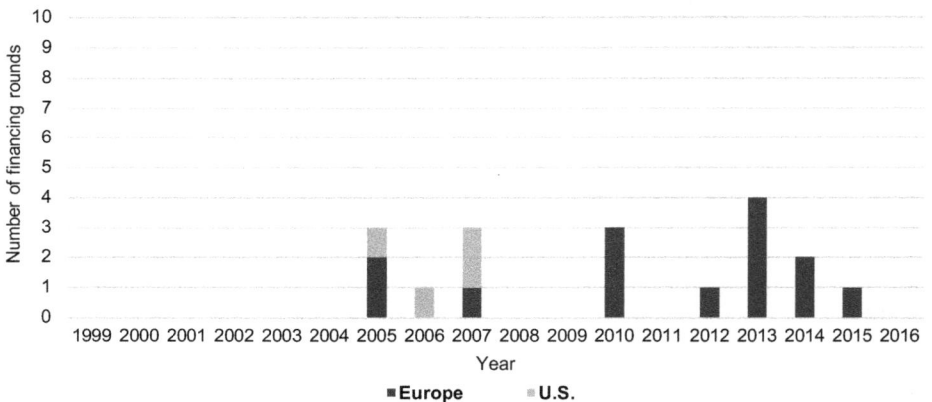

Figure 5.15: Number of fintechs founded in crowdlending in Europe and the U.S. from 1999–2016 for sample April 2000–June 2017.
(Source: own illustration)

Fintechs operating in the crowdlending segment first emerged in 2005 with two start-ups founded in Europe and one in the U.S. In the two years after that, four more fintechs were founded in both regions with the majority of 75% in the U.S. Crowdlending fintechs were also founded in Europe after the financial crisis but not in the U.S. No crowdlending fintechs were launched in the U.S. from 2008 to 2016 suggesting that founders see no niches in this field.

As shown in Figure 5.16 crowdlending deal activity began in 2004 and steadily increased until 2007. The number of financing rounds jumped from 2009 to 2010 and then dropped again until 2012. This seems to be the turning point for the funding of crowdlending fintechs, as deal activity then rose each year, reaching a total of 13 deals in 2015 of which twelve deals were conducted in Europe. The U.S. market already seems to be relatively mature, while the European crowdlending market still has potential for new entrants.

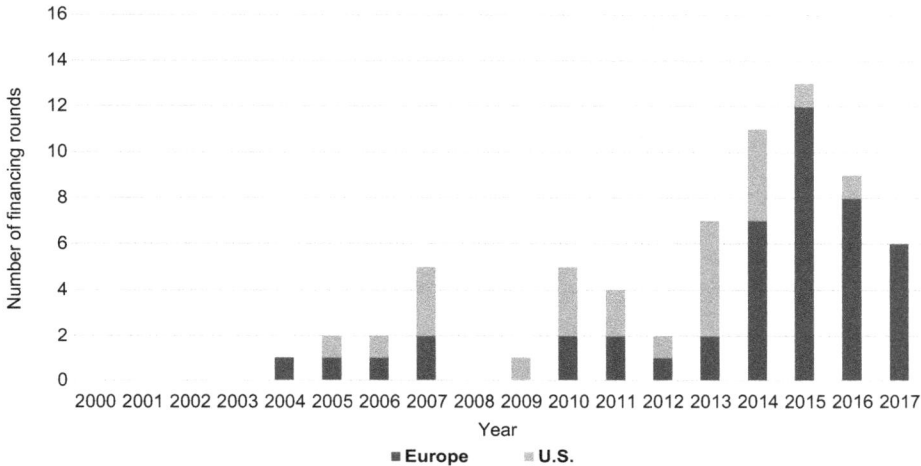

Figure 5.16: Number of financing rounds in crowdlending in Europe and the U.S. for sample April 2000–June 2017.
(Source: own illustration)

In line with the number of financing rounds, the amounts raised started to rise from 2013 onward. While €26.1 million were raised in 2012, more than seven times that amount was raised in 2013, as funding amounted to €216.0 million. In 2014 the amount raised reached an impressive €1.1 billion, predominately driven by the U.S. and the IPO of Lending Club in December. The amount raised then declined in the following three years, which can be led back to the decline in funding in the U.S. European crowdlending fintechs had a record inflow of investments in 2015, with €513.4 million compared to an accumulated €467.5 million in all previous years (see Figure 5.17). European crowdlending is certainly trying to catch up with its U.S. counterparts regarding maturity and scalability. Table 5.4 shows the median amounts raised for each financing round and region.

Seed investments in Europe in crowdlending amount to a median value of €2.0 million. This value can not be compared to the U.S. because no seed investments in the U.S. were secured. In the subsequent round A, U.S. fintechs managed to raise 57% higher amounts than European crowdlending start-ups. However, this observation seems to be the exception to the rule, as European fintechs managed to

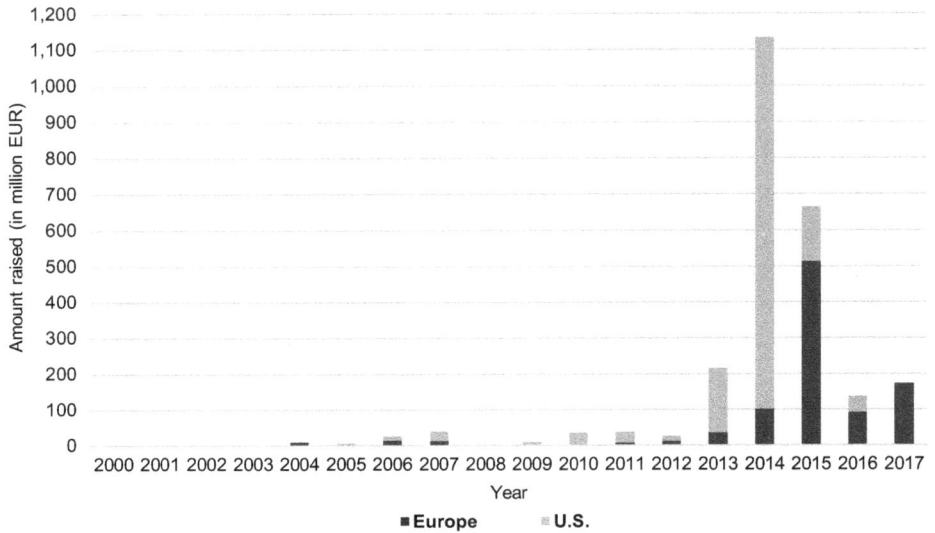

Figure 5.17: Overview of annual amount raised in crowdlending in Europe and the U.S. for sample April 2000–June 2017 (in € m).
(Source: own illustration)

Table 5.4: Median amount raised in crowdlending in Europe and the U.S. for sample April 2000–June 2017 (in € m).

	Seed	A	B	C	D	E	F	IPO
Overall Median	2.0	4.6	11.8	18.1	17.4	25.4	71.2	696.3
Median Europe	2.0	3.7	12.0	26.8	48.1	88.1	95.1	n/a
Median U.S.	n/a	5.8	9.4	16.6	14.1	13.0	47.2	696.3
Sample size n	6	13	10	5	3	4	2	1

(Source: own illustration)

obtain higher funding amounts in all the other financing rounds. But as the sample size is pretty small, we have to be careful with interpretations.

U.S. crowdfunding fintechs require more time to refinance

In Figure 5.18 the median increase in amount raised between two successive financing rounds in the crowdlending space is shown. A differentiation between Europe and the U.S. is made and is based on the underlying sample size as follows: Seed/A $n = 5$; A/B $n = 10$; B/C $n = 5$; C/D $n = 3$; D/E $n = 3$; E/F $n = 2$.

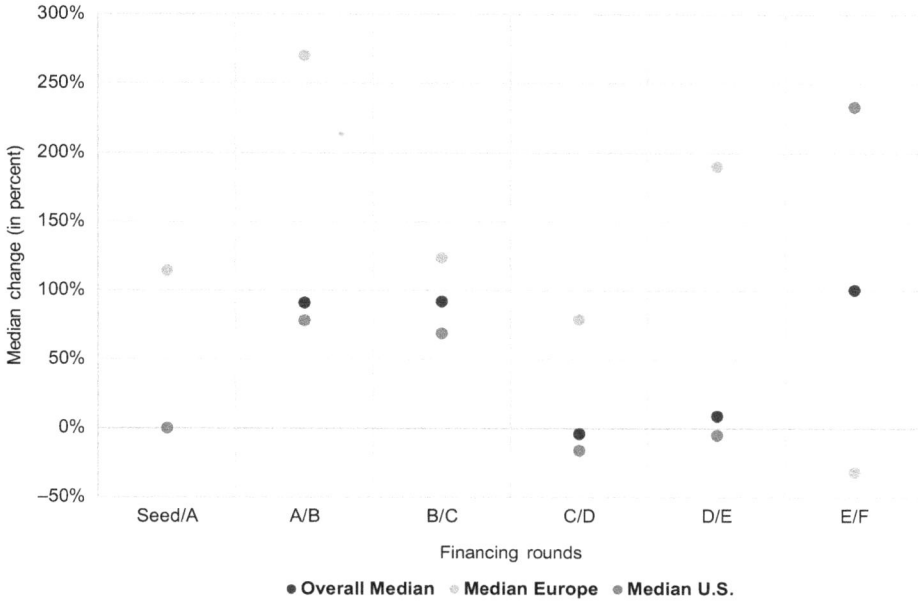

Figure 5.18: Median change in amounts raised between two successive financing rounds in crowdlending for sample April 2000–June 2017 (in percent).
(Source: own illustration)

The median increase from seed investment to financing round A in Europe is 114%. Since no seed investments for the U.S. could be collected, a value can not be derived. The subsequent comparison for the change from financing round A to B shows a median of 270% for Europe while it is only 78% in the U.S., resulting in a gap of 192%. This difference diminishes to 55% for the B/C round comparison as the median is 69% in the U.S. and 124% in Europe. The European median then decreases to 79% in the next comparison, while the U.S. median change amounts to negative 16%. The U.S. fintechs are not able to secure higher funding from financing round C to D. It is surprising that both regions manage to boost their funding in the D/E round comparison, even though the U.S. value is still negative. From financing round E to F this trend is turned around, as the European median is negative 32%, whereas the U.S. median increase is 232%.

The median time difference between two successive financing rounds may provide some clarity as to why the median change in amounts raised has negative values. The sample size for Figure 5.19 is the same as for Figure 5.18 (Seed/A $n = 5$; A/B $n = 10$; B/C $n = 5$; C/D $n = 3$; D/E $n = 3$; E/F $n = 2$).

Figure 5.19 shows that the median time to close financing round A after the seed investment in Europe is approximately 1.5 years. This value decreases to 1.1 years for financing round B, which compares to 1.6 years in the U.S. This means crowdlending

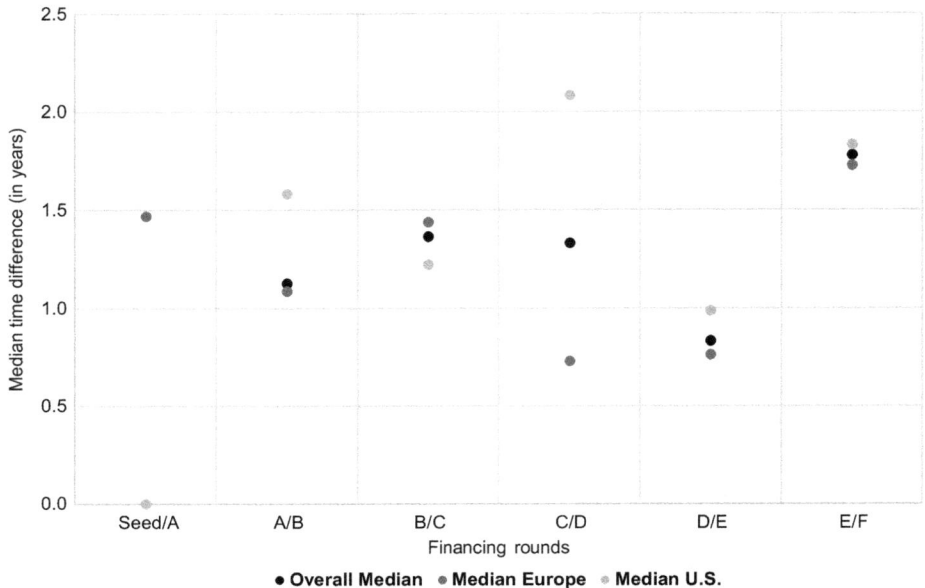

Figure 5.19: Median time difference in years between two successive financing rounds in crowdlending for sample April 2000–June 2017.
(Source: own illustration)

fintechs in the U.S. require 45% more time to close round B despite having a considerably lower median increase in amount raised (78% vs. 270%). This difference completely vanishes as European crowdlending fintechs require roughly three more months in the B/C round comparison than their U.S. counterparts. In all the following three comparisons, U.S. fintechs always require more time to close the successive financing round. However, this gap narrows from 1.4 years in the C/D round comparison to approximately one month in the E/F round comparison. This could mean that U.S. fintechs struggle more to secure follow-up financing in later stage financing.

U.S. crowdlending fintechs appear more mature, as less financing activity takes place but if they do finance, it is more difficult for these fintechs to raise funds. European crowdlending fintechs are not as mature as U.S. crowdlenders because there still is considerable financing activity.

Summary

Volumes in real estate crowdfunding have increased in recent years due to low interest rates and a high demand in the housing market. Donation-based as well as reward-based crowdfunding business models show a stable development but lack a high growth story as the overall market is limited and both segments probably will stay niche markets. In terms of volume, crowdlending is the most important business model in the segment of crowdfunding; but the market shares on the worldwide credit markets are still below a level at which traditional banks would consider them to be a danger to their own business model. In relation to the market volume for loans, China remains the dominant player for crowdlending, followed by the U.S. and Europe.

The median change in financing amounts raised between two successive rounds in crowdlending is generally more than +100% from Seed to round A, from round A to B and from round B to C; it slows down from round C to D and shows significant differences in the later phases D/E and E/F. In the later phases the changes could be negative if growth expectations are not reached or could be more than +200% in case the fintech performs better than expected. The median time difference between two successive financing rounds is between 1 year and 1.5 years for the first three financing rounds and in the later financing rounds the spread widens to 0.7 years and 2 years.

6 Balance-sheet lending from fintechs providing credit & factoring

A main delineation within fintech lending exists between business models that provide loans to borrowers just like traditional banks, and marketplace lending, which avoids ownership of loans by matching borrowers with creditors. Since in the former default risk remains on the balance sheet, this activity is referred to as balance-sheet lending.[292] P2P or marketplace lenders face the challenge of balancing supply with demand. Balance sheet lenders need stable and cheap funding with equity and debt to provide loans to customers. The credit market is always attractive for new entrants. Marcus by Goldman Sachs was created as a start-up to enter consumer banking. In 2016, Marcus launched unsecured personal loans for the mass market and quickly became very profitable in this completely new area for an investment bank. In the following, a number of initiatives by fintech start-ups in the field of loans are presented.[293]

6.1 Profitable platforms for SME loans from OnDeck

One of the leading players in this segment is U.S.-based OnDeck. Its founders took advantage of the financing gap faced by small businesses and expanded their credit access by assessing credit worthiness on the basis of actual business performance, rather than exclusively considering the owner's credit standing. The online platform enables applying for a loan at any time and accelerates the funding process through its proprietary credit scoring methodology. Moreover, OnDeck assures instant availability of funding through its cooperation with Visa and Ingo Money and thus reduces the waiting time from one or two business days to only a few seconds.[294] Initially, OnDeck's service was only available to U.S. customers. However, a strategic partnership with Australian MYOB providing business software and accounting solutions additionally opened the Australian and Canadian markets to the fintech.[295]

OnDeck's focus on young businesses provides a key advantage. The platform enters the business lifecycle earlier than most of its competitors, which opens the opportunity of generating switching costs for its borrowers (see Figure 6.1). OnDeck

---

292 Morgenthaler 2016, pp. 206–207; Ziegler et al. 2018, p. 28; Bank for International Settlements and Financial Stability Board 2017, p. 15.
293 McDonald et al. 2019.
294 OnDeck Capital, Inc. 2018a, 2018b.
295 MYOB Technology Pty Ltd 2018a, 2018b.

https://doi.org/10.1515/9783110704907-006

Key partners	Key activities	Value propositions	Customer relationships	Customer segments
Capital providers 3rd party providers for credit data verification Referring partners, funding advisors as additional loan originators Visa & Ingo Money for provision of instantly available funding White label provider for JP Morgen Chase Shareholders Regulatory authorities	Online onboarding Credit scoring of business activities, owners Platform/ algorithm development and maintenance Marketing, user acquisition	Free use of platform Access to capital for SMEs, either as term loans or credit lines Credit assessment also based on actual cash flows and not only on creditworthiness of business owner	Online User experience, convenience Online blog On-demand support 24/7	SMEs Institutional investors for investments in securitized SME loan portfolio for sale with a premium on OnDeck marketplace
	Key resources	Quick credit decision	**Channels**	
	Online platform Scoring algorithm Data network Partners	Instant funding availability Credit for borrowers with poor history of creditworthiness	Online platform Social media Mail & phone Strategic partners, network of funding advisors and affiliates	

Cost structure	Revenue streams
Development and maintenance of algorithm/platform Fixed, marketing and personnel expenses Fees paid to capital providers Commissions to referring partners and funding advisors Potentially cost entailed in the cooperation	Origination fee Monthly maintenance fee Interest income Origination & servicing fee on loans issued by JPMorgan Chase through OnDeck's white label platform

Figure 6.1: Business Model Canvas – OnDeck.
(Source: own illustration)

rewards repeating users with lower one-time origination fees on consecutive loan utilization.[296] Borrowers requesting their first loan on the platform are required to pay an origination fee of 0% to 5.0% on the loan volume.[297]

Since its launch in 2007, the fintech has successively expanded its product range. It provides short- and long-term loans at volumes of between $5,000 and

---

296 OnDeck Capital, Inc. 2020, 2018c.
297 OnDeck Capital, Inc. 2018b.

$50,000 over a term of 3 to 36 months as well as lines of credit with a maximum amount of $100,000.[298] Users of the latter product might additionally have to pay a monthly maintenance charge of $20.[299] Interest rates on loans depend on the assigned OnDeck credit score and therefore vary from borrower to borrower. As a rough indication, in 2017 the weighted average annual interest rate was equal to 45.2% for term loans and 32.7% for lines of credit.[300] OnDeck's service has relatively high costs compared to Lending Club. However, its strong value proposition of convenience, fast funding and extended capital access offsets that disadvantage.[301] One could critically ask who would want a loan for 32 or 45% and why these are allowed, as in many countries of the world such rates would be considered to be usurious. However, there obviously seems to be a market for such high interest rates.

The success of OnDeck's business model is underlined by an impressive $8 billion issued in loan volume since 2007.[302] OnDeck approaches clients via different channels. With a contribution of 52% in origination volume, OnDeck's primary channel is marketing through direct mail, online, radio and TV. In addition, the company has integrated several strategic partners, such as banks, payment processors or small business-focused service providers, as well as a large base of funding advisors in its distribution network.[303]

White label partnership with JPMorgan

Next to traditional debt facilities, OnDeck uses securitizations as well as a marketplace to sell excess SME loan capacity to institutional investors at a premium.[304] In 2015 the fintech entered into an arrangement with JPMorgan Chase (JPM), which promised a powerful combination of JPM's broad customer base and OnDeck's technology.[305] But the cooperation with JPMorgan was terminated in August 2019.

Although there were some obstacles such as regulatory complications and compliance risk at the beginning of the arrangement, the partners issued their first loan in 2016. JPM marketed the product as "Chase Business Quick Capital" at volumes of up to $200,000 and pre-scored its borrowers based on its existing business customer

---

298 OnDeck Capital, Inc. 2018a, 2018b.
299 OnDeck Capital, Inc. 2018b.
300 OnDeck Capital, Inc. 2017a, p. 8.
301 Cabural 2015; OnDeck Capital, Inc. 2017a, p. 7.
302 OnDeck Capital, Inc. 2018a.
303 OnDeck Capital, Inc. 2017a, p. 11, 2018d, p. 13.
304 OnDeck Capital, Inc. 2015, 2017a, p. 14, 2018d, p. 14.
305 Renton 2015.

relationships. Next to the approval process, JPM's activities also included the provision of capital for backing the loans, therefore keeping risk on their own balance sheet.[306] On the other end of the partnership, the fintech licensed its platform as a white label solution and took "care of sales, servicing, collections, and customer service."[307]

The arrangement allowed JPM to close a gap in its business model by providing small business loans to customers it could previously not serve. For JPM the advantage of the cooperation was the high profitability of the business. For this additional offer JPM earned relatively high annual percentage rates ranging from 9% to 25%. The individual rate depended on the credit risk. For the platform, the white label solution yielded income from fees earned for the origination and servicing of each loan. Although the participation per loan was rather small, in a scaled-up scenario it easily added up to significant volumes. As an additional advantage, these 'technological' revenues did not involve risk for OnDeck. OnDeck's intention was to increase the interest also of other banks to join and to leverage the loan platform.[308]

Revenues, costs and risk management

OnDeck relies on partnerships, which of course entail commission payments. Along with the operation's primary expenses for platform and algorithm, other costs include the following: origination fees, maintenance charges, income from the white label solution provided to JPM, and most importantly interest rate payments.[309] The interest rate charges of OnDeck tend to be relatively high and compensate for the risk associated with issued loans on the own balance sheet. However, in order to reduce risk, the platform automatically deducts repayments and collects them in a weekly or even daily frequency.[310] The most decisive risk mitigation measure is the lender's proprietary credit scoring algorithm OnDeck score, which at the same time presents its major competitive edge.

The algorithm is fed with data about platform users and their businesses, including business credit scores obtained from third parties, payment history, a firm's cash flow characteristics, social media reviews and others. Designed to cope with distinct cash flow profiles, the algorithm assesses more than 2,000 data points per application and as a result yields a credit profile.[311] The application of the algorithm

---

306 Macheel 2017; OnDeck Capital, Inc. 2017b; Renton 2015.
307 Taylor 2017.
308 JPMorgan Chase & Co. 2018; Renton 2015; Taylor 2017.
309 Eifler 2018.
310 OnDeck Capital, Inc. 2018b.
311 Eifler 2018; Kiisel 2018; Li 2015.

procedure intends to take less time for credit decisions compared to traditional banks. Furthermore, due to its machine learning capability, the algorithmic software self-improves the more data it processes. An increasing number of SMEs using the platform implies more credit information. More data, in turn, improves the software's credit scoring ability and, ultimately, enhanced software takes smarter risks. Thus, OnDeck's data network results in an effective feedback loop.[312]

Although OnDeck represents the most prominent example of balance sheet lenders, several other fintechs have already achieved a solid position in balance-sheet lending. Affirm, for example, successfully provides installment loans at the POS and Avant, another personal loan issuer, built a loan portfolio of $6.5 billion. Further platforms include Aire, Bluevine, Bondstreet, borro, bread finance and common bond.[313]

In jurisdictions outside the U.S. balance sheet lending business models play a less prominent role.[314] U.K.-based LendInvests' "receivables participation," for example, entitles investors to receive payments from LendInvest covered by the debt service of borrowers.[315] Other fintechs, like one of China's largest lending-industry participants CreditEase, use a hybrid approach between balance-sheet and crowd-funding-based lending.[316]

6.2 Frictionless consumer lending from Avant

The U.S. fintech Avant offers loans for consumers who have been rejected by traditional credit institutions and generally for individuals with "fair" or "bad" Fair Issac and Company (FICO) credit scores. With its credit products, Avant covers a gap in the lending market. Private customers with a credit rating of less than "fair" will have difficulties in obtaining loans, and if possible, can only do so under poor conditions. When applying for a loan at traditional credit institutions, these customers go through a lengthy and complex application procedure with uncertain prospects of success. Avant's co-founder John Sun recognized a need for credit products specifically tailored for consumers with a less than "fair" credit score.[317]

FICO scores are calculated based on reports from Experian, Transunion and Equifax containing the credit behavior of the retail customers. Limited data means a credit rating of limited significance. Avant has developed a new scoring model applying machine learning techniques and other Big Data methods to replace the

---

312 Punch Card Research 2016.
313 Avant, LLC 2020e; Crunchbase 2020a, 2020b.
314 Bank for International Settlements and Financial Stability Board 2017, p. 15.
315 LendInvest Limited 2020.
316 Deer et al. 2015, p. 11.
317 Avant, LLC 2020e; CreditLoan 2020.

Key partners	Key activities	Value propositions	Customer relationships	Customer segments
Experian, Transunion and Equifax as credit data providers	Own credit scoring	Simple and fast online application process	Online	Retail clients with below-average FICO credit scores
	Continuous enhancement for digital customer onboarding		Frictionless user experience and convenience	
Institutional Marketplace partners to finance originated loans		Instant loan approval		Institutional investors for investments in securitized loan portfolio for sale with a premium on Avant Institutional Marketplace
	Direct mail customer targeting with pre-approved loans	Credit availability next business day	Online blog as personal finance knowledge base	
Banking licence from WebBank to originate consumer credit products in the U.S.	Digital customer acquisition	Credit rating assessment with additional focus on online data analytics	Daily, long opening hours for direct customer service	
	White label solutions			
Regulatory authorities	Loan securitization			

	Key resources		Channels	
	Data generated during the application process		Marketing: social media, website, direct mail, phone	
	Data from credit providers and other financial records		Loan application: Online platform	
	Machine learning and Big Data		Loan securitization: Avant Loans Funding Trust	
	Credit scoring algorithm			

Cost structure	Revenue streams
Development and maintenance of algorithm/platform	Origination fee
Fixed, marketing and personnel expenses	Fees for late/dishonoured payments
Losses from write-offs for bad loans	Interest income
	Credit card fees

Figure 6.2: Business Model Canvas – Avant.
(Source: own illustration)

traditional FICO methodology. Avant's new scoring formula incorporates more than 10,000 variables into its credit scoring process. The new model includes standard FICO data such as loan repayment history, but also includes data analysis of, for example, the time of day when the application was submitted, how responses were input into the online application and "metadata" such as details on the device used for completing the loan application. The scoring algorithm allows Avant to process new loan applications in a streamlined process and to approve them immediately.

The goal is to transfer the credit amount to the applicant's bank account on the next business day.[318]

With targeted direct mailings, Avant reaches potential borrowers who have already been pre-approved in-house for a loan or credit card. Avant also engages in digital marketing and operates an online blog as a personal finance knowledge base. For institutional investors, Avant has established a marketplace for the sale of its securitized loans via the Avant Loans Funding Trust.[319]

Avant has originated more than 800,000 loans via its partner WebBank for private individuals in the U.S. and more than 80,000 loans for retail clients in the U.K. In the U.S. the offered loan amounts range from $2,000 to $35,000 with a loan maturity between 24 and 60 months. The effective annual interest rate for loans ranges from 9.95% to 35.99%. Administration fees of between 0 and 4.75% must also be paid at the moment of origination and are deducted from the loan amount. Avant also offers a credit card in addition to secured and unsecured credit products. The card provides a credit line of between $300 and $1,000 with an annual percentage rate of 24.49% to 25.49%, and an annual fee of $39.[320]

Figure 6.2 depicts the Business Model Canvas for Avant.

6.3 Venture financing in credit & factoring

Table 6.1 shows 181 global financing rounds for credit fintechs between January 2017 and April 2020 with a total of nearly $2 billion raised with a median of $5.5 million. The median amount raised per financing round per credit fintech was $11.8 million in the U.S. and $5.8 million in Europe. The data available for China shows only 5 financing rounds between January 2017 and April 2020 compared to 45 financing rounds in Europe and 59 financing rounds in the U.S. As the data for China is not significant, the analysis of credit fintechs focuses on the U.S. and Europe.

Table 6.2 shows the venture capital financing rounds for factoring fintechs. Only very little data is publicly available and only a few deals were carried out in factoring between January 2017 and April 2020. The median amount raised per financing round for factoring fintechs was $1.2 million in the U.S. and $0.7 million in Europe. No data is available for China and the further analysis of factoring financing rounds will focus on the U.S. and Europe.

---

318 CreditLoan 2020; Avant, LLC 2020a.
319 Avant, LLC 2020d; Avant, LLC 2020c; U.S. Securities and Exchange Commission 2020.
320 AvantCredit of UK, LLC 2020; Avant, LLC 2020b, 2020g, 2020f, p. 1.

Table 6.1: Credit fintechs overview of venture capital financing statistics for sample January 2017–April 2020.

Location	Number Financing Rounds	Median Money Raised	Total Money Raised	Total Pre-Money Valuation
China	5	$20,500,000	$89,511,000	n/a
Europe	45	$5,834,949	$253,514,467	$43,286,301
U.S.	59	$11,860,000	$1,164,884,264	$622,000,000
World	181	$5,537,531	$1,960,544,595	$749,786,301

(Source: own illustration with data from Crunchbase 2020e)

Table 6.2: Factoring fintechs overview of venture capital financing statistics for sample January 2017–April 2020.

Location	Number Financing Rounds	Median Money Raised	Total Money Raised	Total Pre-Money Valuation
China	n/a	n/a	n/a	n/a
Europe	4	$770,000	$3,044,589	$6,011,986
U.S.	n/a	n/a	n/a	n/a
World	5	$1,243,108	$13,044,589	$6,011,986

(Source: own illustration with data from Crunchbase 2020e)

In the area of credit & factoring a total of 52 fintechs were founded in the sample April 2000 to June 2017. The detailed split of the credit & factoring fintechs founded in Europe and the U.S. each year is shown in Figure 6.3.

The first two credit & factoring fintechs were founded in the U.S. in 2000 and 2001. It took another five years before credit & factoring fintechs appeared on the European fintech scene. In the next six years the number of fintechs founded increased each year, with the exception being 2010 where not one single fintech was established in Europe or the U.S. The rise in new credit & factoring fintechs was predominately driven by the U.S. The level of eleven new start-ups in 2012 represents the peak of founding activity overall, as the number has steadily decreased since 2012.

High number of VC financing rounds

Figure 6.4 highlights the development of the number of financing rounds across both regions since 2000. In total, 166 financing rounds took place for credit &

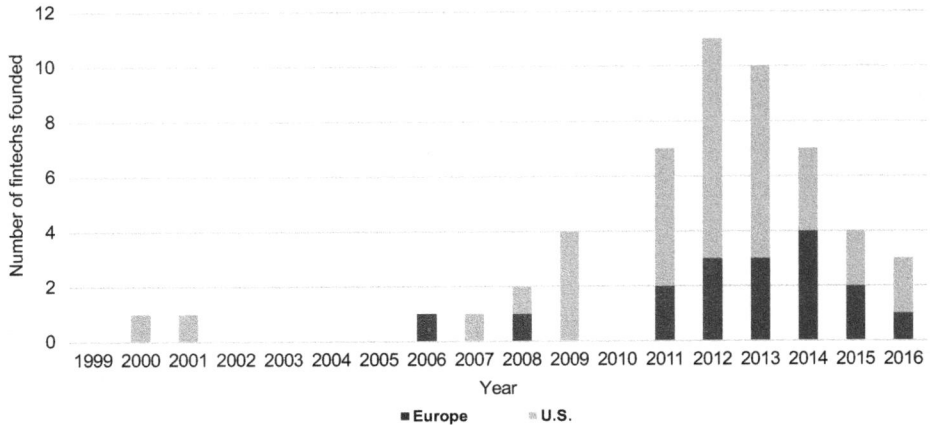

Figure 6.3: Number of fintechs founded in credit & factoring in Europe and the U.S. from 1999–2016 for sample April 2000–June 2017.[321]
(Source: own illustration)

factoring fintechs, which is the second-highest number of the analyzed fintech segments – after alternative payment methods where 241 deals were identified.

The number of financing rounds peaked at 35 deals in 2014 (see Figure 6.4). This development was mainly driven by the strong growth in funding in the U.S. In 2015 deal activity increased by two in the U.S. and stood at 27 deals. Nevertheless, since the deal count in Europe declined by three financing rounds, overall funding activity was down one. The number of financing rounds continued to decrease in 2016 and 2017. Despite a decreasing trend in financing rounds, it can not be said whether credit & factoring in both regions is considered to be reaching maturity, as overall deal activity is still comparatively high. It is necessary to evaluate the amount raised to determine whether the credit & factoring segment is moving toward maturity (see Figure 6.5).

Credit & factoring funding increased from €3.2 million in 2006 to €88.0 million in 2010, implying a CAGR of 129%. After a drop of €5.4 million in 2011, the amount raised skyrocketed in the next four years and stood at roughly €2.5 billion in 2015, predominately driven by the U.S. In 2016 the amount raised only reached 29% of the amount raised in the previous year, indicating that 2015 was a record year as underlined by the €1 billion round E funding of SoFi. The June 2017 figure is already well above the full year 2016 figure of €715.6 million. These findings indicate that

---

[321] Please note that the year of foundation of one fintech operating in this segment is not known and hence excluded in the graph.

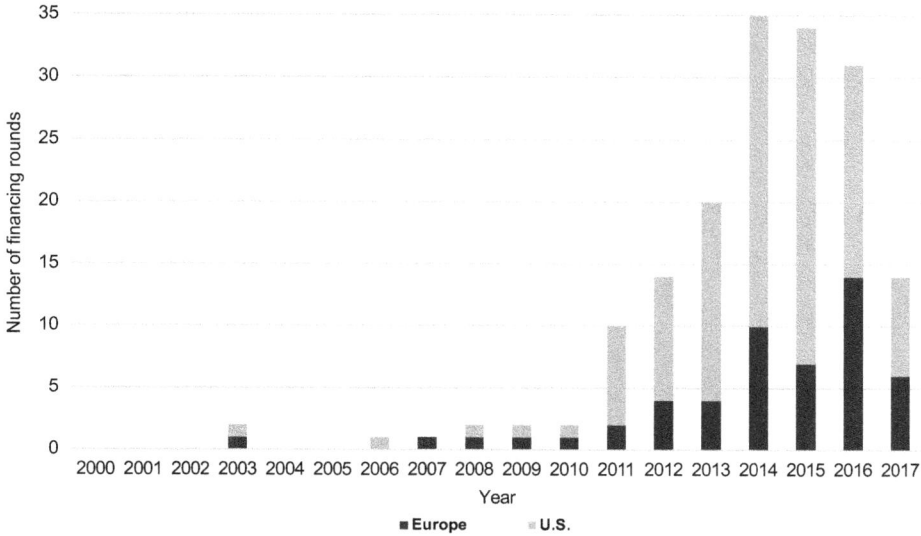

Figure 6.4: Number of financing rounds in credit & factoring in Europe and the U.S. for sample
April 2000–June 2017.
(Source: own illustration)

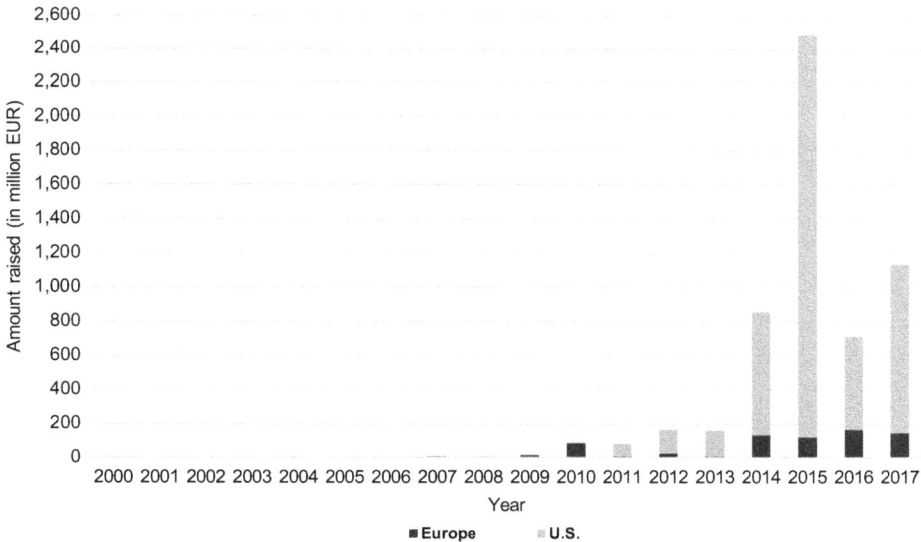

Figure 6.5: Annual overview of amount raised in credit & factoring in Europe and the U.S. for
sample April 2000 June 2017 (in € m).
(Source: own illustration)

both regions are moving toward maturity as the average amount raised and the predominance of more late stage financing rounds is increasing.

Table 6.3 compares the median amounts raised for each financing round for Europe and the U.S. Almost no difference in the median seed amount raised between Europe and the U.S. can be observed. In contrast, U.S. credit & factoring fintechs achieve a 49% higher funding in financing round A than the European start-ups in this field (€7.0 million vs. €4.7 million). This gap almost vanishes in the subsequent round B, where both regions manage to raise a little more than €18.0 million, before it then widens by 29% in favor of U.S. fintechs in financing round C again.

Table 6.3: Median amount raised in credit & factoring in Europe and the U.S. for sample April 2000–June 2017 (in € m).

	Seed	A	B	C	D	E	F	IPO
Overall Median	1.3	6.1	18.1	31.9	44.4	87.3	472.6	117.9
Median Europe	1.3	4.7	18.1	24.8	81.4	16.8	n/a	n/a
Median U.S.	1.2	7.0	18.2	32.0	44.1	118.6	472.6	117.9
Sample size *n*	18	37	30	23	10	6	1	2

(Source: own illustration)

In financing round D, European credit & factoring fintechs managed to collect 85% more capital than their U.S. counterparts (median €81.4 million vs. €44.1 million). This observation is once again completely turned around in financing round E where the U.S. median amounts to €118.6 million, while the European median amounts to just €16.8 million. No clear pattern can be observed up to financing round D. However, for the late stage financing rounds E and F, as well as the IPO, U.S. fintechs appear to be more successful, as the median is either higher or there is not even a public record for a European deal.

Credit & factoring fintechs move toward maturity

In Figure 6.6 the median change in amounts raised between two successive financing rounds is compared across the two regions. The underlying sample size is as follows: Seed/A $n = 10$; A/B $n = 27$; B/C $n = 23$; C/D $n = 10$; D/E $n = 6$; E/F $n = 1$.

European fintechs achieve a significantly higher increase from the original seed investment to financing round A than U.S. fintechs, as the difference is roughly three times as much as in the U.S. For the round A/B comparison, this gap narrows to 64% (Europe 253% vs. U.S. 189%). The gap then widens again with the next two

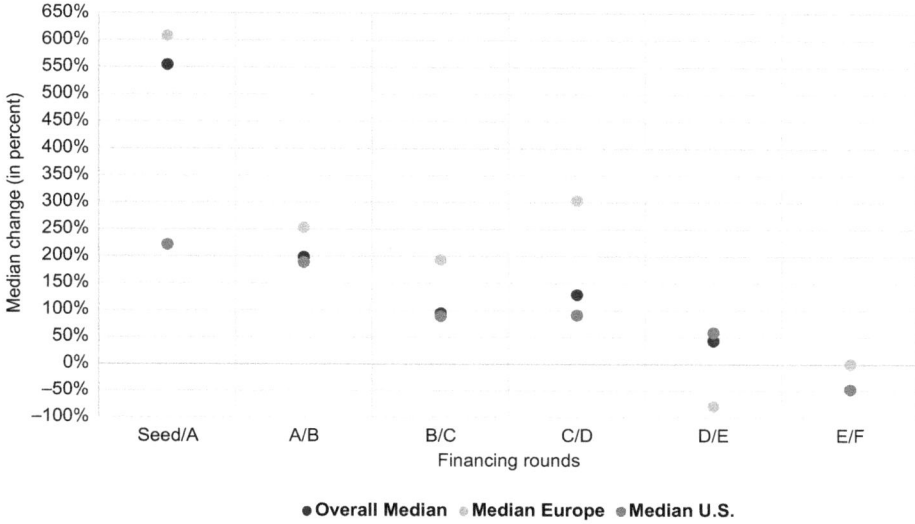

Figure 6.6: Median change in amounts raised between two successive financing rounds in credit & factoring for sample April 2000–June 2017 (in percent). (Source: own illustration)

comparisons, before ultimately resulting in the median of the U.S. outpacing the European one (58% vs. – 79%). The results of the round D/E comparison are actually not astonishing as the European fintechs recorded a sharp increase in median change from the round B/C comparison to the round C/D comparison, making it more difficult to achieve even higher round E funding. European fintechs appear to be more successful in raising early stage funding. With regard to late stage financing there is no clear tendency toward one region, as European fintechs achieve a higher median increase from financing round C to D, which is then mitigated by the negative value in the round after that. Additionally, no information on Europe is available for the round E/F comparison. Another way of comparing the regions and their trends in terms of financing rounds is the median time between two successive financing rounds. The underlying sample size is the same as for the previous analysis.

Figure 6.7 ilustrates that U.S. credit & factoring fintechs take around 0.8 years to close financing round A after the seed investment, while the European counterparts need a year. Consequently, this is one explanation why the U.S. median change is three times less than the European one. Yet, it can certainly not fully explain the huge difference. For the next two comparisons (round A/B and round B/C) European fintechs need around half a year longer than U.S. start-ups in this segment. This could once again explain why the median increase in amount raised is not as high in the U.S. as it is in Europe. To raise round D financing after round C

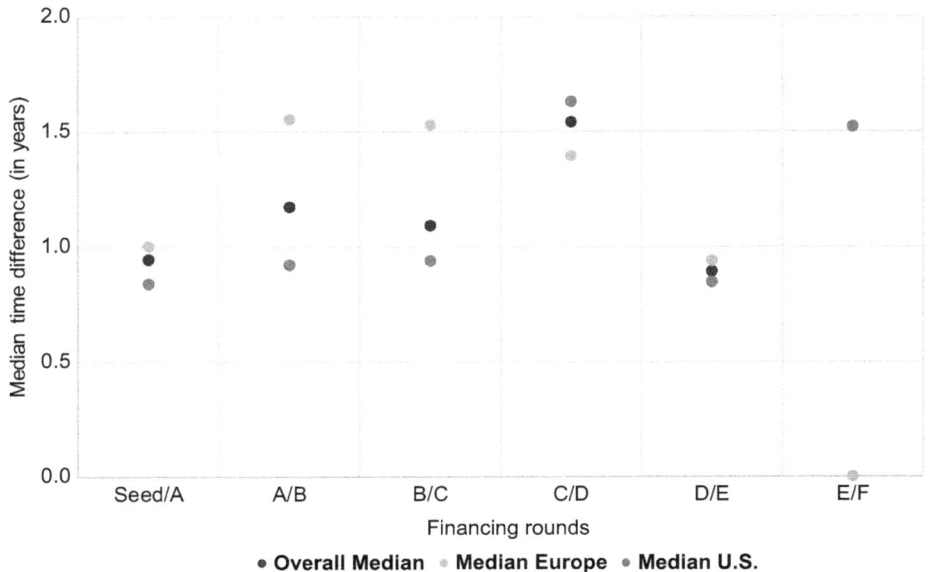

Figure 6.7: Median time difference in years between two successive financing rounds in credit & factoring for sample April 2000–June 2017.
(Source: own illustration)

takes 1.4 years in Europe, while it takes 1.6 years in the U.S. This is surprising, as fintechs in Europe have a three times higher median increase than in the U.S., despite closing the following round quicker. No significant statements can be made for the round D/E comparison, as the median time between the financing rounds is about the same and no data is available for the round E/F comparison in Europe. Credit & factoring fintechs in both regions seem to be moving toward maturity. However, the U.S. seems to be slightly advanced, as the segment also appeared on the U.S. fintech landscape a few years earlier.

Summary

Credit & factoring fintechs often have small- and medium-sized companies as customers as well as institutional investors. The key partners are the capital providers, third-party providers for credit data verification, credit card companies and regulatory authorities. They use online platforms, social media and e-mail to contact potential clients. Once the clients are successfully acquired in a pure online onboarding procedure, the fintechs use algorithm-based credit scorings to derive ratings from the company's cash flows. Credit & factoring fintechs generate revenues from origination fees, monthly maintenance fees and interest income.

Credit & factoring fintechs are moving toward maturity. The changes in the size of the financing rounds generally become smaller from financing round to financing round. It starts with an increase of up to +600% financing volume from seed to round A, and decreases for the next three rounds to +200 and +100%. In the later financing rounds D to F the financing volumes increase only slightly or might even decrease.

7 The future of personal finance management

Personal finance management (PFM) systems primarily help clients to gain a quick and uncomplicated overview of their own financial situation. PFM applications automatically classify transactions into different categories and check their compliance with budget targets. Ideally, PFM tools also help users to optimize their financial situation. This includes the comparison of a user's own payment behavior with that of other customers, the individual proposal for the use of different bank and insurance products or the forecast of a user's own asset development (see Figure 7.1). From the point of view of financial institutions, PFM tools can be used to collect useful data on customer behavior via data mining, which can facilitate cross-selling and improve process efficiency. The combination of customer relationship management (CRM) and PFM within the bank creates new possibilities for analyzing customer needs and identifying starting points for a targeted customer approach. In addition, a good PFM tool can increase customer loyalty and satisfaction, boost the take-up of services and convince new customers. PFM offers considerable simplification potential for classic forecast calculations, such as retirement provision, which are still often carried out by consultants in personal meetings. Instead, PFM can take on the role of a personal advisor. The

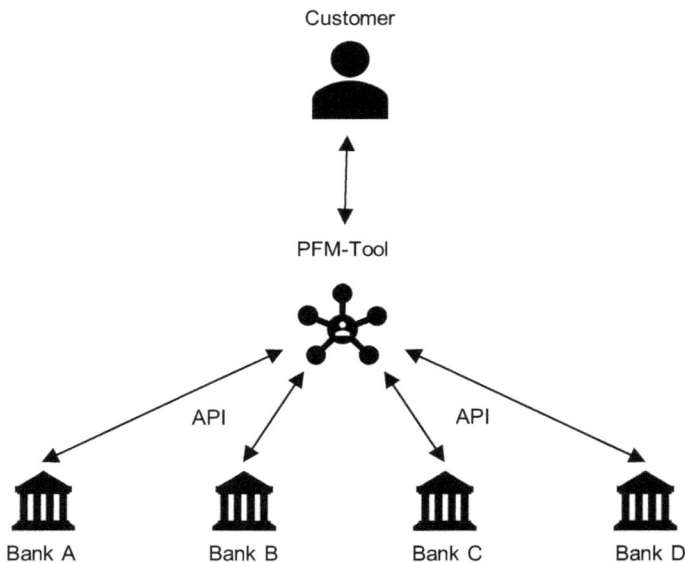

Figure 7.1: Interaction between customer and banks through Personal Finance Management tools. (Source: own illustration)

https://doi.org/10.1515/9783110704907-007

Table 7.1: Market overview Personal Finance Management.

Company	Headquarter	Founding	Total Funding Amount	Customer Size	Customer Regions	Description
Mint	U.S.	2006	$31.8M	20M	USA	Accessible aggregation of financial life and free advice on how to save money.
Credit Karma	U.S.	2007	$868M	85M	USA	Credit assessment, scoring, debt management and account monitoring.
Meniga	U.K.	2009	$34.5M	65M	Europe	Leading white label provider for traditional banks.
51Xinyongka	CHN	2013	$459M	100M	Asia	Credit card management solutions offering data analysis of credit card bills, accounting, credit facilitation and transaction management.

(Source: Data from Crunchbase and company websites)

necessary data for creating a pension calculation, such as income, age and savings, is automatically extracted from the application and the calculated results are visualized within the PFM tool.[322]

The fintech or PFM tool of a bank can suggest individually suitable products for customers to improve their financial situation. The security criterion is a key hygiene and success factor for the acceptance of PFM tools.[323] European regulators are accelerating the development of PFM with the revised Payment Services Directive 2 (PSD-2). The PSD-2 opened the payment market, leading to new services and increased competition for established institutions. Banks need to create system interfaces that allow authorized third parties to access a customer's financial information. The new regulation allows any financial institution to become the central PFM provider and to expand existing customer data or acquire new customers. At the same time, competition from new service providers or fintechs is also increasing.[324]

---

322 Fischer and Wagner 2017, p. 178; Beth and Fischer 2020.
323 Fischer and Wagner 2017, pp. 188–189.
324 Thiele et al. 2017, pp. 1–3.

7.1 Business Model Canvas – Mint

The American software company Intuit Inc. acquired the PFM provider Mint for $170 million in 2009. At that time, Mint had merely about one million users (April 2016: more than 20 million users). In addition to the PFM application, Mint operates QuickBooks, an online accounting software and TurboTax, Intuit's accounting software solution that provides free tax billing, efile taxes and income tax returns.[325]

Mint has some key partners in the business model. Lending Club, the leading peer-to-peer lending platform in the U.S., cooperates with Mint to support consumers to use less debit card debt and pay less interest. Most LendingClub users (71.37%) use loans granted to refinance existing loans or repay their credit card debt.[326] In 2019 LendingClub brokered approximately 920,000 loans totaling about $12.3 billion.[327]

Mint has developed a new method to help children to develop money management skills. In collaboration with Scholastic, an interactive game and free teaching materials were developed for teachers, students and families. The materials were available in about 30,000 classrooms in 2011.[328]

Automatic data categorization as key activity

Mint has had a significant growth in value – from $0 to $170 million in just two years. To achieve this, the company built financial blogs on the internet and created a brand name even before launching their PFM product. The Mint team wrote blog posts, conducted interviews with well-known financial experts, designed infographics and created all sorts of content to reach the target group of mainly young people looking for a better way to meet their financial needs. Mint used social media, in particular Reddit and Search Engine Optimization (SEO), which accounted for about 20% of Mint's total traffic. Mint was quickly considered a trusted source of financial information and many interested private investors subscribed to its newsletter.[329]

The early success of Mint can be linked to a very simple product innovation. Long and tedious processes were shortened and simplified by automation. When a user first logs in to Mint, all the user's financial transactions can be retrieved from the user's

---

325 CBInsights 2017.
326 Data as of December, 31 2019.
327 Lending Club 2010; LendingClub 2019b.
328 Shontell 2011; Schoolastic 2020.
329 CBInsights 2019.

bank, including credit and debit cards. The data is automatically categorized, which is something that could not be offered by competitors.[330]

Value propositions

Mint gives users a cost-free overview of their financial activities, displayed on the website or on the smartphone. All transactions are automatically categorized and graphically displayed. An easy-to-understand financial overview and specific suggestions for saving measures are designed to help customers optimize their financial situation.[331]

In addition to the complete overview, customers get a free credit card rating. The rating value is generated in a continuous process and the users are notified immediately if the rating changes. Customers can also activate other notifications, such as reminders for outstanding invoices, overdraft warnings or unusual account movements. Mint's financial management system also provides investment tracking, allowing users to evaluate their portfolio. The PFM advises on optimization and savings potentials, for example, brokerage fees.[332]

Mint promises its users high security standards through banking standards such as 128-bit SSL encryption and a four-digit PIN. In addition, Mint is permanently monitored by online security services such as TrustE and VeriSign.[333]

Customer relationships and sales channels

In order to use banking apps, customers generally have to provide authentication through a PIN, synchronize with the bank account and various credit cards, enter personal data and a range of other information. Making this experience as simple and stress-free as possible is both a challenge and an opportunity for a PFM provider. Mint solved this problem with a high degree of automation and a simple user interface.[334]

A Stanford study found that 46% of the nearly 3,000 participants surveyed believed that the credibility of a website depends on its design. The Mint team therefore developed a Web 2.0 website with 3D tabs, buttons and shadow effects. The color gradients and the airbrush effects were tailored to the visual credibility of users with green colors and orange accents.[335]

---

330 CBInsights 2019.
331 Mint 2020d.
332 Mint 2020a, 2020b.
333 Mint 2020c.
334 CBInsights 2019.
335 Fogg et al. 2002, pp. 6–7; CBInsights 2019.

Mint targets all retail banking clients or consumers (B2C) who wish to control and manage their financial behavior. Intuit also provides PFM as a white label solution for banks and other financial service providers.[336] Mint uses various marketing channels, especially the internet and social media. In addition, strategic partnerships with Lending Club and the parent company Intuit play a key role in expanding the customer base.

Revenue from commission for recommendations

Mint is not listed separately in Intuit's financial statements but is summarized under the category Consumer with TurboTax and Open Financial Exchange (OFX). Mint generates its revenues with a commission model. For recommendations of credit cards, loans or insurance contracts, Mint receives a commission from the respective provider. The website is used to generate advertising revenue. Other companies can buy advertising space on the homepage or in the app. Mint uses targeted advertising based on users' financial history. Another source of revenue is the implementation of white labels for banks and other financial service providers. Further sales potential could result from the sale of anonymized data to companies for the analysis of consumer behavior.[337] Intuit generated total revenues of $6.74 billion at the fiscal year (FY) ending July 31, 2019, with the Consumer segment accounting for approximately 41% ($2.78 billion). Intuit Group's total operating income of $3.61 billion was 48% for TurboTax, Mint and OFX.[338]

7.2 Business Model Canvas – Credit Karma

Credit scores and credit reports are transferred to Credit Karma by its key partners National Credit Bureaus, TransUnion and Equifax. Users receive their credit score and credit report on a weekly basis. In addition, consumers receive information on what influences their score and how it can be improved. Credit Karma provides personalized recommendations on cheaper credit cards and loans. The company generates revenues mainly through commission income. Credit Karma does not offer loans from traditional banks, but from online platforms such as Lending Club, OnDeck and Marcus by Goldman Sachs.[339]

---

336 Wisniewski 2013.
337 CBInsights 2019.
338 Intuit 2019, pp. 28, 35, 39.
339 Credit Karma.

Free credit scores as key activity and value proposition

At the time of the launch of Credit Karma, the only ways to get a credit report or score was via websites like TrueCredit and FreeCreditReport.com. Registration on these sites, however, was not free. Credit Karma released credit scores for free and gained a large user base. Many of these users are U.S. citizens with a poor credit rating – which is the case for about a third of the U.S. population. Most of these users are not only interested in their score but also want to improve it. The company has therefore developed a specific USP with access to a large amount of user data, in particular regarding U.S. citizens with poor credit ratings.[340]

Cost-free credit monitoring is also provided. The service checks the data of users and notifies them of any significant changes. Various credit cards are offered according to different categorizations like credit score, sports, cashback, students and airlines. Users are also able to evaluate the card providers. The loans are structured as personal loans, home loans, auto loans, student loans and business loans. Furthermore, Credit Karma provides cost-free calculators and simulators including the Credit Score Simulator, Debt Repayment Calculator, Simple Loan Calculator and Amortization Calculator. These applications are accessible for all visitors to the website.[341]

Customer relationships and segments

More than 30% of Credit Karma's five million monthly website visitors visit mainly because of the free tools. This includes a debt repayment calculator and the credit score simulator. Both tools are highly relevant value drivers for both general traffic and customer acquisition. When users register, further functions are unlocked. Credit Karma targets consumers who are looking for a cheap loan or credit card. People with low credit scores generally visit Credit Karma because it is free and does not involve any additional financial burden. It offers financial products tailored to their financial needs. Credit Karma is at the top of Google search results because of its cost-free tools that, in turn, increase the acceptance and credibility of the website.[342]

Revenue from commission of product partners

Credit Karma is free of charge for users, but receives a commission from its partners, for example, the bank that finances the loan or issues the credit card. It has full

---

340 CBInsights 2019.
341 Credit Karma.
342 CBInsights 2019.

transparency about what a customer must pay for existing credit card debt or credit interest and can therefore offer cheaper products. If the customer makes use of these possibilities, Credit Karma receives a commission. In 2017 Credit Karma's turnover grew by 37%, resulting in an annual turnover of $682 million. The large part of revenue comes from commissions, and margins can vary widely depending on the key partner. The Credit Karma management expects double-digit growth for the future.[343]

7.3 Business Model Canvas – Meniga

The key partners of Meniga are a number of banks. In 2015 Meniga integrated its PFM software into the Banco Santander Group. Santander is one of the largest banks in the world with around 144 million customers.[344] Consorsbank in Germany is part of BNP Paribas and expanded its online presence with the Meniga PFM.[345] ING Direct was the first bank in Spain to expand its online banking via Meniga. ING is a Dutch-based financial institution providing banking, insurance and asset management services to more than 85 million private, corporate and institutional customers in 40 countries worldwide.[346] Starting in 2013 the Meniga PFM was implemented at comdirect bank in Germany for its 2.5 million users in multiple stages.[347] mBank is part of the Commerzbank Group in Poland, the Czech Republic and Slovakia and is the largest Central European online bank with more than five million customers. mBank has worked on Europe's most ambitious next-generation online banking project, which includes deeply integrated personal finance functions, event-driven CRM, Facebook integration, P2P payments and more. Meniga's APIs have been used since 2013 to completely redesign the banking experience.[348] Meniga is based in Finland, Iceland, Sweden, Singapore, Poland and the U.K., but works with selected partners around the world including Accenture and SamLink.[349]

Application programming interface and PFM activities

Meniga offers the development and maintenance of application programming interfaces (APIs) that comply with current legal requirements.[350] It uses its PFM website

---

343 Verhage 2018; Banco Santander S.A. 2019, p. IV.
344 Kristjánsson 2015d.
345 Kristjánsson 2015b.
346 Kristjánsson 2015c; Crunchbase 2020c.
347 Kristjánsson 2015a.
348 Luciano 2016; Pankin 2015.
349 Meniga 2020a; Samlink 2020.
350 Meniga 2020b.

in Iceland as a platform to test products and innovations. Iceland is extremely digitalized and a good test market for futuristic products. For example, 90% of all payment transactions are card based, and the country has a high penetration of broadband connections as well as high usage of mobile applications. Twenty-five percent of Icelandic households use the PFM platform, so there is a constant pool of valuable suggestions. Meniga keeps close contact with its users to better understand their needs and requirements.[351]

Data consolidation and enrichment as value propositions

Meniga provides various digital banking products. PFM allows banks to personalize online banking and to deliver a unique customer experience. Meniga Business Finance gives SME customers a real-time view of their finances and enables them to improve their cash conversion cycle time. The engagement platform enhances customer relationships through deep insights into their financial behavior, which allows individualized advice and product recommendations. Meniga also has card-linked offers. Its algorithms analyze customer transaction history and other relevant customer data to provide personalized quotes for card customers. And Meniga also provides consumer data analytics. Banks can offer real-time market trends to business customers, enabling them to compare customer data, such as sales volume and market share, with individual competitors. Meniga's business philosophy focuses on data consolidation and data enrichment to personalize the banking experience.[352]

Customer segments and sales channels

Islandsbanki is one of the oldest and largest banks in Iceland. In 2009 the bank introduced Meniga's PFM software. The solution was well received by the bank's customers and staff, with more than 20% of the bank's online users registering within six months of the launch. Eighty-nine percent of users said they wanted to recommend the Meniga PFM solution to their friends. In the end, 88% of the users stated that they would use Meniga PFM regularly in the future. Meniga's customer segment is currently exclusively B2B, which includes banks and financial service providers. The benefits of its products are communicated mainly via its own website with awards and distinctions for its innovative products and comments from key

---

351 Magnusson 2016.
352 Meniga 2019.

customers. All cooperation partners support the website with quotes from executives describing the benefits of partnering with Meniga and the PFM solution.[353]

Main revenue from software licenses

The loss for the financial year 2018/2019 amounted to €1.6 million. The loss was primarily due to heavy investment in Meniga's marketing and data analytics solutions, reflected in an increase of administrative costs of 19.9% year-on-year to €15.7 million. Revenues in the 2018/2019 financial year rose by 17.4% year-on-year to €13.5 million. Meniga's annual revenue from long-term maintenance contracts and subscription-like license fees rose to approximately €7.9 million, an increase of 49% over the previous year. Meniga acquired multiple new customers, both in its digital banking and rewards business. Meniga has completed the introduction of its software to customers in Italy, Greece and Sweden. License revenues are expected to increase in the near future. Meniga secured €3.0 million in equity investments from new and existing investors to support its expansion.[354]

7.4 Business Model Canvas – u51.com

51 Credit Card Inc. (51Xinyongka), also known as u51.com, provides a credit card management application by analyzing user data from credit card bills, applications and payment transactions. The company provides detailed credit card information from local banks and provides credit and other financial services so customers can search and compare terms when applying for credit cards.[355]

China UnionPay is the only credit card organization in China and an important key partner of u51.com. Members include major Chinese banks such as the Bank of China, China Merchants Bank and the state-owned investment company CITIC China International Trust and Investment Corporation. The platform does not offer credit cards from UnionPay, but from Western providers such as MasterCard and Visa.[356]

Value propositions for more than 100 million users

The most important partner for u51.com is the company's credit card organization UnionPay. This collaboration has enabled u51.com to build a Chinese customer

---

353 Ómarsson 2018.
354 Companies House 2019, pp. 2, 4, 9–10.
355 Pitchbook 2019; 51 Credit Card 2020b.
356 UnionPay International 2020.

base of more than 83 million registered users. The number of credit cards we have managed cumulatively of the credit card platform in 2016, 2017, 2018 and 2019 amounted to 106.3 million, 123.0 million, 118.6 million and 138.7 million, respectively, corresponding to a CAGR of 9.27% in 2019.[357] u51.com provides the four products "51 Credit Card Manager," "51 Characters," "51 People" and "Give Flowers."[358] The 51 Credit Card Manager uses different categories to help customers compare all credit card offers. The platform helps users to compare and break down offers by category: young family, women's credit cards, tourism, intensive users, hotel, aviation, gourmet, car and sports. In 2015 the company expanded its product portfolio to include "51 Characters," an asset manager and "51 Person Loan," its own lending platform. "Give you flowers" has been specially developed for young customers and is intended to shorten the process of traditional borrowing.[359]

Sales channels supported by "Uncle Bo"

At the end of June 2019, 138.7 million credit cards were managed on the platform, enabling record RMB115.8 billion of credit card repayment transactions.[360] u51. com's customer base lies in the B2C segment aiming at Chinese credit card users who want to compare credit card and credit terms online or manage them via the platform.[361] 51Xinyongka promoted its products with its chief product experience officer, Wu Xiubo, also known in China as "Uncle Bo," who is a nationally known personality. He is a successful Chinese actor, musician, producer, as well as an advertising ambassador and was the chief product experience officer.[362] Due to a personal scandal of Uncle Bo, his name no longer appears on the website in 2020.

High revenue growth

Operating expenses increased at a CAGR of 120.6% from RMB255.7 million in 2015 to RMB2,746.4 million in 2018.[363] The two largest cost blocks in 2018 were origination and servicing costs as well as sales and marketing costs, each accounting for more than 20% of total costs. In addition, R&D expenses accounted for 12% of the company's total

---

357 51 Credit Card 2019a, p. 8, 2019c, p. 4.
358 Product no longer mentioned on the company website as of March 2020.
359 51 Credit Card 2020b.
360 51 Credit Card 2019c, p. 4, 2019b, p. 2.
361 51 Credit Card 2020a.
362 51 Credit Card.
363 Hong Kong Exchanges and Clearing 2018, p. 13; 51 Credit Card 2019a, p. 125.

costs.[364] Revenues increased at a CAGR of 215.3% from RMB89.7 million in 2015 to RMB2,812.0 million in 2018. The adjusted operating profit or loss,[365] amounted to a loss of RMB147.6 million in 2015, a profit of RMB86.6 million in 2016, a profit of RMB777.2 million in 2017 and an operating profit of RMB65.3 million in 2018, respectively.[366] Operating margins were 31.1% in 2017 and 0.02% in 2018 and the adjusted net profit margins[367] were 24.3% and 17.3%, respectively.[368] The company generates revenue primarily from credit facilitation and service fees, which accounted for around 73% of total revenue in 2018. The loan facilitation volume amounted to RMB815.3 million in 2015, to RMB10,299.3 million in 2016, to RMB33,890.6 million in 2017 and to RMB20,457.4 million in 2018.[369]

7.5 Venture capital financing of PFM start-ups

PFM tools from fintechs belong to the area of personal finance but could also be seen as a service supporting payment functions for the account of the customer. PFM is therefore generally not shown as a separate segment in public data banks. More than $3.9 billion were invested in U.S. fintechs in the general category of personal finance between January 2017 and April 2020 in 122 financing rounds. In Europe $2.6 billion were invested in the same period in 59 financing rounds for personal finance.[370] The following, more detailed analysis of foundations and financing rounds focuses on a sample of PFM fintechs in Europe and the U.S. as the data available for China is not significant.

Figure 7.2 illustrates the annual split of 40 PFM fintechs launched for the sample April 2000 to June 2017 in Europe and the U.S. Only two PFM fintechs were founded in the period from 1999 to 2006. In the following years, between three and six fintechs were founded each year. Founding activity in the U.S. peaked in 2009 when five new PFM fintechs were launched and has stagnated at a level of one or two new companies ever since. In contrast, more fintechs have emerged in the PFM field in Europe in recent years, reaching the highest level of new fintechs in 2015. Market participants in Europe either still see potential in the PFM market or – in the absence of a one-off effect – believe in a slowly maturing market. On the other

364 51 Credit Card 2019a, pp. 125, 239.
365 Excluding share-based compensation expenses.
366 51 Credit Card 2019a, p. 125; Hong Kong Exchanges and Clearing 2018, p. 313.
367 Excluding share-based compensation expenses, Fair value (gain)/loss of preferred shares, Fair value gain of financial liability at FVPL, Extinguishment gain of preferred shares and listing expenses.
368 51 Credit Card 2019a, pp. 20, 125.
369 Hong Kong Exchanges and Clearing 2018, pp. 4–5; 51 Credit Card 2019a, p. 13.
370 Data as of April 30, 2020 from Crunchbase 2020e.

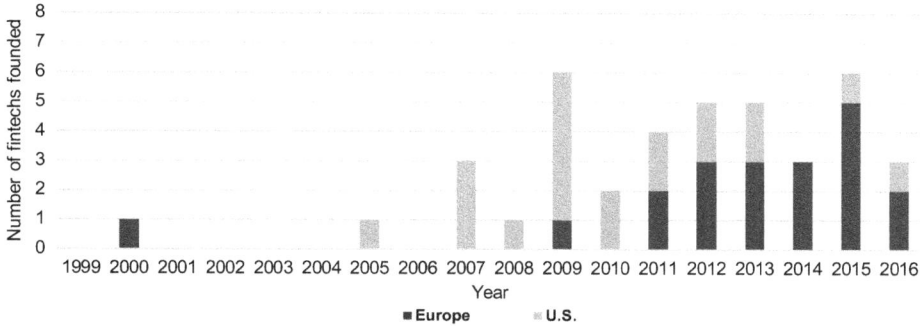

Figure 7.2: Number of fintechs founded in Personal Finance Management in Europe and the U.S. from 1999–2016 for sample April 2000–June 2017. (Source: own illustration)

hand, the U.S. PFM market appears to be relatively mature based on the development in number of new fintechs in this segment over the last years.

During the first seven years of the millennium the only PFM financing round where data was publicly available was closed in 2006. After another year of no financing round taking place, the number significantly increased from two deals in 2008 to 23 in 2016. The number of financing rounds has continuously increased in Europe since the first deal took place in 2010. For instance, six years after the first deal, in 2016, 12 deals were realized. The development of annual amounts raised will be evaluated next to gain further visibility if prior findings can be confirmed or not (see Figure 7.3).

Figure 7.4 shows that fintech funding in PFM was very limited prior to 2008. The amount raised then increased from €1.4 million in 2008 to €61.5 million in 2011, mainly driven by an increase in deal count in the U.S. as well as initial deals in Europe. In 2012 funding dropped by almost 62% even though the number of financing rounds only decreased by 10%. The explanation for that lies in the average amount raised, which plumped from €4.9 million to €0.6 million in Europe and from €6.5 million to €3.7 million in the U.S. After this decline, PFM fintechs managed to grow their funding massively at a CAGR of 153.7% so that the total amount raised in 2015 amounted to €385.2 million. This impressive development was particularly due to the U.S. market. In which the average amount raised saw a more than sevenfold increase.

In 2016 PFM funding amounted to €238.8 million, implying a drop of 38%. The main reason was the decreasing average amount raised in Europe. The share of U.S. PFM funding did not decline as much as the deal count in recent years, allowing for the conclusion that investments became larger to enhance growth in a market moving toward maturity. In Europe the data rather suggests that the PFM

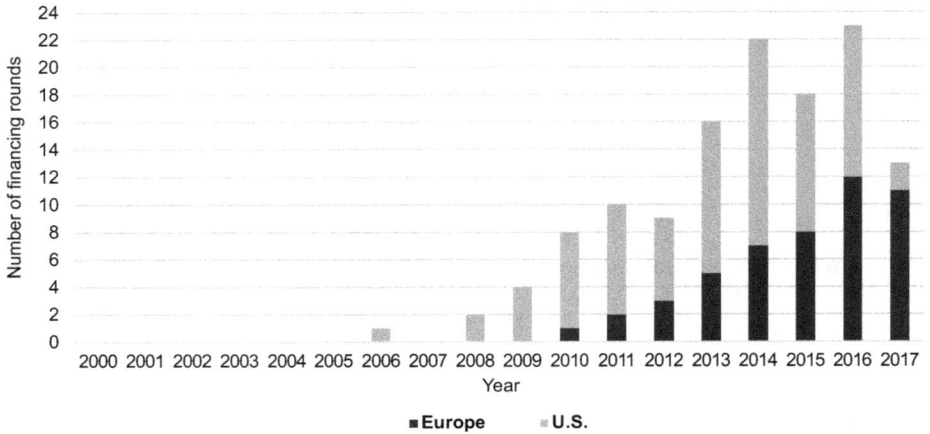

Figure 7.3: Number of financing rounds in Personal Finance Management in Europe and the U.S. for sample April 2000–June 2017.
(Source: own illustration)

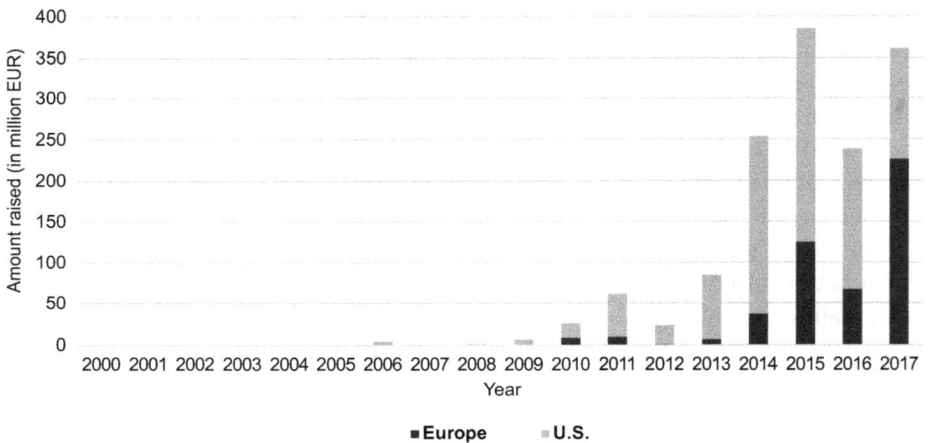

Figure 7.4: Annual overview of amount raised in Personal Finance Management in Europe and the U.S. for sample April 2000–June 2017 (in € m).
(Source: own illustration)

market's maturity is far behind that of the U.S. market, as the number of deals still increased. However, the share of annual amounts raised fails to proportionally demonstrate this development. A closer look at the median amount raised in each of the financing rounds therefore helps to better understand the situation.

Table 7.2 illustrates that differences between Europe and the U.S. regarding Seed and round A funding are negligible. For both regions, the median Seed round capital

Table 7.2: Median amount raised in Personal Finance Management in Europe and the U.S. for sample April 2000–June 2017 (in € m).

	Seed	A	B	C	D	E	F	IPO
Overall Median	1.1	5.5	10.2	23.1	124.9	n/a	n/a	n/a
Median Europe	1.1	5.5	9.0	23.1	n/a	n/a	n/a	n/a
Median U.S.	1.1	5.4	10.2	27.2	124.9	n/a	n/a	n/a
Sample size *n*	22	27	18	7	3	0	0	0

(Source: own illustration)

raised is €1.1 million and approximately €5.5 million in the following financing round A. In financing round B, the median amount raised in Europe is €9.0 million, whereas PFM fintechs in the U.S. raise a median of €10.2 million, implying an approximately 13% higher funding in round B for U.S. PFM fintechs. This gap in funding even further widens in financing round C, where €27.2 million are collected in the U.S. compared to an amount of €23.1 million in Europe. Growth and later stage financing rounds in the U.S. achieve higher funding than in Europe. However, it should be noted that the sample size of $n = 7$ for the median in financing round C is relatively small. For the financing round D, data could only be obtained for the U.S. and hence can not be compared to Europe. Likewise, no data was available for financing rounds E and F as well for IPOs, possibly indicating that PFM fintechs do not yet complete late stage financing. An interpretation for this could be that those fintechs do not require that much follow-on financing or that the market as a whole is not mature yet.

Figure 7.5 presents the difference in amounts raised between two successive financing rounds in percent. The underlying data sample is distributed as follows: Seed/A $n = 13$; A/B $n = 16$; B/C $n = 7$; C/D $n = 3$; D/E $n = 0$; and E/F $n = 0$.

The median increase between Seed investment and financing round A amounts to 398% in the U.S., which is 64% more than in Europe. This difference further increases to 83% for the comparison of financing rounds A and B where the median in Europe is 87%, while the U.S. increase is roughly 171%. This pattern of increasing gaps is refuted by the comparison of financing rounds B and C. Here, in fact, the median growth in amount raised in Europe is 328% and only 143% in the U.S. One could therefore draw the conclusion that it is easier for U.S. PFM fintechs to grow their funding in the early stage, whereas it seems to be easier for the European counterparts to achieve faster growing funding during growth funding rounds (e.g., from B to C). Data on later stage financing rounds is not available.

The last PFM comparison between Europe and the U.S. is shown in Figure 7.6 and consists of the same sample size as for Figure 7.5.

At 1.16 years versus 0.71 years, the time between Seed round and financing round A is almost six months shorter in Europe than in the U.S. This could explain

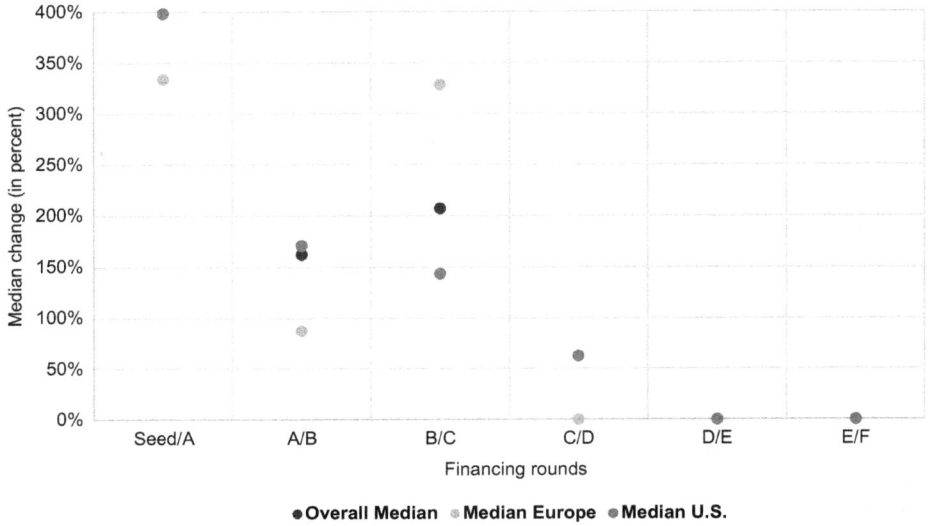

Figure 7.5: Median change in amounts raised between two successive financing rounds in Personal Finance Management for sample April 2000–June 2017 (in percent).
(Source: own illustration)

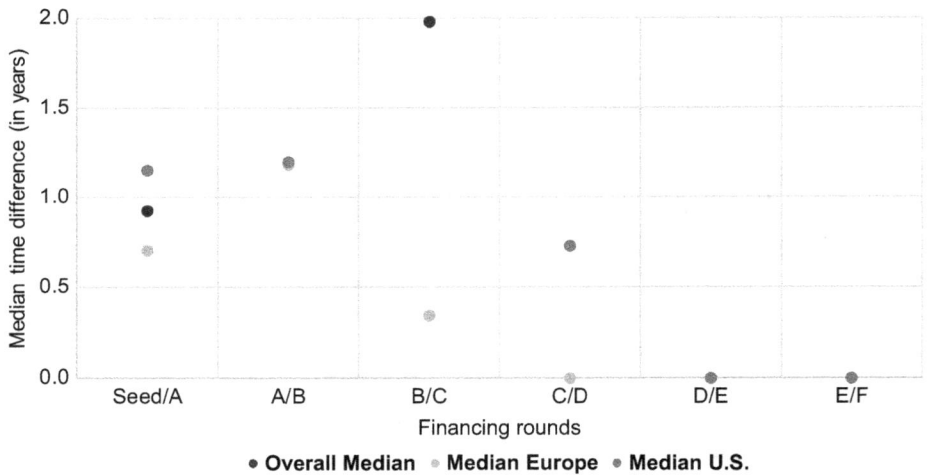

Figure 7.6: Median time difference in years between two successive financing rounds in Personal Finance Management for sample April 2000–June 2017.
(Source: own illustration)

why fintechs in Europe did not increase their amount raised from Seed to round A by as much as the U.S. start-ups in the PFM field. Nevertheless, this interpretation is invalidated by a closer look at the time between round A and round B, which is roughly 1.2 years for both regions and hence almost identical, despite a significantly higher percentage increase in amount raised (171% in the U.S. vs. 87% in Europe). The value of about four months for Europe appears to be affected by the small sample size and the methodology, which only calculates the date difference in years between the respective latest follow-on financing rounds (e.g., A-II and B-II). As a result, no further comparison is possible between Europe and the U.S. in terms of time between two successive financing rounds. In summary, it can be stated that the U.S. PFM market appears to be more mature as highlighted by the development of new fintechs in this field and the implicitly increased average amount raised, derived from the number of deals and the annual amount of financing.

Summary

Mint pioneered individual financial planning and developed the first user-friendly PFM solution. Credit Karma offers credit checks and credit reports free of charge and has gained a large user base. The site is very popular because of its free simulators and calculators. Meniga is the European market leader for PFM solutions in the B2B segment. U51.com is the largest Chinese credit card management platform, which also serves as a comparison marketplace for credit card and credit terms. Compared to Europe, PFM fintechs in the U.S. have seen much stronger customer growth as well as much higher funding volumes with venture capital.

Figure 7.7 summarizes the components of the business model for PFM tools. Key partners are banks and credit card providers. PFM supports the automation of categorization in payments and most of the time the tools are free of charge for the users. Revenues mainly come from partner commissions.

Key partners	Key activities	Value propositions	Customer relationships	Customer segments
Financial institutions, banks and credit card providers	PSD-2 opens access to the payments market	Easy management, control of financial transactions	High degree of automation, simple user interface	Retail banking clients or consumers (B2C)
Strategic partnerships with other fintechs, e.g., Lending Club, OnDeck or Marcus by Goldman Sachs	Trustworthy online presence	Overview of financial situation		White label solution for banks, other financial service providers
	Cost-free calculators	Automated categorization, visualization, evaluations		
	Key resources		**Channels**	
	Development and maintenance of APIs with compliance to current legal requirements	Free of charge	Social media, e.g., Reddit	
		Insight into the client's financial situation, habits	Search engine optimization	
		Gateway to the client relationship		

Cost structure	Revenue streams
High investments in marketing and data analysis solutions as well as for development of APIs to key partners	Commission model and affiliate marketing

Figure 7.7: Business Model Canvas – Personal Finance Management.
(Source: own illustration)

8 The impact of blockchain technology

8.1 Use cases for more efficiency in banking

The global blockchain market size is expected to grow with a CAGR of 69.4% between 2019–2025, from $1.5 billion in 2018 to $57.6 billion by 2025.[371] Banks are facing the perspective of shifting their operational financial systems and processes to blockchain, which is also true for their existing systems of risk evaluation (see Figure 8.1). This would significantly simplify the processes, eliminating costly and sometimes redundant pieces of infrastructure. The growing popularity of blockchain is justified by the benefits provided by the core characteristics of the technology – such as providing transparency, openness and efficiency while using the capabilities of modern technological advancement. Efficiency gains, transactional advantages and increasingly transparent regulatory aspects enabled by blockchain are expected to benefit the financial services industry in particular.[372]

Blockchain provides efficiency gains in many industries beyond finance, including media and entertainment, government and the public sector, healthcare and life sciences, retail and e-commerce, automotive, the energy sector and many others.[373] Figure 8.2 provides an overview of service providers and application areas of blockchain technology. Fintechs differentiate offered services for the three areas of application and solutions, middleware, and infrastructure protocols. Application areas for blockchain are payments, exchanges, smart contracts, governance, compliance, and capital markets. The shift toward the common usage of blockchain will not happen overnight, but the perspectives of cost cutting and efficiency advancement will continue to fuel the interest in investing in blockchain.[374]

8.2 The importance of blockchain – "let the code speak for itself"

Key elements of blockchain architecture

In 2008 an author with the pseudonym Satoshi Nakamoto developed a technical concept for electronic money in a paper called "Bitcoin: A Peer-to-Peer Electronic Cash System." "Let the code speak for itself" summarizes the basic principle for the mode of operation of a blockchain, because in standard processes of financial

---

371 Grand View Research Inc. 2019.
372 Business Insider Intelligence 2017.
373 Blockchain Market by Provider, Application & Organization Size 2018.
374 Business Insider Intelligence 2017.

https://doi.org/10.1515/9783110704907-008

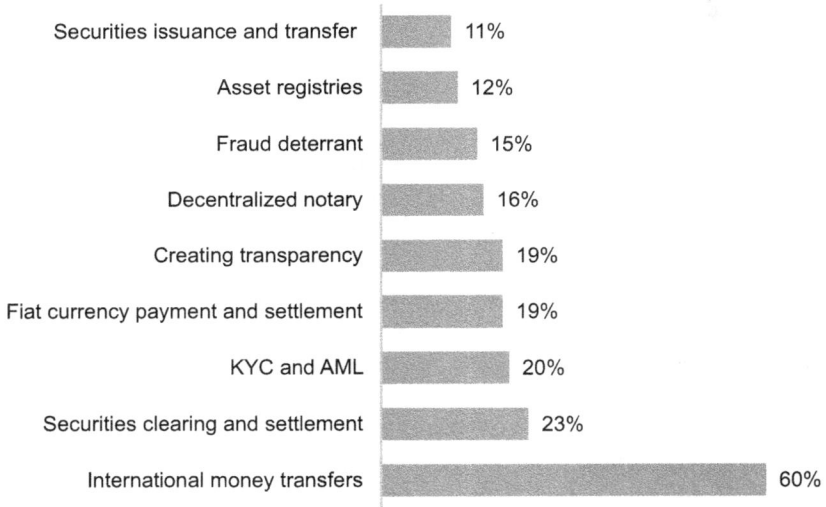

Securities issuance and transfer	11%
Asset registries	12%
Fraud deterrant	15%
Decentralized notary	16%
Creating transparency	19%
Fiat currency payment and settlement	19%
KYC and AML	20%
Securities clearing and settlement	23%
International money transfers	60%

Figure 8.1: Blockchain use cases for banks.
(Source: own illustration with data from Business Insider 2017)

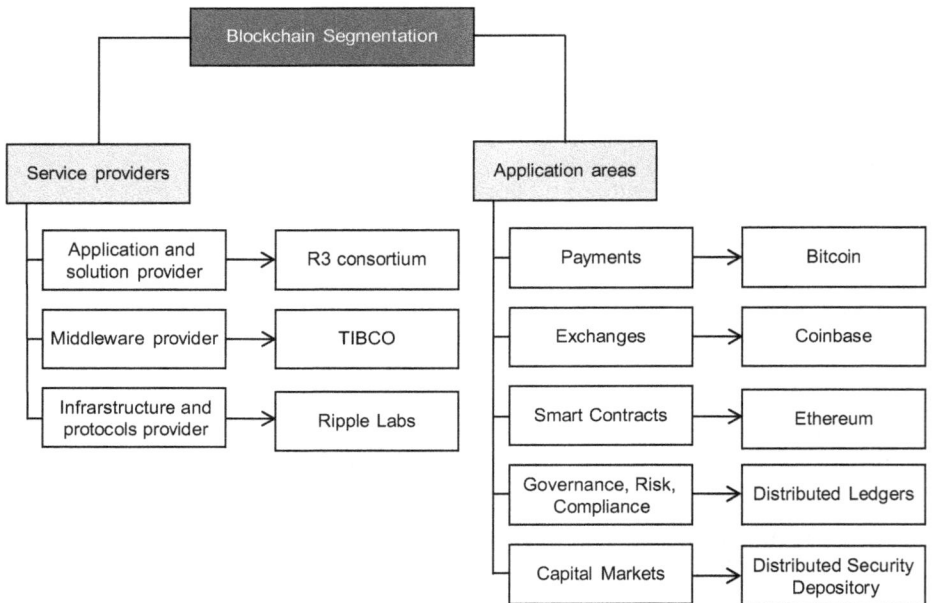

Figure 8.2: Segments of the blockchain industry.
(Source: own illustration)

services not all the functions are explained in a code.[375] Blockchain, the technology behind Bitcoin, is an ever-growing digital registry of digital events or transactions, which is decentralized with no central authority, distributed among the network participants (see Figure 8.3), chronologically updated as new transactions are added, and practically immutable.[376] It is important to highlight that blockchain does not equal Bitcoin, as cryptocurrencies are just one of the many possible applications of blockchain technology. As many stories of fraud or speculation with cryptocurrencies exist in the media, it is crucial to stress the difference to understand blockchain.

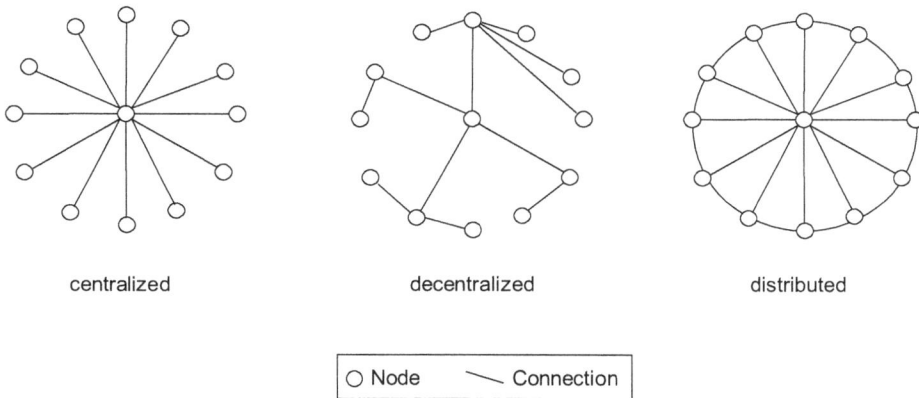

centralized   decentralized   distributed

○ Node   ⌒ Connection

Figure 8.3: Comparison of network architectures.
(Source: own illustration adapted from Baran 1964, p. 2)

Each block consists of transactions communicated to the system in the previous block as well as a mathematical reference (hash) to a previous block, so that a chain is formed. Once on the blockchain, it is nearly impossible for transactions to be modified or erased. In addition to the Merkle root, a block header contains the hash value of the previous block header and a dedicated field Nonce (Number Only Used Once). Several new transactions are collected in the transaction data part of a block. The individual transactions are then combined in a "Merkle Tree" (hash tree) and encrypted until a unique hash value remains (see Figure 8.4). This is called the "Merkle Root."[377]

---

375 Tapscott and Tapscott 2016, p. 23.
376 Nakamoto 2008.
377 Brühl 2017, pp. 136–137.

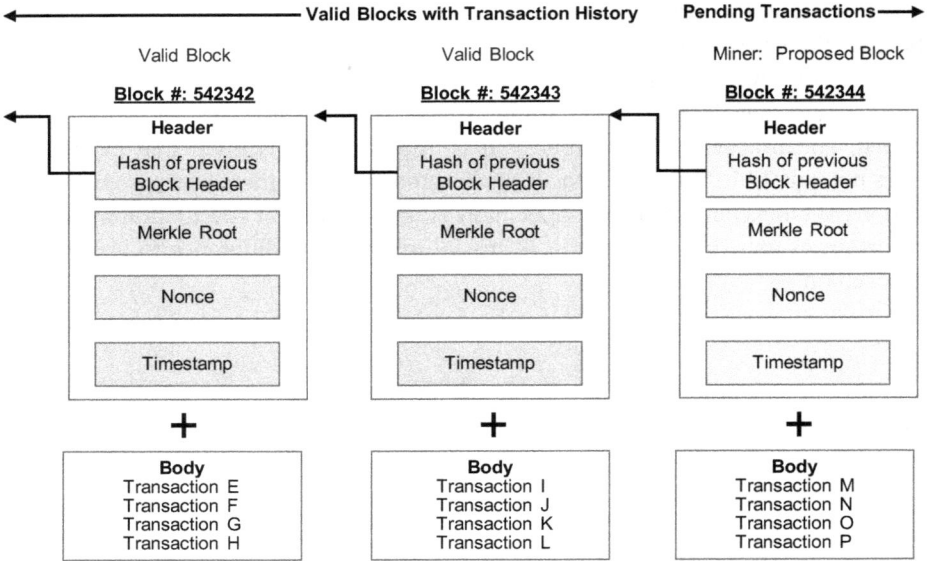

Figure 8.4: Chaining of blocks to a blockchain.
(Source: own illustration adapted from Bitcoin.org 2020 and Parker 2019)

Business, technical and legal aspects of blockchain

Mougayar defines three aspects of blockchain capabilities: business, technical and legal. From a business perspective, blockchain refers to a network of exchange enabling peer-to-peer transactions which are real-time, secure and do not require a third-party intermediary. From a technical viewpoint, one could understand blockchain as a database that provides an open-source distributed ledger. Legally, blockchain is a mechanism for validating transactions based on algorithms and does not require intermediary support. Blockchain thus becomes a virtual enforcer that is active twenty-four hours a day, seven days a week.[378]

Supporters of the blockchain believe that the concept of trust is effectively reinvented. It is no longer established by powerful centralized financial intermediaries, but instead by cryptographic proof – the method to prove the validity and finality of transactions. Individuals can exchange digital messages in a secure manner, knowing their message can not be manipulated and system nodes are working for them not against them. The lack of manipulation enables individual users to transact with one another directly, as well as to participate in financial markets without a central authority. From a theoretical perspective, blockchain has the potential to

---

378 Mougayar 2016, pp. 61–85

at least reestablish if not completely change the role and function of traditional banks.[379] Some critics of blockchain will argue that blockchain does not replace deposits or loans, and it can not create money. It is just another technology that may or may not make some banking services more efficient.

From a technical perspective, blockchain solves the notorious Byzantine Generals' problem (double-spending problem) – the computer communication problem formerly proven to be unsolvable.[380] It manages to do so by enabling a distributed network of independent individuals to arrive at an agreement (consensus) regarding each blockchain transaction, to cryptographically capture that consensus in the system and to make that entry impossible to falsify.[381] Finally, from a legal perspective, blockchain is in the position to undertake the role of a virtual notary,[382] who validates transactions around the clock, for Bitcoin transactions on average within 9.41 minutes[383] of the transaction's initiation and independently of the geographical location of the transacting parties.[384]

Blockchain construction

Let us assume you communicate your wish transaction to a blockchain, and it is accepted to the network along with other pending transactions in the same timeframe. Now each transaction must be verified by network miners called nodes to be connected to the block. Through a complex validation process called mining, legitimate transactions are bundled into a block. Miners randomly iterate selected character strings (nonce), until the hash of a block corresponds with the target value of the network.[385] The process is implemented by network nodes in order to find a new block of the transactions that are valid. The quickest node to find such a new block receives a reward in form of a cryptocurrency. Your transaction becomes part of the blockchain only as soon as it has been connected to a block and loaded by each of the distributed network miners. Thus, each transaction can be accurately verified and tracked via sequential linking of the blocks, which minimizes the possibility of fraudulent manipulations of a transaction.[386]

---

379 Morabito 2017, pp. 5–7.
380 Francis 2016.
381 Campbell 2015.
382 Shuringa 2017.
383 As of March 4, 2020.
384 Bitinfocharts 2020a.
385 Andersen 2016, pp. 2–3.
386 Nakamoto 2008.

The generalized blockchain process

The five basic steps for the creation of a blockchain are visualized in Figure 8.5.[387]
These are as follows:

1. *Transaction definition:* The sender generates an encrypted signature as a cryptographic result of the private key, public key and the transaction message.
2. *Transaction validation:* The network nodes validate the transaction messages by decrypting the digital signature. This data is held temporarily until it is used to create a new block.
3. *Block creation:* During the mining process, transactions are aggregated into a block and sent to the entire network for verification.
4. *Block validation:* The new block created during the mining process is validated by the consensus algorithm on the network.
5. *Block chaining:* When all transactions are validated, the new block is appended to the blockchain and the information is distributed to the entire network.

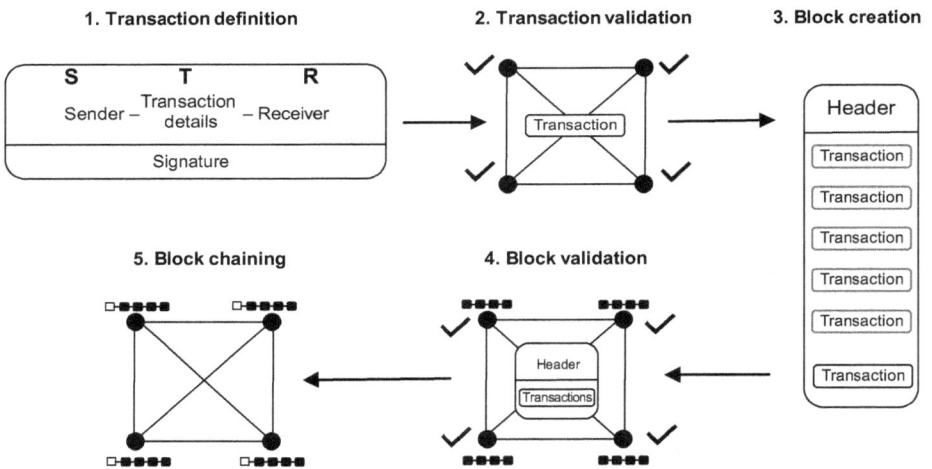

Figure 8.5: Creation of a blockchain.
(Source: own illustration adapted from Frøystad and Holm 2015, p. 10)

---

387 Frøystad and Holm 2015, p. 11.

Smart contracts as blockchain version 2.0

The blockchain version 1.0 includes the cryptographic currency Bitcoin and the same decentralized payment system as originally designed by the pseudonym Satoshi Nakamoto.[388] Today, there are a large number of so-called alternative coins that are based on the Bitcoin or its blockchain. Version 2.0 includes the use of smart contract models, where transactions are automatically executed if a set of pre-defined conditions has been met. At the basic level, smart contracts represent pieces of software, not contracts in the legal sense, which are executed by a network of nodes using a consensus mechanism based on the pre-programmed contract code (see Figure 8.6).[389]

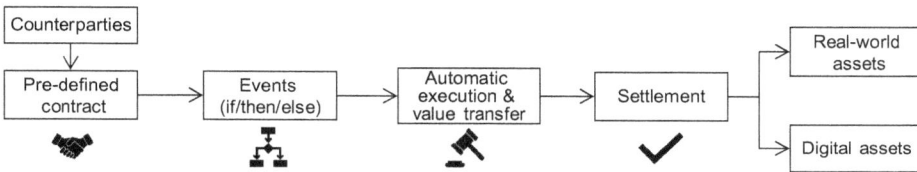

Figure 8.6: Smart contract process.
(Source: own illustration)

The transacting parties agree on the terms and desired outcome of the contract, then the agreement is coded into business logic ("if/then/else" clause) and finally the contract is encrypted into blockchain. In a blockchain, whenever consensus is reached on authentication and verification, the smart contract is added to the block. Network updates after execution and all network computers are automatically updated so that their ledger copy contains the latest smart contract transaction. Once added to the blockchain, the transaction can not be changed.[390]

Smart contracts enable the interaction of real-world assets with the Internet of Things (IoT), such as smart property, smart financial services, smart insurance and so forth. For example, let us consider the usage of a smart contract for insurance against flight delay. When booking a flight online, you take out insurance in case the flight is delayed. The smart contract looks up the departure time of the flight online and if the fact of delay is indeed confirmed (validated by an oracle[391]) the

---

388 Nakamoto 2008.
389 Cant et al. 2016, pp. 2–4.
390 Cant et al. 2016, pp. 3–5.
391 Blockchain oracle is an independent third-party data feed, which provides data from outside a blockchain network (such as departure times, weather temperature, successful payment, price fluctuations and so on) for usage in smart contracts. Smart contracts self-execute once certain values provided by an oracle are reached. See: Types of Oracles 2019.

smart contract automatically reimburses the agreed amount back to the individual's digital wallet.[392]

While reducing risk of error and manipulation, as well as establishing contractual trust between the transacting parties, smart contracts also have their disadvantages. The top challenges named by legal experts include the questionable legal enforceability of smart contracts, which poses the dilemma of whether smart contracts are legally binding or not. Also, their irrevocability depends on the difficulty of allowing a digital self-executing contract to be voidable. Furthermore, the entire protection of personal information is also a major challenge, as the blockchain is decentralized and all network nodes have access to personal data. As Shuringa suggests, to harvest the full potential of blockchain as an effective virtual notary, the digital progression must be carried out with foresight and step by step, while addressing these challenges collectively among legal professionals, building clear understanding of the repercussions and devising a clear plan for protection.[393]

8.3 Benefits for the financial services industry

Several innovation technology thinkers claim that with blockchain we have entered a new industrial era, undergoing a transit into cyber physical systems.[394] Today, innovation and value-adding activities in companies depend not only on the availability of information, but also on skillful value management.[395] One could even go a step further and say that the companies that fail to accept the paradigm shift of the fourth wave of industrial revolution – namely the shift from the reliance on capital, land and labor as major factors of production to the reliance on time, data management and efficiency of raising capital – will lose relevance in the future. Don Tapscott, a business executive specializing in blockchain, claimed that storing, moving, exchanging and lending value is at the core of the financial services industry.[396] By potentially overtaking and changing the "movement of value," blockchain has created a historic opportunity for the industry on the one hand, and an existential threat on the other. In either scenario, the implications for the financial services industry could be massive, as the role of banks as financial intermediaries could be reinvented, and new intermediaries and cooperation mechanisms could emerge.

---

392 Terekhova 2017.
393 Shuringa 2017.
394 Gutierrez 2017.
395 Sameeh 2017.
396 Shin 2016.

As an advocate of the technology, Don Tapscott goes as far as suggesting three reasons to move the entire monetary system to blockchain, which would benefit consumers, banks and authorities: cost reduction and efficiency gains, a new financial system of inclusion and performance, mitigation of risks through higher transparency.[397] In theory, blockchain can completely replace financial intermediaries. Today's payments involve several intermediaries, such as banks, clearing houses and central banks. Due to the many different intermediaries and their own settlement systems, there are time and cost disadvantages that can theoretically be eliminated by the blockchain. Especially for international transfers, fees, exchange rate risk and settlement time could be reduced, as parties act directly with each other. In capital market trading, blockchain can also reduce costs, transaction times and operational risks. Transactions could be paper free, with blockchain securing contract content and smart contracts monitoring contract execution. Transactions would be triggered automatically, and the relevant information stored in the blockchain.[398]

8.4 Business Model Canvas with blockchain use case payments

Cross border payment volume is increasing steadily at about 5% per year. The costs to the receiver of funds remain relatively high, for example, The World Bank estimates average costs of 7% for an amount of $200.[399] Additionally, a certain amount of uncertainty results from the inability to track funds during the transfer process, meaning that the final amount that will be received and the exact time of reception remain unknown until the actual receipt.[400]

Blockchain could be particularly helpful for transacting parties by fixing current problems in terms of cost, speed and security. Long settlement periods exist since transaction information must be validated per transaction per bank, often resulting in high rejection rates. Settlement delays arise due to a country's inability to handle real-time settlement or more burdensome regulatory compliance. There is a lack of transparency and widespread miscommunication of errors due to only limited control over accuracy and up-to-date information, which also varies from bank to bank. Further funds are kept in nostro accounts, which again translates into opportunity and hedging costs.[401]

Conducting money transfers around the globe using blockchain would not only bring benefits to the end customer but could also lead to massive operational and

---

397 Cocking 2016.
398 Schlatt et al. 2016, pp. 32–37.
399 McWaters 2016, p. 47; The World Bank 4/8/2019.
400 Manchiraju et al., p. 12.
401 McWaters 2016, pp. 50–52.

liquidity cost reduction due to real-time settlement, enable new business models and help establish more efficient designs of regulatory oversight. Disruptions in money transfers are increasingly forcing financial institutions to make strategic decisions.[402]

Key partners and activities

Given the high R&D costs related to implementing blockchain into international money transfers, banks alternatively could team up with other banks for the optimization of costs, for economic purposes and to generate economies of scale (see Figure 8.7). Banks, which possess large investment budgets, generally well-educated staff and large customer bases, could join forces with blockchain start-ups, provisioning necessary infrastructure and relevant support services centered on the needs of customers. For example, Santander has launched an app based on blockchain for assisting international payments.[403] SAP, the third-largest software manufacturer in the world, has partnered with Ripple and two banks, ATB Financial in Canada and Reisebank of Germany, to work together on enhancing the efficiency of global payments.[404] While most of the blockchain R&D activities take place in consortia consisting of banks and blockchain start-ups, few banks choose to explore implementation possibilities on their own.

Banks could either strategically concentrate on manufacturing products or on distribution, for example, customer and channel management. While the distribution strategy is more suitable for banks in areas with competitive advantages, the manufacturing model could be applied by banks looking to build up first-class solutions for international money transfers, revolving around product leadership and extensive technological expertise. Sample activities in the area of global money transfers include exchanging crypto tokens into local currency and vice versa, utilizing the blockchain network for offering visual dashboards for tracking payments which are in progress, the coordination of smart contracts for multiple/standardized payments or shared know your customer (KYC) processes to verify the identity, suitability, and risks involved with maintaining a business relationship with a client.

Key resources and value propositions

To enable blockchain-based transfers, banks must secure physical, human and financial resources. Building up a blockchain infrastructure and middleware requires

---

402 McWaters 2016, p. 52.
403 Browne 2018.
404 SAP News 2016.

Key partners	Key activities	Value propositions	Customer relationships	Customer segments
Technology service providers for implementation, support and marketing activities Banks for creation of permitted blockchain network Blockchain start-ups for acquisition of technological know-how and agility Regulators for reviewing transaction history and anti money laundering – reduction of compliance risk and uncertainty	Exchanging crypto-tokens into local currency Utilization of blockchain network for KYC processes Offering visual dashboards for tracking payments Smart contracts coordination	Top performance – enabling real-time payments Cost reduction – via elimination of redundant intermediaries Risk reduction – eliminating uncertainty while funds are in transit	Consulting and software developement for implementation and maintainance Automated services	Multi-sided platform Retail clients Corporate clients
	Key resources	Usability – allows worldwide banking access for unbanked people Innovations – digital identification, smart contracts, tokenization	**Channels**	
	Physical – blockchain infrastructure & middleware Extremely well-trained staff Financial – investments in blockchain capacities		Online for simple and small-scale applications On-site for complex applications	

Cost structure	Revenue streams
Costs for energy and software developement Spreading fixed costs for building up infrastructure among partners of the permitted blockchain	Revenue from new value-adding product range extensions and differentiation activities enabled by blockchain Fees from software developement, licensing and maintainance

Figure 8.7: Business Model Canvas – blockchain applications.
(Source: own illustration)

banks with strong and flexible IT as well as a workforce that supports international money transfer transactions. At a basic level, blockchain from a technological perspective is a protocol, which does not require much investment. However, the determining factor in the usability of the technology is defined by the respective software and the professional developers. Banks require a significant initial investment to advance such infrastructure, employ professional developers and overcome their legacy systems. That is the reason why banks are primarily engaging in multiple trial projects but are more reluctant to opt for extensive investments in the technology as compared to financial technology start-ups.

Fintechs could help consumers in developing countries to solve their banking needs.[405] Money transfers in developing economies still have high fees and are not realized in real time. Enabling money transfers in real time especially for developing countries eliminates the volatility of currencies. By circumventing redundant intermediaries like SWIFT or correspondent banks, transacting parties can save on very high fees deducted from the original amount transferred, which can vary from 3% to as much as 10% depending on volume and value of transactions.[406] By enabling real-time digital dashboards for reviewing the status of money at any given minute during the transfer, banks provide a unique value proposition in terms of risk reduction. Today, it is impossible to track money while in transit, thus increasing uncertainty about the exact arrival time and associated fees in case of delays. Making use of smart contracts managed by their banks, clients can automate processes, which required massive manual effort before, and reduce error rates by using a single source of truth stored on blockchain.

Establishing a new revenue model

Customers are adjusting expectations and changing their preferences toward real-time multi-channel capabilities, such as inquiries about the status of money during transit and real-time problem solving. Banks will respond by delivering value with consideration of clients' sensitivity to costs, openness to virtual delivery and increased speed. Customers principally appreciate better online banking tools, which blockchain enables in terms of speed, cost and security.

Enabled by blockchain, banks could provide value-adding services for international money transfers by coordinating digital identity security, providing a visual dashboard for the funds in transit to reduce risk and uncertainty, and by improving customers' financial stability by supervising smart contracts. According to MX Technologies, such a revenue model is experiencing and will continue to experience growth as opposed to declining revenue models such as bill pay and fee-based mobile banking and solid revenue models such as loan provisioning.[407]

After the global financial crisis, banks succeeded in their ambition to cut costs and improve efficiency mainly by restructuring some of their functions, that is, procurement, finding a balance between inhouse operations and outsourcing as well as dropping riskier business lines. The gains however have been almost offset with increased expenditure on ever-growing complex regulatory compliance processes.[408]

---

405 Kendall 2017.
406 Higginson 2016, p. 53.
407 Dabkowski 2018.
408 Thomson Reuters 5/9/2016.

Cooperation between fintechs and banks

Traditional banks could suffer from a crack in their business model. Typically, a retail bank generates revenues for payments and accounts, financing and investing, which allows it to distribute margins, that is, earn lower margins in competitive areas and higher margins in other areas. According to the McKinsey Quarterly Report, 59% of a bank's after-tax returns come from fee products resulting from origination, administration or sales of balance sheet items, yielding an average return on investment (ROI) of 22%. At the same time, balance sheet or credit provisioning, for example, asset liability management, account for 41% of a bank's after-tax return with an average ROI of only 6%. Hence traditional banks have started looking for ways to leverage the benefits of blockchain, exploring the potential use cases to simplify their existing processes and reduce the cost structures and evaluating possibilities to cooperate.[409]

8.5 Venture capital financing and Blockchain start-up landscape

The fintech area of blockchain is one of the most dynamic fintech segments worldwide. Table 8.1 shows the global venture capital investments for 466 blockchain fintech financing rounds for the sample January 2017 to April 2020. Overall, more than $2.3 billion were invested in only three years with a pre-money valuation of $29 billion. The median amount raised per fintech financing round was $1.4 million in the U.S. and $0.7 million in Europe. The available data for China with only 14

Table 8.1: Blockchain fintechs overview of venture capital financing statistics for sample January 2017–April 2020.

Location	Number Financing Rounds	Median Money Raised	Total Money Raised	Total Pre-Money Valuation
China	14	$10,000,000	$102,168,277	n/a
Europe	142	$750,000	$452,673,554	$1,115,645,744
U.S.	190	$1,450,000	$1,565,464,623	$27,208,810,000
World	466	$1,000,667	$2,314,336,571	$29,017,632,196

(Source: own illustration with data from Crunchbase 2020e)

---

409 Dietz et al. 2016.

financing rounds is not significant. The analysis of financing rounds for blockchain therefore focuses on the U.S. and Europe.

The blockchain market is distributed across several regions around the globe, as indicated in Figure 8.8, with North America dominating the scene with 47% of all blockchain start-ups.[410] Most blockchain R&D activity takes place in consortia consisting of leading financial institutions and fintechs that have the technological expertise. In Europe, a consortium of thirteen banks including Deutsche Bank, HSBC, Société Générale, Unicredit, Natixis, KBC and Rabobank is cooperating to build the blockchain-powered trade finance platform "we.trade," developed by IBM using Hyperledger Fabric. To achieve network effects, the consortium is planning to engage further banks, freight companies, shippers and credit agencies.[411]

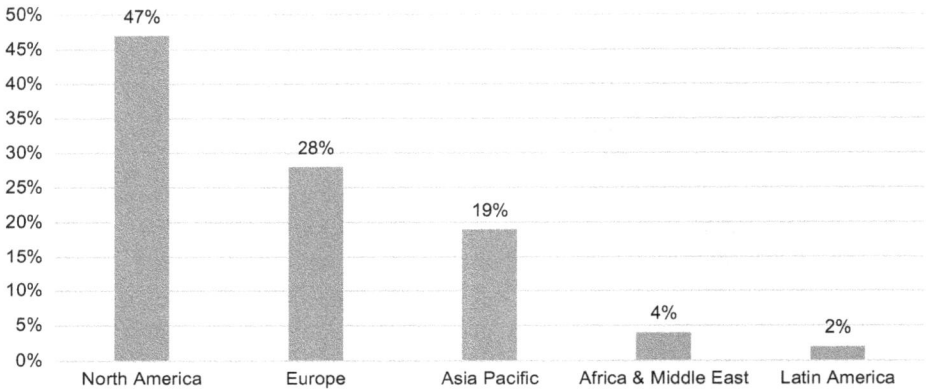

Figure 8.8: Blockchain start-ups geography with closing date May 2017. (Source: own illustration with data from Hileman and Rauchs 2017, p. 33)

In the U.S. the R3 consortium based in New York includes over 80 banks, financial institutions, regulators and technology firms working together to develop Corda, the multi-purpose blockchain-based platform specifically designed for financial services.[412] Some banks have chosen to individually work on possibilities of incorporating blockchain technology into their business model, for example for the integration of data transfer or conducting transactions within the organization. The Bank of Ireland has conducted a proof-of-work on a blockchain to trace if transactions meet the MiFID II regulation by taking the data from multiple systems in its Global Markets division and securing an immutable, distributed and reliable database throughout

---

410 Ball 2017.
411 we.trade 2020; Groenfeldt 2017.
412 Ball 2017.

the full trade cycle. MiFID II is the regulation on financial markets that applies across the European Union, and is primarily aimed at securing competitive financial markets, protecting investors and regulating financial instruments.[413]

Summary

Payments are not the only use case of a blockchain, but they are the best known and in the form of cryptocurrencies, like Bitcoin, the most controversial. In contrast to other networks, the blockchain uses a distributed network of participants where all rules are pre-defined in the program code. Smart contracts extend the functionality of the blockchain and enable the application for physical goods or other services. However, the efficient integration of the blockchain into the financial system will take time as most traditional players do not yet accept the technology. It is also unclear how many years it will take the regulators to approve the new applications for blockchain technology.

---

413 Bank of Ireland 2018.

9 How serious are cryptocurrencies?

9.1 Cryptocurrencies and tokens

Digital tokens are used to represent diverse valuable assets on a blockchain. There are two types of digital tokens: blockchain-intrinsic tokens such as Bitcoin (BTC) on the Bitcoin blockchain, Ethereum (ETH) on the Ethereum blockchain and asset-backed tokens such as "I owe you" (IOU) tokens used by Ripple.[414] In the first case, tokens are a fundamental part of the blockchain, which could not run without them. Although the tokens have value that can be externally traded on exchanges, they are primarily used to motivate network miners to validate transactions. For example, on the Bitcoin blockchain miners receive BTC as a reward.[415]

In the case of asset-backed tokens, digital tokens are claims on underlying assets that can be tangible, intangible, fungible or non-fungible. Records of basically anything can be stored on blockchain – from diamonds, land and gold to various kinds of financial securities. Traditionally, the representation of ownership of an asset is proven by some sort of paper (e.g., a certificate), which makes the sale or transfer easier. Financial securities custody is already administered paperless. But blockchain enables users to prove ownership without central control for many more assets of our world, thus reducing cumbersome data management processes. Tokenization represents a process of securing ownership rights of an asset, for example, stocks, bonds, copyright or oil by creating a digital token representing ownership of the asset, which is stored on a blockchain.[416] It is possible to transfer the usage rights for a defined period of time, for example, property lease contracts, as well as to transfer only partial rights, for example, a right to listening to a song under specific conditions – each transaction is recorded on the blockchain. Eventually, the token holders will want to exchange it for the underlying asset and to claim the asset back; they will then need to address the respective token issuer and must have faith in the liquidity of the token issuer.[417]

Tokenization could be compared to the securitization process. In tokenization, claims on real-world assets are converted into a digital token, whereas in securitization, claims on assets are translated into a financial security instrument. A tokenized loan origination process can be described as follows: as soon as the borrower of funds and the lender have agreed upon a loan contract, a new digital token is created on a blockchain, which includes all supporting information, such as ownership data, underwriting process details, creditworthiness scores and so forth.[418]

---

414 Buterin 2014; Ripple 2014.
415 Nakamoto 2008, p. 4.
416 Cameron-Huff 2017.
417 Lewis 2015, pp. 6–9.
418 Cameron-Huff 2017.

https://doi.org/10.1515/9783110704907-009

With the help of supporting services, for example, coding a smart contract, it is possible to automate loan servicing and manage securities trading and payments of the security on secondary markets. The loan origination lifecycle on primary markets and securitization process on secondary markets is then more efficient and transparent and causes lower costs.[419]

Obviously, tokens are a transparent way of managing and exchanging valuable assets based on blockchain technology, but one must keep in mind the downsides. While having an internal value – for example, the current price of Bitcoin – it is not meant to represent any underlying asset.[420] In the case of asset-backed tokens, one big assumption is the ability of the token issuer to return the underlying asset in exchange for respective tokens on demand of the token holder. A further critical factor is ensuring token consistency, that is, for an asset-backed token to maintain its value and the trust of the general public. It must be warranted that any change in the real-world asset owned or a change of its amount is reflected in the respective digital token stored on a blockchain.[421]

Bitcoin as the first cryptocurrency

Bitcoin is the first blockchain-based cryptocurrency with its white paper published in 2008 under the pseudonym Satoshi Nakamoto, the true identity of the author or group of authors is unknown. Bitcoin consists of a virtual currency, a P2P network and a wallet as open source software. The core of the application is the blockchain as a public and decentralized database.[422] Bitcoin was designed to eliminate weaknesses in electronic payment methods, for example, the solution of the "double-spending problem." Bitcoin prevents double-spending through mining with the Proof of Work (PoW) process. An intermediary who checks the transaction for double-spending is thus not required. There is no central bank for bitcoins. As a means of inflation protection, the total number is limited to 21 million bitcoins. In addition to the absolute quantitative limitation, something of a growth restriction is also in place through the generation of coins by the mining community. The higher the mining activities, for example, through the constant increase in the performance of the mining hardware or a high interest in mining, the more computing power is needed to calculate new hashes and create new blocks. A bitcoin can be divided into up to eight decimal places so that it can be distributed to many users. At the same time, this provides the possibility of making micro-payments. Another advantage of bitcoins is their pseudo-anonymity, as each user can have multiple accounts

---

419 Sindle et al. 2017, pp. 10–20.
420 Lewis 2015, pp. 5–6.
421 Cameron-Huff 2017.
422 Nakamoto 2008.

or wallets that are not associated with personal information. In addition, the transaction costs are low, and a transfer takes about 10 minutes on the main Bitcoin blockchain.[423]

Sequence of a bitcoin transaction

For the execution of transactions, each participant must first connect to the blockchain network. The appropriate software (wallet) is used for this purpose. The wallet represents the virtual purse of the user and fetches all relevant data, such as the current state of the blockchain, from the network (see Figure 9.1).[424]

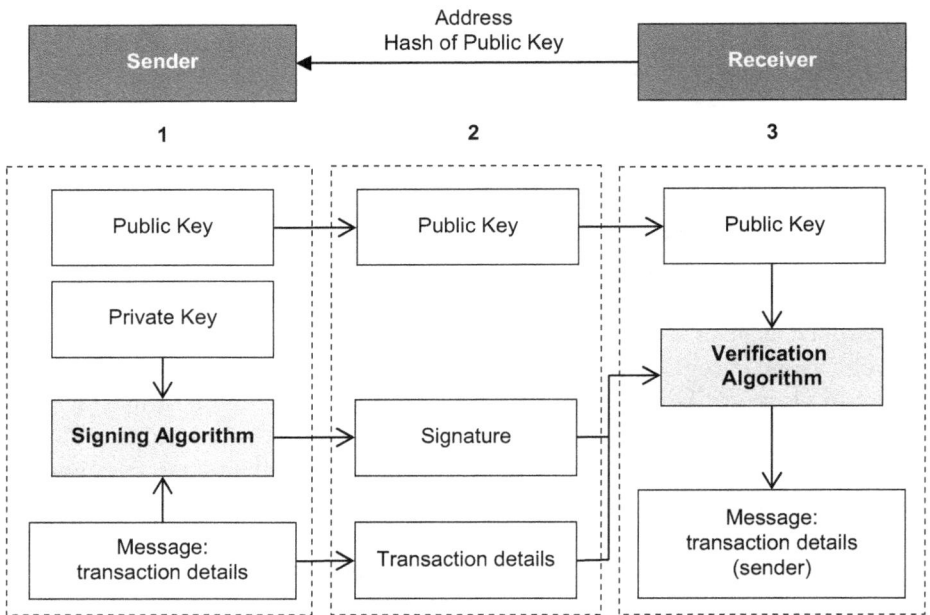

Figure 9.1: Sequence of a bitcoin transaction.
(Source: own illustration adapted from CryptoCompare 2015)

(1) Each wallet has a public key as account address and a private key. Both keys are mathematically linked. However, it is not possible to derive the private key from the

---

423 Nakamoto 2008; Nakamoto et al. 2016.
424 Brühl 2017, p. 136.

public. To initiate a transfer by the sender, the Bitcoin address of the receiver is required. The signing algorithm combines the transaction message – for example, containing the number of bitcoins sent to the address of the receiver – and the private key of the sender to generate the signature as the cryptographic result. (2) This data is then sent to the recipient via the network. (3) The signature can be verified via the sender's public key and the transaction message. It is checked whether the signature matches the sender's public key, because the signature can only be generated by the private key owner. Furthermore, the signature is generated uniquely for each transaction and can not be reused.[425]

The bitcoin protocol is open source and can be used and modified by anyone. Other cryptocurrencies that have functions similar to Bitcoin are called altcoins or alternative coins. Bitcoin Cash was created during a spin-off of the original bitcoin cryptocurrency on August 1, 2017. It focuses on increasing the size of the block, resulting in more transactions per block. Block generation takes approximately 12 minutes and the block size is approximately 8 MB.[426]

Bitcoin Cash tried to establish its block sizes and transaction speed as a competitive advantage over Bitcoin. But Bitcoin Cash's transaction volume and network usage lag far behind the volume of Bitcoin.[427] The hard fork passed without a hitch, but renewed disputes within the team led to another hard fork. In November 2018 the Bitcoin Cash network split again.[428]

Litecoin as a fast alternative

A faster alternative to Bitcoin is the cryptocurrency Litecoin. The block generation takes two and a half minutes because the Litecoin follows a different cryptographic algorithm during the PoW process (scrypt instead of SHA-256). Furthermore, the total offer is limited to 84 million, which is four times more than Bitcoin or Bitcoin Cash.[429]

Ripple Labs Inc

Ripple Labs Inc. (Ripple) and its cryptocurrency XRP must be distinguished. In contrast to Bitcoin, Ripple is not trying to replace the banks as intermediaries but merely provides RippleNet as an efficient platform for connecting the payment systems of existing banks. The cryptocurrency XRP complements RippleNet as a bridge

---

425 Brühl 2017, p. 136.
426 Hays et al. 2017, pp. 18–19.
427 Bitinfocharts 2020b.
428 Ross 2018.
429 Hays et al. 2017, pp. 18–19.

currency in order to enable payment transactions as quickly as possible even in illiquid currency markets.[430] The company Ripple cooperates with various banks and financial service providers such as UniCredit, SBI Remit, Santander and American Express.[431]

Ripple enables money transfers from one financial institution to another in real time and with cryptographic encryption. Unlike the crypto-pioneer Bitcoin, Ripple does not manage a classic blockchain, but a large decentralized database. Ripple's register contains IOUs that banks or other financial institutions issue to each other. The register is not held by the mining process, but by Ripple's own matching algorithm. The algorithm uses the network less heavily than the PoW process and runs from the P2P network every two to five seconds.[432] In addition, Ripple is "premined," meaning that all coins were already emitted when the system was put into operation. There is a total of 100 billion XRP, of which approximately 39 billion are in circulation, 6.25 billion are held by Ripple Labs Inc. and 55 billion have been deposited in a trustee wallet.[433]

The payment network Ripple allows quick and almost free currency exchange and (international) transfers. Banks interact directly with each other via the network without intermediaries. Ripple gateways are selected validation nodes such as banks and crypto exchanges. The gateways reduce the consensus mechanism and thus the transaction duration to a few seconds.[434]

A transaction on RippleNet proceeds as follows (see Figure 9.2): (1) A foreign customer contacts his bank to send a payment to a domestic customer of another bank. (2) The sending bank asks the receiving bank for an estimate of the transaction costs and the exchange rate. (3) If the sender accepts the conditions, the recipient is supplied with the relevant compliance information. (4) Once the sender approves the payment, the validator on RippleNet checks that both parties comply with the agreed terms. (5) Funds are immediately debited and credited to the subledgers of the sender and the receiver. (6) If necessary, the recipient forwards the payment to the domestic customer via various channels. (7) The receiver notifies the sender that the payment has been delivered. (8) The sender and the receiver confirm that the transaction is complete and notify their customers.[435]

Ripple's own cryptocurrency XRP has two functions: it protects against network spam and can be used as a bridge currency in trading with other currencies. To prevent the Ripple network from being deliberately overloaded with transactions, a 0.00001 XRP fee is payable on each transaction. The minimum fee is deducted from

---

430 Brühl 2017, pp. 138–139; Ripple Labs Inc. 2020a.
431 Ripple Labs Inc. 2020b.
432 BTC-Echo 2019.
433 Ripple Labs Inc. 2017.
434 Schlatt et al. 2016, pp. 32–33.
435 Ripple Labs Inc. 2020a, p. 2; Schlatt et al. 2016, pp. 32–33.

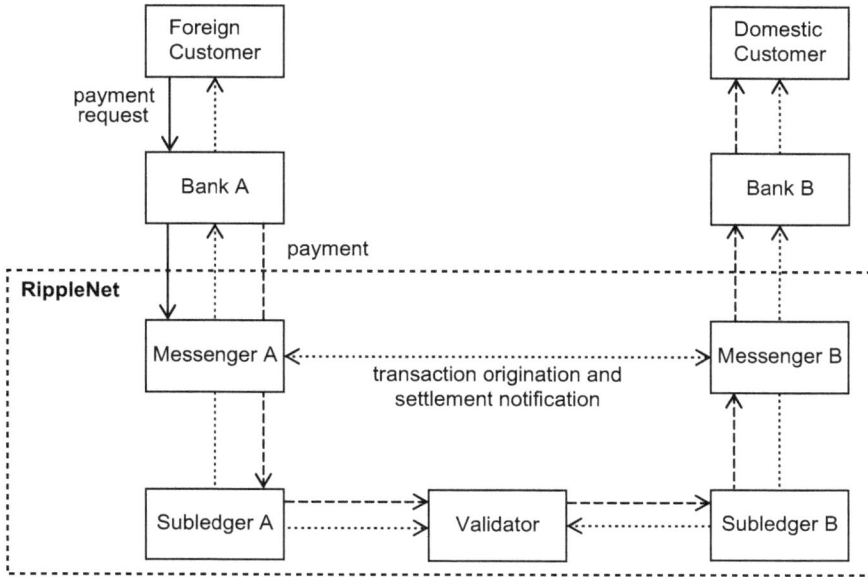

Figure 9.2: Transaction process RippleNet.
(Source: own illustration adapted from Ripple Labs Inc. 2020a, p. 2)

a security of 20 XRP that each participant must deposit on the network. This fee leads to the rapid bankruptcy of spammers. XRP can be used as a bridge currency and enables even faster and inexpensive transactions as long as the desired currency pair for the cryptocurrency is liquid. In addition, Ripple Labs Inc. thus RippleNet are financed by the growth of the value of the issued coins.[436]

Ethereum

Ethereum extends the idea of Bitcoin. The focus is not on a digital currency but on decentralized technologies – smart contracts and DApps, which use a specially developed cryptocurrency called Ether within the network. The main idea of the Ethereum founder is the creation of decentralized autonomous organizations (DAOs) within the Ethereum network.[437] The basic structure of Ethereum is similar to that of Bitcoin. It uses blockchain technology and PoW schematics and extends them with dynamic functions and smart contracts. To develop the network, the de-

---

436 Ripple 2014, pp. 14–16.
437 Buterin 2014, pp. 1, 13–14.

velopment team regularly uses hard forks. In 2016 team discussions led to the separation of Ethereum into Ethereum Classic (ETC) and the Ethereum (ETH) described here .[438]

The Ethereum blockchain is not a pure cryptographic register of transactions, but instead verifies the correctness of automatically running transaction chains or smart contracts. The Ethereum programming language can be seen like children's' Lego building blocks as it allows you to code arbitrarily complex contracts and relationships completely negotiated through the blockchain.[439]

Figure 9.3 shows an overview of some cryptocurrencies in terms of total supply, price and market capitalization. The logarithmic scaling of the figure accounts for the exponential development of the cryptocurrencies. The respective value proposition of each cryptocurrency influences price, supply and market capitalization.

Some in the crypto scene see the value proposition of Bitcoin as the best long-term store of value. Its limited supply of 21 million coins leads to the highest price and the largest market capitalization in comparison to its competitors. Bitcoin is the oldest cryptocurrency and forms the basis for many other digital currencies. Compared to Bitcoin Cash or Litecoin, the Bitcoin technology focuses on more traditional methods regarding block generation and block size. Nevertheless, the first cryptocurrency to be developed enjoys greater popularity.

The value proposition of XRP focuses on fast transactions, requiring high liquidity guaranteed by a large supply of tokens. Most of the XRP supply is not traded publicly. However, pricing based on the few XRP traded on crypto exchanges still results in the lowest price in Figure 9.3. The market capitalization of all available XRP tokens is close to that of Bitcoin and Ethereum.

Ethereum is currently probably the second-most important cryptocurrency. It has expanded the idea of the Bitcoin and brings the blockchain to a new level, where Ethereum enables the infrastructure for smart contracts and initial coin offerings (ICO).[440] Figure 9.3 shows that Ethereum achieves a high price and market capitalization, despite the largest supply of coins in comparison with Bitcoin and XRP.

9.2 Good or bad perspectives for cryptocurrencies?

In 2008 Satoshi Nakamoto released the bitcoin whitepaper and software, marking the beginning of the current blockchain movement. Since then, the ecosystem has developed rapidly, and the question arises as to how blockchain and cryptocurrencies will develop in the future. The development of blockchain technology is still in

---

438 Buterin 2014, pp. 18–21; Cryptolist 2019.
439 Buterin 2014, p. 34.
440 Ross 2018.

Panel A: Circulating Supply from January 2009–March 2020

Panel B: Price in U.S. Dollar from January 2012–March 2020

Panel C: Market Capitalization in U.S. Dollar from January 2012–March 2020

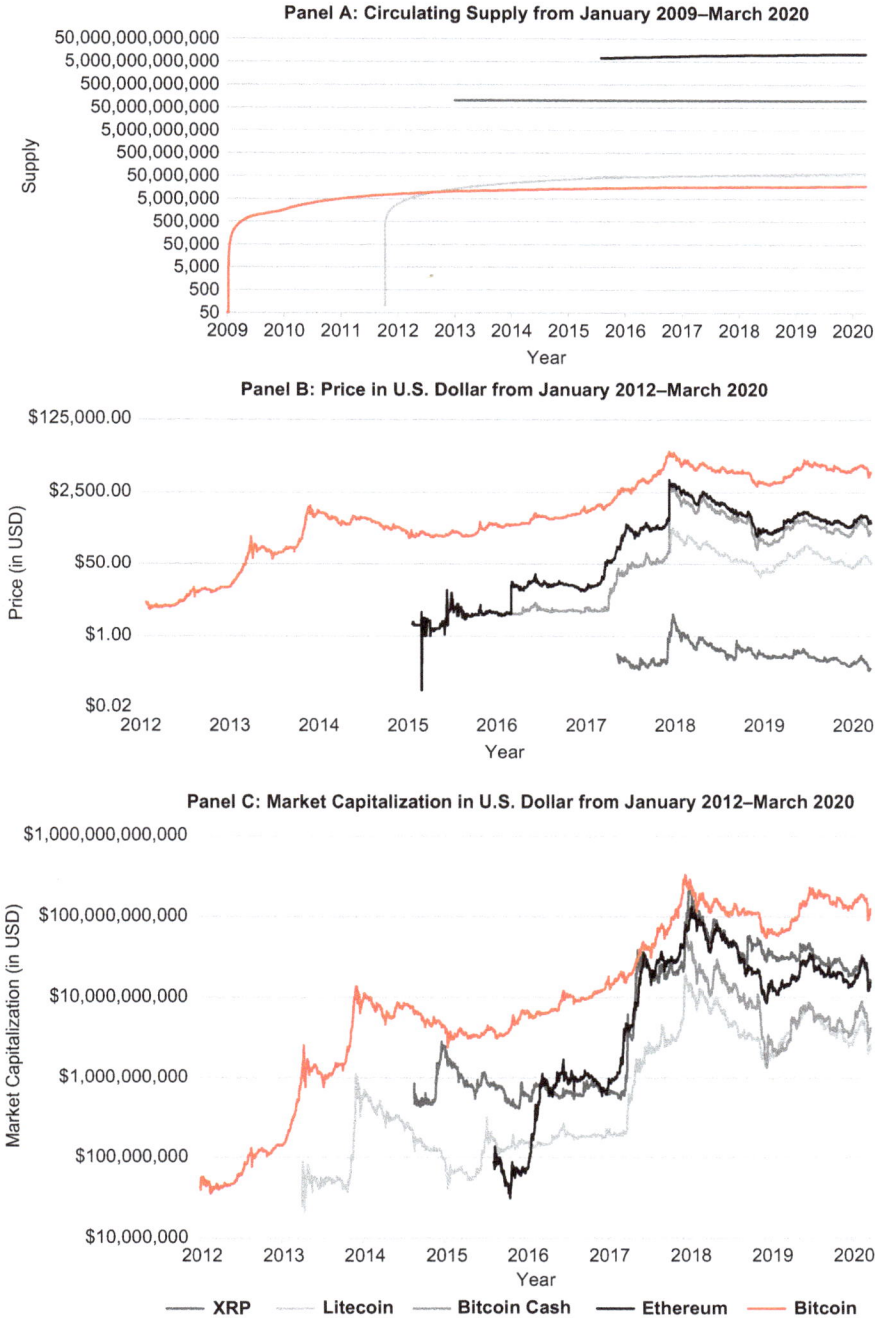

Figure 9.3: Supply, price and market capitalization of cryptocurrencies.
(Source: own illustration with data from CoinMetrics 2020)

an initial phase. However, it can be said that the blockchain is the beginning of a new era. More and more research institutions and companies, especially from the financial sector, are testing the potential of the new technology.

Blockchain technology will certainly become more important in the future. But we can assume that in the next few years perhaps half of all current coins might disappear due to advancing technological development and the improved performance of new cryptocurrencies. At the beginning of 2017, Bitcoin still had a share of more than 85% in the total crypto market capitalization. The second largest currency at that time was Ethereum with a share of less than 5%. By the end of May 2018, Bitcoin's market share fell to around 39% and Ethereum's climbed to almost 17%. The high volatility of the cryptocurrency market is illustrated by the Bitcoin comeback in March 2020, with a market share of approximately 65% in comparison to Ethereum with just under 9%. In the same time frame, XRP doubled its market share to about 4%, with market capitalization being much more volatile than Bitcoin or Ethereum. Bitcoin Cash, born out of a hard fork, had a market share of just over 2% in March 2020.[441] In the future, large cryptocurrencies will face increasing competition from smaller, more efficient competitors. Bitcoin and Ethereum need to be constantly improved by their developer communities to avoid being replaced.

ICO as the new IPO

An Initial Coin Offering (ICO) is a way for blockchain start-ups to collect money outside of the venture capital world. A start-up issues a digital token, which represents a sort of value or is of value itself and offers it for sale in an initial offering. This is very similar to an IPO. However, instead of a security, the investor receives a digital coin token, which is put onto a blockchain and can then be traded anywhere in the world.[442] The value of these tokens will increase as the volume of the platform activity increases.[443] The usual prerequisite for an ICO is a team that presents the key parameters of the project in a whitepaper (20–30 pages) and a website and social media team to handle marketing, sale of the tokens and customer support (see Figure 9.4).[444]

Figure 9.4: Initial Coin Offering roadmap.
(Source: own illustration)

441 CoinMarketCap 2020b.
442 Griffith 2017.
443 Chester 2017.
444 Nimführ 2017; Schiller 2019.

During the ICO campaign, investors can exchange tokens for already established cryptocurrencies. For this purpose, the project website publishes an address
for the transferal of the money. Offer period and pricing are different for each ICO
campaign. After a successful ICO, the funds raised should be used to work on the
project. The company also registers and trades the tokens on crypto exchanges (see
Figure 9.5).[445]

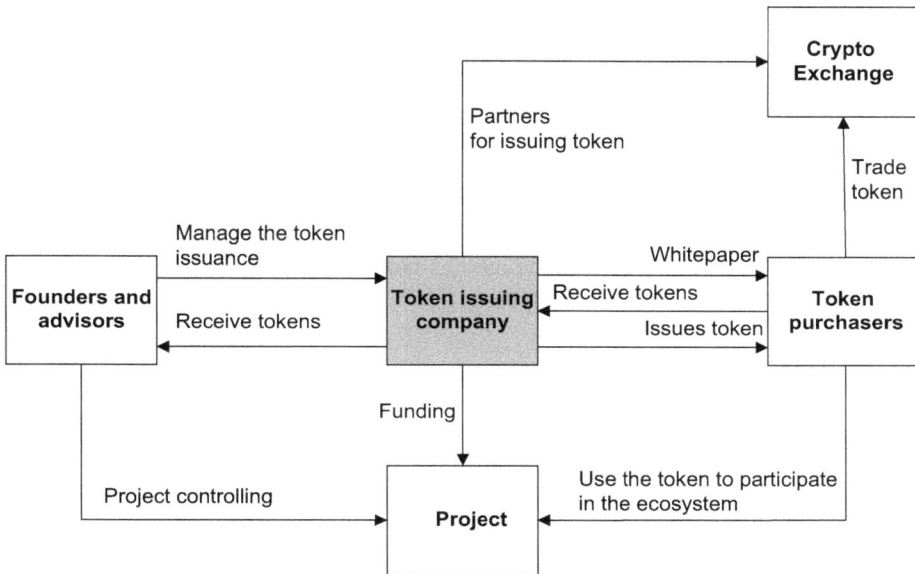

Figure 9.5: Initial Coin Offering project structure.
(Source: own illustration adapted from PwC 2020)

Due to the legal classification of the purchased tokens problems with an ICO can
arise. In case the investor buys the tokens with profit expectations regarding the
business activities of the organization conducting the ICO, the tokens are classified
as a security under U.S. law. Therefore, the fulfillment of the disclosure requirements for publicly traded companies requires considerable financial and organizational resources. For example, important information on the financial situation of
the organization must be disclosed for investor protection. The similar effort of rais-

---

445 Nimführ 2017; Schiller 2019.

ing capital through an ICO compared with an IPO, significantly reduces the ICO's attractivity, especially for young, innovative start-ups with limited resources. It makes no difference whether the organization acts in a decentralized or autonomous fashion, the purchase and sale of the tokens is only possible with cryptocurrencies or the tokens can only be used in a blockchain network.[446]

Crypto exchanges

Crypto exchanges are online platforms that enable merchants, consumers and traders to trade cryptocurrencies and tokens. They enable their users to create their own crypto wallets and buy or sell cryptocurrencies by connecting to their bank accounts. Coinbase raised a total of $547.3 million in funding over nine rounds and was the first crypto unicorn with a value of around $ 8 billion.[447] Coinbase provides two trading platforms, one with the same name and Coinbase Pro for advanced traders. Worldwide, the crypto exchange has more than 30 million users with trading possibility in 28 countries (see Table 9.1).[448]

Table 9.1: Landscape of crypto exchanges.

Name	Headquarter	Established	Trading Pairs	24h Volume (in million USD)	Fee
Coinbase	USA	2012	> 57	~ 240	0% – 0.5%
Binance	Japan	2017	> 632	~ 3,972	0.012% – 0.1%
Bitfinex	Hong Kong	2012	> 277	~ 106	0% – 0.2%
Kraken	USA	2011	> 140	~ 197	0% – 0.26%
Bitstamp	Luxembourg	2011	> 14	~ 137	0% – 0.5%
Bitcoin AG	Germany	2011	BTC, BCH, BTG, ETH	not reported	0.8% – 1.0%, plus 0.1% Fidor fees

(Source: Data retrieved as of March 31, 2020 from company websites and CoinMarketCap 2020a)

Binance is a cryptocurrency exchange founded in China and operating out of Japan that offers a huge list of cryptocurrencies. It is a famous exchange because it charges the lowest fees in the crypto industry.[449] Another crypto exchange with headquarters in Hong Kong is Bitfinex. The exchange handles large daily volumes

---

446 U.S. Securities and Exchange Commission 2011, 7/25/2017, pp. 17–18.
447 Peterson 2017; Crunchbase 2020d.
448 Coinbase 2020b, 2020a.
449 Xiao 2017; Beigel 2019.

in trading between Bitcoin and U.S. dollars. Bitfinex was hacked in 2016 and deposits worth \$72 million were stolen. The affected customers were compensated with BFX tokens, which could be converted into U.S. dollars.[450]

Kraken is a cryptocurrency exchange headquartered in San Francisco, California. The exchange has a large daily trading volume between Bitcoin and Euro. Bitstamp is one of the largest and oldest European cryptocurrency exchanges with headquarters in Luxembourg. In January 2015, Bitstamp suspended its service after a hack in which almost 19,000 Bitcoins were stolen. The exchange reopened almost one week later.[451] Bitcoin AG is not a crypto exchange but a marketplace. It operates Germany's first Bitcoin marketplace in cooperation with Munich-based Fidor Bank AG. More than 800,000 registered users (as of June 2019) trade and store cryptocurrencies via Bitcoin AG. In addition, Bitcoin AG is the world´s only trading platform with a direct interface to the traditional banking system. The strategic partnership with Fidor Bank AG enables users to automatically process payments for the purchase and sale of digital currencies directly from their own bank account.[452]

Tax treatment favorable for long-term retail investors

In the U.S., virtual currencies are treated like property for federal tax purposes. This means that cryptocurrency is not treated like currency but that the general tax principles for real estate transactions apply.[453]

China does not recognize virtual currencies as legal tender and currently does not have any tax framework. The government has taken a series of regulatory measures to stop activities related to cryptocurrencies. For the purposes of investor protection and financial risk prevention, these measures include the illegality of initial coin offers, the restriction of cryptocurrency trading platforms and the prohibition of bitcoin mining.[454]

In Germany, bitcoins are a financial instrument in the form of accounting units in accordance with §1 (11) sentence 1 Banking Act, comparable to foreign exchange. But they are no legal tender. Cryptocurrencies do not fall under withholding tax in accordance with § 43 (5) German Income Tax Law. Gains realized are considered as a private sales transaction (§12 Income Tax Law) and are taxed at the personal income tax rate (§ 32a). No taxes are payable if the crypto funds are held for longer than 12 months (§ 31) or the exemption limit of 600 euros is not exceeded.[455]

---

450 Magas 2018.
451 Hays et al. 2017, pp. 24–26.
452 Bitcoin Deutschland AG 2020.
453 Internal Revenue Service 2014, p. 2.
454 Zhang 2018, p. 30.
455 Henkelmann and Dahmen 2019; Lohnsteuerhilfe Bayern e.V. 2018.

Commercial income generation with cryptocurrencies, according to § 23 Income Tax Law, is income from an independent, sustainable operation, which is undertaken with profit intention and represents a participation in general commercial trade. This includes mining combined with selling cryptocurrencies, running an online exchange and operating a cryptocurrency ATM.[456]

9.3 Business Model Canvas for cryptocurrencies

Figure 9.6 applies the Business Model Canvas to the cryptocurrency sector. The most important element for a cryptocurrency is the development team. Well-known developers such as Vitalik Buterin, who developed Ethereum at the age of 21, help to inspire developers in the entire blockchain and crypto industry. For some in the crypto scene Buterin is a kind of hero or role model and motivates other developers to join his cause. Other key partners include crypto exchanges, which enable trading in the currency. The currency is often listed on several larger but also many small exchanges.

Cryptocurrencies are not only used as an investment, but also as a means of payment. The creator of a payment transaction uses a wallet software to execute the payment. The software gives each participant access to the crypto network and enables the payments transaction with cryptocurrencies. An essential part for transactions is the mining or verification process, which provides computing power for transaction processing, security and synchronization of all users in the network.

When it comes to customer relationships and sales channels, cryptocurrencies have shown only very limited engagement in online marketing measures, due to their operation distributed across numerous network participants. Customers must therefore take the initiative and collect information about the currency. The central element for information on the currency is the cryptocurrency website – for the potential distribution via an ICO as well as for all other types of messages. The customer segments of cryptocurrencies include retail clients and consumers, young persons with an affinity to current trends and IT or financial services providers.

The cost structure essentially consists of the staff costs for the developers. The costs for mining a block or verification process depend on several factors of the underlying blockchain. The popularity of a cryptocurrency strongly influences the performance. Further factors are the leadership, the developments of competitors, news, forks or quotations on other crypto exchanges.

---

456 WINHELLER Rechtsanwaltsgesellschaft mbH 2020b, 2020a.

Key partners	Key activities	Value propositions	Customer relationships	Customer segments
Crypto exchanges to trade digital currency Corporate partners using the cryptocurrency Users, investors and speculators Validators or miners for transaction processing and network safeguarding	Continuous development of cryptocurrency Consistent provision of information on functional upgrades, ICOs, forks and general messages **Key resources** Liquidity and currency trading pairs provided by exchanges Experienced software developers Continuous community support and promotion	High risk and return investment profile Offer for medium of exchange, store of value and unit of account Independence from financial system No access restrictions for movement of funds Opportunity to participate in a new market	Rare use of direct online marketing Focus on community-driven approach Creation of entrepreneurial thinking and enhancement of individual responsibility **Channels** Project website Community website Crypto exchanges Social media	Retail clients People with an independent spirit looking for more freedom Persons with affinity to current trends and IT Financial services providers

Cost structure	Revenue streams
Costs for software developers, energy, hardware, and marketing depending on consensus algorithm, number of developers, block size, market volume, and blockchain network activity	Trading fees, bid/ask spreads, and wallet administration fees depending on popularity during and after the ICO, competitors, and blockchain-based services

Figure 9.6: Business Model Canvas – Cryptocurrencies. (Source: own illustration)

9.4 Venture capital financing of start-ups in blockchain & cryptocurrencies

The fintech area of cryptocurrencies counted 313 financing rounds in the world for the sample January 2017 to April 2020. Table 9.2 shows a median of money raised per financing round of $2 million for the U.S. and $1.2 million globally. Overall, more than $2.6 billion were invested in only three years with a pre-money valuation of $41 billion. The available data for China with only three financing rounds is not significant. The detailed analysis of financing rounds for cryptocurrencies therefore focuses on the U.S. and Europe.

Within the blockchain & cryptocurrencies segment, a total of 23 fintechs have been founded for the sample April 2000 to June 2017. An annual overview of the number of venture capital-financed fintechs founded in Europe and the U.S. is shown in Figure 9.7.

Table 9.2: Cryptocurrencies fintechs overview of venture capital financing statistics for sample January 2017–April 2020.

Location	Number Financing Rounds	Median Money Raised	Total Money Raised	Total Pre-Money Valuation
China	3	$7,000,000	$22,954,000	n/a
Europe	84	$897,592	$237,408,136	$97,322,917
U.S.	133	$2,000,000	$2,148,296,154	$39,624,642,458
World	313	$1,204,287	$2,629,548,613	$41,329,142,728

(Source: own illustration with data from Crunchbase 2020e)

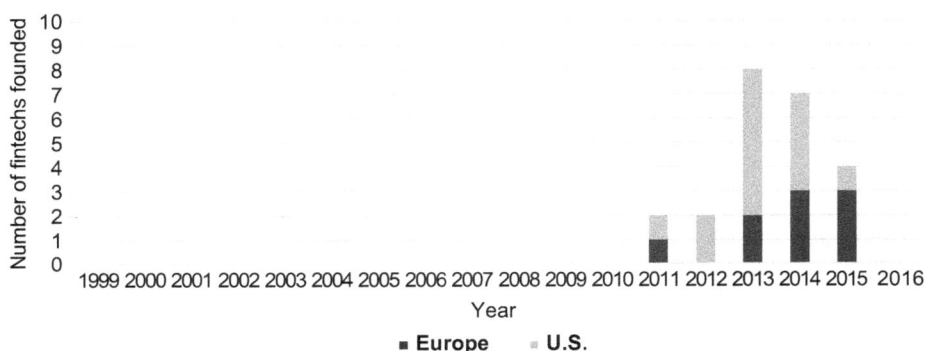

Figure 9.7: Number of fintechs founded in blockchain & cryptocurrencies in Europe and the U.S. from 1999–2016 for sample April 2000–June 2017.
(Source: own illustration)

Blockchain and cryptocurrencies is one of the youngest segments in the fintech landscape as shown by Figure 9.7. The first fintech in this field emerged in both Europe and the U.S. in 2011. Another two fintechs were founded in the U.S. in 2012, before in 2013 eight fintechs were founded. It can be said that potential founders then saw limited new opportunities to enter the blockchain & cryptocurrencies market, as there were no foundations in 2016.

The number of financing rounds rose sharply between 2012 and 2014, mainly driven by an increasing deal count in the U.S. and the first financing rounds being closed in Europe (see Figure 9.8). From 2015 to 2017, deal activity fluctuated around eight financing rounds per year as the U.S. saw a small drop in deal count while it was more volatile in Europe.

The amount raised skyrocketed from just €0.5 million in 2012 to €162.9 million in 2014, implying a CAGR of 1,763%. Two factors are responsible for this development: the very high funding in the U.S. and the first €25.0 million being raised in

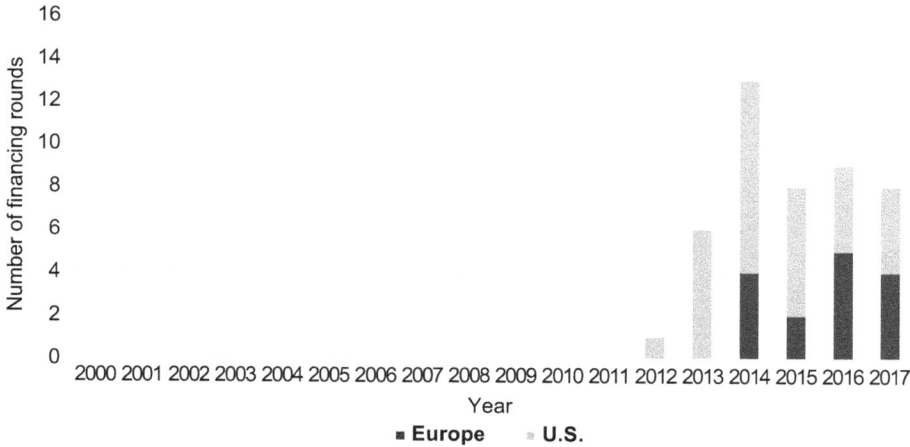

Figure 9.8: Number of financing rounds in blockchain & cryptocurrencies in Europe and the U.S. for sample April 2000–June 2017.
(Source: own illustration)

Europe. In the following two years, the annual amount raised declined by roughly €30.0. In 2017 financing amounts in Europe increased dramatically. Considering that the overall deal count decreased from 2016 to 2017, the average amount raised per deal must have increased. This could mean that blockchain & cryptocurrencies in both regions are striving for growth and maturity quickly (see Figure 9.9).

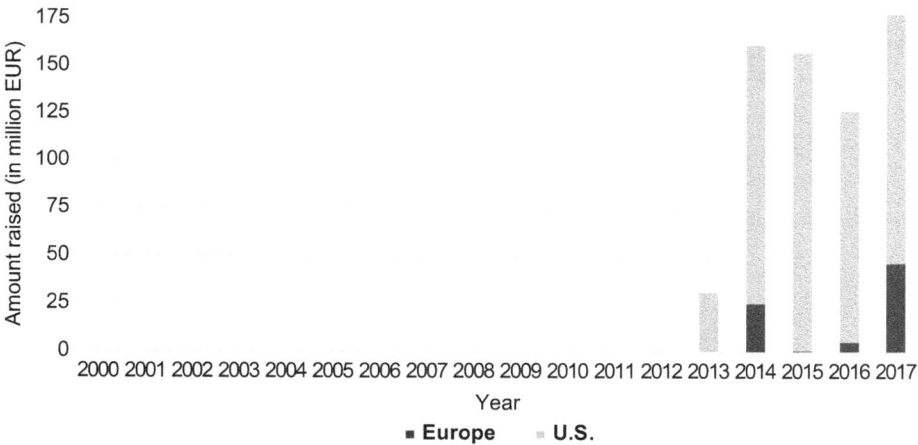

Figure 9.9: Annual overview of amount raised in blockchain & cryptocurrencies in Europe and the U.S. for sample April 2000–June 2017 (in € m).
(Source: own illustration)

In Table 9.3 the median amount raised in each of the respective financing rounds is compared for Europe and the U.S.

Table 9.3: Median amount raised in blockchain & cryptocurrencies in Europe and the U.S. for sample April 2000–June 2017 (in € m).

	Seed	A	B	C	D	E	F	IPO
Overall Median	1.4	12.0	14.1	43.9	n/a	n/a	n/a	n/a
Median Europe	0.5	5.7	35.9	n/a	n/a	n/a	n/a	n/a
Median U.S.	2.0	16.4	10.1	43.9	n/a	n/a	n/a	n/a
Sample size *n*	13	12	4	2	0	0	0	0

(Source: own illustration)

U.S. blockchain & cryptocurrency fintechs appear to raise significantly higher funds in the early stage, which is evidenced by the U.S. seed median of €2.0 million being four times the European median and the round A median being a little less than three times the European median in financing round A. This snapshot is reversed in financing round B where the European median of €35.9 million compares to the U.S. median of €10.1 million. This indicates that early stage financing in this segment is easier in terms of amount raised in the U.S., while follow-up financing could be simpler for European fintechs. This finding can not be fully proven, as no comparisons after financing round B are possible due to the lack of information on European blockchain & cryptocurrency late stage financing rounds.

In the next step the median change in amounts raised between two successive financing rounds is evaluated and depicted in Figure 9.10. The graph is based on the following sample size: Seed/A $n = 7$; A/B $n = 2$; B/C $n = 2$; C/D $n = 0$; D/E $n = 0$; E/F $n = 0$.

European and U.S. blockchain fintechs achieve a large increase in their round A funding compared to the seed investment. However, the U.S. managed to raise 183% more in this comparison than the European counterparts (817% vs. 634%). This gap widens to 237% for the round A/B comparison, as the U.S. median is 288% and the European median is 57%. This finding is in line with the previous finding that U.S. fintechs manage to secure higher earlier stage funding than fintechs in Europe.

Lastly, the median time between two successive financing rounds is assessed. The sample size corresponds to the one in Figure 9.10 (Seed/A $n = 7$; A/B $n = 2$; B/C $n = 2$; C/D $n = 0$; D/E $n = 0$; E/F $n = 0$).

U.S. blockchain & cryptocurrency fintechs have less problems in securing early stage financing than their European counterparts. This is evidenced by the comparison of seed and round A as well as the round A/B comparison in both of which the U.S. requires less time to close the next financing round. This fact is particularly

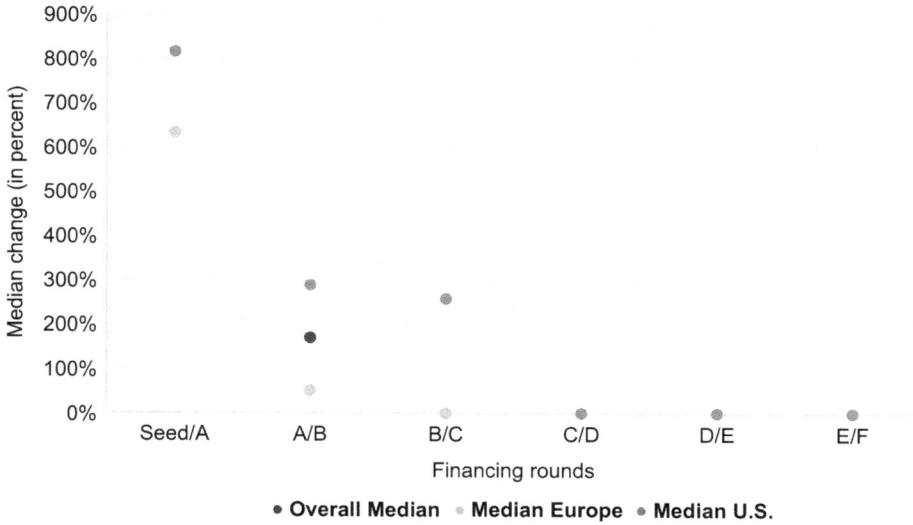

Figure 9.10: Median change in amounts raised between two successive financing rounds in blockchain & cryptocurrencies for sample April 2000–June 2017 (in percent). (Source: own illustration)

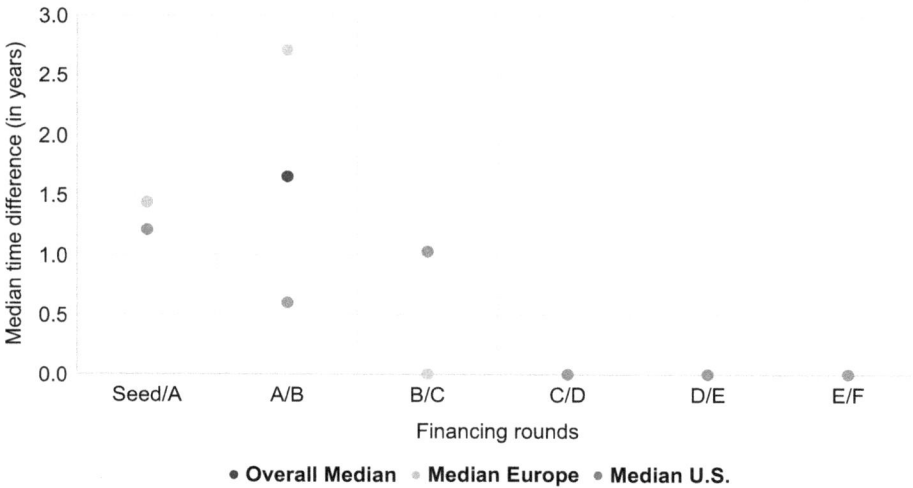

Figure 9.11: Median time difference in years between two successive financing rounds in blockchain & cryptocurrency for sample April 2000–June 2017. (Source: own illustration)

underlined by the difference of more than two years in medians (Europe 2.7 years vs. U.S. 0.6 years, see Figure 9.11). The good news for venture capitalists is that both regions are not mature regarding blockchains & cryptocurrencies yet.

Summary

Tokens on a blockchain contain intrinsic values or consist or represent the tokenization of goods from outside the network. Crypto exchanges offer information and liquidity for thousands of different tokens with specific use cases. Sometimes the ICO helps to finance start-up companies, but a bad design of the token offering can lead to legal pitfalls. The future of the young industry of blockchain and cryptocurrency start-ups strongly depends on the approval of regulators and the innovation of individual developer communities.

10 Big data and AI

Artificial intelligence (AI) in the area of banks and fintechs is often applied in the forms of machine learning and chatbots. The integration of AI in financial services just started a few years ago and will surely increase. Some banks already operate chatbots for service functions and others use test chatbots for information and client knowledge, for example, on capital market products. Banks also use test chatbots to replace consulting functions but still have to show that they can cope with regulatory issues and the liability for potentially erroneous consulting or investment advice. It is important to understand that consulting in financial questions could have other impacts for the consumer than a conversation with Google Assistant, Siri – Apple's voice-controlled personal assistant – or Alexa by Amazon. From a regulatory view it is much easier to develop and test household conversations, for example with Alexa, than to implement investment advice chatbots for banks. The management of the bank could be made liable for wrong investment recommendations or losses of investors due to the answers of the machine.

So far there is no official definition for the term big data. It is often referred to as collecting masses of data, the size of which exceeds the capacity and capability of traditional database and software tools to capture, store, process and analyze. Big data is always associated with the so-called five Vs, which are explained below (see Figure 10.1):[457]

- *Volume:* Every purchase on Amazon, every tweet and every search on Google leads to a massive amount of data. Google processes around 12 billon search queries in the U.S. every month,[458] 15% of all searches are queries that have never been made before. The volume of search queries is constantly increasing due to the growing number of internet users.[459]
- *Variety:* In addition to the structured data traditionally managed by enterprise information systems, the majority of big data includes unstructured data ranging from text, log files, audio, video and image files.
- *Veracity:* The reliability of the data is not always guaranteed, especially when published by third parties. The data source and the quality of the available data represent a key aspect of big data.
- *Velocity:* The data is frequently updated and can be quickly analyzed during collection/generation without having to enter it into databases (i.e., real-time analysis).

---

457 Morabito 2015, pp. 8–9.
458 The number contains only search queries made from private desktop computers or from corporate locations that reflect the user's specific intent to interact with the search results.
459 Heshmore 2017; comScore 2020; Gomes 2017.

https://doi.org/10.1515/9783110704907-010

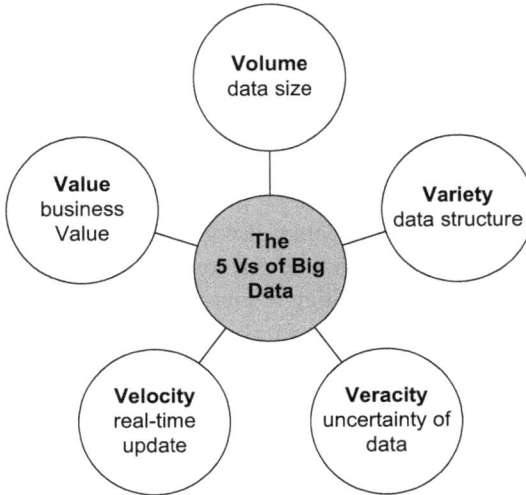

Figure 10.1: The 5 Vs of big data.
(Source: own illustration adapted from Emmanual 2015, p. 2)

– *Value:* By predicting new trends based on data analytics, traditional financial service providers and fintechs can give their customers additional value by offering them new services.[460]

10.1 Impact of big data on the traditional banking sector

The core requirements of banks include the persistent storage of customer and account as well as their business transaction-related data and its periodic updating. These are highly standardized processes that are usually completely represented by information technology (IT). IT systems in the banking sector are traditionally focused on bulk processing of large volumes of data. The application landscape has inevitably led to a silo-like structure of data management. Due to the large amounts of data processed in the finance sector, it is no surprise that this industry plays a prominent role in the public debate about the economic potential of big data. The banking industry is currently facing a variety of challenges regarding IT infrastructure, regulatory requirements, competitors and current customer trends. Data structures traditionally focus on accounts and custody accounts. Banking applications are generally not designed for a customer centric view. Putting the customer at the center of banking IT means a paradigm shift. Form a customer view, an evaluation of the central account and depot systems requires the inclusion of all sources of

---

460 Emmanual 2015, p. 2.

knowledge, including all existing channels of the bank and their networking. Banks must compete with companies in which the evaluation and commercialization of customer data has always been part of the business model.[461]

Finance companies benefit from knowing their customers and their living conditions and preferences. Many large data applications are available for financial companies, where offers are tailored to the specific life situations of the customers. Marketing activities can be made more effective by focusing on the needs of customers. Risks and customer scores can be individually predicted. Tailor-made offers and more flexible reactions to the changing circumstances of a customer's life contribute to improving the consulting services. Regardless, big data applications and technologies are slowly being integrated into the banking system. In order to explore the real potential of big data in the banking industry, it is necessary to look at the business and service areas of a bank individually.[462]

For example, Bank of America (BoA) uses big data technology to process and analyze data from its full customer set. The bank monitors its customers' "journeys" through websites, call centers, tellers and other channels to understand the paths that customers follow through the bank and how this path affects the purchase of financial services. The bank uses transaction models to determine which customers are using a credit card or mortgage that could benefit from refinancing with a competitor, and then makes an offer when the client contacts the bank through online banking, call center or branches. In addition, the various sales channels can communicate with each other, so that a customer who starts online without completing the form can receive a follow-up offer on another channel such as e-mail or in a branch.[463]

The Chinese Bank CITIC uses big data to better align marketing for credit-card customers with their needs. For this purpose, the CITIC database collects basic customer demographics information, including transaction data, customer attributes, residence information and online behavior information, including transaction and risk preferences, and social networking activities. Traditional credit approval methods use indicators such as income and employer. CITIC can now validate credit card customers by analyzing online information resources that are closely related to consumer behavior, thus helping to understand customers' online purchasing behavior. At the same time, the bank can retrieve up-to-date economic information to understand customers' offline behavior and the local economic ecosystem. In this context, the bank can decide whether to accept new customers or not. With such extensive customer data, CITIC Bank is now able to innovatively target its customers. The application website, for example, contains credit card options based on customers' purchasing power, real estate value and working position. In addition, the database

---

461 Geenen et al. 2015, pp. 134–138.
462 Gronau et al. 2016, p. 475.
463 Groenfeldt 2013.

enables CITIC Bank's Credit Card Center to strengthen its research and development capabilities for precision marketing applications. But CITIC's big data applications go beyond the credit card business. CITIC Bank is also cooperating with China UnionPay for the introduction of POS merchant net loans to offer "loans in a second" by analyzing UnionPay's transaction data.[464]

10.2 Business Model Canvas for big data

The competitive advantage of internet companies lies in their access to a large amount of customer data and search volumes are increasing as the number of internet users grows.[465] Baidu, the Chinese equivalent of Google, contains consumer behavior and customer preference data that can be used for credit checking through in-depth analysis before transactions are approved.[466] Baidu is the fourth most popular homepage in the world according to the Alexa ranking, while 93.9% of the website visitors are from China.[467] Due to the large number of users, other companies like Google, eBay and Apple also generate a massive amount of information and data. This data can be used for the entire group to expand business, especially in the sector of financial services.

Figure 10.2 shows the Business Model Canvas for big data. Platforms like eBay, Alibaba, Amazon and search engines like Google or Baidoo are the main collectors of data. They are therefore key partners for banks and fintechs. As a value proposition, big data enhances decision making, understanding customer behavior and customer segmentation. The key infrastructure is IT, the database and analysis tools. Big data helps to reduce costs but also provides new revenue potentials due to client-tailored products.

Alibaba's "Ali Finance" with Alipay, Ali Small Micro Finance and the company's money-market fund Yu'e Bao has successfully gained access to the banking sector. The key to Ali Finance's success in achieving its current market position was large amounts of data. With its central e-commerce platform, Alibaba is building new businesses that further enhance core value. As the platform evolves, the customer base is growing, customer loyalty is improving and Alibaba's innovation and business development capabilities are increasing. Ali Finance can easily access credit customer data and credit information to effectively manage risk. In its data analysis model, Ali Finance adjusts various weights in real time to make the analysis more accurate and ensure that the debt ratio does not increase.[468]

---

464 ATKearney 2014.
465 Heshmore 2017.
466 ATKearney 2014.
467 Alexa 2018b.
468 ATKearney 2014.

Key partners	Key activities	Value propositions	Customer relationships	Customer segments
Platforms as data providers: Marketplaces: eBay, Taobao, Alibaba, Amazon Search engines: Google, Baidu Payment applications: Google Wallet, Apple Pay, PayPal, Alipay, WeChat Pay, online banking, credit cards Own customer data Cooperation with fintechs, other financial services providers and integration of PFM tools	Set up customer database with high volume, variety, veracity and velocity Set up marketplaces and payment applications	Enhancement of decision-making Critical insights into understanding customer behaviors Development of new business strategies to keep pace with changing consumer demands Classification of customers to enhance customized offers	Enhancement of relationship with customers while improving profitability Banks and insurance companies analyze customer defaults and choose best possible customers	Retail banks and insurance companies Websites and marketplaces for B2C and B2B More data allows more applications and more customers who can be reached
	Key resources Efficient and flexible IT infrastructure Tools to capture, store, process and analyze data	Enabling of new AI applications	**Channels** All channels Focus on online channels	

Cost structure	Revenue streams
IT Infrastructure Well-trained and experienced staff	Revenue from target-oriented marketing, better understanding of customer needs, development of innovative and tailored new products

Figure 10.2: Business Model Canvas – Big data.
(Source: own illustration)

Ali Small Micro Finance can retrieve and use company e-commerce business data together with third-party certified information before issuing a loan to assess the company's business, loan terms and repayment capabilities.[469] Throughout the lifecycle of an outstanding loan, Alipay and the future logistics system monitor a company's information flow, logistics and cash flow to identify potential risks and provide advance alerts. Alibaba adjusts users' credit ratings by closely monitoring real-time data. Transactions, fluctuations in orders and changes in cash flows to Alipay accounts can result in a credit adjustment. Once a red line is breached, Ali Small Micro Finance triggers repayment in advance and recovers funds through

---

469 Yan et al. 2015, p. 5.

various channels to reduce the debt ratio. For overdue loans, Ali Small Micro Finance monitors corporate operations, re-evaluates ratings and limits, or closes online shops for defaulting customers. Furthermore, Ali can inform other online customers about the potential risks. All these measures serve to strengthen the credit evaluation and monitoring process of corporate customers.[470]

10.3 AI and chatbot Inga from ING

AI implementations in the form of chatbots may be used at the interface to the customer. A chatbot provides a first efficient contact point for better customer service. Risks are inherent in an impersonal, error-prone, purely mechanical approach and isolated solutions without a designated pathway to support staff. If a bot capitulates in the case of complex, individual customer enquiries by reaching a dead end, financial institutions risk a poor user experience and thus losing customer acceptance. For the successful implementation of a chatbot, a financial institution needs a proper range of available functions, but also a customer-friendly conversational design and integration into existing banking and organizational infrastructures.[471]

ING is currently developing Inga, a chatbot intended to offer a better service to private customers without replacing the existing support staff. For the development of Inga, ING has focused on avoiding common mistakes in the design of chatbots. Customers have a low error tolerance toward bots, as even unexpected behavior during an interaction can cause a customer to cancel the request. Users are also skeptical about sharing their personal information with a bot. In order to avoid inconsistency between the capabilities of a chatbot and customer expectations, the functionality and limitations of the program must be transparently communicated.[472]

The conversational flow via text or voice is central to customer acceptance and loyalty to a chatbot as a support channel. For Inga, the necessary interaction paths and background processes are depicted in Figure 10.3. At the beginning of the customer interaction, Inga's skills and functions are introduced in order to establish trust and realistic expectations. During the conversation, Inga uses natural language processing to recognize the concern and emotional state of the conversational partner. Inga's dialogue flow is additionally supported by combining the information and contract history of the customer with the institution. Experience gained from inquiries on similar topics by other customers as well as past interactions with the

470 ATKearney 2014.
471 Wei et al. 2018, pp. 370–372; ING online 2018; Mishevski 2018.
472 Mishevski 2018; Seeger et al. 2017, p. 2; ING online 2019, p. 31.

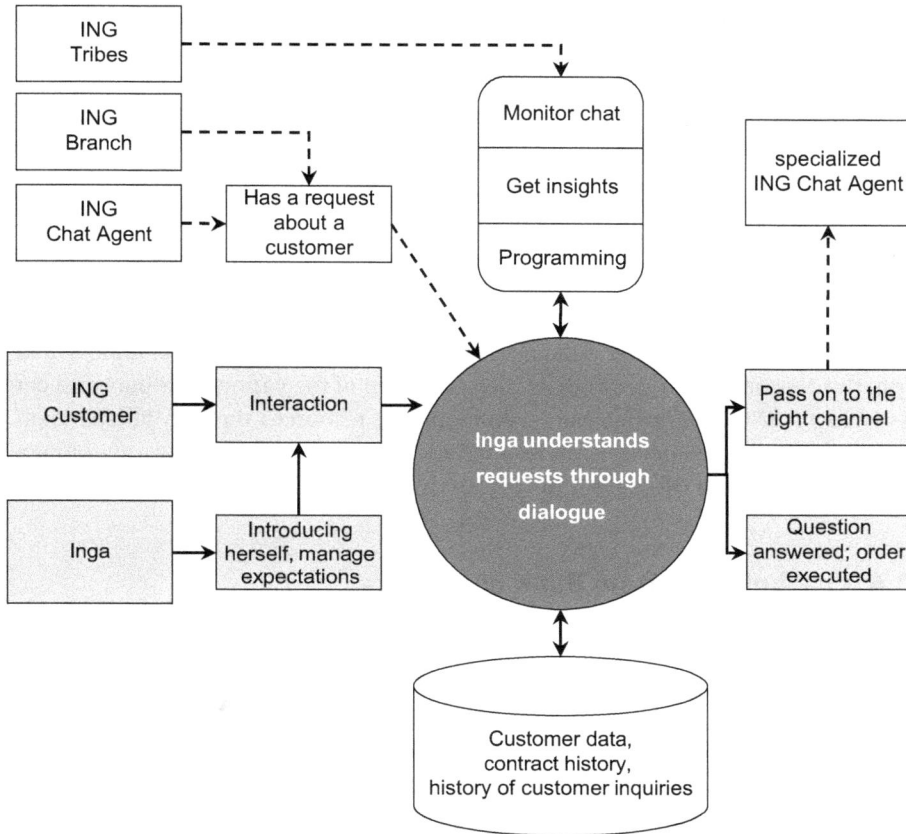

Figure 10.3: ING process for chatbot Inga.
(Source: own illustration adapted from Mishevski 2018)

conversational partner also contribute to user-friendliness. The functional scope of Inga is accessible to customers as well as to ING support and branch employees. If Inga can not answer an inquiry or execute a task, the conversational partner is seamlessly forwarded to a suitable support staff member. At ING a so-called Tribe is responsible for the programming, chat monitoring and analysis of Inga, and organized as an interdisciplinary cross-functional team. Using the answers to repeated questions, Inga is designed to relieve the workload of employees who can thus concentrate more on consulting customers.[473]

ING has decided in favor of a slower, gradual introduction of Inga in its private customer business. In a reduced functional scope, the chatbot is available under

---

473 Mishevski 2018; Phillips 2019; ING online 2019, p. 30.

the name Inge for Dutch private customers in the service portal Mijn ING. Inge presents the search results, provides transaction information and helps customers with investment decisions or transfer orders.[474]

Parallel to Inge, ING is also developing other chatbots. The Kijk Vooruit chat bot, for example, is also available to private customers in the Netherlands. As a forecasting tool, Kijk Vooruit answers questions about upcoming account activity and potentially triggered overdrafts. For ING, this decentralized, flexible development approach creates opportunities for the creation of functional scope and conversation design geared to specific customer segments. The ING tribes responsible for the respective chatbot can quickly make decisions in order to integrate functions that meet changed customer demands. Without a standardized development platform, the decentralized operation and development of the various chatbots also carries risks for ING. Inefficient use of development resources through independent, decentralized competence centers in a rapidly developing technology environment could also mean that ING risks falling behind.[475]

10.4 Chatbot Erica from Bank of America

With its chatbot Erica, Bank of America (BoA) has decided on a more uniform solution within its banking app, which is centrally controlled and continuously developed. Similar interaction paths and background processes as shown in Figure 10.3 form the structural basis for Erica. In comparison to the independent chatbot implementations of ING, BoA bundles all functionality within Erica to form a larger and constantly growing range of services for its private customers in the U.S.[476]

Erica offers BoA customers a wide range of functions with deep integration into the bank's product offerings. Erica reports weekly on the financial situation of the client and answers questions on revenues and expenses by account, category and time period. As a member of the Zelle payment network, BoA has also firmly integrated the Zelle service into Erica. Customers can use Erica to make real-time transfers to U.S. bank accounts and check on the status of transactions. A central part of Erica is its integration with credit and debit card products. Clients can use Erica to request and activate a new card, block an existing card and access the associated rewards program. With Erica, customers can sign up to the rewards program and receive help if they have further questions. Erica can redeem earned bonus points directly, for example, for loan interest discounts,

---

474 Mishevski 2018; ING online 2019, p. 31.
475 ING online 2019, pp. 31–32; Adel 2019; Mishevski 2018.
476 Bank of America online 2019a, S. 6, 15, 189, 2019c.

savings interest boosts or discounts for custodian fees for investment and trading accounts.[477]

BoA plans to expand Erica's range of services even further. The available functions have convinced customers of different age groups to regularly use Erica as a flexible point of contact for their financial questions and inquiries. For BoA, Erica creates opportunities by serving as an efficient interface within the institute's banking app. Flexible, direct service increases customer satisfaction and loyalty, while additional cross-selling potential is created by integrated products and services.[478]

Figure 10.4 shows the Business Model Canvas for a banking chatbot. Regulatory authorities and financial service providers are the central partners to enable legally compliant operations and to supply complementary financial services. The cooperation with key partners is critical for clients to accept the offered chatbots. Professionally designed and programmed, the value proposition of the chatbot is an always available, fast and client-tailored customer service. The most important resources and activities focus on deep knowledge of customer needs as well as the technical implementation of accessible and direct communication channels by the chatbots.

10.5 Machine learning with contract intelligence from JPMorgan

With Contract Intelligence (COiN), JPMorgan has now entered the legal industry. JPMorgan and Cloudera developed COiN for automated document review based on unsupervised machine learning. The review classifies documents relating to legal disputes or official investigations according to their relevance to litigations. Documents classified as significant form the data basis of the legal due diligence. The objective is to develop a comprehensive understanding of the central factual and legal issues of a case.[479]

JPMorgan's development of COiN is incentivized by increasing quality problems and compliance costs in the standardized commercial credit business. Per year, 360,000 hours are spent manually checking the bank's 12,000 annual loan agreements. In terms of quality, 80% of errors in loan management occur during the time-consuming, manual document review. The machine learning program addresses this unsatisfactory status quo and manages the error-free analysis of credit agreements in seconds. The vital enabling factors are 150 learned attributes with

---

477 Bank of America online 2019a, 6, 15, 189; Bank of America 5/28/2019, pp. 1–2; Bank of America online 2019b.

478 Bank of America 5/28/2019, pp. 1–2.

479 Blythe 2018; Cloudera [2018], p. 11; JPMorgan Chase & Co. 2017, p. 49; Remus and Levy 2015, pp. 18–22.

Key partners	Key activities	Value propositions	Customer relationships	Customer segments
Lawmakers to enable processing, linking and analysis of customer information Financial services companies to provide products and platforms for the extension of functions AI service providers e.g., IBM Watson Conversational content providers Test and training partners	Design of individual chatbot considering brand image Evaluation and monitoring of chat activities Intensive simulation of customer interactions as development basis Analysis of customer requirements for functionality and interaction **Key resources** Competence in customer support via telephone and chat Knowledge about predictive analysis, speech recognition, natural language processing and database organization Knowledge of customer target groups and expectations	Fast, direct, personal customer service around the clock Further information and advice about financial services and financial planning Relevant information at the right time to enhance fast financial decision-making Replace call-centers Reduce costs by automated answers to service and consulting requests	Individualized conversational experience for clients based on earlier conversations, similar requests and customer data **Channels** Online customer portal App of the bank Social media	Private and business customers Own employees in customer support or specialized department and branch office Retail banking and insurance companies

Cost structure	Revenue streams
Set-up of chatbot	Cross-selling of financial services
Establishing and maintaining a uniform customer data structure	Enhancement of profitability by reduction of costs for services and customer consultation
Unification and standardization of services and banking systems	Enhancement of sales through faster response to customer requests

Figure 10.4: Business Model Canvas – chatbots in banking. (Source: own illustration)

which the image recognition software used in COiN filters critical data and clauses from the documents.[480]

---

480 JPMorgan Chase & Co. 2017, p. 49; Blythe 2018.

The functional scope of the COiN program is strongly limited to standardized documents. In the medium-term, JPMorgan aims to further develop COiN for more complex tasks. The use of COiN for credit-default swaps and custody agreements is planned. In addition to simple classification, the program may also be used for the interpretation of legal texts and the analysis of corporate communications in the future.[481]

The automation of the staff-intensive, manual checking of documents achieved with COiN through the technology partnership with Cloudera that began in 2009, provides JPMorgan with various internal and external opportunities. Fast, clean and redundancy-free processes help the financial group to compete with fintechs. IT-driven efficiency improvements have been only slowly introduced in the legal industry. The expertise gained in the data analysis and evaluation of legal documents has helped the bank to create new business areas that have traditionally been reserved for law firms and legal consulting firms.[482]

Figure 10.5 depicts the Business Model Canvas for the use of machine learning for intelligent contract analysis. The coordination with many stakeholders along the capturing and document analysis process is necessary to implement a COiN software. As a value proposition, the automated, fast and error-free document analysis provides cost savings by reducing the workload of employees in the legal department. The rapid analysis of documents decreases the process time for the entire organization. The key resources for success are flexible and efficient IT as well as expertise in the field of language recognition.

10.6 Venture capital financing for artificial intelligence

The fintech area of artificial intelligence (AI) has seen many foundations around the world in recent years. Table 10.1 shows 260 financing rounds globally with 11 in the U.S., 80 in Europe and 52 in Asia for the sample January 2017 to April 2020. Overall, more than $1.4 billion were invested in only three years. The median amount raised per fintech financing round was $2.4 million in the U.S. and $2.2 million in Europe. Only 11 financing rounds are shown for China, but the median of $25 million is very high.

---

481 Son 2017.
482 Son 2017; Simon et al. 2018, p. 234.

Key partners	Key activities	Value propositions	Customer relationships	Customer segments
Technology partners with access to key resources Customers to simplify document exchange and capture Legislators to enable the external use of software	Preparation of content and samples to train the algorithm Process definition and monitoring of the document capture and subsequent use of the analysis results Quality control of analysis results	Automated classification, organization and monitoring of contract documents Quality improvement and cost reduction in document review Interpretation and risk assessment of document content	Individual support and consulting for implementation and customization for the intended use case	Use for financial institutions within compliance department Other financial institutions, law firms, trading or manufacturing companies
	Key resources Flexible access to computing capacities Know-how of automated image processing, database organization, pattern and language recognition		**Channels** Direct distribution and implementation on-site or as SaaS platform	

Cost structure	Revenue streams
Set-up of a digital document management system Customization costs of software for the specified use case	Additional revenues through fast, clean, redundancy-free processes with high-quality results Revenues from commercialization as on-site implementation or as SaaS platform

Figure 10.5: Business Model Canvas – contract intelligence with machine learning. (Source: own illustration)

Table 10.1: AI fintechs overview of venture capital financing statistics for sample
January 2017–April 2020.

Location	Number Financing Rounds	Median Money Raised	Total Money Raised	Total Pre-Money Valuation
Asia	52	n/a	$343,987,830	n/a
China	11	$25,000,000	$219,653,851	n/a
Europe	80	$2,247,175	$215,357,230	$87,402,305
Singapore	14	n/a	$41,300,000	n/a
U.S.	111	$2,435,000	$899,542,888	$1,787,760,000
World	260	$2,251,780	$1,470,006,208	$1,876,713,003

(Source: own illustration with data from Crunchbase 2020e)

Summary

The features of volume, variety, veracity, velocity and value of data for products and services define the classification of the concept of big data for IT-sytems. The analysis of customer data supports the development of client-tailored financial products. Big Data also provides the basis for the application of machine learning in the form of a chatbots. The first examples of chatbots can improve the variety of communication and client channels but are still in the test phase. Fintechs or banks could even offer new services outside the world of financial products, if big data and AI are combined.

11 Venture capital financing and fintech valuations

Venture capital is needed to finance the growth prospects of fintechs worldwide. Figure 11.1 illustrates the total money raised in different regions of the world as well as the number of financing rounds with venture capital for a period of 28 years. The financing rounds in Figure 11.1 comprise angel and seed financing as well as all further venture capital financing rounds. From April 1992 until April 2020 more than $102 billion were raised for fintechs worldwide in 8,448 financing rounds. The highest financing volume was recorded by the U.S. with $35 billion followed by China with $33 billion. Only 153 financing rounds with a total volume of $543 million were realized in Africa. That is less than in Singapore in both categories. In India $6.2 billion were raised for fintechs, in Germany $2.6 billion and $10.6 billion in the U.K. The total for all South America amounted to only $1.9 billion in 317 financing rounds. The illustration shows clearly where the regions of financial innovation in

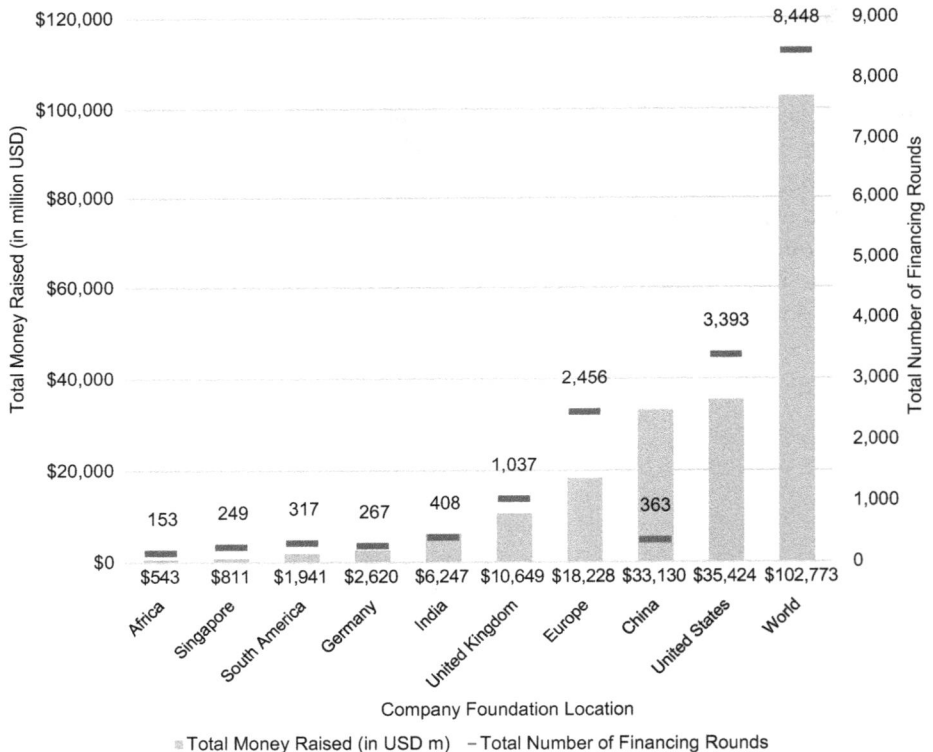

Figure 11.1: Total money raised and total number of financing rounds per company foundation location for sample April 1992–April 2020.
(Source: own illustration with data from Crunchbase 2020e)

https://doi.org/10.1515/9783110704907-011

the world can be found. Figure 11.1 also shows 28 years of worldwide financing development in the fintech area. It is important to point out that the highest proportion of the overall amount financed was raised in the last five years.

11.1 Global Fintech funding and Europe versus the U.S.

Due to the lack of detailed information on financing rounds in China, the empirical analysis covering the sample of 379 fintechs concentrates on Europe and the U.S. Relevant data on financing rounds and valuation for the sample April 2000 to June 2017 was identified in the empirical study for both regions. The fintechs were classified into the five segments Financing, Investment, Payment & Account, Service & Support with Comparison Sites & Search Engines and Infrastructure & IT as well as adjacent fields like Insurtech or Healthtech. The underlying data on the 379 fintechs and the financing rounds was gathered from company research including CB Insights, Financial Technology Partners, Mercer Capital, Mergermarket, Pitchbook, Raymond James and Thomson Reuters, crunchbase.com, empirica-software.com, fintechranking. com, letstalkpayments.com, app.dealroom.co and tech.eu. Although important publicly available databases were screened, the study naturally can not guarantee that the presented picture is complete, as some VC fintech fundings may not be included or other databases containing additional fintech deals might exist.[483]

Fintech business models clustered into alternative payment methods total 70 fintechs or 18.7% overall and represent the largest share, while the subcategory comparison sites & search engines accounts for the smallest portion, with only 1.3 % or five fintechs (see Figure 11.2). For the 379 fintechs in the database, a total of 1,096 financing rounds for the sample April 2000 to June 2017 were compiled, with an overall amount raised of approximately €23.2 billion. Data includes seed rounds, angel investments, venture rounds A to F, IPOs and acquisitions as well as financing rounds where the exact round is unknown.

Research concept for the sample of 379 fintechs

For a sample of 379 fintechs all financing rounds and acquisitions for the sample April 2000 June 2017 were analyzed in EUR and converted from GBP or USD into EUR using the historical exchange rate at the date of the transaction. Angel investments and so-called unknown rounds were disregarded for the analysis of consecutive financing rounds, as angel investments sometimes took place before seed rounds and

---

[483] In general a complete and global database with venture capital data does not exist see: Kaplan and Lerner 2016.

Others, 10
Healthtech, 7
Insurtech, 24
Crowdfunding, 19
Crowdlending, 18
Infrastructure & IT, 60
Credit & Factoring, 53
Comparison Sites & Search Engines, 5
Social Trading, 6
Blockchain & Cryptocurrencies, 23
Robo-Advice, 32
Personal Finance Management, 40
Alternative Payment Methods, 70
Savings, 12

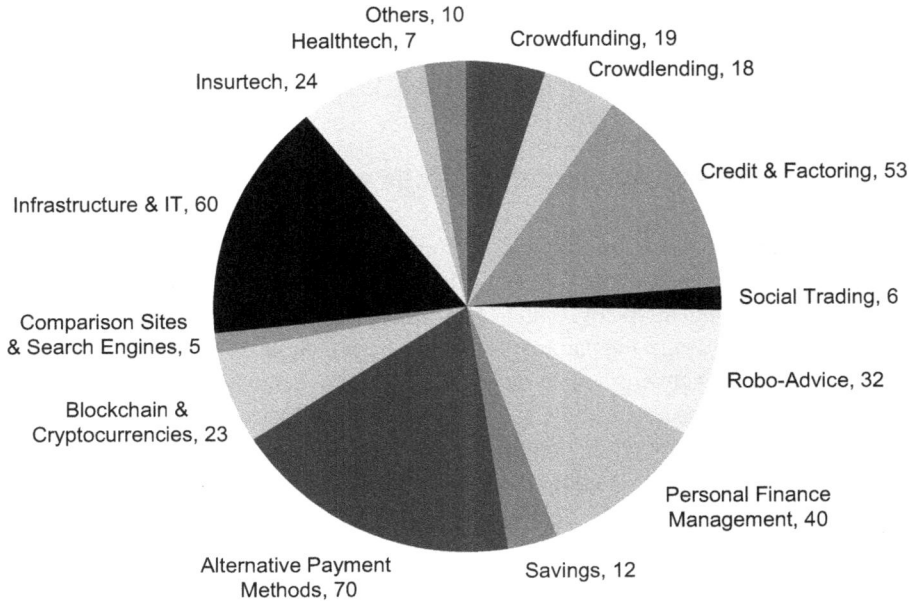

Figure 11.2: Split of 379 fintechs in the database into 14 subsegments for sample April 2000–June 2017.
(Source: own illustration)

at other times after the seed round, which made it impossible to compare. Unknown rounds were not analyzed, as it was simply not known whether they were standalone financing rounds or a follow-on round of a previous one (e.g., second round B). However, both kinds of financing rounds were included in the comparison of Europe and the U.S. In case of follow-on financing rounds, the amounts were accumulated for comparative purposes while for the time between financing rounds the latest dates of each round were compared.

An emphasis was put on year-over-year comparisons, such as the overall amount raised or the number of deals in Europe and the U.S. since 2000, before analyzing the financing rounds for patterns by comparing the amounts raised in the previous funding rounds (e.g., round A) with the amounts in the following ones (e.g., round B). The annual split of fintechs founded per segment was also analyzed to detect where founders and entrepreneurs saw improvement potential for financial services. The segment comparisons were conducted on a median basis as the effect of outliers should be diminished as much as possible. This methodology is consistent with other research on this topic such as from CB Insights or Pitchbook.

Number of fintech financing rounds

Figure 11.3 illustrates the number of financing rounds per company foundation location for the sample January 2017 to April 2020. Historically, the first fintechs were founded in the U.S. and the U.S. dominated the fintech market, followed by Europe. But the competitive situation has changed dramatically, as China has led the number of financing rounds in recent years. For the sample January 2017 to April 2020 China counted 1,526 financing rounds, the U.S. 1,357 financing rounds and for Europe the number was just 582. India had 216 financing rounds and Singapore (with 130 financing rounds) still had a higher number than Africa with only 103 rounds. Europe must pay attention regarding its fintech investments, as in the first years of the fintech evolution Europe was nearly as good as the U.S. But in recent years China and the U.S. have dominated the world market. South America and Africa are far behind the rest of the world.

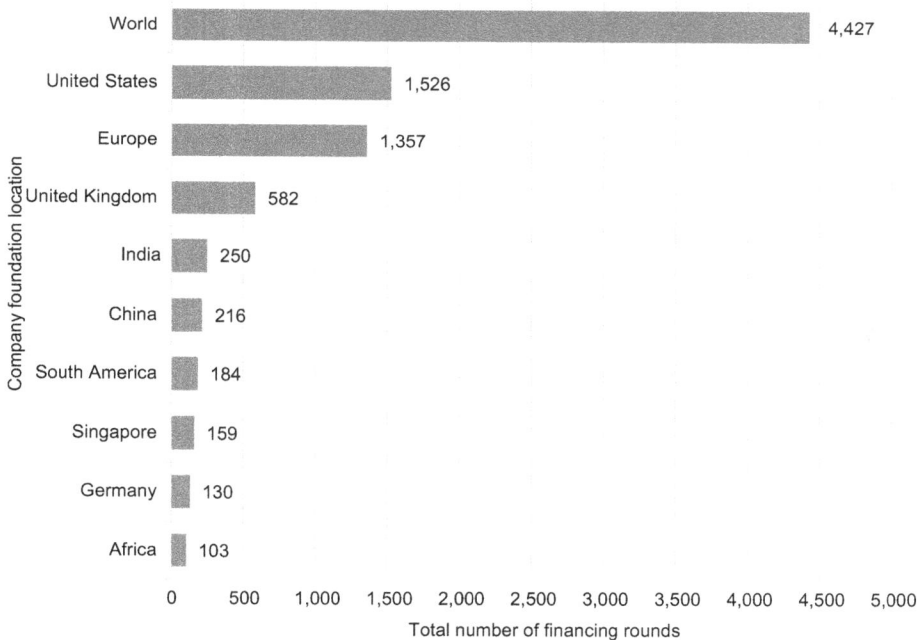

Figure 11.3: Total number of financing rounds per company foundation location for sample January 2017–April 2020.
(Source: own illustration with data from Crunchbase 2020e)

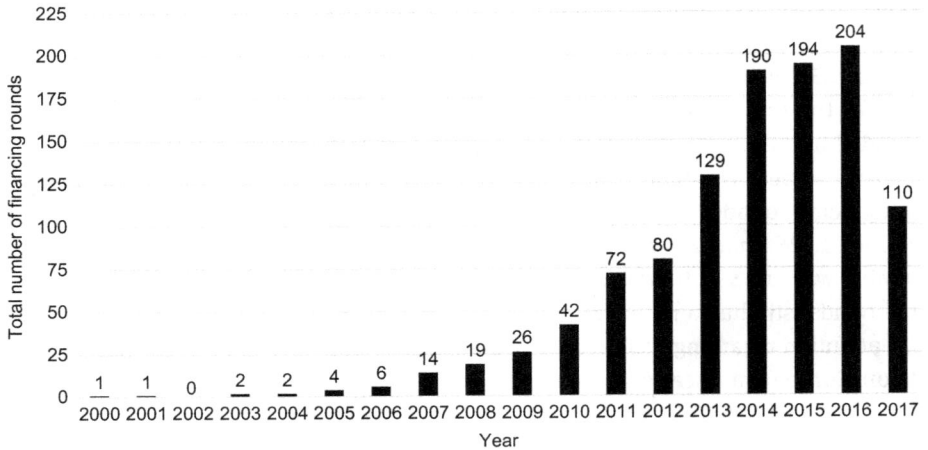

Figure 11.4: Annual overview of financing rounds for sample April 2000–June 2017.
(Source: own illustration)

A more detailed analysis is possible for our sample of only 379 fintechs between April 2000 and June 2017 (see Figure 11.4). A total of 1,096 financing rounds were compiled, split between 486 European and 610 U.S. deals, which is equivalent to 44.3% and 55.7%. The number of financing rounds does not fully correspond with the figures of CB Insights, as the underlying database relies on different sources including but not limited to CB Insights.

At the beginning of the millennium, only occasional fintech funding rounds took place. From 2005 the number of fintech deals increased until 2016, with the most significant increase of 110 deals between 2012 and 2014. The share of each of the regions is highlighted in the next chart.

After 2006 the majority of deals were closed in the U.S., reaching its maximum of 78.9% in 2008. After 2008 the percentage share of European deals increased each year to a level even higher than the U.S. in 2017 (see Figure 11.5).

Leading position of China in recent capital raised

Figure 11.6 illustrates that in recent years the highest total amount raised was in China with $24 billion, followed by the U.S. with $20 billion and Europe with $13 billion. So not only has China had the highest volume in recent financing rounds, but it also leads when it comes to the overall amount raised. Singapore, as a very small country, has underlined its role as a financial center, as $695 million were raised between January 2017 and April 2020. In Europe the two most important fintech markets are the U.K. and Germany.

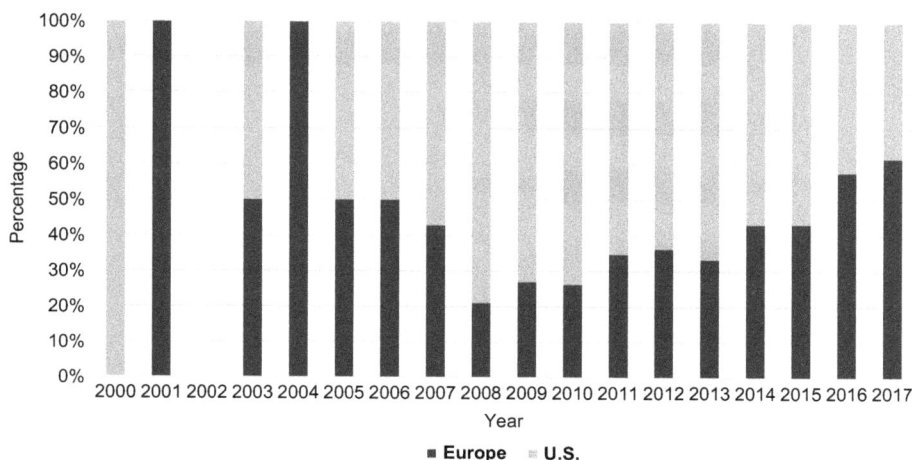

Figure 11.5: Percentage of overall deals in Europe and the U.S. for sample April 2000–June 2017. (Source: own illustration)

In the 1,096 financing rounds of the sample from 2000 until mid 2017 a total of €23.2 billion was raised (see Figure 11.7). The vast majority of 71.8% was collected in the U.S.[484]

In the period from 2000 to 2006, a combined value of only €88.8 million was raised. The explanation is that overall fintech funding was in an early stage. In the next six years, fintech funding massively increased from €89.9 million in 2007 to €996.2 million in 2013, representing a CAGR of 49.3%. However, in the aftermath of the financial crisis, 2012 was the only year in which the amount raised decreased in comparison to the previous year. Funding more than quintupled in 2014 and reached its peak of close to €6.8 billion in 2015. In 2016 the amount raised dropped by 28.3%, which might be due to the cooldown of the fintech hype and the emphasis on sustainable business models in niche segments.

In order to determine the differences in funding regarding Europe and the U.S., the amount raised in each region as a percentage of the total funding in each year was compared. Due to the extremely low number of deals until 2006, the share of capital raised in Europe and the U.S. during this period is not considered significant. In 2007 Europe accounted for 60.2% of the overall amount raised, despite the lower number of deals, while in 2008 the opposite was the case and the U.S. raised 78.9% of all capital in that year (see Figure 11.8).

---

484 Please note that the amounts raised do not fully correspond with the figures of CB Insights as the underlying database relies on different sources including but not limited to CB Insights.

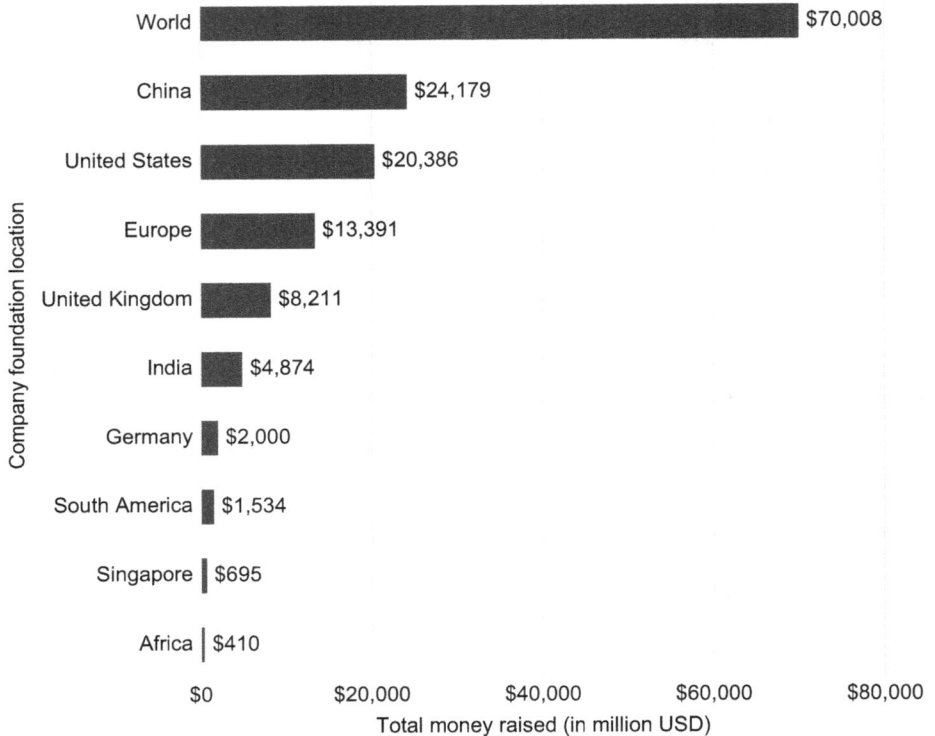

Figure 11.6: Total money raised per company foundation location for sample January 2017 – April 2020 (in € m).
(Source: own illustration with data from Crunchbase 2020e)

In 2009 Europe once again raised more capital than the U.S., with a share of 55.5%. Since then, more capital has been raised in the U.S. than in Europe each year, without a clear trend being observable. This development is remarkable when taking into consideration that the previous analysis showed that Europe's share of deal activity has been increasing since 2008 and is currently well above 61%. The average amount raised in the U.S. has been steadily increasing in recent years. This supports the conclusion suggesting that the fintech market in the U.S. is more mature in comparison to the European market – hence, the larger average funding or a higher number of bigger-sized deals.

Niche markets in Europe open for new fintechs

In Europe, 486 financing rounds took place in the sample April 2000 to June 2017 (see Figure 11.9). The deal activity in fintech funding was marginal between 2000 and

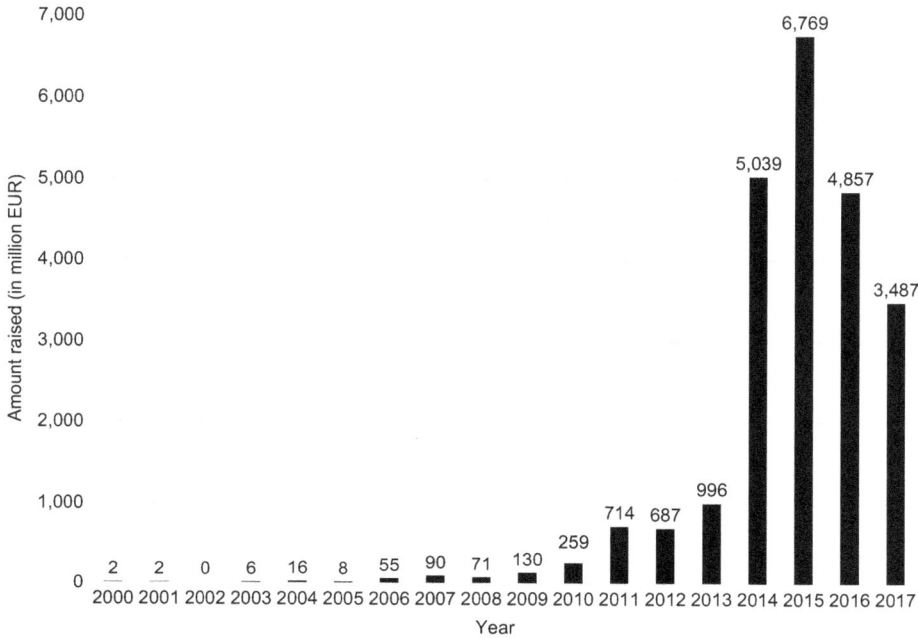

Figure 11.7: Annual overview of amount raised for fintechs for sample April 2000–June 2017 (in € m).
(Source: own illustration)

2006, before doubling in 2007 compared to the previous year. It then dropped back to four deals in 2008. In the next eight years, deal activity increased continuously each year, especially between 2013 and 2014, where the financing rounds almost doubled within one year. The deal count of 118 in 2016 is the yearly maximum up to date even though 68 deals were already closed by June 2017, suggesting a new record year. This leads to the conclusion that the European fintech market is still far from being mature. Nevertheless, a closer look at Table 11.1 must be taken to uncover deal activity trends for the various segments.

Infrastructure & IT represents the main segment of deal activity until 2008, followed by crowdlending and alternative payment methods. In 2009 initial deals in robo-advice, social trading and credit & factoring took place apart from in the already emphasized segments. In the years after that, all remaining segments including crowdfunding and PFM started to attract attention. Blockchain & cryptocurrencies was the last of the segments to close at least one financing round.

According to the sample, healthtech is the only segment not represented in a single financing round in Europe. In contrast to that, a strong focus was placed on alternative payment methods, infrastructure & IT, PFM and credit & factoring during the last five years of the observation period. One conclusion of these findings could be that the European fintech market still provides possibilities in every niche, as deal activity is very diversified, leading to the assumption that the market is not mature.

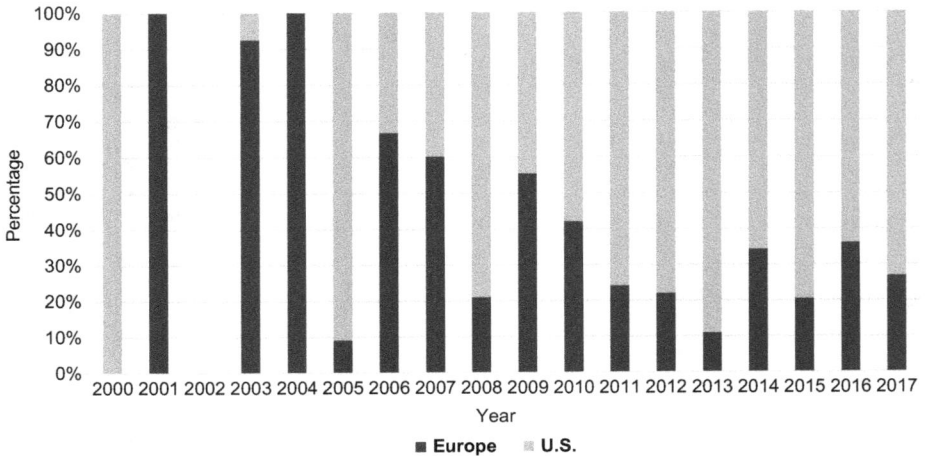

Figure 11.8: Percentage of overall amount raised in Europe and the U.S. for sample April 2000–June 2017 (in percent).
(Source: own illustration)

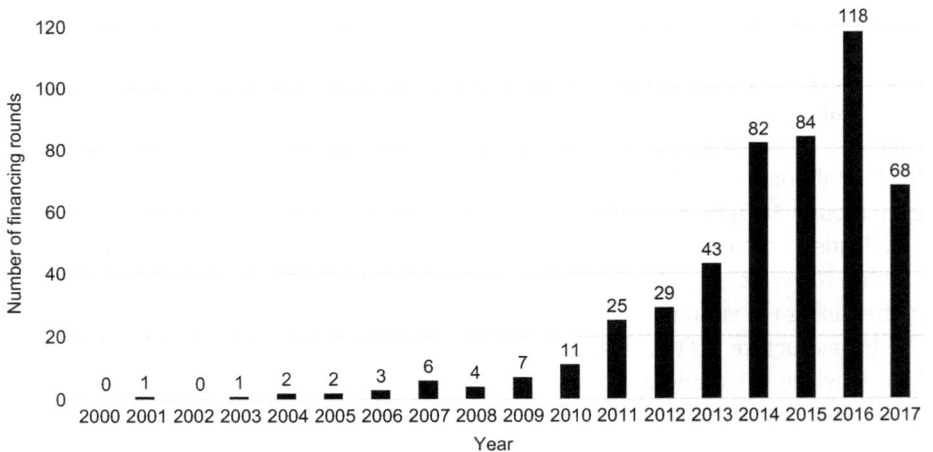

Figure 11.9: Annual overview of financing rounds in Europe for sample April 2000–June 2017.
(Source: own illustration)

Table 11.1: Percentage of each segment compared to overall fintech funding activity in Europe for sample April 2000–June 2017.

Segment	2000	2001	2002	2003	2004	2005	2006	2007	2008	2009	2010	2011	2012	2013	2014	2015	2016	2017
Crowdfunding	n/a	0.0%	n/a	0.0%	0.0%	0.0%	0.0%	0.0%	0.0%	0.0%	18.2%	0.0%	3.4%	0.0%	6.1%	6.0%	6.8%	4.4%
Crowdlending	n/a	0.0%	n/a	0.0%	50.0%	50.0%	33.3%	33.3%	0.0%	0.0%	18.2%	8.0%	3.4%	4.7%	8.5%	14.3%	6.8%	8.8%
Credit & Factoring	n/a	0.0%	n/a	0.0%	0.0%	0.0%	0.0%	16.7%	25.0%	14.3%	9.1%	8.0%	13.8%	9.3%	12.2%	8.3%	11.9%	8.8%
Social Trading	n/a	0.0%	n/a	0.0%	0.0%	0.0%	0.0%	16.7%	0.0%	14.3%	9.1%	4.0%	3.4%	0.0%	3.7%	2.4%	0.8%	1.5%
Robo-Advice	n/a	0.0%	n/a	0.0%	0.0%	0.0%	0.0%	0.0%	0.0%	14.3%	0.0%	4.0%	6.9%	4.7%	3.7%	7.1%	7.6%	7.4%
Personal Finance Management	n/a	0.0%	n/a	0.0%	0.0%	0.0%	0.0%	0.0%	0.0%	0.0%	9.1%	8.0%	10.3%	11.6%	8.5%	9.5%	10.2%	16.2%
Savings	n/a	0.0%	n/a	0.0%	0.0%	0.0%	0.0%	0.0%	0.0%	0.0%	0.0%	4.0%	0.0%	2.3%	3.7%	4.8%	7.6%	5.9%
Alternative Payment Methods	n/a	0.0%	n/a	0.0%	0.0%	50.0%	0.0%	16.7%	0.0%	28.6%	36.4%	32.0%	37.9%	48.8%	26.8%	20.2%	18.6%	16.2%
Blockchain & Crypto-currencies	n/a	0.0%	n/a	0.0%	0.0%	0.0%	0.0%	0.0%	0.0%	0.0%	0.0%	0.0%	0.0%	0.0%	4.9%	2.4%	4.2%	5.9%
Comparison Sites & Search Engines	n/a	0.0%	n/a	0.0%	0.0%	0.0%	0.0%	0.0%	0.0%	0.0%	0.0%	0.0%	0.0%	2.3%	2.4%	3.6%	2.5%	0.0%
Infrastructure & IT	n/a	100.0%	n/a	100.0%	50.0%	0.0%	66.7%	16.7%	75.0%	28.6%	0.0%	24.0%	10.3%	11.6%	14.6%	13.1%	12.7%	16.2%
Insurtech	n/a	0.0%	n/a	0.0%	0.0%	0.0%	0.0%	0.0%	0.0%	0.0%	0.0%	0.0%	6.9%	4.7%	4.9%	8.3%	9.3%	7.4%
Healthtech	n/a	0.0%	n/a	0.0%	0.0%	0.0%	0.0%	0.0%	0.0%	0.0%	0.0%	0.0%	0.0%	0.0%	0.0%	0.0%	0.0%	0.0%
Others	n/a	0.0%	n/a	0.0%	0.0%	0.0%	0.0%	0.0%	0.0%	0.0%	0.0%	8.0%	3.4%	0.0%	0.0%	0.0%	0.8%	1.5%

(Source: own illustration)

Similarly to the number of deals, fintech funding in Europe was at a very low level until the mid-2000s, with the exception of 2004 where two deals raised a total of €15.9 million (see Figure 11.10). The overall amount raised increased from 2005 to 2007 before dropping sharply by roughly €39 million in 2008. After that, European funding of fintechs picked up pace in the next three years to reach a level of €172.5 million in 2011, before declining by more than €62 million in the following two years, so that in 2013 €109.7 million were raised. The following massive jump between 2013 and 2014 to €1,728.6 million, implying an annual growth rate of 1,475%, suggests that in 2014 the hype surrounding fintechs reached Europe. While capital raised in Europe fell by 20% in 2015 to €1,386.7 million, it reached a new all-time high of € 1,750.7 million in 2016.

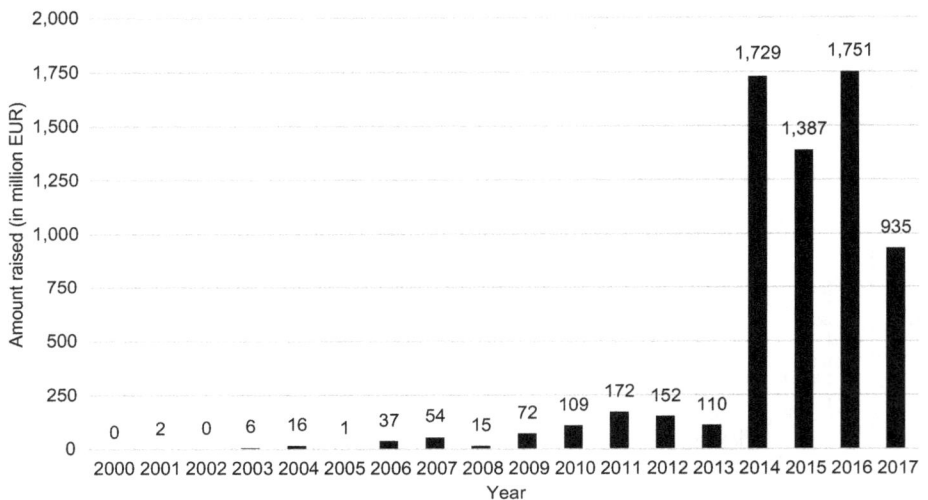

Figure 11.10: Annual overview of amount raised in Europe for sample April 2000–June 2017 (in € m). (Source: own illustration)

11.2 Allocation of money raised per financing round and business model

From seed and angel funding to rounds E and F in Europe

The fintech funding amount raised in 2000 to 2005 is based on a handful of deals. For the two years after that, the majority of capital raised is allocated to the financing rounds A and B. Yet 43% of the overall amount raised in 2006 and approximately 18% in 2007 are associated with growth financing rounds C and D. For 2008 and 2009, large parts of funding in Europe can not be assigned to a specific round and are therefore defined as unknown. The focus of funding then shifted from mainly growth financing in 2010 to early stage financing across seed and financing rounds A and B in 2014 (see Table 11.2).

Nonetheless, there was one IPO in Europe in 2014 that was responsible for approximately 46% of the total amount raised. After that, fintech funding varied across all sorts of financing rounds without any clear pattern, especially since the unknown rounds account for a significant proportion. However, the fact that several IPOs as well as a number of later stage financing rounds (e.g., rounds F) took place, suggest that the European fintech market is slowly moving toward a certain maturity.

It must be noted that although both crowdlending and alternative payment methods each closed one deal in 2005, crowdlending accounts for more than 90% of the overall amount raised in that year, implying a much higher amount raised compared to the alternative payment methods segment (see Table 11.3). The crowdlending transaction was an A-round, whereas the other transaction concerned seed financing. In Europe, most money was invested in alternative payment methods, followed by crowdlending, credit & factoring and PFM.

From seed and angel funding to round F in the U.S.

Similar to the development in Europe, deal activity was very low between 2000 and 2006. From 2007 onward the number of financing rounds climbed annually irrespective of the then prevailing financial crisis. One could even assume that the financial crisis actually fueled fintech deal activity in the U.S. much quicker than in Europe. The peak was in 2015 with 110 deals closed in the U.S. (see Figure 11.11).

Until the mid-2000s, the only deals closed in the U.S. were in alternative payment methods. From 2005 to 2007 crowdlending had the highest deal activity along with several deals in credit & factoring, PFM, infrastructure & IT and social trading. In subsequent years, the number of robo-advice and healthtech deals started to increase in the U.S. fintech market, before all remaining segments showed some deal activity until 2012. Deal activity was well diversified across all segments except for social trading and savings where almost no financing rounds took place. In summary, a strong emphasis in the U.S. fintech funding market was on alternative payment methods, infrastructure & IT, credit & factoring as well as robo-advice (see Table 11.4).

Vast fintech funding amounts were raised in the U.S. in the aftermath of the financial crisis. Fintech funding in the U.S. actually began in 2005, as no significant amounts were raised prior to that. In the following five years, the amounts increased more than twentyfold to €149.5 million. The average amount per financing round declined from €6.0 million in 2006 to €4.8 million in 2010. However, this trend can potentially be explained by the assumption that investors might have

Table 11.2: Percentage of each fintech funding type series compared to overall amount raised in Europe for sample April 2000–June 2017.

Financing Round	2000	2001	2002	2003	2004	2005	2006	2007	2008	2009	2010	2011	2012	2013	2014	2015	2016	2017
Seed	n/a	0.0%	n/a	0.0%	0.0%	8.3%	0.0%	0.0%	2.7%	0.2%	2.5%	3.0%	4.3%	7.4%	1.7%	2.8%	3.6%	3.1%
A	n/a	100.0%	n/a	0.0%	0.0%	91.7%	13.8%	20.8%	12.2%	2.1%	9.8%	8.4%	20.4%	45.8%	9.2%	9.4%	9.5%	15.6%
B	n/a	0.0%	n/a	100.0%	0.0%	0.0%	43.2%	61.3%	0.0%	28.7%	6.2%	7.5%	27.1%	3.3%	21.4%	16.0%	14.5%	11.5%
C	n/a	0.0%	n/a	0.0%	38.3%	0.0%	0.0%	17.9%	0.0%	0.0%	80.2%	67.4%	21.3%	24.5%	3.3%	27.8%	9.7%	6.5%
D	n/a	0.0%	n/a	0.0%	0.0%	0.0%	43.0%	0.0%	45.0%	0.0%	0.0%	0.0%	0.0%	0.0%	8.7%	5.0%	6.6%	5.8%
E	n/a	0.0%	n/a	0.0%	0.0%	0.0%	0.0%	0.0%	0.0%	0.0%	0.0%	0.0%	0.0%	0.0%	0.0%	11.3%	0.0%	3.9%
F	n/a	0.0%	n/a	0.0%	0.0%	0.0%	0.0%	0.0%	0.0%	0.0%	0.0%	0.0%	0.0%	0.0%	0.0%	0.0%	0.0%	10.2%
Angel	n/a	0.0%	n/a	0.0%	0.0%	0.0%	0.0%	0.0%	0.0%	0.6%	1.2%	0.3%	1.1%	3.8%	0.5%	0.2%	0.1%	0.0%
Unknown	n/a	0.0%	n/a	0.0%	61.7%	0.0%	0.0%	0.0%	40.1%	68.5%	0.0%	13.3%	25.9%	15.2%	9.4%	27.4%	12.9%	43.4%
IPO	n/a	0.0%	n/a	0.0%	0.0%	0.0%	0.0%	0.0%	0.0%	0.0%	0.0%	0.0%	0.0%	0.0%	45.9%	0.0%	43.1%	0.0%

(Source: own illustration)

Table 11.3: Percentage of each segment compared to overall amount raised in Europe for sample April 2000–June 2017.

Segment	2000	2001	2002	2003	2004	2005	2006	2007	2008	2009	2010	2011	2012	2013	2014	2015	2016	2017
Crowdfunding	n/a	0.0%	n/a	0.0%	0.0%	0.0%	0.0%	0.0%	0.0%	0.0%	1.7%	0.0%	2.7%	0.0%	0.2%	1.4%	3.1%	1.4%
Crowdlending	n/a	0.0%	n/a	0.0%	61.7%	91.7%	43.2%	25.3%	0.0%	0.0%	2.4%	4.8%	7.9%	32.9%	6.0%	37.0%	5.3%	18.5%
Credit & Factoring	n/a	0.0%	n/a	0.0%	0.0%	0.0%	0.0%	8.2%	12.2%	21.8%	78.4%	5.2%	18.0%	9.0%	7.9%	8.8%	9.5%	15.7%
Social Trading	n/a	0.0%	n/a	0.0%	0.0%	0.0%	0.0%	2.4%	0.0%	6.8%	1.8%	3.5%	7.5%	0.0%	1.8%	0.8%	0.1%	1.3%
Robo-Advice	n/a	0.0%	n/a	0.0%	0.0%	0.0%	0.0%	0.0%	0.0%	0.2%	0.0%	0.4%	4.8%	1.0%	2.5%	2.0%	4.2%	1.4%
PFM	n/a	0.0%	n/a	0.0%	0.0%	0.0%	0.0%	0.0%	0.0%	0.0%	8.5%	5.7%	1.1%	6.0%	2.2%	9.0%	3.8%	24.2%
Savings	n/a	0.0%	n/a	0.0%	0.0%	0.0%	0.0%	0.0%	0.0%	0.0%	0.0%	0.7%	0.0%	0.0%	0.6%	2.6%	8.3%	5.1%
Alternative Payment Methods	n/a	0.0%	n/a	0.0%	0.0%	8.3%	0.0%	2.8%	0.0%	0.6%	7.2%	73.7%	48.4%	40.9%	28.6%	29.4%	54.8%	12.2%
Blockchain & Cryptocurrencies	n/a	0.0%	n/a	0.0%	0.0%	0.0%	0.0%	0.0%	0.0%	0.0%	0.0%	0.0%	0.0%	0.0%	1.5%	0.0%	0.3%	5.0%
Comparison Sites & Search Engines	n/a	0.0%	n/a	0.0%	0.0%	0.0%	0.0%	0.0%	0.0%	0.0%	0.0%	0.0%	0.0%	1.8%	0.2%	1.4%	3.0%	0.0%
Infrastructure & IT	n/a	100.0%	n/a	100.0%	38.3%	0.0%	56.8%	61.3%	87.8%	70.5%	0.0%	5.9%	8.3%	4.6%	47.2%	2.5%	3.9%	8.2%
Insurtech	n/a	0.0%	n/a	0.0%	0.0%	0.0%	0.0%	0.0%	0.0%	0.0%	0.0%	0.0%	0.4%	3.8%	1.4%	5.0%	3.6%	6.2%
Healthtech	n/a	0.0%	n/a	0.0%	0.0%	0.0%	0.0%	0.0%	0.0%	0.0%	0.0%	0.0%	0.0%	0.0%	0.0%	0.0%	0.0%	0.0%
Others	n/a	0.0%	n/a	0.0%	0.0%	0.0%	0.0%	0.0%	0.0%	0.0%	0.0%	0.1%	0.8%	0.0%	0.0%	0.0%	0.1%	0.7%

(Source: own illustration)

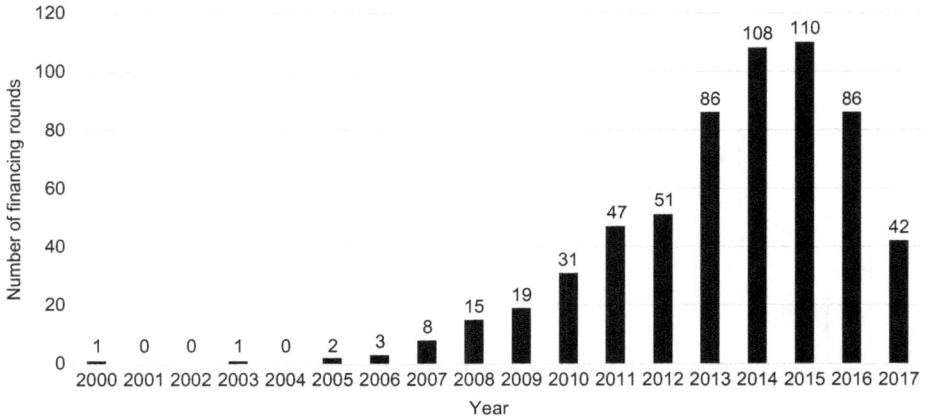

Figure 11.11: Annual overview of financing rounds in the U.S. for sample April 2000–June 2017. (Source: own illustration)

wanted to minimize their investments during the peak of the financial crisis to decrease risk. From 2011 to 2015, annual fintech funding in the U.S. grew dramatically and reached its all-time high of €5,382.4 million (see Figure 11.12).

With regard to the maturity of the U.S. fintech market, it can be stated that the previous finding, according to which a higher degree of maturity is indicated, is supported by the figures on amounts raised, as the deal count has been decreasing disproportionately compared to the amounts raised. Consequently, this leads to an increase in average amount raised per financing round, hinting at increasing maturity (see Table 11.5).

Due to the low number of deals that took place until the mid-2000s, the explanatory power during this time is very low, except for the fact that all amounts raised during that time were related to early stage investments, that is, seed investments and A-rounds. In the 10 years after that, the focus of funding gradually shifted from early stage investments to growth investments or later stage investments, even including financing rounds F. For instance, the share of financing rounds D to F in relation to the overall amount raised in a specific year increased from 7.3% in 2010 to 33.0% in 2017. Additionally, the IPOs that took place in every year after 2014 can also be interpreted as investors seeing limited growth possibilities for their investments, implying advanced maturity.

First venture capital investments in payments and crowdfunding

In contrast to Europe, it can be more definitively concluded that the U.S. fintech market, as a whole, is reaching maturity. The interesting question in this context is

Table 11.4: Percentage of each fintech segment compared to overall funding activity in the U.S. for sample April 2000–June 2017.

Segment	2000	2001	2002	2003	2004	2005	2006	2007	2008	2009	2010	2011	2012	2013	2014	2015	2016	2017
Crowdfunding	0.0%	n/a	n/a	0.0%	n/a	0.0%	0.0%	0.0%	0.0%	0.0%	0.0%	2.1%	0.0%	2.3%	2.8%	4.5%	2.3%	4.8%
Crowdlending	0.0%	n/a	n/a	0.0%	n/a	50.0%	33.3%	37.5%	0.0%	5.3%	9.7%	4.3%	2.0%	5.8%	3.7%	0.9%	1.2%	0.0%
Credit & Factoring	0.0%	n/a	n/a	0.0%	n/a	0.0%	33.3%	0.0%	6.7%	5.3%	3.2%	17.0%	19.6%	18.6%	23.1%	24.5%	19.8%	19.0%
Social Trading	0.0%	n/a	n/a	0.0%	n/a	0.0%	0.0%	12.5%	6.7%	0.0%	0.0%	0.0%	0.0%	1.2%	0.9%	0.9%	0.0%	0.0%
Robo-Advice	0.0%	n/a	n/a	0.0%	n/a	0.0%	0.0%	0.0%	20.0%	10.5%	9.7%	6.4%	7.8%	10.5%	11.1%	10.9%	11.6%	14.3%
Personal Finance Management	0.0%	n/a	n/a	0.0%	n/a	0.0%	33.3%	0.0%	13.3%	21.1%	22.6%	17.0%	11.8%	12.8%	13.9%	9.1%	12.8%	4.8%
Savings	0.0%	n/a	n/a	0.0%	n/a	0.0%	0.0%	0.0%	0.0%	0.0%	0.0%	0.0%	0.0%	1.2%	0.0%	0.9%	0.0%	0.0%
Alternative Payment Methods	100.0%	n/a	n/a	100.0 %	n/a	50.0%	0.0%	25.0%	33.3%	42.1%	35.5%	29.8%	29.4%	18.6%	13.9%	14.5%	11.6%	14.3%
Blockchain & Cryptocurrencies	0.0%	n/a	n/a	0.0%	n/a	0.0%	0.0%	0.0%	0.0%	0.0%	0.0%	0.0%	2.0%	7.0%	8.3%	5.5%	4.7%	9.5%
Comparison Sites & Search Engines	0.0%	n/a	n/a	0.0%	n/a	0.0%	0.0%	0.0%	0.0%	0.0%	0.0%	0.0%	3.9%	1.2%	0.0%	1.8%	1.2%	0.0%
Infrastructure & IT	0.0%	n/a	n/a	0.0%	n/a	0.0%	0.0%	25.0%	13.3%	10.5%	9.7%	17.0%	15.7%	11.6%	12.0%	11.8%	14.0%	16.7%
Insurtech	0.0%	n/a	n/a	0.0%	n/a	0.0%	0.0%	0.0%	0.0%	0.0%	3.2%	0.0%	3.9%	2.3%	2.8%	2.7%	12.8%	4.8%
Healthtech	0.0%	n/a	n/a	0.0%	n/a	0.0%	0.0%	0.0%	6.7%	0.0%	3.2%	4.3%	2.0%	2.3%	2.8%	6.4%	4.7%	7.1%
Others	0.0%	n/a	n/a	0.0%	n/a	0.0%	0.0%	0.0%	0.0%	5.3%	3.2%	2.1%	2.0%	4.7%	4.6%	5.5%	3.5%	4.8%

(Source: own illustration)

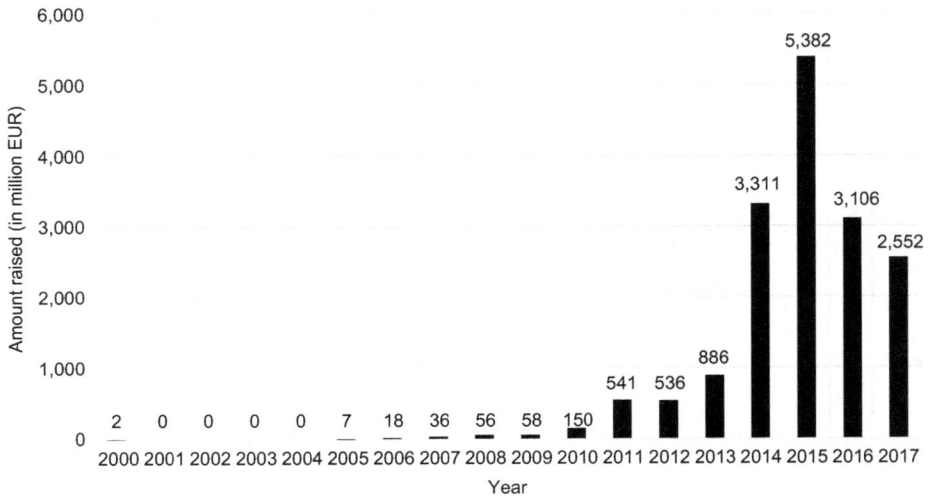

Figure 11.12: Annual overview of fintech funding amount in the U.S. for sample
April 2000–June 2017 (in € m).
(Source: own illustration)

which segments are still regarded to be attractive. Table 11.6 helps to identify the
trends of recent funding activity in the U.S.

With respect to trends in amounts raised in the U.S. for a specific segment, the
main message concerns deal activity as depicted in Table 11.6: alternative payment
methods were the forerunners in raising funds in the U.S. From 2005 to 2007, crowdlending had the largest share of annual amount raised, despite several deals also taking place in credit & factoring, PFM, infrastructure & IT and social trading. One may
thus conclude that crowdlending funding was well above the average compared to
the other segments, as it accounts for 37.5% of deals but at the same time constitutes
75.0% of all funds raised in 2007. In subsequent years the amount of robo-advice and
healthtech deals started to increase on the U.S. fintech market before all remaining
segments showed some deal activity by 2012. In the period from 2008 to 2012, alternative payment methods as well as credit & factoring secured above-average amounts
raised per round when comparing their deal share to the funding share. In most recent years the highest funding amount in relation to the number of deals was
achieved for healthtechs. This trend was also observable for the credit & factoring
segment.

Table 11.5: Percentage of each funding type series compared to overall amount raised in the U.S. for sample April 2000–June 2017.

Financing Round	2000	2001	2002	2003	2004	2005	2006	2007	2008	2009	2010	2011	2012	2013	2014	2015	2016	2017
Seed	0.0%	n/a	n/a	0.0%	n/a	18.6%	0.0%	0.0%	0.2%	5.8%	4.5%	1.3%	3.7%	5.5%	1.1%	0.5%	0.8%	0.3%
A	100.0%	n/a	n/a	100.0%	n/a	81.4%	0.0%	54.9%	22.7%	64.5%	22.7%	16.0%	7.4%	16.5%	9.3%	7.6%	12.0%	25.6%
B	0.0%	n/a	n/a	0.0%	n/a	0.0%	82.5%	0.0%	65.2%	16.3%	20.8%	28.1%	34.6%	20.1%	11.9%	15.4%	11.5%	9.6%
C	0.0%	n/a	n/a	0.0%	n/a	0.0%	0.0%	42.0%	0.0%	9.0%	41.2%	36.0%	5.5%	19.8%	18.1%	19.6%	20.3%	10.1%
D	0.0%	n/a	n/a	0.0%	n/a	0.0%	0.0%	0.0%	0.0%	0.0%	7.3%	9.8%	35.2%	9.3%	13.0%	11.1%	13.9%	14.2%
E	0.0%	n/a	n/a	0.0%	n/a	0.0%	0.0%	0.0%	0.0%	0.0%	0.0%	2.2%	5.8%	4.3%	5.6%	25.9%	14.0%	0.3%
F	0.0%	n/a	n/a	0.0%	n/a	0.0%	0.0%	0.0%	0.0%	0.0%	0.0%	0.0%	0.0%	0.0%	2.3%	2.2%	0.0%	18.5%
Angel	0.0%	n/a	n/a	0.0%	n/a	0.0%	0.0%	3.1%	11.8%	0.3%	0.0%	0.0%	0.0%	0.7%	0.0%	0.0%	0.0%	0.0%
Unknown	0.0%	n/a	n/a	0.0%	n/a	0.0%	17.5%	0.0%	0.0%	4.1%	3.6%	6.8%	7.8%	23.7%	12.7%	11.7%	23.6%	18.5%
IPO	0.0%	n/a	n/a	0.0%	n/a	0.0%	0.0%	0.0%	0.0%	0.0%	0.0%	0.0%	0.0%	0.0%	25.9%	5.9%	3.8%	3.0%

(Source: own illustration)

Table 11.6: Percentage of each fintech segment compared to overall amount raised in the U.S. for sample April 2000–June 2017.

Segment	2000	2001	2002	2003	2004	2005	2006	2007	2008	2009	2010	2011	2012	2013	2014	2015	2016	2017
Crowdfunding	0.0%	n/a	n/a	0.0%	n/a	0.0%	0.0%	0.0%	0.0%	0.0%	0.0%	0.3%	0.0%	0.1%	0.9%	1.0%	1.9%	3.1%
Crowdlending	0.0%	n/a	n/a	0.0%	n/a	81.4%	56.6%	75.0%	0.0%	16.3%	22.4%	5.4%	2.6%	20.3%	31.2%	2.8%	1.4%	0.0%
Credit & Factoring	0.0%	n/a	n/a	0.0%	n/a	0.0%	17.5%	0.0%	11.4%	1.8%	1.6%	13.6%	26.1%	17.1%	21.9%	43.9%	17.7%	38.8%
Social Trading	0.0%	n/a	n/a	0.0%	n/a	0.0%	0.0%	2.1%	7.4%	0.0%	0.0%	0.0%	0.0%	1.1%	0.0%	0.1%	0.0%	0.0%
Robo-Advice	0.0%	n/a	n/a	0.0%	n/a	0.0%	0.0%	0.0%	9.6%	9.2%	7.4%	5.3%	3.1%	8.4%	6.3%	3.3%	9.1%	5.5%
Personal Finance Management	0.0%	n/a	n/a	0.0%	n/a	0.0%	25.9%	0.0%	2.5%	12.0%	11.0%	9.5%	4.1%	8.8%	6.5%	4.8%	5.5%	5.3%
Savings	0.0%	n/a	n/a	0.0%	n/a	0.0%	0.0%	0.0%	0.0%	0.0%	0.0%	0.0%	0.0%	0.2%	0.0%	0.3%	0.0%	0.0%
Alternative Payment Methods	100.0%	n/a	n/a	100.0%	n/a	18.6%	0.0%	10.5%	44.6%	42.9%	42.9%	43.0%	57.1%	16.9%	17.3%	13.2%	18.4%	2.9%
Blockchain & Cryptocurrencies	0.0%	n/a	n/a	0.0%	n/a	0.0%	0.0%	0.0%	0.0%	0.0%	0.0%	0.0%	0.1%	3.5%	4.1%	2.9%	3.9%	5.2%
Comparison Sites & Search Engines	0.0%	n/a	n/a	0.0%	n/a	0.0%	0.0%	0.0%	0.0%	0.0%	0.0%	0.0%	0.2%	0.4%	0.0%	0.4%	1.0%	0.0%
Infrastructure & IT	0.0%	n/a	n/a	0.0%	n/a	0.0%	0.0%	12.4%	20.9%	11.1%	2.9%	11.3%	3.9%	11.6%	5.3%	5.9%	11.5%	7.4%
Insurtech	0.0%	n/a	n/a	0.0%	n/a	0.0%	0.0%	0.0%	0.0%	0.0%	2.0%	0.0%	1.0%	5.3%	1.2%	0.3%	8.9%	2.7%
Healthtech	0.0%	n/a	n/a	0.0%	n/a	0.0%	0.0%	0.0%	3.6%	0.0%	7.9%	10.3%	0.9%	5.3%	2.6%	9.3%	19.0%	27.7%
Others	0.0%	n/a	n/a	0.0%	n/a	0.0%	0.0%	0.0%	0.0%	6.7%	1.9%	1.4%	0.9%	1.1%	2.7%	11.9%	1.7%	1.4%

(Source: own illustration)

11.3 Patterns in funding size of successive financing rounds

The vast majority of fintechs raises up to €2.5 million in the seed round and as much as €10.0 million in the subsequent financing round A. All apart from nine fintechs raised at most €5.0 million in the seed round, before raising up to €30.0 million in the following round. One striking element is that alternative payment methods account for three of these larger A-rounds between €24.7 million and €28.8 million after seed investments varying from €0.4 million to €2.8 million.

Out of the nine outliers, the credit & factoring segment achieved the highest amount raised in financing round A with €32.8 million, after having initially raised €1.2 million in the seed round. In contrast to that, one alternative payment methods fintech collected an impressive €19.2 million of seed capital, while then only raising €3.8 million in round A. Two out of the nine outliers are related to insurtechs, meaning that this segment is less predictable in terms of capital raising in the seed stage and financing round A.

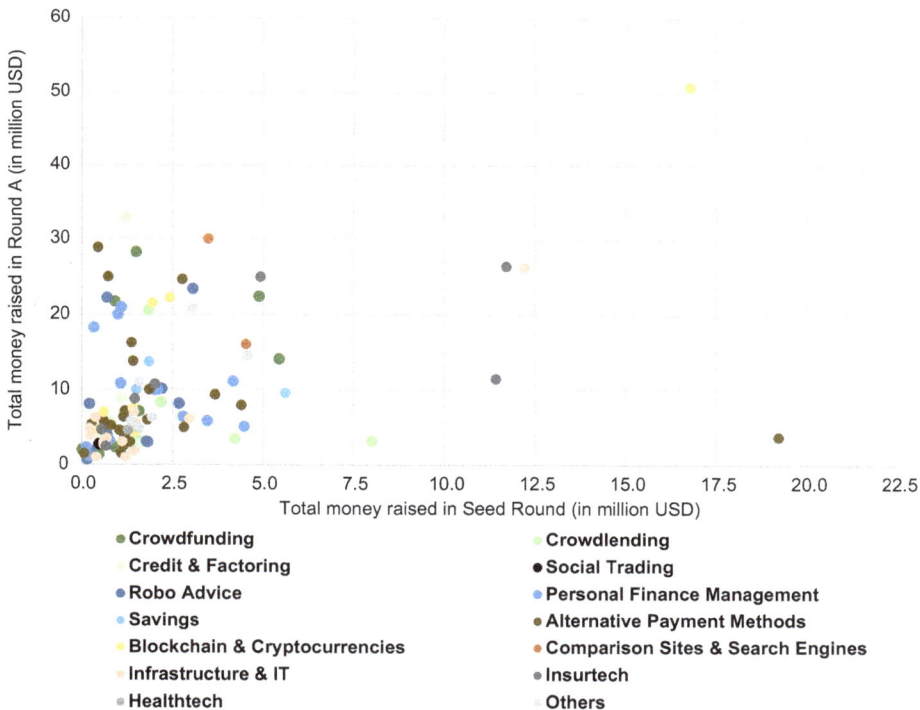

Figure 11.13: Comparison of total money raised between seed round and financing round A for sample April 2000–June 2017, *n* = 104 (in € m).
(Source: own illustration)

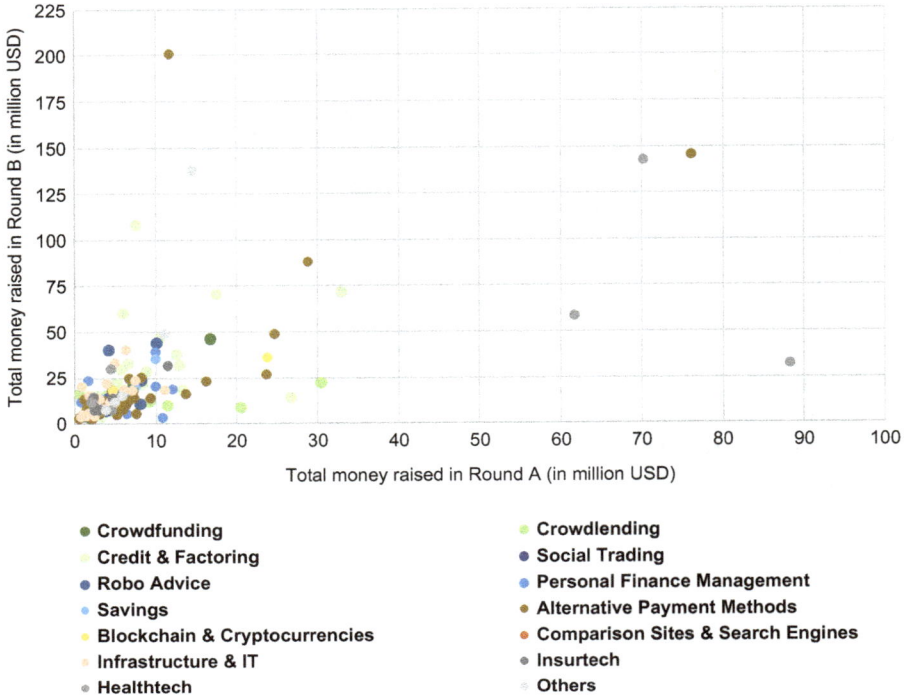

Figure 11.14: Comparison of total money raised between financing rounds A and B for sample April 2000–June 2017, *n* = 146 (in € m).
(Source: own illustration)

Comparison between financing rounds A and B

Most of the fintech start-ups raise up to €10.0 million in financing round A and €40.0 million in the following round B. However, as depicted in Figure 11.13, the number of fintechs that raise an amount that is outside of the range of the majority of fintechs significantly increases in comparison to the seed round and financing round A. For instance, the number of outliers rises from nine in the seed and A-round, equaling 8.6% of the sample, to 30 for the financing rounds A and B (20.5% of the sample). Consequently, one finding is that deviations increase over time. Within the outliers, one fintech in alternative payment methods managed to raise €200.6 million in financing round B after receiving €11.7 million of funds in the prior round. This amounts to growth in amount raised of more than 1,714% from one round to the other (see Figure 11.14). Based on the underlying sample, outliers can particularly be found in alternative payment methods and credit & factoring, with seven outliers each. This suggests that investors are willing to invest more money in the aforementioned segments compared to other segments if they believe in the business model.

Alternative payment methods, credit & factoring and robo-advice are the three segments that have the largest number of outliers compared to the general observable pattern of successive financing rounds. Hence, the conclusion is that investors in these segments more closely follow the development of the respective fintech and challenge the business model more profoundly. Consequently, they are willing to invest more if the business looks promising but will also not hesitate as much as in other segments to cut funding if major obstacles arise.

Fintech segments with the highest funding

Figure 11.15 illustrates the relationship between maximum money raised in a financing round and the accumulated pre-money valuation per company foundation location in the period 2017 until April 2020. The figure compares the accumulated pre-money valuation for fintechs and the highest funding for one single financing round for different world regions. In this observation for recent years, China leads in both criteria followed by a group including the U.S., Europe and India. South America follows at a distance and Africa is even further behind. With Ant Financial, China also

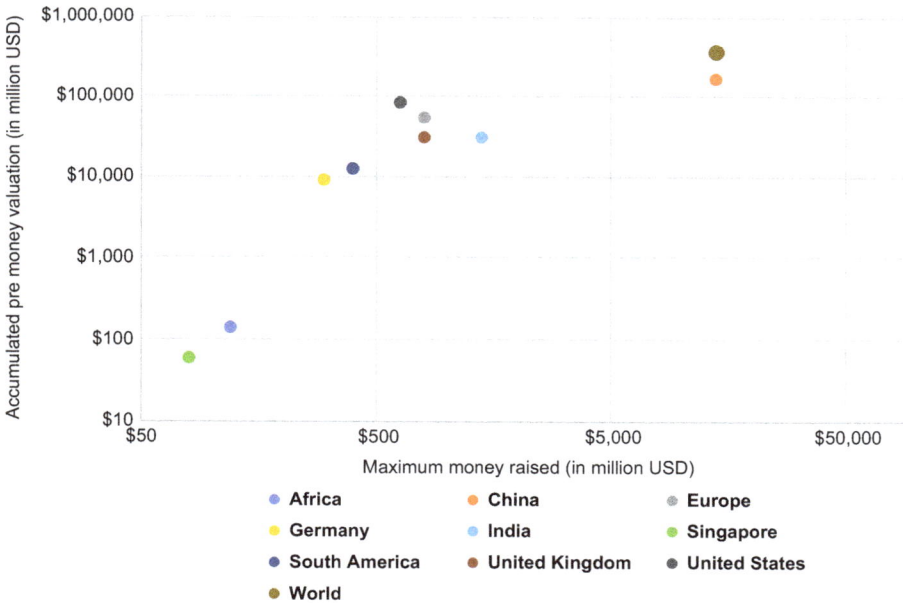

Figure 11.15: Comparison between accumulated pre-money valuation and maximum money raised per company foundation location for sample January 2017–April 2020 (in USD m). (Source: own illustration with data from Crunchbase 2020e)

has the fintech company with the highest pre-money valuation of $136 billion as well as the highest financing amount for a single round with $14 billion. Nevertheless, it must be pointed out that the publicly available data for venture capital investments in China is limited to a few transactions only. We can see trends in financing and differences between fintech business segments. But the data available for the U.S. and for Europe is statistically much more significant and therefore more reliable for systematic comparisons of venture capital financing patterns.

The ranking of the highest funding amounts includes the highest amount of funding during the observation period, the median amount raised and the median difference between successive financing rounds. In addition to that, the frequency of mega rounds is analyzed for financing rounds with a minimum of €50.0 million. The analyses of the three indicators involving the median exclude financing rounds E and F as well as IPOs. A scorecard aggregates the results to determine the best segment in terms of funding, based on the underlying data. The overall number of financing rounds per segment and the total amount raised in million EUR per segment are the two key metrics for the identification of the segment with the highest funding (see Table 11.7).

Out of the approximately 1,100 financing rounds in the underlying data, 241 fintechs can be allocated to alternative payment methods, making it the segment that has closed most financing rounds according to the underlying data. The second-most financing rounds are closed in credit & factoring (166 deals), followed by infrastructure & IT (154 deals). In contrast to that, social trading and comparison sites & search engines only closed 17 and 15 funding rounds during the same period. This means that roughly 16 times more financing rounds have been closed for alternative payment methods than for comparison sites & search engines.

Shifting the focus toward the total amount raised, it becomes apparent that the top two fintech segments in terms of financing rounds also lead in this area, as €5,730.8 million were raised in credit & factoring and €4,965.9 million in alternative payment methods. Credit & factoring fintechs raised approximately €765.0 million more than their counterparts in alternative payment methods, despite closing fewer financing rounds (166 vs. 241). This implies that the average amount raised in credit & factoring is significantly higher than in the payments segment. Comparison sites & search engine fintechs managed to raise €32.3 million more than social trading fintechs, even though these fintechs closed two more financing rounds. This once again suggests that comparison sites & search engines managed to secure a higher average amount raised in comparison to social trading.

Table 11.7: Number of financing rounds and total amount (in € m) raised per segment for sample April 2000–June 2017.

Segment	Number of financing rounds	Total amount raised (in million EUR)
Crowdfunding	39	321.4
Crowdlending	68	2,517.9
Credit & Factoring	166	5,730.8
Social Trading	17	100.0
Robo-Advice	93	1,115.6
Personal Finance Management	126	1,447.4
Savings	24	255.9
Alternative Payment Methods	241	4,965.9
Blockchain & Cryptocurrencies	45	656.4
Comparison Sites & Search Engines	15	132.3
Infrastructure & IT	154	2,407.4
Insurtech	55	675.5
Healthtech	24	2,005.5
Others	29	856.3
Total	**1,096**	**23,188.4**

(Source: own illustration)

Mega funding rounds

The annual split of mega rounds for each segment since 2010 is depicted in Table 11.8. No prior years are shown in this table because no data on mega rounds could be gathered for the time before 2010. The overview on mega rounds shows that financing rounds of €50.0 million or more were not very frequent until 2014, since only a total of seven mega rounds were closed during the time period from 2010 to 2013. Prior to that, no mega rounds could be seen in the underlying data. The deal count of mega rounds experienced a massive jump in 2014 when 24 of these financing rounds were closed in light of the booming fintech market, in particular in terms of funding. This momentum was maintained in 2015, as the number of mega deals rose to 37. In the subsequent year, the deal count for these mega rounds cooled down significantly to 17 deals, mainly driven by less deals in credit & factoring (down nine deals compared to prior year), crowdlending (down four deals), alternative payment methods and others (down three deals each). However, as fintechs become more mature, mega rounds will become more necessary in the future.

Five out of the first seven financing rounds in the observed time frame come from credit & factoring and alternative payment methods. Credit & factoring fintechs closed 24 financing rounds of €50.0 million or more, and companies in the alternative payment methods segment closed 23. One possible explanation for the strong frequency of mega rounds in the two segments could be that competition is greater than in other segments. This results in the necessity to raise large amounts more often to invest in growth and hence limit the attractiveness for other fintechs to enter the segment, or to eliminate existing competition as scalability is reached faster. Fintechs operating in the segments of social trading or comparison sites & searches did not manage to close a mega round. The reasons could be an unprofitable level of risk and return for the equity investor or less capital-intensive business models.

Table 11.8: Mega rounds per segment for sample April 2000–June 2017.

Segment	2010	2011	2012	2013	2014	2015	2016	2017	Total
Crowdfunding	0	0	0	0	0	0	0	1	1
Crowdlending	0	0	0	1	3	4	0	1	9
Credit & Factoring	1	0	1	0	6	10	1	5	24
Social Trading	0	0	0	0	0	0	0	0	0
Robo-Advice	0	0	0	0	1	1	2	1	5
Personal Finance Management	0	0	0	0	2	3	0	3	8
Savings	0	0	0	0	0	0	1	0	1
Alternative Payment Methods	0	2	1	0	7	8	5	0	23
Blockchain & Cryptocurrencies	0	0	0	0	1	1	2	1	5
Comparison Sites & Search Engines	0	0	0	0	0	0	0	0	0
Infrastructure & IT	0	0	0	0	3	3	2	2	10
Insurtech	0	0	0	0	0	0	1	0	1
Healthtech	0	1	0	0	1	4	3	3	12
Others	0	0	0	0	0	3	0	0	3
Total	1	3	2	1	24	37	17	17	102

(Source: own illustration)

Fintech ranking by financing scorecard

Table 11.9 illustrates the average score for each segment to ultimately determine which segment achieves the highest funding. The results are ranked from 1 to 14,

Table 11.9: Financing scorecard for fintechs for sample April 2000–June 2017.

Segment	Amount raised	Number of deals	Median amount raised					Number of mega rounds	Median percentage change in amount raised				Median difference in years				Score
			Seed	A	B	C	D		Seed/A	A/B	B/C	C/D	Seed/A	A/B	B/C	C/D	
Crowdfunding	11	9	12	6	13	2	11	10	10	6	13	11	13	2	6	11	9.13
Crowdlending	3	6	2	11	8	12	9	5	14	13	9	10	11	4	7	4	8.00
Credit & Factoring	1	2	10	8	3	5	3	1	3	3	8	2	2	8	4	7	4.38
Social Trading	14	13	14	14	14	14	8	13	5	1	14	1	12	14	5	10	10.38
Robo-Advice	7	5	3	13	7	10	4	7	7	2	11	3	9	7	12	2	6.81
Personal Finance Management	6	4	11	9	10	9	1	6	9	9	3	4	1	9	13	1	6.56
Savings	12	11	5	5	2	6	11	11	2	8	12	11	5	5	9	11	7.88
Alternative Payment Methods	2	1	8	10	6	13	6	2	6	11	4	7	10	10	10	5	6.94
Blockchain & Cryptocurrencies	10	8	7	3	5	3	11	8	1	7	1	11	8	12	3	11	6.81
Comparison Sites & Search Engines	13	14	1	2	12	11	10	13	4	12	10	9	7	11	2	6	8.56
Infrastructure & IT	4	3	13	12	11	7	7	4	11	4	7	6	14	13	11	9	8.50
Insurtech	9	7	6	4	9	4	5	12	8	5	2	8	3	1	8	3	5.88
Healthtech	5	12	9	1	1	1	2	3	13	14	6	5	6	6	1	8	5.81
Others	8	10	4	7	4	8	11	9	12	10	5	11	4	3	14	11	8.19

(Source: own illustration)

with one indicating the best result in a category. In case two or more segments have the same result in one category, they are allocated the same number in the ranking. In the event of one or several segments having no value in a certain category, they are automatically put in shared last place in the individual ranking. Consequently, it is possible that the last place in the ranking is not represented by number 14 but by number 11, for example.

Table 11.9 clearly shows that credit & factoring is the segment that secures the highest level of funding based on the selection criteria with an average score of 4.38. Healthtechs are positioned second with an average score of 5.88, mainly due to their strong performance in the category "median amount raised." Insurtechs rank third, which is related to the aspect that their performance was not really poor anywhere, except for in the category "number of mega rounds." In strong contrast to the three aforementioned segments, social trading is the lowest-ranked segment with regard to funding. This is shown by the fact that it is the only segment that has a double-digit average score (10.38). Alternative payment methods only rank seventh with a score of 6.94. This is surprising as they ranked best in "number of deals" and held second positions in "overall amount raised" as well as "number of mega rounds." However, the funding statistics of fintechs operating in this segment were comparably poor in the three median categories, especially the median difference in years between financing rounds and median amount raised.

11.4 Features of Fintech Valuation

Fintechs with the highest valuation

The valuation analysis was based on a total of 136 financing rounds in which valuations were publicly disclosed. The median valuation of all segments for each financing round was determined and compared. Table 11.10 illustrates the median valuation per segment for each financing round and acquisition. No information on the valuation could be obtained for social trading and comparison sites & search engines.

In the seed round, blockchain & cryptocurrencies accomplished the highest median valuation with €5.8 million. This is almost five times as much as the median valuation for PFM fintechs, which rank lowest among all segments. Likewise, the median of robo-advisors is substantially higher than the bulk of other fintech valuations in the seed round, amounting to €4.4 million. The robo valuation increases sevenfold in financing round A, as the median stands at €31.2 million. Robo-advisor fintechs rank in the middle of all valuations in the A-rounds. Alternative payment methods have a median valuation of €416.6 million. When comparing the valuation of alternative payment methods in financing round B to round A, it becomes apparent that the value increases approximately fivefold (see Table 11.10).

Table 11.10: Median valuation per segment per funding type series for sample April 2000–June 2017 (in € m).

Segment	Seed	A	B	C	D	E	F	IPO	Acquisition
Crowdfunding	n/a	n/a	n/a	709.8	n/a	n/a	n/a	n/a	50.0
Crowdlending	n/a	12.8	39.2	75.4	170.4	732.8	2,760.6	7,003.5	n/a
Credit & Factoring	2.1	169.0	173.1	572.2	925.9	1,757.4	4,064.4	640.3	n/a
Social Trading	n/a	n/a	n/a	n/a	n/a	n/a	n/a	n/a	n/a
Robo-Advice	4.4	31.2	n/a	647.3	473.8	553.8	n/a	n/a	73.2
Personal Finance Management	1.2	5.5	56.3	156.2	3,086.0	n/a	n/a	n/a	229.0
Savings	n/a	30.0	125.0	n/a	n/a	n/a	n/a	150.0	n/a
Alternative Payment Methods	n/a	54.0	394.8	860.9	743.4	4,526.5	n/a	3,950.2	250.1
Blockchain & Cryptocurrencies	5.8	n/a	n/a	n/a	n/a	n/a	n/a	n/a	n/a
Comparison Sites & Search Engines	n/a	n/a	n/a	n/a	n/a	n/a	n/a	n/a	n/a
Infrastructure & IT	1.4	7.6	58.7	309.0	231.2	80.6	224.9	2,515.2	180.0
Insurtech	1.8	8.1	22.3	n/a	n/a	n/a	n/a	n/a	n/a
Healthtech	n/a	2,494.0	584.0	1,388.1	1,362.3	n/a	n/a	n/a	n/a
Others	n/a	n/a	416.6	4,097.7	n/a	n/a	n/a	n/a	n/a
Sample size *n*	10	15	22	20	18	9	3	9	20

(Source: own illustration)

The highest multiplication of the valuation can be observed for PFM fintechs, as it increases from €5.5 million to €56.3, implying a median increase of 924% (see Table 11.10). Due to this strong growth, PFM left the last rank of the previous financing rounds to insurtechs. Unfortunately, the evolution of the median valuation of insurtechs can not be assessed in further financing rounds as no more public information was available. In the subsequent financing round C, crowdlending therefore ranks last with a median valuation of €75.4 million. It should be noted that the valuation did not even double in comparison to the previous round.

In the credit & factoring segment, the median valuation jumped from €925.9 million in financing round D to €4,064.4 million in financing round F, implying a growth of 334%. This is not surprising, as these financing rounds are used for growth and the achievement of scalability. In the crowdlending segment, the median valuation jumped from €170.4 million in round D to €2,760.6 million in round F, suggesting that growth targets were achieved. In crowdlending, the development of the valuation of a single fintech is included in the form of Lending Club, where the valuations from financing rounds A to F as well as the IPO were available. It is in fact the company that accomplished the highest valuation in this table as it was valued at more than €7.0 billion at its IPO.

Alternative payment methods are another segment that achieved high valuations during an IPO. This is supported by the two IPOs in this segment with a median value of the companies of approximately €4.0 billion. In strong contrast to that, the one IPO that took place in the savings segment valued the company at only €150.0 million. Furthermore, when comparing the median valuations of acquired fintechs, alternative payment methods appear to secure the highest valuation. These fintechs manage to achieve roughly five times higher valuations than their crowdfunding counterparts, which rank last with a median valuation of €50.0 million.

It can be said that PFM and crowdlending generally achieve the lowest valuations in early stage financing rounds. However, both segments seem to be valued much higher once they reach a certain scalability, as evidenced by the impressive IPO valuation of Lending Club. Credit & factoring and alternative payment method fintechs achieved valuations at the upper end of the range in most financing rounds, indicating that investors saw a lot of growth potential from the start.

Example valuation of robo-advisory with EV/AUM multiples

Table 11.11 depicts the EV/AUM multiples gathered for five financing rounds and one acquisition in the robo segment. The enterprise values originated from the sources of the research study, while the historical AUM figures originated from the historical archive of investment advisor reports, published by the SEC. The EV/AUM multiples for robo-advisory fintechs varied from 0.17x to 4.03x.

Table 11.11: EV/AUM multiples robo-advisor segment.

Date	Company	Financing Round	EV (in million EUR)	AuM (in million EUR)	EV/AuM
Oct-14	Wealthfront	D	700.0	1,548.8	0.45x
Feb-15	Betterment	D	450.0	1,400.3	0.32x
Apr-15	Acorns	C	106.0	26.3	4.03x
Aug-15	FutureAdvisor	Acquisition	152.0	600.0	0.25x
Mar-16	Betterment	E	700.0	4,037.1	0.17x
Dec-16	Personal Capital	E	500.0	2,853.5	0.18x
				Median	**0.29x**

(Source: own illustration)

The 4.03x EV/AUM multiple of acorns in financing round C is driven by the very low AUM number of 26.3 million. Hence, this deal can clearly be categorized as an outlier. The adjusted range therefore goes from 0.17x to 0.45x. The median valuation in the robo-advice area amounts to 0.29x of AUM. The EV/AUM multiples then become smaller for later stage financing rounds. For instance, this is evidenced by Betterment, where the round D multiple amounted to 0.32x, whereas the following round E multiple stood at only 0.17x. Robo-advisors generally strive for exponential growth in AUM. Consequently, the EV/AUM multiple declined, despite a jump of €250.0 million in absolute valuation and an almost tripling of AUM within one year.

Fintech valuation with unicorn status and median time

Table 11.12 illustrates the median time of fintechs in one segment to achieve unicorn status, meaning a valuation of $1.0 billion or more. The table also shows the number of unicorns as well as the number of deals. The median time of all the 25 fintechs to achieve unicorn valuation status is seven years. Fintechs in the segment "others" achieved this milestone the quickest, with a median time of three years. The second rank goes to robo-advice, where fintechs required a median of four years to be valued at $1.0 billion or more. It must be taken into account that the median of robo-advice is only based on a single fintech, which is why the result should rather be considered as an indication and not as an outcome with statistical significance.

Credit & factoring fintechs are ranked third, requiring a median of 5.5 years to reach the respective milestone. Infrastructure & IT fintechs need the longest time to accomplish unicorn status, as the median stands at 11.5 years. This is approximately 65% longer than the overall median. The segment of alternative payment methods accounts for six unicorns in the underlying database and is thus the best segment in that regard, followed by crowdlending with five unicorns, and credit & factoring and healthtech with four fintechs each. However, no unicorns could be recorded for 6 out of the 14 segments, including crowdfunding and insurtechs.

Table 11.12: Median time until unicorn valuation status per segment for sample April 2000–June 2017.

Segment	Time in years	Number of unicorns	Number of deals with a valuation
Overall	7.00	25	136
Crowdfunding	n/a	0	2
Crowdlending	8.00	5	11
Credit & Factoring	5.50	4	16
Social Trading	n/a	0	0
Robo-Advice	4.00	1	12
Personal Finance Management	8.00	1	18
Savings	n/a	0	3
Alternative Payment Methods	7.00	6	35
Blockchain & Cryptocurrencies	n/a	0	4
Comparison Sites & Search Engines	n/a	0	0
Infrastructure & IT	11.50	2	20
Insurtech	n/a	0	3
Healthtech	5.50	4	7
Others	3.00	2	5

(Source: own illustration)

Credit & factoring and alternative payment methods are the two segments most likely to secure a high valuation, as these segments are among the upper 25% of median valuations and also displayed a median time until unicorn status that is lower than the overall median (credit & factoring) or in line with the overall median (alternative payment methods).

Summary

Out of 1,096 financing rounds in the underlying data, 241 fintechs can be allocated to alternative payment methods and 166 to credit & factoring. Credit & factoring as well as alternative payment methods are also the fintech segments that have secured high valuations and the highest funding. They have also managed to reach unicorn status in a relatively short time. The median time of the 25 fintechs to achieve unicorn valuation status is seven years. The example of multiples valuation for robo-advisory shows that multiples are decreasing, which could be a sign of lower growth prospects than originally assumed. Nevertheless, the valuation multiples are still very high, which is why venture capitalists generally must pay high prices. PFM and crowdlending achieved the lowest valuation in early stage financing rounds but have significantly higher valuations once a status of scalability is reached. The majority of fintechs raised up to €2.5 million in the seed round and as much as €10.0 million in the subsequent financing round A.

Investors in the U.S. face an increasingly mature market, with late stage financing rounds as well as several exits through IPOs. New investors could either try to invest in one of the late stage financing rounds, which would eventually mean a lower return on investment (ROI) in comparison to an early stage investment, or invest in one of the new start-ups, where the chance of having a sustainable business model in a niche is low but would yield a higher ROI in case of survival. European investors are considered to have more options because the market is less mature and still offers niches for early stage financing rounds.

12 Conclusion: What we can know and can not know about the future of fintechs

Fintech strategy in banking: Collaborate, invest or develop in-house

Global financial managers always try to increase the return on equity and cost-income ratio for their companies.[485] As a consequence, banks have implemented many different instruments of value-based management in the past but not with a focus on technology.[486] The financial sector's future cooperation with technology partners and customers is essential for the value creation of banks. On the one hand, financial institutions want to gain access to data processing and data analysis tools, while on the other hand, the new services to be set up must be developed and improved in cooperation with customers. Traditional players, such as banks, basically have three options on how to deal with fintechs: collaborate with fintechs, acquire fintechs or develop in-house fintech solutions.[487]

Market entry in China is still possible but a few fintech players already dominate the market. The company valuations are too high for acquisitions and therefore the only entry options to the Chinese fintech market are collaboration or own product development. The postponed IPO of Ant Financial in November 2020 shows that the Chinese government intends to implement stricter regulatory processes for fintechs. Fintechs in China could face the same regulatory environment as banks.

The European fintech market, where the deal count has risen constantly while funding has varied at comparably high levels from 2014 until 2019, is still receptive for innovate business models across all segments. However, this still bears the opportunity of non-sustainable fintechs entering or already operating in the European market, as the natural selection due to predatory competition has not yet separated the fintechs with a sustainable business model in a certain niche from the fintechs that could struggle in the long run. Consequently, investing in or acquiring a fintech is an option but the underlying risk appears high.

Nevertheless, there are obviously well established fintechs in Europe, such as the payment fintechs Adyen, Klarna and TransferWise or the robo-advisor Nutmeg. These companies have already achieved high valuations, resulting in the fact that banks would have to invest large sums to obtain a small stake in the respective fintech. Collaboration with a fintech or developing an in-house solution could therefore be the more appropriate approaches, as valuations are already very high. The

---

485 Mitsyk and Fischer 2019.
486 Fischer 2004; Fischer and Tournois 2008.
487 The choice of strategy is e.g. discussed by McCarthy and Mills 2017.

https://doi.org/10.1515/9783110704907-012

decision as to whether a bank should opt for a collaboration or an in-house solution is mainly influenced by the budgetary constraints as well as the urgency to have the product ready for use. Ultimately, as long as valuations are relatively high, collaboration is a suitable option in the European fintech market.

The U.S. fintech market is regarded to be in a more mature stage than the European market. As a result, stronger consolidation is expected in the near future. Due to this consolidation, there will be fewer collaboration opportunities as the fintechs themselves get bigger. Nevertheless, in some areas such as alternative payment methods, collaborations might still make sense in order to reach even more customers. Investments in a fintech are most likely associated with high costs, since the fintechs operating in a maturing market have proven to eliminate competitors with inferior business models. Despite that, fintech acquisitions and not only investments in minority shares could possibly guarantee a competitive advantage if the integration into the bank is managed successfully. In-house solutions could be a valid alternative to an investment or acquisition due to the fact that banks are aware of the increasing maturity of the fintech market in the U.S. and thus fintechs would need to collaborate to reach a broader customer base and scalability.

What we can know about the future of fintechs

Not all fintechs will survive. In our empirical study we analyzed more than 2,000 financing rounds for worldwide venture capital funding with a focus on Europe, the U.S. and China. And of course, at the time this book is published, large fintechs will still exist but several of the small and young fintechs will not have survived. But that is statistically normal for the general evolution of start-ups. Many small and young fintechs will be taken over by competitors or banks. Others will be liquidated in case they do not meet the expectations of the venture capital investors.

The global success potential of fintechs in the area of payments has been underestimated by the traditional banks. The example of Paypal or Alipay dominating the online payment markets in many countries shows that incumbants must take new market entrants more seriously. Because, once the fintechs succeed it will be exceedingly difficult to get back market share. Also, the area of credit & factoring has been one of the most successful fintech segments in terms of getting venture capital. In contrast, so far the future market potentials and growth rates of other fintech segments, like robo advisory or crowdfunding, have been overestimated. And fintechs in the area of social trading will probably stay niche players. Blockchain fintechs will still need several years to establish themselves in the financial industry but they have the potential to sustainably change the financial world. Cryptocurrencies or tokens that keep pace with technological as well as legal developments will complement classical means of payment and traditional asset classes in the long term. Venture capital investments in fintechs developing AI applications have increased strongly in recent years.

We understand the business models of fintechs quite well, as we have shown in the systematically applied Business Model Canvas in this book. Although the content of the key components of the Business Model Canvas is different from fintech segment to fintech segment, our analysis has shown similarities within the segments and across the fintech segments. Often the key partners are regulatory authorities, the onboarding of clients is done online, key resources are dominated by algorithms or software and the sales channels are online or mobile apps. But the key partners of each fintech business model also depend on the specific products and services offered; the value propositions are totally different as are the customer relationships or the customer segments. The only real common feature across all different fintech segments is technology such as software, analytical tools and data processing. Besides technology, the fintech segments require different activities because of the different products and services. Only the large fintech companies like Ant Financial have proven that they can successfully penetrate different financial product areas.

The results of our empirical study show that the fintech market in the U.S. is more mature in comparison to the European market – hence the larger average funding or a higher number of bigger-sized deals. The median time taken by all fintechs analyzed in our empirical study in Europe and the U.S. to achieve unicorn valuation status is seven years. The venture capital market for the financing of fintechs in Europe and the U.S. was in an early phase from 2000 until 2009. In 2010 the venture capital volume and the number of financing rounds registered particularly strong growth, which inceased even further from 2014 until the beginning of 2020 when the COVID-19 crisis also affected the fintech area. But the great advantage of fintechs in the post coronavirus time will be that worldwide the digital economy will play an even more relevant role and therefore technology-focused fintechs will have competitive advantages.

What we can not know about the future of fintechs

It is difficult to predict which specific fintech company will be successful in the future. Nobody was able to forecast the triumphant growth path of Paypal, Alipay and WeChat Pay. And many professional forecasts by experts overestimated growth rates for fintechs in crowdfunding or robo advisory. It is not easy to recognize early in the start-up cycle who will dominate future markets and therefore incumbants are wise to closely monitor the market and stay invested in a portfolio of several fintech companies. But our empirical data of historical venture capital rounds for fintechs shows that certain fintech sectors are more successful with venture capitalists than others. Good data analysis of the financing of fintechs with venture capital will therefore give us valuable hints as to what will be the winner and loser segments.

Several technologies used or offered by fintechs are not in a mature status. With the future acceptance of a common blockchain platform by several important market players, the traditional capital providers or intermediaries could theoretically be completely disrupted. But incumbents might not be interested in changing the existing market standards as the status quo generates revenues for their businesses which could be in danger in the case of technological change. Financial regulators might not allow all theoretical potentials for change due to a lack of experience with the respective technology. Clients could have a problem with the acceptance of contracts that are executed automatically and can not be changed even if errors are discovered at a later stage. The book also covered examples of AI and big data in the area of banking. We discussed existing, exciting forms of AI applied in the forms of machine learning, service chatbots or contract intelligence. But although the integration of AI in financial services started a few years ago, the applications are still very basic and we can only speculate about the future impact on consulting services in the financial sector or on capital markets. All theoretically possible new functions based on innovative technology still have to be tested and to demonstrate that they can cope with regulatory issues as well as the liability for potential errors.

Last but not least

The book covered fintech cases from Europe, the U.S. and China. The biggest fintechs are based in China and it is assumed that in the future China will try to defend its leading position ahead of U.S. fintechs. Europe still lags behind but also counts smaller yet numerous successful fintechs. It remains to be seen in the future and it is questionable whether big techs will really want to enter the banking business, as the returns from projects outside the regulated financial market are currently significantly higher. Big techs will only use the banking business as long as they do not have to come under the umbrella of regulation. So it has not yet been decided whether Alibaba, WeChat, Amazon, Apple, Facebook, Google or Microsoft want to enter the banking business in order to generate a substantial part of income. For many years, the global financial community has discussed the quote from Bill Gates who said that "banking is necessary, banks are not." But banks are still alive to this day. And despite future technological changes, banks will be necessary as long as financial regulators demand a banking license for banking business. Fintechs can grow fast up to a certain point outside of the regulatory umbrella. However, for growth potentials above certain levels, fintechs will have to go under the regulatory umbrella. Fintechs are necessary, banks too.

List of figures

https://doi.org/10.1515/9783110704907-013

List of tables

https://doi.org/10.1515/9783110704907-014

Abbreviations

AAAfx	Triple A Experts
AI	Artificial Intelligence
API	Application Programming Interface
APMs	Alternative Payment Methods
ATM	Automatic Teller Machine
AUM	Assets under Management
B2B	Business-to-Business
B2C	Business-to-Consumer
BaFin	German Federal Financial Supervisory Authority
BoA	Bank of America
BTC	Bitcoin
CAGR	Compound Annual Growth Rate
CAPM	Capital Asset Pricing Model
CFD	Contract for Differences
CTA	Commodities Trading Advisor
COiN	Contract Intelligence
DAOs	Decentralized Autonomous Organizations
DCF	Discounted Cash Flow
ESMA	European Securities and Markets Authority
ETC	Ethereum Classic
ETF	Exchange-Traded Fund
ETH	Ethereum
ETP	Exchange-Traded Products
EUR	Euro
EV	Enterprise Value
FCA	Financial Conduct Authority
FDIC	Federal Deposit Insurance Corporation
Forex	Foreign Exchange Market
FICO	Fair Isaac and Company
FY	Fiscal Year
GAFA	Google, Apple, Facebook and Amazon
GewO	Trade Regulation Germany (Gewerbeordnung)
GmbH	Limited Company
HWM	High Watermark
ICO	Initial Coin Offering
IoT	Internet of things
IOUs	I Owe You
IPO	Initial Public Offering
IT	Information Technology
KYC	Know Your Customer
MiFID	Markets in Financial Instruments Directive
NFA	National Futures Association
NFC	Near Field Communication
OTC	Over the Counter
P2P	Person-to-Person
PBC	Public Benefit Cooperation
PFM	Personal Finance Management

https://doi.org/10.1515/9783110704907-015

Pips	Percentage in Points
PSD-2	Payment Services Directive 2
POS	Point of Sale
PoW	Proof of Work
Q&A	Questions and Answers
R&D	Research and Development
ROE	Return on Equity
ROI	Return on Investment
REIT	Real Estate Investment Trust
RMB	Renminbi (Chinese currency)
SEC	Securities and Exchange Commission
SEK	Swedish Cronar (currency)
SPV	Special Purpose Vehicle
SMB	Small and Medium Business
SME	Small and Medium Enterprises
TACO	Total Cost of Ownership
TER	Total Expense Ratio
TPV	Total Payment Volume
U.K.	United Kingdom
U.S.	United States
USD	US Dollar
USP	Unique Selling Proposition
VAS	Value-Added Services
VC	Venture Capital
VermAnlG	German Capital Investment Act (Vermögensanlagengesetz)
WACC	Weighted Average Cost of Capital
YOY	Year-over-Year

Glossary

AI *Artificial Intelligence*

Alternative payment methods Online systems that enable consumers to manage digital wallets and use mobile devices with biometrics for payments.

Angel Investor Wealthy private investor for start-up companies. The investor expects ownership in the company and the investment is done at a very early financing phase of the company.

API *Application Programming Interface*

Application Programming Interface (API) A computing interface, a program part of a software for other programs to connect to the software.

Artificial Intelligence (AI) Machine or software that tries to copy human behavior regarding learning and problem solving.

Asset manager A company that offers investment products, discusses and determines the individual investment strategy, and executes the rebalancing of the asset classes for clients.

Assets under management (AUM) The volume of client funds that a company or individual manages.

AUM *Assets under management*

Average Value calculated by dividing the sum of the values in a data set by the number of values, also called mean.

B2B *Business-to-Business*

B2C *Business-to-Consumer*

Big data A method of collecting, storing, processing, and analyzing masses of data, beyond the size, capacity, and capability of traditional database and software tools.

Bitcoin The first electronic peer-to-peer blockchain-based cash system and cryptocurrency.

Business-to-Business (B2B) Business relationship between two or more companies.

Business-to-Consumer (B2C) Business relationship between a company and private individuals.

CAGR *Compound Annual Growth Rate*

CAPM *Capital Asset Pricing Model*

Compound Annual Growth Rate (CAGR) Average annual growth rate of an initial value over several years.

Capital Asset Pricing Model (CAPM) Financial model that provides the expected returns for assets with different risks.

CFD *Contract for Differences*

Chatbot AI implementation designed to simulate a conversation via text or voice with a user.

Crowddonating Funding method where a large number of individuals receive no financial or material compensation for providing donations to the beneficiaries.

https://doi.org/10.1515/9783110704907-016

Crowdfunding Funding method where a large number of individual investors can receive different forms of return for contributing with relatively small amounts of money to provide funding for private and business purposes.

COiN *Contract Intelligence*

Commodities Trading The trading of futures contracts, options on futures, retail off-exchange Forex contracts, or swaps. The traded commodities can be, for example, oil, gold, silver, cotton or sugar.

Contract for Differences (CFD) An agreement between a buyer and a seller to exchange the difference in the amount between the price of an underlying asset as of the date of settlement and the initial price fixed in the contract.

Contract Intelligence (COiN) Software for automated document review based on unsupervised machine learning using language recognition.

Cryptocurrency Virtual currency or digital asset for payments operating independently from central banks, e.g. Bitcoin.

Crypto exchanges Online platforms that enable merchants, consumers, and traders to trade cryptocurrencies and tokens.

Crypto wallet Device, physical object, or software storing the public and private key as an account; used to execute payments in a cryptocurrency network.

DCF *Discounted Cash Flow method*

Discounted Cash Flow method (DCF) A company valuation method used for estimating the present value of an investment based on its future cash flows and risk profile.

Enterprise Value (EV) The value of a company as the sum of market value of equity plus the market value of debt.

ETF *Exchange-Traded Fund*

EV *Enterprise Value*

Exchange-Traded Fund (ETF) A financial asset or security designed to track other securities of an underlying index. An ETF replicates an index of stocks, bonds, currencies or commodities.

Factoring In a factoring transaction the sale of accounts receivable to a third party at a discount is realized in order to convert the receivables into cash quickly.

FCA *Financial Conduct Authority*

Financial Conduct Authority (FCA) The financial regulatory entity of the U.K.

Financing round A, B, C, D (Funding round A, B, C, D) Start-up funding rounds are a series of investments for a new business. In each funding round the company is evaluated. The seed financing or angel financing rounds are followed by series A, B, C, D financing rounds of venture capitalists. Usually the money raised per financing round increases in later rounds as the business of the company grows.

Funding round A, B, C, D *Financing round A, B, C, D*

Financing round A (Series A funding) Investors in Series A funding typically come from venture capital companies. The amount invested is higher than in the seed financing phase but lower than in the following B and C rounds.

Financing Round B (Series B funding) Investors in Series B funding typically come from venture capital companies. The amount invested is higher than in the A round and supports the company to grow the business.

Financing Round C (Series C funding) Companies in financing round C have already shown successful development of the business and therefore investors are ready to further invest in new products and expansion.

Future contract A contract to buy a security on a future date at a price fixed today.

Hedge fund Investment fund charging a performance fee. The fund invests in options, futures, stocks, bonds, currencies or commodities, often with complex strategies.

High Watermark (HWM) Calculation principle for performance fees paid by investors to asset managers. The HWM reflects the highest level to which the value of assets rose. The compensation will be paid only after reaching a new maximum value of managed capital.

HWM *High Watermark*

Hyperledger Global enterprise blockchain project that offers frameworks, standards, guidelines, and tools for building open-source blockchains and related applications.

ICO *Initial Coin Offering*

Initial Coin Offering (ICO) Financing method for a business to collect money outside of the venture capital world issuing a blockchain-native digital token representing a sort of value or being of value itself.

Insurtech Internet company that is offering services around the value chain of insurance companies in the form of marketplaces, online product offerings, Peer-to-Peer (P2P) services, or data providers on customers and potential customers.

Internet of things (IoT) Physical or digital machines and sensors connected to the internet that can operate collaboratively and exchange information autonomously.

IoT *Internet of things*

IOUs *I Owe You*

Internal Rate of Return (IRR) The discount rate at which the investment has a net present value of zero. The IRR is typically used as required rate of return from venture capital investors.

IRR *Internal Rate of Return*

I Owe You (IOUs) Document acknowledging debt which does not determine repayment terms.

Initial Public Offering (IPO) A company's first public issue of common stock

IPO *Initial Public Offering*

Key activities Activities creating the value proposition that reaches customers through the chosen channels, build up the customer relationships, and generate revenue.

Key partners Partners minimizing the risks of the operating activities that help to achieve economies of scale and scope as well as to enable access to the necessary resources.

Key resources Tangible or intangible resources that are necessary to deliver the value proposition to the customers.

Kickback Benefits paid to the asset managers by the seller of investment products, e.g., investment funds.

Know Your Customer (KYC) Financial industry-standard that is required to verify the identity, suitability, and risks involved with maintaining a business relationship with a client.

KYC *Know Your Customer*

Leverage Leverage refers to the amount of debt used by a company. It is also a financial strategy to use borrowed money to improve the rate of return on the investment.

Libra Open-source cryptocurrency project promoted by Facebook.

Liquidity (Liquid) Ability to sell an asset or security on short notice and to convert it in cash at close to market price. It is also the ability to execute payment obligations at any time.

Lot A standard lot is the reference size on Forex markets and equals 100,000 units of the base currency.

Machine learning AI implementation that is designed to connect inputs in a large set of data with the desired outputs learning to predict outcomes from data which per se seem uncorrelated or unstructured.

Mean Value calculated by dividing the sum of the values in a data set by the number of values, also called average.

Mean-variance method Financial method that weighs the possible risk of an investment and the possible expected return of the investment. Variance shows the standard deviation for an expected value and is a measure for risk.

Median Statistical measure that defines a value separating the higher half from the lower half of a data sample.

Mega rounds Venture capital financing rounds with a minimum of €50.0 million raised.

Markets in Financial Instruments Directive (MiFID) Regulation on financial markets applying across the European Union, aimed at securing competitive financial markets, protecting investors, and regulating financial instruments.

Micro-payments Financial transaction with very small payment amounts.

MiFID *Markets in Financial Instruments Directive*

Modern portfolio theory (MPT) Financial model to determine the asset allocation and diversification for investors with different risk profiles. The MPT shows the highest expected return for a given market risk.

Money market Market for short-term investments with low risk and low return.

Money Raised Equity capital invested in the company in a financing round. The equity may come from seed or angel or venture capital investors.

MPT *Modern Portfolio Theory*

Mutual fund Financial instrument that collects capital from investors through selling shares of the fund and that invests the capital in stocks, bonds and other asset classes.

Option Financial instrument that gives the holder the right to buy or to sell a financial asset for a specified price and/or at a specified date.

Personal Finance Management (PFM) Analysis and evaluation process helping clients to gain a quick and uncomplicated overview of their financial situation.

PFM *Personal Finance Management*

Portfolio management Process of selecting, monitoring, and rebalancing of financial assets to meet the long-term goals of retail or institutional clients.

Point of Sale (POS) Place where something is publicly sold or where a payment is made.

POS *Point of Sale*

PoW *Proof of Work*

Pre-Money Valuation The value of a company before the going public or before the next financing round with venture capital. The Pre-Money Valuation equals the Post-Money Valuation minus Investment Amount and it is the basis for venture capital investors to calculate how much ownership they might expect.

Private Equity Invested equity in a company that is not publicly traded. Venture capital for start-up companies is a part of private equity but also equity capital to finance management buyouts.

Proof of Work (PoW) Consensus mechanism requiring the solving of challenging but feasible computational tasks or puzzles to prevent the malicious use of computing power, e.g. the mining process for bitcoins.

Proptechs Internet companies that are focusing on real estate offering comparison services as marketplaces, support for online sales, collecting and analyzing the data of target groups or trying to position themselves as gatekeepers for all the needs of homeowners.

Rate of return Total income divided by capital invested.

Return on Equity (ROE) Financial ratio for profit divided by invested equity capital.

Robo-advisory Digital service of investment advisory and automated asset management for private clients.

ROE *Return on Equity*

Seed capital Money raised by a company in the very early phase of a business idea or a business plan. It is raised before institutional venture capital is invested and may come from angel investors or public institutions.

Social trading Fully transparent investment transactions by individuals or professionals shown publicly on trading platforms. Users can automatically track the investments of other traders on the trading platform.**Special Purpose Vehicle (SPV)** A company established for a specific goal to meet clearly defined or temporary objectives.

Spin-off Creation of a new legal company entity through the sale of a division or part of an existing company.

SPV *Special Purpose Vehicle*

Start-up/Startup Young company with a few employees seeking to develop an innovative or scalable business idea. Start-ups have high risks and typically they are financed in the first stage by the founders or the family and in later stages by venture capital.

TACO *Total Cost of Ownership*

TER *Total Expense Ratio*

Total Cost of Ownership (TACO) Financial ratio that is capturing all costs for an investor of an ETF.

Total Expense Ratio (TER) Financial ratio for the yearly cost of an ETF comprising the management fee, administrative charges and further cost of operation in relation to the AUM of the ETF.

Token Digital information on a blockchain representing diverse blockchain-intrinsic or asset-backed values.

Unicorn A start-up company with a valuation of $1.0 billion or more.

Unique Selling Proposition (USP) The perceived benefit of a product, brand, or service, which differentiates itself from its competitors.

USP *Unique Selling Proposition*

VAS *Value-Added Services*

Value-Added Services (VAS) Functions that can be added to a core product or service or can stand alone to enhance the user experience.

Value proposition Product or service for a customer segment, either as an innovation or an existing basic product with more and improved features.

VC method (Venture Capital Method) Valuation method that is combining DCF modeling with multiple valuation to derive a present value for a young non-listed company.

VC *Venture Capital***Venture Capital (VC)** Private equity raised by young companies to finance innovative ideas and business models with high risk.

VermAnlG *Vermögensanlagengesetz*

Vermögensanlagengesetz (VermAnlG) German Capital Investment Act, regulation applying to investments that are publicly offered in Germany.

WACC *Weighted Average Cost of Capital*

Weighted Average Cost of Capital (WACC) Expected return for equity and debt capital invested in a company.

Appendix

List of fintechs in research sample for venture capital rounds for time series analysis of sample April 2000–June 2017

Country	Company	Foundation	Country	Company	Foundation	Country	Company	Foundation
Alternative Payment Methods			U.K.	Currencycloud	2012	U.S.	PaySimple	2006
Belgium	IbanFirst	2012	U.K.	Ebury	2009	U.S.	Qvivr	2014
Denmark	Nets	2003	U.K.	GoCardless	2011	U.S.	Remitly	2011
Denmark	Pleo	2015	U.K.	iZettle	2010	U.S.	Ripple	2012
France	Anytime	2012	U.K.	Kantox	2011	U.S.	Square	2009
France	FAMOCO	2010	U.K.	Revolut	2015	U.S.	Stripe	2010
France	Lemon Way	2007	U.K.	SumUp	2011	U.S.	Transactis	2001
France	Lydia	2013	U.K.	TransferWise	2010	U.S.	Veem	2014
France	Spendesk	2016	U.K.	VocaLink	2007	U.S.	Venmo	2009
Germany	AEVI	2015	U.K.	WeSwap	2010	U.S.	WePay	2008
Germany	BillPay	2009	U.K.	WorldRemit	2010	U.S.	Yapstone	1999
Germany	Cringle	2014	U.K.	YoYo Wallet	2013	U.S.	ZenBanx	2012
Germany	iPAYst	2010	U.S.	Boku	2008	U.S.	Zooz	2010
Germany	Lendstar	2013	U.S.	Braintree	2007	U.S.	Zuora	2007
Germany	OptioPay	2014	U.S.	CardConnect	2006	**Blockchain & Cryptocurrencies**		
Germany	payleven	2012	U.S.	CardFlight	2013	France	Stratumn	2015
Germany	PAYMILL	2012	U.S.	Clinkle	2011	Germany	Coyno	2014
Germany	Payworks	2012	U.S.	Coin	2012	Germany	SatoshiPay	2014
Germany	traxpay	2012	U.S.	Credorax	2008	Italy	Euklid	2015
Ireland	Circle	2013	U.S.	Dwolla	2008	Luxembourg	Blockchain	2011
Ireland	CurrencyFair	2009	U.S.	flywire	2009	Netherlands	coinsnap	2015
Ireland	Plynk	2015	U.S.	Greenlight Financial Technology	2014	Netherlands	Quantoz	2013
Italy	Satispay	2013				U.K.	Elliptic	2013
Luxembourg	Cashcloud	2012	U.S.	LevelUp	2008	U.K.	Wirex	2014
Netherlands	Adyen	2006	U.S.	Marqeta	2010	U.S.	21 Inc	2013
Netherlands	Dimebox	2014	U.S.	Mozido	2008	U.S.	Axoni	2013
Sweden	Klarna	2005	U.S.	Paydiant	2010	U.S.	Bitnet Technologies	2013
Switzerland	MUUME	2013	U.S.	PayNearMe	2009	U.S.	BitPay	2011
U.K.	Azimo	2012	U.S.	Payoneer	2005	U.S.	Blockstream	2014

https://doi.org/10.1515/9783110704907-017

Country	Company	Foundation
U.S.	Chain	2014
U.S.	Coinbase	2012
U.S.	Digital Asset	2014
U.S.	Factom	2015
U.S.	LedgerX	2013
U.S.	Paxos	2013
U.S.	R3	2014
U.S.	TradeBlock	2013
U.S.	Xapo	2012
Comparison Sites & Search Engines		
Denmark	Samlino.dk	2013
Germany	Finanzcheck	2010
Germany	Finanzchef24	2012
U.S.	AlphaSense	2010
U.S.	the zebra	2012
Credit & Factoring		
Germany	Bezahlt.de	2016
Germany	Bilendo	2015
Germany	COMPEON	2012
Germany	Fincompare	unknown
Germany	Fintura	2014
Germany	Kreditech	2012
Germany	Pagido	2013
Germany	Spotcap	2014
Germany	Tradico	2013
Latvia	Creamfinance	2012
Netherlands	Invoice Sharing	2013
U.K.	Aire	2014
U.K.	BillFront	2015
U.K.	borro	2008
U.K.	DueCourse	2014
U.K.	ezbob	2011
U.K.	iwoca	2011
U.K.	wonga	2006
U.S.	Affirm	2012
U.S.	Argon Credit	2013

Country	Company	Foundation
U.S.	AutoGravity	2015
U.S.	Avant	2012
U.S.	AvidXchange	2000
U.S.	Behalf	2011
U.S.	Better Mortgage	2014
U.S.	Billtrust	2001
U.S.	Blend	2012
U.S.	BlueVine	2013
U.S.	Bond Street	2013
U.S.	Bread Finance	2014
U.S.	C2FO	2008
U.S.	CommonBond	2011
U.S.	Earnest	2013
U.S.	Elevate	2014
U.S.	FastPay	2009
U.S.	Finova Financial	2016
U.S.	Fundbox	2012
U.S.	fundera	2013
U.S.	Kabbage	2009
U.S.	LendingHome	2013
U.S.	LendUp	2011
U.S.	nav	2012
U.S.	OnDeck	2007
U.S.	Pave	2012
U.S.	Point	2015
U.S.	Selfscore	2012
U.S.	SoFi	2011
U.S.	Tala	2011
U.S.	Taulia	2009
U.S.	TrueAccord	2013
U.S.	Upgrade	2016
U.S.	Upstart	2012
U.S.	ZestFinance	2009

Country	Company	Foundation
Crowdfunding		
Austria	CONDA	2013
Belgium	Look&Fin	2012
France	Leetchi	2009
France	microDON	2009
France	SmartAngels	2011
France	Lendix	2014
France	Unilend	2013
Germany	Exporo	2014
Germany	Kapilendo	2014
Germany	Startnext	2010
Germany	Auxmoney	2007
Germany	Bitbond	2013
Germany	Lendico	2013
Germany	smava	2005
Sweden	Lendify	2014
Switzerland	Lend	2015
U.K.	BrickVest	2014
U.K.	Crowdcube	2010
U.K.	Prodigy Finance	2007
U.K.	Property Planer	2014
U.K.	SyndicateRoom	2012
U.K.	Funding Circle	2010
U.K.	Lending Works	2012
U.K.	LendInvest	2013
U.K.	MarketInvoice	2010
U.K.	RateSetter	2010
U.K.	Zopa	2005
U.S.	Cadre	2014
U.S.	Fundrise	2012
U.S.	Neighborly	2012
U.S.	Patch of Land	2013
U.S.	PeerStreet	2013

Country	Company	Foundation
U.S.	Sunfunder	2012
U.S.	GreenSky	2006
U.S.	Lending Club	2007
U.S.	LendKey Technologies	2007
U.S.	Prosper	2005
Healthtech		
U.S.	Bright Health	2016
U.S.	Clover Health	2014
U.S.	Collective Health	2013
U.S.	Oscar	2013
U.S.	Outcome	2006
U.S.	Simplee	2010
U.S.	ZocDoc	2007
Infrastructure & IT		
Belgium	Clear2Pay	2001
Belgium	Qover	2016
France	Qonto	2016
Germany	Alyne	2015
Germany	Barzahlen	2011
Germany	bexio	2013
Germany	Candis	2015
Germany	figo	2012
Germany	MAMBU	2011
Germany	payever	2013
Germany	Pay.on	2004
Germany	SMACC	2015
Germany	solarisBank	2016
Germany	Treasury Intelligence Solutions	2010
Germany	Zeitgold	2015
Ireland	AQMetrics	2012
Ireland	moQom	2007
Netherlands	five degrees	unknown

Country	Company	Foundation
Portugal	Feedzai	2009
Spain	Strands	2003
Sweden	BehavioSec	2007
Switzerland	NetGuardians	2007
U.K.	AimBrain	2014
U.K.	Algomi	2012
U.K.	Babel Systems	2008
U.K.	Behavox	2014
U.K.	Contego Fraud Solutions	2011
U.K.	CoVi Analytics	2015
U.K.	Dealflo	2009
U.K.	Dopay	2014
U.K.	Markit	2001
U.K.	Monitise	2003
U.K.	OpenGamma	2009
U.K.	R5FX	2013
U.K.	Ravelin	2014
U.S.	AltX	2012
U.S.	Aria Systems	2002
U.S.	Ayasdi	2008
U.S.	ChartIQ	2012
U.S.	Cloud Lending Solutions	2012
U.S.	Collibra	2008
U.S.	Coupa Software	2006
U.S.	DealCloud	2010
U.S.	Droit Fintech	2012
U.S.	Easy Solutions	2007
U.S.	InvestCloud	2010
U.S.	LMRKTS	2012
U.S.	Lucena Research	2011
U.S.	Onfido	2012

Country	Company	Foundation
U.S.	Persado	2012
U.S.	Personetics	2010
U.S.	Powerlytics	2011
U.S.	Quovo	2010
U.S.	Sift Science	2011
U.S.	Signifyd	2011
U.S.	Symphony	2014
U.S.	Token	2015
U.S.	TradeShift	2009
U.S.	trueEX	2010
U.S.	Yodlee	1999
Insurtech		
France	Shift Technology	2013
Germany	Clark	2015
Germany	Friendsurance	2010
Germany	Getsurance	2016
Germany	massUp	2015
Germany	Simplesurance	2012
Germany	wefox (formerly FinanceFox)	2014
Gibraltar	Quan Template	2013
Ireland	WeSavvy	2015
Norway	Tribe	2016
Sweden	Bima	2010
Switzerland	Knip	2013
U.K.	Boughtbymany	2013
U.K.	Cuvva	2014
U.K.	Kasko	2015
U.S.	Cyence	2014
U.S.	Embroker	2015
U.S.	Goji	2007
U.S.	Ladder	2015
U.S.	Lemonade	2015
U.S.	Metromile	2011

Country	Company	Foundation
U.S.	Next Insurance	2016
U.S.	PolicyGenius	2014
U.S.	Trov	2012
Personal Finance Management		
Finland	Holvi	2011
France	Bankin	2011
Germany	Avuba	2013
Germany	bonify	2015
Germany	moneymeets	2012
Germany	savedroid	2015
Germany	treefin	2014
Iceland	Meniga	2009
Netherlands	AdviceGames	2013
Sweden	Qapital	2012
Sweden	Tink	2012
Switzerland	eWise	2000
U.K.	Atom Bank	2014
U.K.	Curve	2015
U.K.	Monzo	2015
U.K.	Pariti	2014
U.K.	Oval Money	2015
U.K.	Tandem	2013
U.K.	Tide	2016
U.K.	TrueLayer	2016
U.S.	Addepar	2009
U.S.	Check	2007
U.S.	Clarity Money	2016
U.S.	Credit Karma	2007
U.S.	Digiliti Money	2010
U.S.	digit	2013
U.S.	HelloWallet	2009
U.S.	Kapitall	2008
U.S.	LearnVest	2007
U.S.	Level Money	2012

Country	Company	Foundation
U.S.	Linkable	2010
U.S.	MoneyLion	2013
U.S.	Moven	2011
U.S.	NerdWallet	2009
U.S.	Payoff	2009
U.S.	Plaid	2012
U.S.	riskalyze	2011
U.S.	Roofstock	2015
U.S.	Simple	2009
U.S.	TradeKing	2005
Robo-Advice		
France	Yomoni	2014
Germany	Cashboard	2014
Germany	easyfolio	2009
Germany	LIQID	2016
Germany	Scalable Capital	2014
Germany	Vaamo	2013
Ireland	Rubicoin	2014
Netherlands	Pritle	2014
Sweden	Pensionera	2014
U.K.	Huddlestock	2014
U.K.	Moneyfarm	2011
U.K.	MortgageGym	2016
U.K.	Nutmeg	2010
U.S.	Acorns	2012
U.S.	AdvisorEngine	2014
U.S.	Betterment	2008
U.S.	blooom	2013
U.S.	Ellevest	2014
U.S.	Financial Guard	2009
U.S.	FutureAdvisor	2010
U.S.	Hedgeable	2009
U.S.	Honest Dollar	2014

Country	Company	Foundation
U.S.	jemstep	2008
U.S.	MarketRiders	2008
U.S.	motif	2010
U.S.	Personal Capital	2009
U.S.	Prumentum Group	un-known
U.S.	Robinhood	2013
U.S.	SigFig	2007
U.S.	Stash	2015
U.S.	Trizic	2012
U.S.	Wealthfront	2011
Savings		
Germany	Deposit Solutions	2011
Germany	N26	2013
Germany	Raisin	2013
Germany	Savedo	2014
Luxembourg	MyBucks	2011
Sweden	Kollektiva	2014
U.K.	Monese	2013
U.K.	Pockit	2014
U.K.	Starling Bank	2014
U.K.	Swanest	2014
U.K.	Trussle	2015
U.S.	Aspiration	unknown
Social Trading		
Austria	Wikifolio	2008
Germany	SwipeStox	2015
U.K.	ayondo	2008
U.K.	eToro	2007
U.S.	Covestor	2005
U.S.	TradingView	2011
Others		
Germany	Gini	2011
U.K.	Habito	2015

Country	Company	Foundation
U.S.	AcadiaSoft	2009
U.S.	Activehours	2012
U.S.	eShares	2012
U.S.	Gusto (formerly ZenPayroll)	2011
U.S.	Nymbus	2015
U.S.	Quantopian	2011
U.S.	xignite	2003
U.S.	Zenefits	2013

Publication bibliography

51 Credit Card (Ed.): Spokesman. Available online at https://www.u51.com/#/spokesman, checked on 5/27/2020.

51 Credit Card (Ed.) (2019a): 2018 Annual Report. Available online at https://ir.u51.com/u51-web/static/public/file/50689_2018_ANNUAL_REPORT_en.pdf, checked on 2/24/2020.

51 Credit Card (Ed.) (2019b): 2019 Interim Report. Available online at https://ir.u51.com/u51-web/static/public/file/26731_2019_INTERIM_REPORT_en.pdf, checked on 2/24/2020.

51 Credit Card (Ed.) (2019c): 2019 Interim Results Presentation. Available online at https://ir.u51.com/u51-web/static/public/file/08195_2019_Interim_Results_Presentation_en.pdf, checked on 3/24/2020.

51 Credit Card (Ed.) (2020a): Company Profile. Available online at https://www.u51.com/#/company, checked on 2/24/2020.

51 Credit Card (Ed.) (2020b): Offers. Available online at https://www.u51.com/product, checked on 2/24/2020.

Accenture (Ed.) (2016): Fintech and the evolving landscape: Landing points for the industry. Available online at https://www.accenture.com/t20161011t031409z__w__/us-en/_acnmedia/pdf-15/accenture-fintech-evolving-landscape.pdf#zoom=50, checked on 9/5/2019.

Adarlo, Sharon (2018): Will small clients be claimed by chatbots? Available online at https://www.financial-planning.com/news/whats-the-word-on-chatbots-in-wealth-management, updated on 4/18/2018, checked on 12/16/2019.

Adel, Florine van den (2019): Bankieren met een Chatbot. Edited by ING online. Available online at https://www.ing.nl/de-ing/achtergronden/vernieuwen/bankieren-met-een-chatbot.html, updated on 1/30/2019, checked on 5/16/2019.

Adyen (Ed.) (2018): How the payments industry evolved. Learn about key players and big changes in this brief history, covering 40 years of the payments industry. Available online at https://www.adyen.com/blog/how-the-payments-industry-evolved, updated on 5/16/2018, checked on 6/29/2020.

Adyen (Ed.) (2019): Alipay and Adyen Partner to Streamline Global Payment Experiences for Users, Merchants and Businesses. Available online at https://www.adyen.com/press-and-media/2019/alipay-and-adyen-partner-to-streamline-global-payment-experiences-for-users-merchants-and-businesses, updated on 8/28/2019, checked on 7/14/2020.

Adyen (Ed.) (2020a): Find a partner. We partner with leading technology solutions to give your customers the best experiences. Available online at https://www.adyen.com/partners/network, checked on 6/29/2020.

Adyen (Ed.) (2020b): Global Acquiring. Fast global payment processing. Available online at https://www.adyen.com/global-payment-processing, checked on 6/29/2020.

Adyen (Ed.) (2020c): Mobile payments. Available online at https://www.adyen.com/knowledge-hub/guides/optimize-your-mobile-payments, updated on 7/2/2020, checked on 7/2/2020.

Adyen (Ed.) (2020d): Online payments. Accept payments with cards, wallets, and key local payment methods on your website and mobile app. Available online at https://docs.adyen.com/checkout, checked on 7/2/2020.

Adyen (Ed.) (2020e): Our story. Available online at https://www.adyen.com/about, checked on 6/29/2020.

Adyen (Ed.) (2020f): Payments 101 for fast-growing businesses. Available online at https://www.adyen.com/de_DE/landing/online/us/payments-101, checked on 6/29/2020.

Adyen (Ed.) (2020g): 2019 Annual report. Available online at https://www.adyen.com/de_DE/investor-relations/publication-annual-report-2019, checked on 6/29/2020.

https://doi.org/10.1515/9783110704907-018

Alexa (2018a): Alexa Top 500 Global Sites. Available online at https://www.alexa.com/topsites, checked on 10/9/2018.

Alexa (2018b): Baidu.com Traffic, Demographics and Competitors – Alexa. Edited by Alexa. Available online at https://www.alexa.com/siteinfo/baidu.com, checked on 12/17/2018.

Alexa (2018c): Top Sites in China – Alexa. Available online at https://www.alexa.com/topsites/countries/CN, checked on 10/9/2018.

Alibaba Group (2018a): Alibaba Group Agrees to 33% Equity Stake in Ant Financial. Available online at https://www.alibabagroup.com/en/news/press_pdf/p180201a.pdf, checked on 2/10/2019.

Alibaba Group (2018b): Alibaba Group Announces March Quarter 2018 Results and Full Fiscal Year 2018 Results, p. 6. Available online at https://www.alibabagroup.com/en/news/press_pdf/p180504.pdf, checked on 10/9/2018.

Alibaba Group (Ed.) (2019): Our Businesses. Available online at https://www.alibabagroup.com/en/about/businesses, checked on 9/5/2019.

Alipay (2019a): Main flows. Edited by Alipay for global business. Available online at https://intl.alipay.com/doc/barcode/barcoderecon, updated on 5/17/2019, checked on 5/18/2019.

Alipay (2019b): Introduction. Edited by Alipay for global business. Available online at https://global.alipay.com/doc/barcode/barcodeintro, updated on 5/17/2019, checked on 5/18/2019.

Allayannis, Yiorgos; Becker, Joseph M. (2019): A Global Fintech Overview. Edited by Harvard Business School Publishing. Darden School of Business. Available online at https://hbsp.harvard.edu/product/UV7736-PDF-ENG?itemFindingMethod=Bundle+Page, checked on 6/24/2020.

Allayannis, Yiorgos; Cartwright, Kayla (2017): Cutting through the Fog: Finding a Future with Fintech. Edited by Harvard Business School Publishing. Darden School of Business. Available online at https://hbsp.harvard.edu/product/UV7225-PDF-ENG?itemFindingMethod=Bundle+Page, checked on 6/24/2020.

Amazon Pay (Ed.) (2019): Online-Bezahldienst für E-Commerce Händler. Available online at https://pay.amazon.com/de, checked on 12/9/2019.

Amazon Payments Inc online (Ed.) (2019): Using Amazon Pay. Available online at https://pay.amazon.com/using-amazon-pay, checked on 9/5/2019.

Andersen, Nicolai (2016): Vorstellung der Blockchain-Technologie. In *Deloitte*. Available online at https://www2.deloitte.com/content/dam/Deloitte/de/Documents/Innovation/Vorstellung%20der%20Blockchain-Technologie.pdf, checked on 2/19/2019.

AngelList (2015): Economics of Syndicates. Available online at https://angel.co/economics-syndicates, checked on 10/29/2018.

AngelList (2018a): Jobs at AngelList. A platform for startups. Available online at https://angel.co/angellist/jobs, checked on 10/29/2018.

AngelList (2018b): Syndicates / For Investors. Overview. Available online at https://angel.co/syndicates/for-investors, checked on 10/29/2018.

AngelList (2018c): Most Frequently Asked Questions. SYNDICATES. How much do syndicates cost? Available online at https://angel.co/help/syndicates/syndicates-cost, updated on 12/21/2018, checked on 10/29/2018.

AngelList (2020): Done Deals. Available online at https://angel.co/done-deals, updated on 1/8/2020, checked on 1/8/2020.

Ant Financial (11/6/2018): Bridging the trust gap in the "New Renting Economy". Zhima Credit Management Team. Available online at https://www.antfin.com/zhima-open-letter.htm, checked on 9/5/2019.

Ant Financial (Ed.) (2019): Ant Family. Available online at https://www.antfin.com/family.htm, checked on 12/9/2019.

ArtistShare (2018): About us. Available online at https://www.artistshare.com/about, checked on 10/4/2018.

Athwal, Nav (2014): The Investor's Guide To Real Estate Crowdfunding. Available online at https://www.forbes.com/sites/groupthink/2014/08/19/the-investors-guide-to-real-estate-crowdfunding/#31fe6ccd6d32, updated on 8/19/2014, checked on 10/19/2018.

ATKearney (Ed.) (2014): Big Data: The Next Leading Edge in the Financial Industry. Available online at https://www.atkearney.com/financial-services/article?/a/big-data-the-next-leading-edge-in-the-financial-industry, checked on 12/17/2018.

ATKearney (2015): Hype vs. Reality: The coming Waves of "Robo" Adoption. Available online at https://www.atkearney.de/financial-services/article?/a/hype-vs-reality-the-coming-waves-of-robo-advisors, checked on 9/26/2018.

Avant, LLC (2020a): How fast will my loan be funded? Available online at https://support.avant.com/article/18-funding-speed, checked on 6/1/2020.

Avant, LLC (Ed.) (2020b): What is the relationship between Avant and WebBank? Available online at https://support.avant.com/article/340-what-is-the-relationship-between-avant-and-webbank, checked on 6/1/2020.

Avant, LLC (Ed.) (2020c): Get your Personalized Loan Offer. Available online at https://www.myavantoffer.com/, updated on 1/22/2020, checked on 6/1/2020.

Avant, LLC (Ed.) (2020d): My AvantCard Offer. Available online at https://www.avant.com/content/myavantcard/, updated on 5/8/2020, checked on 6/1/2020.

Avant, LLC (2020e): About us. Available online at https://www.avant.com/about_us, updated on 5/29/2020, checked on 6/1/2020.

Avant, LLC (Ed.) (2020f): Cardmember Agreement. Available online at https://www.avant.com/cardmember-agreement/, updated on 5/29/2020, checked on 6/1/2020.

Avant, LLC (Ed.) (2020g): Terms of Use. Available online at https://www.avant.com/terms-of-use/, updated on 5/29/2020, checked on 6/1/2020.

AvantCredit of UK, LLC (Ed.) (2020): Personal Loans. Available online at https://www.avantcredit.co.uk/, updated on 6/1/2020, checked on 6/1/2020.

BaFin (2007): Merkblatt zur Erlaubnispflicht von Kreditvermittlungsplattformen. Available online at https://www.bafin.de/SharedDocs/Veroeffentlichungen/DE/Merkblatt/mb_070514_kreditvermittlungsplattform.html, checked on 9/14/2018.

BaFin (2016): Plattform zur Signalgebung und automatisierten Auftragsausführung – Signal Following oder Social Trading. Available online at https://www.bafin.de/DE/Aufsicht/FinTech/Signalgebung/signalgebung_node.html, checked on 8/14/2018.

BaFin (2017a): Social Trading – Plattformen zur Signalgebung und automatisierten Auftragsausführung. Available online at https://www.bafin.de/DE/Verbraucher/Finanzwissen/Fintech/SocialTrading/social_trading_node.html, checked on 8/9/2018.

BaFin (2017b): BaFin restricts CFD trading. Available online at https://www.bafin.de/SharedDocs/Veroeffentlichungen/EN/Pressemitteilung/2017/pm_170508_cfd_en.html, updated on 5/8/2017, checked on 8/9/2018.

BaFin (2018): Crowdlending. Available online at https://www.bafin.de/DE/Aufsicht/FinTech/Crowdfunding/Crowdlending/crowdlending_node.html#doc7851540bodyText2, checked on 9/14/2018.

Ball, Tom (2017): Top 10 biggest blockchain players. Edited by Computer Business Review. Available online at https://www.cbronline.com/news/verticals/fintech/top-10-biggest-blockchain-players, checked on 3/6/2019.

Banco Santander S.A. (Ed.) (2019): 2018 Annual Report. Available online at https://www.santander.com/content/dam/santander-com/en/documentos/informe-anual/2018/IA-2018-Annual%20report-20-en.pdf, checked on 2/19/2020.

Bank for International Settlements; Financial Stability Board (2017): FinTech credit. Market structure, business models and financial stability implications. Available online at https://www.bis.org/publ/cgfs_fsb1.pdf, checked on 9/27/2018.

Bank of America (5/28/2019): Bank of America's Erica® Completes More Than 50 Million Client Requests in First Year. Virtual Financial Assistant Surpasses 7 Million Users. Charlotte, N.C. Available online at https://newsroom.bankofamerica.com/press-releases/consumer-banking/bank-americas-ericar-completes-more-50-million-client-requests, checked on 5/31/2019.

Bank of America online (Ed.) (2019a): 2018 Annual Report. Available online at http://media.corpo rate-ir.net/media_files/IROL/71/71595/BOAML_AR2018.pdf, checked on 5/31/2019.

Bank of America online (Ed.) (2019b): Bank of America Preferred Rewards Program. Available online at https://www.bankofamerica.com/preferred-rewards/, updated on 5/28/2019, checked on 6/2/2019.

Bank of America online (Ed.) (2019c): Meet Erica, Your Financial Digital Assistant From Bank of America. Available online at https://promo.bankofamerica.com/erica/, updated on 5/31/2019, checked on 5/31/2019.

Bank of Ireland (Ed.) (2018): Bank of Ireland and Deloitte announce blockchain proof-of-concept focused on trade reporting. Available online at https://www.bankofireland.com/about-bank-of-ireland/press-releases/2016/bank-of-ireland-and-deloitte-announce-blockchain-proof-of-concept-focused-on-trade-reporting/, updated on 7/3/2018, checked on 3/15/2020.

Baran, Paul (1964): On Distributed Communications: I. Introduction to Distributed Communications Networks. In *United States Air Force Project Rand*. Available online at https://www.rand.org/content/dam/rand/pubs/research_memoranda/2006/RM3420.pdf, checked on 2/19/2019.

Barber, Gregory (2019): Facebook Is Losing Its Cover for Libra As More Members Flee. The departures of Visa, Mastercard, and three others mean that more than ever, Libra is Facebook's cryptocurrency project. Edited by WIRED. Available online at https://www.wired.com/story/facebook-losing-cover-libra-more-members-flee/, updated on 11/10/2019, checked on 12/9/2019.

Bary, Emily (2020): Adyen shares gain after company talks up new merchant wins. Edited by MarketWatch. Available online at https://www.marketwatch.com/story/adyen-shares-gain-after-company-talks-up-new-merchant-wins-2020-02-27, updated on 2/27/2020, checked on 7/30/2020.

Beck, Ralf (2014): Crowdinvesting. Die Investition der Vielen. 3. Aufl. Kulmbach: Börsenmedien.

Beck, Ralf (2015): Wer braucht noch Banken? Wie Start-Ups die Finanzwelt verändern und was uns das nutzt. Kulmbach: Börsenbuchverl.

Beigel, Ofir (2019): Binance Review and Comparison. Edited by 99Bitcoins. Available online at https://99bitcoins.com/bitcoin-exchanges/binance-review/, updated on 12/11/2019, checked on 3/23/2020.

Belleflamme, Paul; Lambert, Thomas; Schwienbacher, Armin (2012): Crowdfunding: Tapping the Right Crowd. In *SSRN Journal*. DOI: 10.2139/ssrn.1578175.

Benke, Alex (2017): Your Money, Your Way: The Betterment Service Plans. Betterment. Available online at https://www.betterment.com/resources/your-money-your-way-the-betterment-ad vice-plans/, updated on 7/26/2017, checked on 9/26/2018.

Benovic, Carol (2016): The Project Review Process: From Submitting to Getting Approved. Edited by Kickstarter, PBC. Available online at https://www.kickstarter.com/blog/everything-you-need-to-know-about-the-project-review-process?lang=de, updated on 6/14/2016, checked on 10/30/2018.

Berman, Larry (2017): Financial planning for the future of AI and robo-advisors. Bloomberg. Available online at https://www.bnnbloomberg.ca/larry-berman-financial-planning-for-the-fu ture-of-ai-and-robo-advisors-1.926796, checked on 9/26/2018.

Beth, Alexander; Fischer, Matthias (2020): Personal Finance Management Tools – Benchmarking von Banken und Fintechs. In *Financial Research Note* 04/2020 (Nr. 06), pp. 1–18. Available online at https://d-nb.info/1208317679/34, checked on 5/29/2020.

Betterment Holdings Inc: ETF Selection for Portfolio Construction: A Methodology. Available online at https://www.betterment.com/resources/research/etf-portfolio-selection-methodology/, checked on 9/26/2018.

Betterment Holdings Inc (2014): Allocation Advice for Betterment Portfolios. Available online at https://www.betterment.com/resources/research/stock-allocation-advice/, updated on 8/19/2014, checked on 9/26/2018.

betterplace.org (Ed.) (2018): Hallo, wir sind betterplace. Wir sind Deutschlands größte Spendenplattform. Available online at https://www.betterplace.org/c/ueber-uns, checked on 9/28/2018.

betterplace.org (2020): Entdecke eines von über 27.000 bewegenden Projekten. Available online at https://www.betterplace.org/de, checked on 1/6/2020.

Bharath, Kumar J. (2017): The Story of PayPal. Edited by Medium. Available online at https://medium.com/@bharath.bkj/the-story-of-paypal-b708efe83064, updated on 5/21/2017, checked on 12/9/2019.

Bitcoin Deutschland AG (Ed.) (2020): Bitcoins Marktplatz, Forum und Informationen. Available online at https://www.bitcoin.de/de/faq/was-ist-bitcoin-de/89.html, checked on 3/23/2020.

Bitcoin.org (Ed.) (2020): Bitcoin Developer Guide. Blockchain Guide. Available online at https://bitcoin.org/en/blockchain-guide#introduction, checked on 4/7/2020.

Bitinfocharts (Ed.) (2020a): Bitcoin Block Time chart. Available online at https://bitinfocharts.com/comparison/bitcoin-confirmationtime.html#1y, updated on 3/4/2020, checked on 3/4/2020.

Bitinfocharts (Ed.) (2020b): Bitcoin, Bitcoin Cash Block Size historical chart. Average block size. Available online at https://bitinfocharts.com/comparison/size-btc-bch.html, updated on 3/15/2020, checked on 3/15/2020.

Blockchain Market by Provider, Application & Organization Size (2018). Available online at https://www.marketsandmarkets.com/Market-Reports/blockchain-technology-market-90100890.html, checked on 3/4/2019.

Blythe, Greg (2018): Bank on AI to shape the future of finance. Edited by Megatrends by HP. Available online at https://hpmegatrends.com/bank-on-ai-to-shape-the-future-of-finance-93520267e63a, updated on 2/28/2018, checked on 4/10/2019.

Borysowich, Craig; Bansal, Sunil (2017): Financial Chatbots. A landscape of white label banking products. With assistance of Bhanu Kohli. The Capital Markets Company NV. Available online at https://www.capco.com/-/media/CapcoMedia/PDFs/Financial-chatbots.ashx, checked on 9/26/2018.

Bouchey, Paul (2004): Questionnaire Quest. New research shows that standard questionnaires designed to reveal investors' risk tolerance levels are often flawed or misleading. In *Financial Planning* 34 (7), pp. 97–99.

Braun, Andreas (2013): Social Trading. Vom Know-how der Champions profitieren. 1. Aufl. München: FBV (Simplified).

Brennan, Matthew (2018): One Billion Users And Counting – What's Behind WeChat's Success? Edited by Forbes. Available online at https://www.forbes.com/sites/outofasia/2018/03/08/one-billion-users-and-counting-whats-behind-wechats-success/#5a9471a8771f, checked on 10/16/2018.

Browne, Ryan (2018): Santander launches a blockchain-based foreign exchange service that uses Ripple's technology. Edited by CNBC. Available online at https://www.cnbc.com/2018/04/12/santander-launches-blockchain-based-foreign-exchange-using-ripple-tech.html, updated on 4/12/2018, checked on 3/6/2019.

Brühl, Volker (2017): Bitcoins, Blockchain und Distributed Ledgers. In *Wirtschaftsdienst* 97 (2), pp. 135–142. DOI: 10.1007/s10273-017-2096-3.

Brylewski, Sarah; Lempka, Robert (2016): Social Trading: die moderne Geldanlage. In Oliver Everling, Robert Lempka (Eds.): Finanzdienstleister der nächsten Generation. Megatrend Digitalisierung: Strategien und Geschäftsmodelle. With assistance of Sabine Leutheusser-Schnarrenberger. 1. Auflage. Frankfurt am Main: Frankfurt School Verlag, pp. 135–150.

BTC-Echo (Ed.) (2019): Was ist Ripple und XRP? Available online at https://www.btc-echo.de/tuto rial/was-ist-ripple-und-xrp/, checked on 2/19/2019.

Business Insider (2017): Here's how banks can save big with blockchain. Available online at https://www.businessinsider.de/heres-how-banks-can-save-big-with-blockchain-2017-1?r= US&IR=T, checked on 11/30/2018.

Business Insider Intelligence (2017): Here's how banks can save big with blockchain. Edited by Business Insider. Available online at https://www.businessinsider.com/heres-how-banks-can-save-big-with-blockchain-2017-1?r=DE&IR=T, updated on 1/19/2017, checked on 3/5/2019.

Business Insider Intelligence (Ed.) (2020): Charles Schwab Intelligent Portfolios Performance Review 2020: Fees, Returns, Robo Investing Services & Competitors. Available online at https://www.businessinsider.com/schwab-intelligent-portfolios-performance-review?r= DE&IR=T, updated on 7/1/2020, checked on 8/17/2020.

Buterin, Vitalik (2014): Ethereum White Paper. A next Generation Smart Contract & decentralized Application Platform. Available online at http://blockchainlab.com/pdf/Ethereum_white_ paper-a_next_generation_smart_contract_and_decentralized_application_platform-vitalik-bu terin.pdf, checked on 2/19/2019.

Cabural, Marie (2015): OnDeck Capital and Lending Club: Both Compelling but Different. Available online at https://www.valuewalk.com/2015/01/ondeck-capital-vs-lending-club/, checked on 11/23/2018.

Cameron-Huff, Addison (2017): Op Ed: How Tokenization Is Putting Real-World Assets on Blockchains. Edited by Bitcoin Magazine. Available online at https://bitcoinmagazine.com/ar ticles/op-ed-how-tokenization-putting-real-world-assets-blockchains/, updated on 3/30/2017, checked on 3/3/2019.

Campbell, Dug (2015): The Byzantine Generals' Problem. Edited by dugcampbell.com. Available online at https://www.dugcampbell.com/byzantine-generals-problem/, checked on 3/5/2019.

Cant, Bart; Khadikar, Amol; Ruiter, Antal (2016): Smart Contracts in Financial Services: Getting from Hype to Reality. Edited by Capgemini Consulting. Available online at https://www.capgemini. com/consulting-de/wp-content/uploads/sites/32/2017/08/smart_contracts_paper_long_0. pdf, checked on 3/5/2019.

Carroll, Dan (2017): Introducing Path. A Better Financial Planning Experience. Wealthfront. Available online at https://blog.wealthfront.com/introducing-path/, checked on 9/26/2018.

CB Insights (2018a): Banks Are Finally Going After Fintech Startups. Available online at https:// www.cbinsights.com/research/top-us-banks-fintech-acquisitions/, updated on 2/13/2018, checked on 9/26/2018.

CBInsights (2017): Unbundling Intuit: The Fintech Startups Attacking the Tax & Accounting Software Giant. Edited by CBInsights. Available online at https://www.cbinsights.com/research/unbun dling-intuit-expert-intelligence/, checked on 2/18/2019.

CBInsights (2018b): What The Largest Global Fintech Can Teach Us About What's Next In Financial Services. Available online at https://www.cbinsights.com/research/ant-financial-alipay-fin tech/, updated on 10/4/2018, checked on 9/5/2019.

CBInsights (Ed.) (2019): We Analyzed 7 Of The Fastest-Growing Personal Finance Apps Of All Time To Figure Out The Secrets To Their Success – Here's What We Learned. Available online at https://www.cbinsights.com/research/personal-finance-apps-strategies/, updated on 4/24/2019, checked on 2/13/2020.

Charles Schwab & Co Inc. (Ed.) (2019a): Automated Investing | Schwab Intelligent Portfolios. Available online at https://intelligent.schwab.com/, checked on 12/16/2019.

Charles Schwab & Co Inc. (2019b): Frequently Asked Questions: A Zero Advisory Fee Service. Available online at https://intelligent.schwab.com/public/intelligent/faq-intelligent-portfolios/pay-no-advisory-fees.html, checked on 9/26/2018.

Charles Schwab & Co Inc. (2019c): How it works. Available online at https://intelligent.schwab.com/public/intelligent/how-it-works, checked on 12/16/2019.

Charles Schwab & Co Inc. (2019d): Schwab Intelligent Portfolios Premium™. Robo-advice meets 1:1 professional guidance. Available online at https://www.schwab.com/public/schwab/investment_advice/intelligent_advisory, checked on 12/16/2019.

Chen, Jessie (2016): Everything you ever wanted to know about WeChat – UX Collective. UX Collective. Available online at https://uxdesign.cc/wechat-the-invincible-app-a-key-to-business-success-in-china-8e9a920deb26, checked on 10/17/2018.

Chen, Lulu (2018): Ant Financial Annual Profit Jumps 65% Ahead of Anticipated IPO. Edited by Bloomberg. Available online at https://www.bloomberg.com/technology, checked on 10/7/2018.

Cheng, Evelyn (2018): How Ant Financial grew larger than Goldman Sachs. Edited by CNBC. Available online at https://www.cnbc.com/2018/06/08/how-ant-financial-grew-larger-than-goldman-sachs.html, checked on 10/7/2018.

Chester, Jonathan (2017): A New Way To Raise Money: The Initial Coin Offering. Edited by Forbes. Available online at https://www.forbes.com/sites/jonathanchester/2017/06/12/a-new-way-to-raise-money-the-initial-coin-offering/#734af32e5fb5, updated on 6/12/2017, checked on 3/9/2019.

China Internet Network Information Center (Ed.) (2019): The 44th Statistical Report on Internet Development in China. Available online at https://cnnic.com.cn/IDR/ReportDownloads/201911/P020191112539794960687.pdf, checked on 6/1/2020.

Cloudera (Ed.) ([2018]): The rise of machines. How People and Technology will shape the Future of Finance. Available online at https://www.cloudera.com/content/dam/www/marketing/resources/whitepapers/Banking-and-Finance-Whitepaper.pdf?daqp=true, checked on 4/12/2019.

Cocking, Simon (2016): Fintech Innovation and Disruption. Blockchain Insights with Don and Alex Tapscott. Edited by Irish Tech News, updated on 11/8/2016, checked on 3/5/2019.

Cohen, Jeremy (2016): A Study on the History and Functionality of Real Estate Crowdfunding. Available online at http://repository.upenn.edu/joseph_wharton_scholars/19, checked on 10/25/2018.

Coinbase (Ed.) (2020a): What countries are buys and sells available in? Available online at https://help.coinbase.com/en/coinbase/trading-and-funding/buying-selling-or-converting-crypto/what-countries-are-buys-and-sells-available-in.html, updated on 3/21/2020, checked on 3/23/2020.

Coinbase (Ed.) (2020b): About. Available online at https://www.coinbase.com/about, updated on 3/23/2020, checked on 3/23/2020.

CoinMarketCap (Ed.) (2020a): 24 Hour Volume Rankings (Exchange). Available online at https://coinmarketcap.com/rankings/exchanges/reported/, updated on 3/31/2020, checked on 3/31/2020.

CoinMarketCap (Ed.) (2020b): Percentage of Total Market Capitalization (Dominance). Available online at https://coinmarketcap.com/charts/, updated on 3/23/2020, checked on 3/23/2020.

CoinMetrics (Ed.) (2020): CM Lookup (Assets/Metrics by API Key, Data Dictionary). Available online at https://coinmetrics.io/tools/, updated on 3/24/2020, checked on 4/7/2020.

Companies House (Ed.) (2019): Group Strategic Report, Report of the Directors and Consolidated Financial Statements for the Year ended 31 March 2019 for Meniga Limited.

Available online at https://beta.companieshouse.gov.uk/company/08822710/filing-history, checked on 2/24/2020.

comScore (Ed.) (2020): Comscore Explicit Core Search Query Report. Total U.S. – Desktop Home & Work Locations. Available online at https://www.comscore.com/Insights/Rankings?country=US#tab_search_query/, updated on 4/7/2020, checked on 4/7/2020.

Consorsbank (2017): Herzlich Willkommen im Max-Morlock-Stadion! Available online at https://max-morlock-stadion-2017.de/, checked on 11/29/2018.

Contracts for Difference Verband e.V. (2017): CFD-Markstudie: Typologisierung von CFD-Investoren. Statistik im Auftrag des Contracts for Difference Verband e.V. Available online at https://www.cfd-portal.com/wp-content/uploads/CFD_Marktstudie_2017.pdf, checked on 12/23/2019.

Coresight Research (Ed.) (2017): Amazon Pay Places: Amazon's Next Conquest Could Be Mobile Payments. Available online at https://coresight.com/research/amazon-pay-places-amazons-next-conquest-could-be-mobile-payments/, updated on 8/8/2017, checked on 9/3/2018.

Credit Karma: Credit Karma – How it works. Available online at https://www.creditkarma.com/faq/howitworks, checked on 2/18/2019.

CreditLoan (Ed.) (2020): The Story Behind Avant's Success. Available online at https://www.creditloan.com/blog/story-behind-avants-success/#table-of-contents, updated on 5/9/2020, checked on 6/1/2020.

Crowdcircus (2018): Wie funktioniert Immobilien Crowdinvesting? Available online at https://crowdcircus.com/de/news/wie-funktioniert-immobilien-crowdinvesting, updated on 4/2/2018, checked on 10/25/2018.

Crunchbase (Ed.) (2019a): AngelList. Available online at https://www.crunchbase.com/organization/angellist, checked on 9/28/2018.

Crunchbase (Ed.) (2019b): Ant Financial. Available online at https://www.crunchbase.com/organization/alipay#section-locked-charts, checked on 10/7/2018.

Crunchbase (Ed.) (2019c): eToro. Available online at https://www.crunchbase.com/organization/etoro#section-overview, updated on 12/23/2019, checked on 8/20/2018.

Crunchbase (Ed.) (2019d): PayPal, checked on 10/1/2018.

Crunchbase (Ed.) (2019e): Revolut. Available online at https://www.crunchbase.com/organization/revolut#section-locked-charts, checked on 12/9/2019.

Crunchbase (Ed.) (2019f): Skrill (Moneybookers). Available online at https://www.crunchbase.com/organization/moneybookers#section-overview, checked on 12/9/2019.

Crunchbase (Ed.) (2019g): Tencent Holdings. Available online at https://www.crunchbase.com/organization/tencent#section-overview, checked on 12/9/2019.

Crunchbase (Ed.) (2019h): wikifolio. Available online at https://www.crunchbase.com/organization/wikifolio#section-overview, checked on 12/23/2019.

Crunchbase (Ed.) (2019i): ZuluTrade. Available online at https://www.crunchbase.com/organization/zulutrade, checked on 12/23/2019.

Crunchbase (Ed.) (2020a): Affirm. Available online at https://www.crunchbase.com/organization/affirm, checked on 11/23/2018.

Crunchbase (Ed.) (2020b): Avant. Available online at https://www.crunchbase.com/organization/avant-credit#section-overview, checked on 11/23/2018.

Crunchbase (Ed.) (2020c): ING Group. Available online at https://www.crunchbase.com/organization/ing-group#section-overview, checked on 2/19/2020.

Crunchbase (Ed.) (2020d): Coinbase. Available online at https://www.crunchbase.com/organization/coinbase#section-overview, updated on 3/23/2020, checked on 3/23/2020.

Crunchbase (Ed.) (2020e): Fintech Founding Rounds. Data consists of Angel, Pre-Seed, Seed, Series A-J and unknown (unclassified) financing rounds listed in the crunchbase.com database

between 04/02/1992and 04/30/2020. Available online at https://www.crunchbase.com/
search/funding_rounds, updated on 5/11/2020, checked on 5/11/2020.

Crunchbase (Ed.) (2020f): Stripe. Available online at https://www.crunchbase.com/organization/
stripe, updated on 6/4/2020, checked on 5/22/2020.

Crunchbase (Ed.) (2020g): Scalable Capital. Available online at https://www.crunchbase.com/orga
nization/scalable-capital, updated on 8/7/2020, checked on 8/17/2020.

Crunchbase (Ed.) (2020h): Personal Capital. Available online at https://www.crunchbase.com/organi
zation/personal-capital/company_financials, updated on 8/17/2020, checked on 8/17/2020.

Crunchbase (Ed.) (2020i): Klarna. Available online at https://www.crunchbase.com/organization/
klarna, updated on 11/9/2020, checked on 11/9/2020.

CryptoCompare (Ed.) (2015): How do digital signatures in Bitcoin work? Available online at https://
www.cryptocompare.com/wallets/guides/how-do-digital-signatures-in-bitcoin-work/, updated
on 2/12/2015, checked on 4/13/2020.

Cryptolist (Ed.) (2019): Was ist Ethereum? Kryptowährungen und Coins einfach erklärt. Available
online at https://www.cryptolist.de/ethereum, checked on 2/19/2019.

Dabkowski, Kenneth (2018): Banks Must Change Their Revenue Model to Survive: A Focused Look
at Consumers and Data. Edited by Money Summit. Available online at https://www.mx.com/
moneysummit/revenue-models-data, updated on 3/1/2018, checked on 3/3/2019.

Dapp, Thomas-Frank (2016): Robo advice – when machines manage your assets. (Fintech #8).
Deutsche Bank Research. Available online at http://www.dbresearch.com/servlet/reweb2.
ReWEB?rwnode=RPS_EN-PROD$DEU&rwsite=RPS_EN-PROD&rwobj=ReDisplay.Start.class&do
cument=PROD0000000000448038, checked on 9/26/2018.

Deer, Luke; Jackson, Mi; Yu, Yuxin (2015): The rise of peer-to-peer lending in China: an overview
and survey case study. Edited by Association of Chartered Certified Accountants. Available
online at https://www.accaglobal.com/content/dam/ACCA_Global/Technical/manage/ea-
china-p2p-lending.pdf, checked on 9/17/2019.

Defren, Timo; Groll, Alexander; Jamin, Gösta (2017): Anlagekonzepte auf Basis der Weisheit der Masse.
Eine Konkurrenz für passiv verwaltete Produkte? In Wilhelm Niehoff, Stefan Hirschmann (Eds.):
Aspekte der Digitalisierung in Banken. Köln: Bank-Verlag GmbH (Die Bank), pp. 201–211.

Deloitte GmbH Wirtschaftsprüfungsgesellschaft (2016): The expansion of Robo-Advisory in
Wealth Management. A closer look and analysis. Available online at https://www2.deloitte.
com/content/dam/Deloitte/de/Documents/financial-services/Deloitte-Robo-safe.pdf,
checked on 9/26/2018.

Deng, Iris; Chen, Celia (2018): The WeChat story: how Tencent's super-app changed China. Edited
by South China Morning Post. Available online at https://www.scmp.com/tech/article/
2159831/how-wechat-became-chinas-everyday-mobile-app, updated on 10/5/2018, checked
on 10/16/2018.

Dietz, Miklos; Härle Philipp; Khanna, Somesh (2016): A digital crack in banking´s business model.
Edited by McKinsey & Company. Available online at https://www.mckinsey.com/industries/finan
cial-services/our-insights/a-digital-crack-in-bankings-business-model, checked on 3/6/2019.

Doering, Philipp; Neumann, Sascha; Paul, Stephan (2015): A Primer on Social Trading Networks –
Institutional Aspects and Empirical Evidence. In *Presented at EFMA Annual Meetings 2015,
Breukelen/Amsterdam*. DOI: 10.2139/ssrn.2291421.

Dorfleitner, Gregor; Fischer, Lukas; Lung, Carina; Willmertinger, Philipp; Stang, Nico; Dietrich,
Natalie (2018): To Follow or Not to Follow – An Empirical Analysis of the Returns of Actors on
Social Trading Platforms. DOI: 10.2139/ssrn.3108422.

Dorfleitner, Gregor; Hornuf, Lars (2016): FinTech-Markt in Deutschland. With assistance of Matthias
Schmitt, Martina Weber. Available online at https://www.google.com/url?sa=t&rct=j&q=
&esrc=s&source=web&cd=1&cad=rja&uact=8&ved=2ahUKEwiur8rvv7DeAhVMqYsKHbJdAcsQF

jAAegQICBAC&url=>https//%3A%2F%2Fwww.bundesfinanzministerium.de%2FContent%2FDE
%2FStandardartikel%2FThemen%2FInternationales_Finanzmarkt%2F2016-11-21-Gutachten-
Langfassung.pdf%3F__blob%3DpublicationFile%26v%3D3&usg=
AOvVaw07wPOqef6pvcnNRTx8ZFeehttps//%3A%2F%2Fwww.bundesfinanzministerium.de%
2FContent%2FDE%2FStandardartikel%2FThemen%2FInternationales_Finanzmarkt%2F2016-11-
21-Gutachten-Langfassung.pdf%3F__blob%3DpublicationFile%26v%3D3&usg=
AOvVaw07wPOqef6pvcnNRTx8ZFee, checked on 10/31/2018.

Doyle, Simon (2016): New robo-advisor uses A.I. to take on active investing. Edited by Money
Sense. Available online at https://www.moneysense.ca/save/investing/new-robo-advisor-
uses-a-i-to-take-on-active-investing/, updated on 8/4/2016, checked on 9/26/2018.

Dragt, Bruce (2018): Alternative Payment Methods Are Taking Over Global Online Businesses.
Edited by PaymentsJournal. Available online at http://www.paymentsjournal.com/alternative-
payment-methods-are-taking-over-global-online-businesses/, checked on 10/1/2018.

Eifler, Miranda (2018): The OnDeck Score: Making Targeted Small Business Lending Decisions in
Real Time. Edited by OnDeck Capital, Inc. Available online at https://www.ondeck.com/resour
ces/ondeckscore, checked on 11/23/2018.

Emmanual, Jonathan (2015): What's the big deal? Big data in the financial services sector. Edited
by Bird&Bird. Available online at https://www.twobirds.com/~/media/whats-the-big-deal-big-
data-in-the-financial-services-sector-by-jonny-emmanuel.pdf, checked on 12/10/2018.

ESMA (2012): MiFID Questions and Answers. Investor Protection & Intermediaries.

eToro (2014): To risk or not to risk? Available online at https://www.etoro.com/blog/product-up
dates/risk-score/, updated on 6/2/2014, checked on 12/23/2019.

eToro (2017): Terms and Conditions. Affiliate Program Agreement. Available online at https://www.
etoropartners.com/media/aff-prog-effective-as-of-feb-2017.pdf, updated on 2/2/2017,
checked on 8/20/2018.

eToro (2018a): Can I invite my friend to eToro? Available online at https://www.etoro.com/en/
help#/path/My-Account/521262/Can-I-invite-my-friend-to-eToro.htm, checked on 12/23/2019.

eToro (2018b): CopyPortfolios. Available online at https://www.etoro.com/investing/copyportfo
lios/#, checked on 12/23/2019.

eToro (2018c): Plattformen – Historie. Available online at https://www.etoro.com/de/trading/plat
forms/, checked on 12/23/2019.

eToro (2018d): Popular Investor level requirements and benefits. Available online at https://www.
etoro.com/en/help#/path/Copy-Trading/886382132/Popular-Investor-level-requirements-and-
benefits.htm, checked on 12/23/2019.

eToro (2018e): Promote the World's Leading social investment network. Available online at https://
www.etoropartners.com/, checked on 12/23/2019.

eToro (2018f): Regulierung und Lizenz. Available online at https://www.etoro.com/de/customer-
service/regulation-license/, checked on 12/23/2019.

eToro (2018g): What are CopyPortfolios? Available online at https://www.etoro.com/customer-ser
vice/help/955033442/what-are-copyportfolios/, checked on 12/23/2019.

eToro (2018h): What does responsible trading mean? Available online at https://www.etoro.com/
en/help#/path/Copy-Trading/815849/What-does-responsible-trading-mean.htm, checked on
12/23/2019.

eToro (2019a): Become a Popular Investor on eToro Get copied, get paid. Available online at
https://www.etoro.com/en/popular-investor, checked on 12/23/2019.

eToro (2019b): Welcome to eToro. Available online at https://content.etoro.com/lp/practice_ac
count/, checked on 12/23/2019.

Eule, Alex (2018): As Robo-Advisors Cross $200 Billion in Assets, Schwab Leads in Performance.
Edited by Dow Jones & Company Inc. Available online at https://www.barrons.com/articles/as-

robo-advisors-cross-200-billion-in-assets-schwab-leads-in-performance-1517509393, updated on 2/3/2018, checked on 9/5/2019.

European Commission (2018): Crowdfunding. Available online at https://ec.europa.eu/info/busi ness-economy-euro/growth-and-investment/financing-investment/crowdfunding_en, updated on 3/8/2018, checked on 9/14/2018.

Everling, Oliver; Lempka, Robert (Eds.) (2016): Finanzdienstleister der nächsten Generation. Megatrend Digitalisierung: Strategien und Geschäftsmodelle. With assistance of Sabine Leutheusser-Schnarrenberger. Frankfurt School Verlag GmbH. 1. Auflage. Frankfurt am Main: Frankfurt School Verlag.

Fiebert, Andrew (2018): Fundrise Review: Diversify with Online Real Estate Investing. Available online at https://www.listenmoneymatters.com/fundrise-review/, checked on 10/31/2018.

Financial Conduct Authority (2016): Copy Trading. Available online at https://www.fca.org.uk/ firms/copy-trading, updated on 5/15/2016, checked on 8/9/2018.

Financial Technology Partners (2017): WEALTHTECH. The Digitization of Wealth Management. Available online at http://finte.ch/WealthTechReport, checked on 9/26/2018.

Fischer, Matthias (Ed.) (2004): Handbuch Wertmanagement in Banken und Versicherungen. 1. Aufl. Wiesbaden: Gabler.

Fischer, Matthias (2017): Robo Advisory und automatisierte Vermögensverwaltung. In *Zeitschrift für das gesamte Genossenschaftswesen* 67 (3), pp. 183–193. DOI: 10.1515/zfgg-2017-0019.

Fischer, Matthias (2020): Erfolgsbewertung von Fintechs durch die Analyse von Venture Capital Finanzierungsrunden. In: *Zeitschrift für das gesamte Genossenschaftswesen*, 70 (3), pp. 161–175. DOI: https://doi.org/10.1515/zfgg-2020–0012.

Fischer, Matthias; Tournois, Nadine (Eds.) (2008): La création de valeur dans la banque. Paris: Vuibert (Entreprendre).

Fischer, Matthias; Wagner, Dominik (2016): Die Wissenslücken der Deutschen bei der Geldanlage. Eine empirische Untersuchung. 1. Auflage 2017. Wiesbaden: Springer Gabler (essentials). Available online at http://www.springer.com/.

Fischer, Matthias; Wagner, Dominik (2017): Personal Finance Management als Basis für Robo Advice. In Wilhelm Niehoff, Stefan Hirschmann (Eds.): Aspekte der Digitalisierung in Banken. Köln: Bank-Verlag GmbH (Die Bank), pp. 177–189.

Fogg, B. J.; Soohoo, Cathy; Danielson, David; Marable, Leslie; Stanford, Julianne; Tauber, Ellen R. (2002): How Do People Evaluate a Web Site's Credibility? Results from a Large Study. Stanford University. Available online at https://www.google.com/url?sa%3Dt%26rct%3Dj%26q%3D% 26esrc%3Ds%26source%3Dweb%26cd%3D1%26cad%3Drja%26uact%3D8%26ved% 3D2ahUKEwi_w4Tpms7nAhWFlFwKHbadBREQFjAAegQIAxAB%26url%3D https//%3A%2F% 2Fdejanmarketing.com%2Fmedia%2Fpdf%2Fcredibility-online.pdf%26usg% 3DAOvVaw0xWIUOlk_rBDcIMJ0F3beV, checked on 2/13/2020.

Francis, Philip (2016): Blockchain, The Byzantine Generals Problem, and The Future of Identity Management. Edited by Medium. Available online at https://medium.com/@philfrancis77/ blockchain-the-byzantine-general-problem-and-the-future-of-identity-management-6b50a2eb815d, checked on 3/5/2019.

Friedberg, Barbara A. (2020): 2012 Robo-Advisors With the Most AuM. Who's Winning the Digital Investment Competition. Available online at https://www.roboadvisorpros.com/robo-advisors-with-most-aum-assets-under-management/, checked on 7/8/2020.

Friedman, Zack (2017): Amazon Banks On Its $3 Billion Loan Club. Edited by Forbes. Available online at https://www.forbes.com/sites/zackfriedman/2017/07/25/amazon-bank/ #7afc10156256, updated on 7/25/2017, checked on 9/5/2019.

Frøystad, Peter; Holm, Jarle (2015): Blockchain: Powering the Internet of Value. In *EvryLabs*. Available online at https://www.finyear.com/attachment/637653/, checked on 6/11/2019.

Fundrise, LLC (2018a): A New Portfolio Theory for the Technology Generation: Invest Like a Billion Dollar Institution. Available online at https://fundrise.com/education/blog-posts/a-new-portfo lio-theory-for-the-technology-generation-invest-like-a-billion, checked on 10/31/2018.

Fundrise, LLC (2018b): Frequently Asked Questions. Available online at https://fundrise.com/educa tion/faq, checked on 10/31/2018.

Fundrise, LLC (2018c): Investment. Available online at https://fundrise.com/investments, checked on 10/31/2018.

Fundrise, LLC (2018d): Meet the innovations behind our powerful new approach. Available online at https://fundrise.com/e-direct-investing, checked on 10/31/2018.

Fundrise, LLC (2018e): Save 20 – 40% vs. traditional investments through our end-to-end approach. Available online at https://fundrise.com/pricing, checked on 10/31/2018.

Fundrise, LLC (2018f): We follow a rigorous, institutional underwriting process. Available online at https://fundrise.com/real-estate-expertise?cta=Expert%20Analysis&utm_campaign=impactra dius&irgwc=1&utm_medium=cpa&utm_source=businessinsider&clickid= UdTV4F1tUTmFTI93JAT1yyfAUkg1slx5V24XwY0, checked on 10/31/2018.

Geenen, Wilhelmus van; Dorschel, Werner; Dorschel, Joachim (2015): Big Data in der Kreditwirtschaft. In Joachim Dorschel (Ed.): Praxishandbuch Big Data. Wirtschaft – Recht – Technik. With assistance of Joachim Dorschel. Wiesbaden: Springer Gabler, pp. 134–146.

Gierczak, Michael M.; Bretschneider, Ulrich; Haas, Philipp; Blohm, Ivo (2016): Crowdfunding: Outlining the New Era of Fundraising. In Dennis Brüntje, Oliver Gajda (Eds.): Crowdfunding in Europe. State of the Art in theory and practice. Cham: Springer (FGF studies in small business and entrepreneurship), pp. 7–23.

Global Banking & Finance Review (2011): Copy trading vs. mirror trading, which should you be doing? Available online at https://www.globalbankingandfinance.com/copy-trading-vs-mirror-trading-which-should-you-be-doing/, checked on 8/19/2018.

Gomes, Ben (2017): Our latest quality improvements for Search. Edited by Google. Available online at https://blog.google/products/search/our-latest-quality-improvements-search/, updated on 4/25/2017, checked on 4/7/2020.

Grabianowski, Ed; Pollette, Chris; Crawford, Stephanie (2019): How PayPal Works. https://www. howstuffworks.com. Available online at https://money.howstuffworks.com/paypal3.htm, updated on 5/3/2019, checked on 9/5/2019.

Grand View Research Inc. (Ed.) (2019): Blockchain Technology Market Size, Share, Industry Report, 2019–2025. Available online at https://www.grandviewresearch.com/industry-analysis/block chain-technology-market, checked on 3/4/2020.

Graziani, Thomas (2018): WeChat impact report 2018: all the latest WeChat data – WalktheChat. Available online at https://walkthechat.com/wechat-impact-report-2016/, checked on 10/17/2018.

Greenberg, Julia (2015): Fundrise lets common folk invest in posh real estate ventures. Available online at https://www.wired.com/2015/12/fundrise-wants-to-let-anyone-own-a-piece-of-a-sky scraper/, updated on 3/12/2015, checked on 10/31/2018.

Griffith, Erin (2017): Why Startups Are Trading IPOs for ICOs. Edited by Fortune. Available online at http://fortune.com/2017/05/05/ico-initial-coin-offering/, updated on 5/5/2017, checked on 3/9/2019.

Groenfeldt, Tom (2013): Banks Use Big Data To Understand Customers Across Channels. Edited by Forbes. Available online at https://www.forbes.com/sites/tomgroenfeldt/2013/06/11/banks-use-big-data-to-understand-customers-across-channels/, checked on 12/15/2018.

Groenfeldt, Tom (2017): 7 European Banks Form Blockchain Consortium For SMEs. Edited by Forbes. Available online at https://www.forbes.com/sites/tomgroenfeldt/2017/06/28/7-euro pean-banks-form-blockchain-consortium-for-smes/#7987b0023818, checked on 3/6/2019.

Gronau, Norbert; Thim, Christof; Fohrholz, Corinna (2016): Business Analytics in der deutschen Praxis. In *CON* 28 (8-9), pp. 472–479. DOI: 10.15358/0935-0381-2016-8-9-472.

Guo, Jia (2017): Alibaba's Yu'e Bao becomes world's largest money market fund – China business and technology news from April 28, 2017. Edited by Supchina. Available online at https://supchina.com/2017/04/28/alibabas-yue-bao-becomes-worlds-largest-money-market-fund-china-business-technology-news-april-28-2017/, checked on 10/9/2018.

Gutierrez, Carlo (2017): The "Internet of Value": 8 Top Sectors Being transformed by Blockchain. Edited by Altoros. Available online at https://www.altoros.com/blog/the-internet-of-value-8-top-sectors-being-transformed-by-blockchain/, updated on 5/4/2017, checked on 3/5/2019.

Hackerbay (2015): Angellist: A Zero Capital, Infinite Carry Venture Capital Fund. Available online at https://medium.com/@hackerbayteam/angellist-a-zero-capital-infinite-carry-venture-capital-fund-d37fee8b6328, updated on 6/14/2015, checked on 10/29/2018.

Hahn, Christopher; Naumann, Daniel (2014): Start-up Phase. In Christopher Hahn (Ed.): Finanzierung und Besteuerung von Start-up-Unternehmen. Praxisbuch für erfolgreiche Gründer. Wiesbaden: Springer Gabler, pp. 127–197.

Hays, Demelza Kelso; Stoeferle, Ronald-Peter; Valek, Mark J. (2017): crypto research.report. In *Incrementum Crypto Research Report* (1st Edition). Available online at http://cryptoresearch.report/wp-content/uploads/2017/12/Incrementum-Crypto-Research-Report-Edition-1-German-version.pdf, checked on 2/19/2019.

Henkelmann, Stefan; Dahmen, Lennart J. (2019): Blockchain & Cryptocurrency Regulation 2020 Germany. Edited by Global Legal Insights. Global Legal Group. Available online at https://www.globallegalinsights.com/practice-areas/blockchain-laws-and-regulations/germany, checked on 3/31/2020.

Heshmore (2017): How much data does google handle?? Heshmore. Available online at https://www.heshmore.com/how-much-data-does-google-handle/, checked on 12/10/2018.

Higginson, Matt (2016): How Blockchain could disrupt cross-border Payments. The distributed-ledger technology is being tested for its ability to deliver benefits for various forms of payment. In *Banking Perspectives*, pp. 52–62. Available online at https://www.theclearinghouse.org/-/media/new/tch/documents/banking-perspectives/2016q4bankingperspectives.pdf, checked on 3/6/2019.

Hileman, Garrick; Rauchs, Michel (2017): Global blockchain benchmarking study. Edited by Cambridge Centre for Alternative Finance.

Hong Kong Exchanges and Clearing (Ed.) (2018): Post Hearing Information 51 Credit Card Inc. Available online at http://www3.hkexnews.hk/listedco/listconews/sehk/2018/0713/ltn20180713106.pdf, checked on 2/18/2019.

Hua, Sha (2018): Plötzlich in der ersten Liga – was das teuerste Fintech der Welt auszeichnet. Die Alibaba-Tochter Ant Financial könnte bald zu einer der wertvollsten Firmen weltweit werden. Ein Eckpfeiler des Erfolgs: die Bezahlplattform Alipay. Edited by Handelsblatt. Available online at https://www.handelsblatt.com/finanzen/banken-versicherungen/ant-financial-ploetzlich-in-der-ersten-liga-was-das-teuerste-fintech-der-welt-auszeichnet/22663308.html?ticket=ST-9995180-kVHdcyC3bFe49cto9kcx-ap2, checked on 10/7/2018.

ING online (Ed.) (2018): Robo talk. Available online at https://www.ing.com/Newsroom/All-news/Robo-talk.htm, updated on 4/5/2018, checked on 5/23/2019.

ING online (Ed.) (2019): 2018 ING Group Annual Report. Available online at https://www.ing.com/About-us/Annual-reporting-suite/Annual-Report/2018-Annual-Report.htm, checked on 5/16/2019.

Inside Amazon Videos (2014): The Amazon Lending team. Edited by YouTube. Available online at https://www.youtube.com/watch?v=2kyeV2fxqdQ, updated on 1/9/2014, checked on 9/5/2019.

Internal Revenue Service (2014): Notice 2014–21. In *Internal Revenue Bulletin* (2014–16). Available online at https://www.irs.gov/irb/2014-16_IRB#NOT-2014-21, checked on 3/3/2019.

Intuit (2019): FORM 10-K. For the fiscal year ended July 31, 2019. Edited by Intuit. Available online at https://s23.q4cdn.com/935127502/files/doc_financials/quarterly/2019/q4/817655_007_Print_CLEAN.pdf, updated on 8/30/2019, checked on 2/13/2020.

Jacobs, Harrison (2018): One photo shows that China is already in a cashless future. Business Insider. Available online at https://www.businessinsider.de/alipay-wechat-pay-china-mobile-payments-street-vendors-musicians-2018-5?r=US&IR=T, updated on 5/29/2018, checked on 10/1/2018.

JD.com (2018): Corporate Factsheet, p. 1. Available online at http://1cn9a51rqjf725dws347pvfp.wpengine.netdna-cdn.com/wp-content/uploads/2018/08/JD-corporate-factsheet.pdf, checked on 10/17/2018.

Jessop, Simon; Hunnicutt, Trevor (2017): BlackRock takes Scalable Capital stake in Europe 'robo-advisor' push. Reuters. Available online at https://www.reuters.com/article/us-blackrock-scalablecapital-idUSKBN19A322, updated on 6/20/2017, checked on 9/26/2018.

JPMorgan Chase & Co. (Ed.) (2017): Annual Report 2016. Available online at https://www.jpmorganchase.com/corporate/investor-relations/document/2016-annualreport.pdf, checked on 4/10/2019.

JPMorgan Chase & Co. (Ed.) (2018): Chase Business Quick Capital®. a new way to get fast funding for your business. Available online at https://www.chase.com/business/quickcapital-loan/faq.

Juengerkes, Bjoern Erik (2016): FinTechs and Banks – Collaboration is Key. In Susanne Chishti, Janos Barberis (Eds.): The FinTech book. Chichester: Wiley, pp. 179–182.

Kaplan, Steven N.; Lerner, Josh (2016): Venture Capital Data: Opportunities and Challenges. Available online at https://www.hbs.edu/faculty/Publication%20Files/17-012_10de1f93-30e4-4a98-858c-4137556ec037.pdf, checked on 6/24/2020.

Kaufman, Adam (2018): Intro To Real Estate Crowdfunding: Not All Models Are Created Equal. Available online at https://www.forbes.com/sites/forbesrealestatecouncil/2018/08/13/intro-to-real-estate-crowdfunding-not-all-models-are-created-equal/#12b21b527bc2, updated on 8/13/2018, checked on 10/19/2018.

Kendall, Jake (2017): Fintech Companies Could Give Billions of People More Banking Options. Edited by Harvard Business Review online. Available online at https://hbsp.harvard.edu/product/H03EQQ-PDF-ENG?Ntt=HBR+fintech+2020+fintech*&itemFindingMethod=Search, updated on 1/20/2017, checked on 6/24/2020.

Kern, Andreas (2017): Wikifolio: Social Trading. In Victor Tiberius, Christoph Rasche (Eds.): FinTechs. Disruptive Geschäftsmodelle im Finanzsektor. Wiesbaden: Springer Gabler (Edition Bankmagazin), pp. 189–198.

Kickstarter, PBC (Ed.) (2018): Unser Ziel ist es, die Umsetzung kreativer Projekte zu ermöglichen. Available online at https://www.kickstarter.com/about?ref=global-footer, checked on 9/28/2018.

Kickstarter, PBC (Ed.) (2020a): Creator Handbook. Available online at https://www.kickstarter.com/help/handbook, checked on 2/6/2020.

Kickstarter, PBC (Ed.) (2020b): Gebühren in Deutschland. Available online at https://www.kickstarter.com/help/fees?ref=faq-basics_fees, checked on 1/6/2020.

Kickstarter, PBC (Ed.) (2020c): Kickstarter in Zahlen. Available online at https://www.kickstarter.com/help/stats?ref=about_subnav, checked on 1/6/2020.

Kickstarter, PBC (Ed.) (2020d): Most Funded Projects. Available online at https://www.kickstarter.com/discover/most-funded, updated on 1/8/2020, checked on 1/8/2020.

Kiisel, Ty (2018): What Is a Business Credit Score? Available online at https://www.ondeck.com/resources/business-credit-score, checked on 11/23/2018.

Kinzel, Mirjam (2018): Wer darf ein Projekt anlegen und was muss beachtet werden? Edited by betterplace.org. Available online at https://www.betterplace.org/c/hilfe/projekt-anlegen, updated on 10/2/2018, checked on 1/6/2020.

Klarna Bank AB (Ed.) (2016): Annual report 2015. Klarna AB. Available online at https://reports.klarna.com/investor-relations/2015/Annual-report-Klarna-AB-2015-EN.pdf, checked on 7/9/2020.

Klarna Bank AB (11/19/2018): Klarna launches 'Boost' to supercharge SME growth. Nyman, Johanna. Available online at https://www.klarna.com/international/press/klarna-launches-boost-to-supercharge-sme-growth/, checked on 7/9/2020.

Klarna Bank AB (Ed.) (2020a): Bezahle mit Klarna. Available online at https://www.klarna.com/de/smooooth/, checked on 7/8/2020.

Klarna Bank AB (Ed.) (2020b): Europäische Standardinformation für Verbraucherkredite. Available online at https://cdn.klarna.com/1.0/shared/content/legal/de_de/consumer_credit.pdf, checked on 7/8/2020.

Klarna Bank AB (Ed.) (2020c): Mit Klarna verkaufen. Available online at https://www.klarna.com/de/verkaeufer/, checked on 7/8/2020.

Klarna Bank AB (Ed.) (2020d): Sofortüberweisung. Einfach und direkt bezahlen. Available online at https://www.klarna.com/sofort/, checked on 7/8/2020.

Klarna Bank AB (Ed.) (2020e): Annual report 2019. Klarna Bank AB. Available online at https://www.klarna.com/assets/2020/04/Klarna_Bank_AB_publ_Annual_Report_2019_EN.pdf, checked on 7/8/2020.

Klarna Inc. (Ed.) (2018): WebBank Klarna Credit Account Agreement. Available online at https://cdn.klarna.com/1.0/shared/content/legal/en_us/account/terms.pdf, updated on 10/11/2018, checked on 7/8/2020.

Klarna Inc. (Ed.) (2020a): 4 interest-free installments. Available online at https://www.klarna.com/us/customer-service/csc/4-interest-free-installments/, checked on 7/8/2020.

Klarna Inc. (Ed.) (2020b): About us. Available online at https://www.klarna.com/us/about-us/, updated on 7/8/2020, checked on 7/8/2020.

Klarna Inc. (Ed.) (2020c): Klarna for business. Available online at https://www.klarna.com/us/business/, checked on 7/8/2020.

Klarna Inc. (Ed.) (2020d): Monthly financing. Available online at https://www.klarna.com/us/customer-service/csc/monthly-financing/, checked on 7/8/2020.

Klarna Inc. (Ed.) (2020e): Pay later in 30 days. Available online at https://www.klarna.com/us/customer-service/csc/pay-later-in-30-days/, checked on 7/8/2020.

Klarna Inc. (Ed.) (2020f): Pricing. Available online at https://www.klarna.com/us/business/pricing/, checked on 7/8/2020.

Knezevic, Dejan; Teelucksingh, Gary (2017): Transformative Nature of Artificial Intelligence (AI) in Wealth Management. Capco. Available online at https://www.capco.com/-/media/CapcoMedia/transformative-nature-of-artificial-intelligence-in-wealth-management.ashx, checked on 9/26/2018.

Kocianski, Sarah (2016): THE ROBO ADVISING REPORT. Market forecasts, key growth drivers, and how automated asset management will change the advisory industry. Business Insider. Available online at https://intelligence.businessinsider.com/post/the-robo-advising-report-market-forecasts-key-growth-drivers-and-how-automated-asset-management-will-change-the-advisory-industry-2016-5, checked on 9/26/2018.

Konakanchi, Prashanth (2004): Paypal.Com´s Business Model.

Kotas, Carsten (2018): Real Estate Crowdfunding in Deutschland – Eine empirische Untersuchung vom 01. 01.2012-31.12.2017. In *Arbeitspapiere der FOM* (69).

Kothari, Rohit; Bansal, Tarun (2017): Robo Advisors. Tracxn Robo Advisors Report June 2017. Traxcn. Available online at https://www.slideshare.net/Tracxn/tracxn-research-robo-advisors-report-june-2017-77327211, checked on 9/27/2018.

Kowlessar, Astrid (2016): The Scorecard Pre-Money Valuation Method For Pre-Revenue Startups Explained. Available online at https://magazine.startus.cc/scorecard-pre-money-valuation-method-explained/, checked on 9/26/2018.

KPMG and H2 Ventures (2017): Fintech100. Leading Global Fintech Innovators, p. 12, checked on 10/6/2018.

Kristjánsson, Kristján (2015a): Comdirect bank launches PFM Service powered by Meniga. Edited by Meniga. Available online at https://blog.meniga.com/comdirect-bank-launches-pfm-ser vice-powered-by-meniga-b2b801018728, updated on 9/24/2015, checked on 2/19/2020.

Kristjánsson, Kristján (2015b): Consors Bank takes the lead with Meniga. Edited by Meniga. Available online at https://blog.meniga.com/consors-bank-takes-the-lead-with-meniga-e8f1a8e64183, updated on 9/24/2015, checked on 2/19/2020.

Kristjánsson, Kristján (2015c): Meniga powers ING Direct into the future. Available online at https://blog.meniga.com/meniga-powers-ing-direct-into-the-future-7d0f2fabbd75, updated on 9/24/2015, checked on 2/19/2020.

Kristjánsson, Kristján (2015d): Santander and Meniga partner to deliver world class personal finance management to Santander's. Available online at https://blog.meniga.com/santander-and-meniga-partner-to-deliver-world-class-personal-finance-management-to-santander-s-8c913b69af76, updated on 11/10/2015, checked on 2/19/2020.

Kumar, Arbin; Bansal, Ritik (2020): Tracxn Sector Report Robo Advisors. April 2019. Edited by Tracxn. Available online at https://de.slideshare.net/Tracxn/tracxn-robo-advisors-startup-land scape, checked on 8/17/2020.

Kuzmina, Anna (2018): Alipay & WeChat Pay: history and strategy – What the money – Medium. Medium. Available online at https://medium.com/what-the-money/alipay-wechat-pay-history-and-strategy-af1b19d66556, checked on 10/16/2018.

Lee, David K.C.; Teo, Ernie G. S. (2015): Emergence of Fintech and the Lasic Principles. In *SSRN Journal*, pp. 5–9. DOI: 10.2139/ssrn.2668049.

Lending Club (Ed.) (2010): Lending Club Selected as Mint.com Goals Launch Partner to Help Consumers Pay Off Credit Card Debt, Keep More of Their Money. Lending Club Offers Lower Cost Personal Loans to Help Pay Off Credit Card Debt, updated on 6/30/2010, checked on 2/18/2019.

LendingClub (2018a): About the Trading Platform. Available online at https://www.lendingclub.com/investing/investor-education/about-the-trading-platform, checked on 10/25/2018.

LendingClub (Ed.) (2018b): Amounts for personal loans. Available online at https://help.lending club.com/hc/en-us/articles/213706198-Amounts-for-personal-loans, checked on 12/23/2019.

LendingClub (2018c): Business loan amounts, rates, and fees. Available online at https://help.lend ingclub.com/hc/en-us/articles/215496568-Business-loan-amounts-rates-and-fees, checked on 10/28/2018.

LendingClub (Ed.) (2018d): Turning automated investing on and off. Available online at https://www.lendingclub.com/investing/investor-education/automated-investing, checked on 10/25/2018.

LendingClub (2018e): What is a LendingClub Note? Available online at https://www.lendingclub.com/investing/investor-education/what-is-a-lendingclub-note, checked on 10/25/2018.

LendingClub (2019a): Business Loans up to $500K funds in as little as a few days. Available online at https://www.lendingclub.com/business/?utm_source=LC&utm_medium=link&utm_cam paign=pl_top_nav&u=1, checked on 12/23/2019.

LendingClub (2019b): Lending Club Statistics. Available online at https://www.lendingclub.com/info/statistics.action, updated on 12/31/2019, checked on 4/7/2020.

LendingClub (2019c): Personal Loans up to $40,000. Available online at https://www.lendingclub.com/loans/personal-loans, checked on 12/23/2019.

LendingClub (2019d): Rates and Fees. Available online at https://www.lendingclub.com/public/rates-and-fees.action, checked on 10/25/2018.

LendingClub Asset Management, LLC (2018): About Us. Available online at https://www.lcam.com/, checked on 10/25/2018.

LendInvest Limited (Ed.) (2020): How does the investment contract work? Available online at https://www.lendinvest.com/help/investors/managing-my-investments/#how-does-the-investment-contract-work, checked on 9/17/2019.

Levy, Benjamin (2015): The Rise of Angel(List) and how it is rapidly changing the game of angel investing. Edited by BootstrapLabs. Available online at https://bootstraplabs.com/blog/2015/05/06/the-rise-of-angellist-and-how-it-rapidly-is-changing-the-game-of-angel-investing/, updated on 5/6/2015, checked on 10/29/2018.

Lewis, Antony (2015): A gentle introduction to digital tokens. Edited by Bits on Blocks. Available online at https://assets.ctfassets.net/sdlntm3tthp6/RChVLUNxAGimseMUQWokQ/b846d6a79b15881e137bcb5c7c37c2e7/A-Gentle-Introduction-To-Digital-Tokens-WEB.pdf, updated on 10/29/2015, checked on 3/3/2019.

Li, Jennifer (2015): OnDeck: Solving for Nonconsumption with Simple, Fast and Convenient Financing. Edited by Harvard Business School Digital Initiative. Available online at https://www.hbs.edu/openforum/openforum.hbs.org/goto/challenge/understand-digital-transformation-of-business/ondeck-solving-for-nonconsumption-with-simple-fast-and-convenient-financing/comments/c-91ba4a4478a66bee9812b0804b6f9d1b.html, updated on 4/14/2015, checked on 11/29/2018.

Libra Association (Ed.) (2019): libra Whitepaper. Available online at https://libra.org/de-DE/whitepaper/#introduction, checked on 9/5/2019.

Lochmaier, Lothar (2014): Social Trading kommt in Mode. Available online at https://www.wiso-net.de/dosearch/:3:FZS?q=0342-3182.IS.+AND+2014.YR.+AND+5.HN.+AND+58.SE.&explicitSearch=true#DIBA__2014050148, checked on 8/2/2018.

Lochner, Mario (2014): Kein Erfolg an der Börse? Setzen Sie auf die Intelligenz der Masse. Available online at https://www.focus.de/finanzen/boerse/social-trading/social-trading-wie-schlau-ist-die-masse_id_3945316.html, checked on 8/9/2018.

Lohnsteuerhilfe Bayern e.V. (Ed.) (2018): So wird der Handel mit Kryptowährungen versteuert. Available online at https://www.lohi.de/news/article/so-wird-der-handel-mit-kryptowaehrungen-versteuert.html, updated on 7/31/2018, checked on 3/31/2020.

Luciano, Gabrielle (2016): mBank ramps up digital banking with Meniga. Available online at https://blog.meniga.com/mbank-ramps-up-digital-banking-with-meniga-930132bd7403, updated on 8/30/2016, checked on 2/19/2020.

Lunden, Ingrid (2020): Scalable Capital raises $58M at a $460M valuation for its robo-investment platform. Edited by techcrunch. Available online at https://techcrunch-com.cdn.ampproject.org/c/s/techcrunch.com/2020/07/22/scalable-capital-raises-58m-at-a-460m-valuation-for-its-robo-investment-platform/amp/, updated on 7/22/2020, checked on 8/17/2020.

Macheel, Tanya (2017): One year in: How JPMorgan is transforming small-business lending. Edited by Tearsheet. Available online at https://www.tearsheet.co/modern-banking-experience/one-year-in-how-jp-morgan-is-transforming-small-business-lending, updated on 6/21/2017, checked on 11/30/2018.

Magas, Julia (2018): Crypto Exchange Hacks in Review: Proactive Steps and Expert Advice. Available online at https://cointelegraph.com/news/crypto-exchange-hacks-in-review-proactive-steps-and-expert-advice, updated on 8/31/2018, checked on 3/23/2020.

Magnusson, Finnur (2016): How Meniga engages with people through the development process. Edited by Meniga. Available online at https://blog.meniga.com/how-meniga-engages-with-people-through-the-development-process-7f395d1d4078, checked on 2/18/2019.

Manchiraju, Srividya; Vudayagiri, Ganesh; Garg, Gaurav: Top 10 Trends In Payments In 2016. Available online at https://www.capgemini.com/wp-content/uploads/2017/07/payments_trends_2016.pdf, checked on 3/5/2019.

Matonis, Jon (2012): Another Market Not Available to U.S. Citizens. Available online at https://www.forbes.com/sites/jonmatonis/2012/04/09/another-market-not-available-to-u-s-citizens/#531d70d73482, updated on 4/9/2012, checked on 8/20/2018.

Matthiesen, Marie-Louise; Steininger, Bertram I. (2017): Finanzinnovation: Crowdfunding für die Immobilienwirtschaft (Financial Innovation: Crowdfunding for the Real Estate Market).

McAlone, Nathan (2016): This company raised over $1 million on Kickstarter to make the 'world's thinnest watch' – now it's declared bankruptcy and those backers likely won't see a penny. Available online at https://www.businessinsider.de/this-company-raised-over-1-million-to-make-the-worlds-thinnest-watch-now-its-declared-bankruptcy-and-those-backers-probably-wont-see-a-penny-2016-5?r=US&IR=T, updated on 5/6/2016, checked on 10/30/2018.

McCarthy, Brayden; Mills, Karen (2017): How Banks Can Compete Against an Army of Fintech Startups. Edited by Harvard Business Review online. Available online at https://hbsp.harvard.edu/product/H03MS6-PDF-ENG?Ntt=HBR+fintech+2020+fintech*&itemFindingMethod=Search, updated on 4/26/2017, checked on 6/24/2020.

McDonald, Rory; Junnarkar, Samir; Lane, David (2019): Marcus by Goldman Sachs. Edited by Harvard Business School Publishing. Harvard Business School. Available online at https://hbsp.harvard.edu/product/620005-PDF-ENG?Ntt=HBR+fintech+2020+fintech*&itemFindingMethod=Search, checked on 6/24/2020.

McWaters, R. Jesse (2016): The future of financial infrastructure. In *World Economic Forum*. Available online at http://www3.weforum.org/docs/WEF_The_future_of_financial_infrastructure.pdf, checked on 3/5/2019.

Meniga (Ed.) (2019): Products. Available online at https://www.meniga.com/products, checked on 2/18/2019.

Meniga (Ed.) (2020a): About. Available online at https://www.meniga.com/about/, checked on 2/18/2019.

Meniga (2020b): Services. Edited by Meniga. Available online at https://www.meniga.com/services/, checked on 2/18/2019.

Meola, Andrew (2017a): Vanguard Personal Advisor Services Review 2017. Fees, Returns, Investing Services & Competitors. Business Insider. Available online at https://www.businessinsider.de/vanguard-personal-advisor-services-review?r=US&IR=T, checked on 9/26/2018.

Meola, Andrew (2017b): Personal Capital Review 2017. Fees, Returns, Investing Services & Competitors. Business Insider. Available online at https://www.businessinsider.com/personal-capital-review?r=DE&IR=T, updated on 2/8/2017, checked on 9/26/2018.

Meola, Andrew (2017c): Scalable Capital Review 2017. Fees, Returns, Investing Services & Competitors. Business Insider. Available online at https://www.businessinsider.de/scalable-capital-review?r=US&IR=T, updated on 3/22/2017, checked on 9/26/2018.

Meyer zu Schwabedissen, Gustav; Prager, Oliver (2016): Der CFD as „Universal Wrapper" (Basisprodukt) für Next-Generation-Finance-Geschäftsmodelle. In Oliver Everling, Robert Lempka (Eds.): Finanzdienstleister der nächsten Generation. Megatrend Digitalisierung: Strategien und Geschäftsmodelle. With assistance of Sabine Leutheusser-Schnarrenberger. 1. Auflage. Frankfurt am Main: Frankfurt School Verlag, pp. 233–256.

Millward, Steven (2018a): 7 years of WeChat. Techinasia. Available online at https://www.techinasia.com/history-of-wechat, updated on 10/16/2018, checked on 10/16/2018.

Millward, Steven (2018b): 7 years of WeChat DUBL. Techinasia. Available online at https://www.techinasia.com/history-of-wechat, updated on 10/4/2018, checked on 10/6/2018.

Mint (Ed.) (2020a): Free Credit Score & Free Credit Report with No Credit Card. Available online at https://www.mint.com/how-mint-works/credit, checked on 2/13/2020.

Mint (Ed.) (2020b): Investment Tracker & Investment Tracking Software. Available online at https://www.mint.com/how-mint-works/investments, checked on 2/13/2020.

Mint (Ed.) (2020c): Safety & Security for Your Personal Finances. Available online at https://www.mint.com/how-mint-works/security, checked on 2/13/2020.

Mint (Ed.) (2020d): What is Mint, and how does it work? Available online at https://www.mint.com/how-mint-works, checked on 2/13/2020.

Mishevski, Filip (2018): How we designed Inga, a delightful banking chatbot for ING. Edited by A Medium Corporation online. Available online at https://uxdesign.cc/how-we-designed-inga-a-de lightful-banking-chatbot-for-ing-941d18c4646f, updated on 5/14/2018, checked on 5/16/2019.

Mitsyk, Alla; Fischer, Matthias (2019): Global Bank Survey – Empirical Comparison 2008–2017 of Return on Equity and Cost Income Ratio. In Financial Research Note 07/2019 (Nr. 05), pp. 1–21. Available online at https://d-nb.info/1194562280/34, checked on 5/28/2020.

Morabito, Vincenzo (2015): Big Data and Analytics. Cham: Springer International Publishing, checked on 4/23/2019.

Morabito, Vincenzo (2017): Business innovation through blockchain. The B3 perspective. Cham: Springer International Publishing. Available online at https://ebookcentral.proquest.com/lib/gbv/detail.action?docID=4793398.

Morgan, Blake (2017): How Chatbots Will Transform Customer Experience. An Infographic. Forbes. Available online at https://www.forbes.com/sites/blakemorgan/2017/03/21/how-chatbots-will-transform-customer-experience-an-infographic/#13858aa07fb4, updated on 3/21/2017, checked on 12/16/2019.

Morgan Stanley (2015): Can P2P Lending Reinvent Banking? Available online at https://www.mor ganstanley.com/ideas/p2p-marketplace-lending, checked on 9/14/2018.

Morgenthaler, Paul (2016): The Digital Lending Revolution. In Oliver Everling, Robert Lempka (Eds.): Finanzdienstleister der nächsten Generation. Megatrend Digitalisierung: Strategien und Geschäftsmodelle. With assistance of Sabine Leutheusser-Schnarrenberger. 1. Auflage. Frankfurt am Main: Frankfurt School Verlag, pp. 203–216.

Mougayar, William (2016): The business blockchain. Promise, practice, and application of the next Internet technology. With assistance of Vitalik Buterin. Hoboken, New Jersey: John Wiley & Sons Inc. Available online at http://proquest.tech.safaribooksonline.de/9781119300311.

MYOB Technology Pty Ltd (2018a): It's time to celebrate. We're exclusively offering MYOB loans powered by OnDeck to our cu stomers with no repayments until 2019. Available online at https://www.myob.com/au/small-business/ondeck-business-loans, checked on 11/23/2018.

MYOB Technology Pty Ltd (2018b): Set your business up for success. Available online at https://www.myob.com/au, checked on 11/23/2018.

Nakamoto, Satoshi (2008): Bitcoin: A Peer-to-Peer Electroncic Cash System. Available online at https://bitcoin.org/bitcoin.pdf, checked on 2/19/2019.

Nakamoto, Satoshi; Falke, Marco; Jorge, Timón; Wuille, Peter; Todd, Pieter; Pavel, Janik et al. (2016): bitcoin/src/amount.h. Available online at https://raw.githubusercontent.com/bitcoin/bitcoin/08a7316c144f9f2516db8fa62400893f4358c5ae/src/amount.h, checked on 3/11/2020.

National Futures Association (2018a): Commodity Trading Advisor (CTA) Registration. Available online at https://www.nfa.futures.org/registration-membership/who-has-to-register/cta.html, checked on 8/20/2018.

National Futures Association (2018b): Introducing Broker (IB) Registration. Available online at https://www.nfa.futures.org/registration-membership/who-has-to-register/ib.html, checked on 8/14/2018.

Nimführ, Marcel (2017): Was ist ein ICO und wie funktioniert es? – Bitcoin Blase. Edited by Bitcoin-Blase. Available online at https://www.bitcoinblase.at/ico/, updated on 10/2/2017, checked on 2/19/2019.

O'Connor, Matt R. (2016): Lending Club: Sound Business Model At A Discount. Edited by Seeking Alpha. Available online at https://seekingalpha.com/article/3983093-lending-club-sound-busi ness-model-discount, updated on 6/20/2016, checked on 10/30/2018.

Oehler, Andreas; Horn, Matthias; Wendt, Stefan (2016): Benefits from social trading? Empirical evidence for certificates on wikifolios. In *International Review of Financial Analysis* 46, pp.202–210. DOI: 10.1016/j.irfa.2016.05.007.

Ómarsson, Ómar Þór (2018): Íslandsbanki invests €3 million in Meniga's digital banking solutions. Edited by Meniga. Available online at https://blog.meniga.com/%C3%ADslandsbanki-invests-3-million-in-menigas-digital-banking-solutions-f2401a84b006, updated on 11/6/2018, checked on 2/19/2020.

OnDeck Capital, Inc. (Ed.) (2015): OnDeck Announces General Availability of Marketplace Platform to Connect Institutional Investors with Main Street. Available online at https://www.ondeck. com/press-releases/ondeck-announces-general-availability-of-marketplace-platform-to-con nect-institutional-investors-with-main-street, checked on 11/23/2018.

OnDeck Capital, Inc. (Ed.) (2017a): 4Q 2017 Investor Presentation. OnDeck, checked on 11/23/2018.

OnDeck Capital, Inc. (2017b): Chase, OnDeck Extend Existing Relationship. Available online at https://www.ondeck.com/news/chase-ondeck-extend-existing-relationship, checked on 11/30/2018.

OnDeck Capital, Inc. (2018a): About us. Helping small businesses reach their goals. Available online at https://www.ondeck.com/company, checked on 11/23/2018.

OnDeck Capital, Inc. (2018b): Customer Support. We're on top of it. Available online at https://www.ondeck.com/support, checked on 11/23/2018.

OnDeck Capital, Inc. (2018c): Fixed Term Loans. Grow and invest in your business. Available online at https://www.ondeck.com/term-loans.

OnDeck Capital, Inc. (Ed.) (2018d): ondeck. 2017 Annual Report, checked on 11/23/2018.

OnDeck Capital, Inc. (Ed.) (2020): How It Works. Available online at https://www.ondeck.com/how-it-works, checked on 2/19/2020.

OnVista (2020a): US-Dollar – Renminbi Yuan | US Dollar Chinesischer Renminbi Yuan Kurs | Wechselkurs | USD CNY | aktueller Kurs. onvista media GmbH. Available online at https://www. onvista.de/devisen/US-Dollar-Renminbi-Yuan-USD-CNY, checked on 4/1/2020.

OnVista (Ed.) (2020b): USD/SEK | US Dollar Schwedische Krone Kurs | Wechselkurs | USD SEK | aktueller Kurs. Available online at https://www.onvista.de/devisen/USD-SEK-USD-SEK, updated on 7/9/2020, checked on 7/9/2020.

OnVista (Ed.) (2020c): US-Dollar – Kanadischer Dollar. Available online at https://www.onvista.de/ devisen/US-Dollar-Kanadischer-Dollar-USD-CAD, updated on 8/20/2020, checked on 8/20/2020.

Orçun, Kaya (2017): Robo-advice. a true innovation in asset management. Deutsche Bank Research (EU Monitor Global Financial Markets). Available online at https://www.dbresearch.de/PROD/ RPS_DE-PROD/PROD0000000000449125/Robo-advice_%E2%80%93_a_true_innovation_in_ asset_managemen.PDF, checked on 9/26/2018.

Osterwalder, Alexander; Pigneur, Yves (2013): Business model generation. A handbook for visionaries, game changers, and challengers. New York: Wiley&Sons.

Öynhausen, Hauke Christian (2015): Nutzung Kollektiver Intelligenz am Kapitalmarkt. Dissertation. Josef Eul Verlag GmbH.

P2PMarketData (Ed.) (2019a): Crowdfunding in China: A Look at the World's Largest Market. Available online at https://p2pmarketdata.com/crowdfunding-china/, updated on 7/12/2019, checked on 3/15/2020.

P2PMarketData (Ed.) (2019b): The Future of P2P Lending in China: Is There a Time After the Great Cleanup? Available online at https://p2pmarketdata.com/p2p-lending-china/, updated on 7/13/2019, checked on 3/15/2020.

Pan, Wei; Altshuler, Yaniv; Pentland, Alex (2012): International Conference on Privacy, Security, Risk and Trust (PASSAT), 2012 and 2012 International Conference on Social Computing (SocialCom). 3-5 Sept. 2012, Amsterdam, Netherlands; [including workshops. Piscataway, NJ: IEEE. Available online at http://ieeexplore.ieee.org/servlet/opac?punumber=6403618.

Pankin, Vadym (2015): mBank – digital bank that conquered Polish market. Edited by LinkedIn. Available online at https://www.linkedin.com/pulse/mbank-digital-bank-conquered-polish-market-vadym-pankin, updated on 2/27/2015, checked on 2/19/2020.

Parker, Lewis (2019): Bitcoin, Not Blockchain. Edited by Unchained Capital. Available online at https://www.unchained-capital.com/blog/bitcoin-not-blockchain/, updated on 9/9/2019, checked on 9/13/2019.

PayPal (2017): PayPal – Verkäuferschutzrichtlinie. Edited by PayPal. Available online at https://www.paypal.com/de/webapps/mpp/ua/sellerprotection-full, checked on 10/1/2018.

PayPal (2018a): 2017 Annual Report / Form 10-K. Edited by PayPal. Available online at https://investor.paypal-corp.com/secfiling.cfm?filingID=1633917-18-29&CIK=1633917, checked on 10/1/2018.

PayPal (2018b): 2018 Annual Meeting of Stockholders and Proxy Statement & 2017 Annual Report. Available online at https://investor.paypal-corp.com/annuals-proxies.cfm, checked on 10/1/2018.

PayPal (2018c): PayPal Fact Sheet Q4 2017, p. 2. Available online at https://www.paypalobjects.com/digitalassets/c/website/marketing/global/shared/global/about/documents/paypal-fast facts-q417-and-fy17.pdf, checked on 10/1/2018.

PayPal (2018d): PayPal Reports First Quarter 2018 Results. Edited by BusinessWire. Available online at https://www.businesswire.com/news/home/20180425006571/en/PayPal-Reports-Quarter-2018-Results, checked on 10/1/2018.

PayPal (2018e): Wesentliche Hinweise zu unserem Service. Edited by PayPal. Available online at https://www.paypal.com/de/webapps/mpp/ua/servicedescription-full, checked on 10/1/2018.

PayPal (Ed.) (2019a): Fees. Available online at https://www.paypal.com/de/webapps/mpp/paypal-fees, checked on 12/9/2019.

PayPal (Ed.) (2019b): Home. Available online at https://www.paypal.com/de/home, checked on 12/9/2019.

PayPal (Ed.) (2019c): Über PayPal. Available online at https://www.paypal.com/de/webapps/mpp/about, checked on 12/9/2019.

PayPal (Ed.) (2020): 2020 Annual Meeting of Stockholders and Proxy Statement & Annual Report 2019. Available online at https://investor.paypal-corp.com/static-files/6b4a31d7-9941-464d-846d-3859fd7058dc, checked on 8/17/2020.

PayPal DE (Ed.) (2020): Zahlungsmethoden – Zahlungsarten. Available online at https://www.paypal.com/hr/webapps/mpp/accept-payments-online#feeCalculator, checked on 7/8/2020.

Personal Capital Corporation (2019a): Financial Tools. Overview. Available online at https://www.personalcapital.com/financial-software, checked on 12/16/2019.

Personal Capital Corporation (2019b): Wealth Management. Additional Services. Available online at https://www.personalcapital.com/wealth-management/additional-services, checked on 12/16/2019.

Personal Capital Corporation (2019c): Wealth Management. Overview. Available online at https://www.personalcapital.com/wealth-management, checked on 9/26/2018.

Peterson, Becky (2017): Bitcoin exchange Coinbase confirms its unicorn status with $1.6 billion valuation. Edited by Business Insider. Available online at https://www.businessinsider.de/co inbase-now-unicorn-valuation-series-d-funding-2017-8?r=US&IR=T, checked on 2/28/2019.

Phillips, Casey (2019): The Ultimate Chatbot UX Design Strategy for 2019. Edited by Chatbots Magazine online. Available online at https://chatbotsmagazine.com/the-ultimate-chatbot-ux-design-strategy-for-2019-b77b85e36f5a, updated on 1/19/2019, checked on 5/23/2019.

Pirner, Daniel; Fischer, Matthias (2018): Asset Allocation with Black-Litterman in a case study of Robo Advisor Betterment. In *Financial Research Note* 08/2018 (Nr. 04), pp. 1–24. Available online at https://d-nb.info/116404222X/34, checked on 5/29/2020.

Pitchbook (Ed.) (2019): 51credit Company Profile: Stock Performance & Earnings. Available online at https://pitchbook.com/profiles/company/81712-36, checked on 2/18/2019.

Punch Card Research (2016): OnDeck Capital (ONDK) & The Re-Engineering of Small Business Lending. Available online at http://www.punchcardresearch.com/ondeck-capital-ondk-the-re-engineering-of-small-business-lending/, checked on 11/23/2018.

PwC (Ed.) (2017): Global FinTech Report 2017. Redrawing the lines: FinTech's growing influence on Financial Services. Available online at https://www.pwc.com/gx/en/industries/financial-serv ices/assets/pwc-global-fintech-report-2017.pdf, checked on 9/26/2018.

PwC (Ed.) (2020): Initial coin offerings. Legal Frameworks and regulation for ICOs. Available online at https://www.pwc.ch/en/industry-sectors/financial-services/fs-regulations/ico.html, checked on 9/12/2019.

PYMNTS (2015): PayPal-Xoom Acquisition Completed. Edited by PYMNTS. Available online at https://www.pymnts.com/news/2015/paypal-xoom-deal-now-official, checked on 10/1/2018.

PYMNTS (2018): PayPal To Replace eBay In The S&P. Edited by PYMNTS. Available online at https://www.pymnts.com/news/2015/paypal-to-replace-ebay-in-the-sp, updated on 7/14/2018, checked on 10/1/2018.

Qian, Looby (2015): WeChat Red Envelope Digital Campaign – Sheng Li Digital. Edited by Shengli digital. Available online at http://www.shenglidigital.com/blog/wechat-red-envelope-cam paign/, checked on 10/17/2018.

Rao, Leena; Perez, Sarah; Lunden, Ingrid (2013): EBay's PayPal Acquires Payments Gateway Braintree For $800M In Cash. Edited by techcrunch. Available online at https://techcrunch. com/2013/09/26/paypal-acquires-payments-gateway-braintree-for-800m-in-cash/, checked on 10/1/2018.

Rashid, Brian (2017): This $130 Million Fund Is Leading The Way In Real Estate Crowdfunding. Available online at https://www.forbes.com/sites/brianrashid/2017/06/19/this-130-million-fund-is-leading-the-way-in-real-estate-crowdfunding/#6ad388936908x, updated on 6/17/2017, checked on 10/19/2018.

Remus, Dana; Levy, Frank S. (2015): Can Robots Be Lawyers? Computers, Lawyers, and the Practice of Law. In *SSRN Journal*. DOI: 10.2139/ssrn.2701092.

Renton, Peter (2015): An In Depth Look at the OnDeck/JPMorgan Chase Deal. We speak with Noah Breslow, CEO of OnDeck, to get details of their new partnership with JPMorgan Chase. Edited by LendIt Fintech News. Available online at https://www.lendacademy.com/an-in-depth-look-at-the-ondeckjpmorgan-chase-deal/, updated on 12/4/2015, checked on 11/23/2018.

Research and Markets (2018): Global CFD Market 2018-2022. Available online at https://www. researchandmarkets.com/reports/4585492/global-cfd-market-2018-2022, checked on 8/18/2018.

Responsive Capital Management (Ed.) (2019): Evolve Wealth Team Performance. Boost advisor productivity with human-centric AI. Grow revenue and loyalty with better, faster decisions. Available online at https://www.responsive.ai/, checked on 12/16/2019.

Revolut (2019): Deine digitale Banking-Alternative | Revolut. Available online at https://www.revolut.com/de/about, checked on 12/9/2019.

Rey, Jason Del (2018): After 15 years, eBay plans to cut off PayPal as its main payments processor. Edited by recode. Available online at https://www.recode.net/2018/1/31/16957212/ebay-adyen-paypal-payments-agreement, checked on 10/1/2018.

Riethdorf, Cornelius (2017): Startup valuation – how to value an early-stage company? SyndicateRoom. Available online at https://www.syndicateroom.com/learn/investor-tools-re ports/startup-valuation, checked on 9/26/2018.

Ripple (2014): The Ripple Protocol: A Deep Dive for Finance Professionals. Available online at https://assets.ctfassets.net/sdlntm3tthp6/resource-asset-r372/c53076ab408af8495 f928018a8e2e0d9/aa9579ea-c54d-40cb-91e1-c38947b44d4c.pdf, checked on 2/19/2019.

Ripple Labs Inc. (Ed.) (2017): Ripple Escrows 55 Billion XRP for Supply Predictability. Available online at https://ripple.com/insights/ripple-escrows-55-billion-xrp-for-supply-predictability/, checked on 2/19/2019.

Ripple Labs Inc. (Ed.) (2020a): ripple. The World's Most Reliable Global Payments Network. Available online at https://ripple.com/wp-content/uploads/2019/09/RippleNet-Overview.pdf, checked on 3/15/2020.

Ripple Labs Inc. (Ed.) (2020b): Solutions To Send Money Globally, Using Blockchain Technology. Available online at https://ripple.com/ripplenet/, checked on 2/19/2019.

Roderick, Mark (2013): SEC: FundersClub, AngelList Not Required To Register As Broker-Dealers. Available online at https://crowdfundattny.com/2013/04/02/sec-fundersclub-angellist-not-re quired-to-register-as-broker-dealers/, checked on 10/31/2018.

Ronsdorf, Marvin (2014): Crowdfunding. Edited by Henrik Schütt. Deutsches Institut für Bankwirtschaft (Band 11 (c) (11/2014)). Available online at https://deutsches-institut-bankwirt schaft.de/publikationen/Ronsdorf%20Crowdfunding.pdf, checked on 9/12/2019.

Rosov, Sviatoslav (2017): Machine Learning, Artificial Intelligence, and Robo-Advisers. The Future of Finance? CFA Institute. Available online at https://blogs.cfainstitute.org/marketintegrity/ 2017/07/12/machine-learning-artificial-intelligence-and-robo-advisers-the-future-of-finance/, updated on 6/12/2017, checked on 9/26/2018.

Ross, Alex (2018): Bitcoin: Geschichte und Unterschiede von BTC, BCH und BSV. Edited by BTC-Echo. Available online at https://www.btc-echo.de/bitcoin-geschichte-und-unterschiede-von-btc-bch-und-bsv/, updated on 12/13/2018, checked on 2/22/2019.

S&P Dow Jones Indices (7/14/2015): PayPal Holdings Set to Join S&P 100 & 500; Others to Join S&P MidCap 400 and S&P SmallCap 600. New York, NY. Blitzer, David; Guarino, David R. Available online at https://www.spice-indices.com/idpfiles/spice-assets/resources/public/documents/ 206958_ebaypalswiftroserti654.pdf?force_download=true, checked on 12/9/2019.

Sahlman, William A.; Scherlis, Daniel R. (1987 (Revised 2009)): A Method For Valuing High-Risk, Long-Term Investments. The "Venture Capital Method". Harvard Business School (Harvard Business School Background Note, 288–006).

Sameeh, Tamer (2017): The Blockchain Technology and The Fourth Industrial Revolution. Edited by Live Bitcoin News. Available online at https://www.livebitcoinnews.com/blockchain-technol ogy-fourth-industrial-revolution/, updated on 7/19/2017, checked on 3/5/2019.

Samlink (Ed.) (2020): Partners. Available online at https://www.samlink.fi/partners/?lang=en, checked on 2/19/2020.

SAP News (2016): ATB Financial Sends One of the World's First Real-Time Payments From Canada to Germany Using Blockchain Technology Supported by SAPATB Sends Payment via Blockchain with SAP. Edited by SAP News. Available online at https://news.sap.com/2016/07/atb-finan

cial-sends-one-of-the-worlds-first-real-time-payments-from-canada-to-germany-using-block
chain-technology-supported-by-sap/, checked on 3/6/2019.

Scalable Capital Limited (6/20/2017): BlackRock to Take a Minority Equity Stake in Digital
Investment Manager Scalable Capital. München, London. Available online at https://uk.scal
able.capital/press/BlackRock-to-take-a-minority-equity-stake-in-Scalable-Capital, checked on
9/26/2018.

Scalable Capital Limited (5/29/2018): Scalable Capital durchbricht Milliardengrenze. München,
London. Available online at https://de.scalable.capital/presse/scalable-capital-durchbricht-
milliardengrenze, checked on 9/26/2018.

Scalable Capital Limited (8/2/2019): Scalable Capital raises 25 million Euros in latest funding
round. München, London. Available online at https://uk.scalable.capital/press/scalable-capi
tal-25-million-funding-round, checked on 12/16/2019.

Schiller, Kai (2019): Initial Coin Offering (ICO) | Übersicht und Erklärung. Edited by Blockchainwelt.
Available online at https://blockchainwelt.de/initial-coin-offering-ico-zukunft-finanzierung/,
updated on 4/29/2019, checked on 3/18/2020.

Schlatt, Vincent; Schweizern, André; Urbach, Nils; Fridge, Gilbert (2016): Blockchain: Grundlagen,
Anwendungen und Potenziale. Available online at https://www.fim-rc.de/Paperbibliothek/
Veroeffentlicht/642/wi-642.pdf, checked on 2/19/2019.

Schlesinger, Joel (2017): How chatbots and artificial intelligence are changing wealth management.
Edited by The Globe and Mail Inc. Available online at https://www.theglobeandmail.com/re
port-on-business/will-computer-deep-learning-lead-to-higher-earnings/article34842587/,
updated on 5/5/2017, checked on 9/26/2018.

Schoolastic (Ed.) (2020): Financial Wizard. Available online at http://www.scholastic.com/browse/
lessonplan.jsp?id=1410, checked on 2/19/2020.

Seeger, Anna-Maria; Pfeiffer, Jella; and Heinzl, Armin (2017): When Do We Need a Human?
Anthropomorphic Design and Trustworthiness of Conversational Agents. Edited by SIGHCI.
Available online at https://aisel.aisnet.org/sighci2017/15/?utm_source=aisel.aisnet.org%
2Fsighci2017%2F15&utm_medium=PDF&utm_campaign=PDFCoverPages.

Seetharaman, Deepa; Mukherjee, Supantha (2014): EBay follows Icahn's advice, plans PayPal
spinoff in 2015. Edited by Reuters. Available online at https://www.reuters.com/article/us-
ebay-divestiture/ebay-follows-icahns-advice-plans-paypal-spinoff-in-2015-
idUSKCN0HP13D20140930, updated on 9/30/2014, checked on 12/9/2019.

Shin, Laura (2016): How The Blockchain Will Transform Everything From Banking To Government To
Our Identities. Edited by Forbes. Available online at https://www.forbes.com/sites/laurashin/
2016/05/26/how-the-blockchain-will-transform-everything-from-banking-to-government-to-
our-identities/#15c6024b558e, updated on 5/26/2016, checked on 3/5/2019.

Shontell, Alyson (2011): Mint Partners With Scholastic To Invade 30,000 Schools This Fall.
Business Insider. Available online at https://www.businessinsider.com/mint–scholastic-
quest-for-money-game-in-30000-schools-this-fall-2011-3?r=DE&IR=T, updated on 3/30/2011,
checked on 2/19/2020.

Shuringa, Harmen (2017): The legal implications of Blockchain. Edited by ABN Amro. Available
online at https://www.abnamro.com/en/newsroom/blogs/harmen-schuringa/2017/the-legal-
implications-of-blockchain.html, updated on 6/12/2017, checked on 3/5/2019.

Simon, Michael; Lindsay, Alvin F.; Sosa, Loly; Comparato, Paige (2018): The Automation of the
Legal Profession. In *THE YALE JOURNAL OF LAW & TECHNOLOGY* (Volume 20), pp. 234–310.
Available online at https://yjolt.org/sites/default/files/20_yale_j.l._tech._234.pdf, checked
on 4/11/2019.

Sindle, Guy; Santhana, Prakash; Srinivas, Val; Hernandez, Lisa; Maroz, Dzmitry; Goradia, Urval
(2017): Applying blockchain in securitization: opportunities for reinvention. In *Deloitte*.

Available online at https://digitalchamber.org/assets/sfig-blockchain-report.pdf, checked on 3/3/2019.

Sixt, Elfriede (2014): Schwarmökonomie und Crowdfunding: Webbasierte Finanzierungssysteme im Rahmen realwirtschaftlicher Bedingungen: Springer Science and Business Media. Available online at http://search.ebscohost.com/login.aspx?direct=true&scope=site&db=nlebk&db=nlabk&AN=920849.

Social Trading Guru (2018): Social Trading Networks Business Models. Available online at http://socialtradingguru.com/networks/social-trading-business-models, checked on 8/14/2018.

Son, Hugh (2017): This software does in seconds what took lawyers 360,000 hours. Edited by Independent Digital News and Media. Available online at https://www.independent.co.uk/news/business/news/jp-morgan-software-lawyers-coin-contract-intelligence-parsing-financial-deals-seconds-legal-working-a7603256.html, updated on 2/28/2017, checked on 4/10/2019.

Spöde, Sven (2018): Wechat-Mini-Programme: Kleine Anwendungen mit großer Wirkung. t3n Magazin. Available online at https://t3n.de/news/wechat-mini-programme-911797/, updated on 1/16/2018, checked on 10/17/2018.

Steinkühler, Dominik (2017): Mehr Flexibilität im Kreditgeschäft. In Wilhelm Niehoff, Stefan Hirschmann (Eds.): Aspekte der Digitalisierung in Banken. Köln: Bank-Verlag GmbH (Die Bank), pp. 39–43.

Surowiecki, James (2005): The wisdom of crowds. 1. ed. New York, NY: Anchor Books.

Swedroe, Larry (2014): What's the best incentive scheme for fund managers? Available online at https://www.cbsnews.com/news/whats-the-best-incentive-scheme-for-fund-managers/, checked on 8/9/2018.

Tapscott, Don; Tapscott, Alex (2016): Blockchain revolution. How the technology behind Bitcoin is changing money, business, and the world. International edition. New York, New York: Portfolio/Penguin. Available online at https://books.google.de/books?id=NqBiCgAAQBAJ&pg=PT108&dq=tapscott+let+the+code+speak+for+itself&hl=de&sa=X&ved=0ahUKEwipp9np6IDoAhW1QEEAHYOgBDQQ6AEIKTAA#v=onepage&q=tapscott%20let%20the%20code%20speak%20for%20itself&f=false, checked on 3/4/2020.

Taylor, Allen (2017): The Growth of Lending-as-a-Service. Edited by Lending Times. Available online at https://lending-times.com/2017/08/15/the-growth-of-lending-as-a-service/, updated on 8/15/2017, checked on 11/30/2018.

TechNavio (Ed.) (2018): Global Crowdfunding Market 2018–2022. Available online at https://www.technavio.com/report/global-crowdfunding-market-analysis-share, checked on 3/15/2020.

Tencent (2016): 2015 Annual Report, p. 3. Available online at https://www.tencent.com/en-us/articles/1700051460102129.pdf, checked on 10/16/2018.

Tencent (2018): 2018 Second Quarter Corporate Overview, p. 8. Available online at http://www.tencent.com/attachments/CorporateOverview2Q18.pdf, checked on 10/17/2018.

Tencent (Ed.) (2020): Tencent Holdings Limited 2019 Annual Report. Incorporated in the Cayman Islands with limited liability. Available online at https://cdc-tencent-com-1258344706.image.myqcloud.com/uploads/2020/04/02/ed18b0a8465d8bb733e338a1abe76b73.pdf, checked on 8/17/2020.

Terekhova, Maria (2017): AXA turns to smart contracts for flight-delay insurance. Edited by Business Insider. Available online at https://www.businessinsider.de/axa-turns-to-smart-contracts-for-flight-delay-insurance-2017-9?r=US&IR=T, updated on 9/15/2017, checked on 3/5/2019.

Tertilt, Michael; Scholz, Peter (2018): To Advise, or Not to Advise – How Robo-Advisors Evaluate the Risk Preferences of Private Investors. In *JWM* 21 (2), pp. 70–84. DOI: 10.3905/jwm.2018.21.2.070.

The Vanguard Group Inc. (2014): Vanguard Personal Advisor Services. Available online at https://personal.vanguard.com/pdf/r119.pdf?2210113091, checked on 9/27/2018.

The Vanguard Group Inc. (Ed.) (2018): Frequent questions about Vanguard advice. Available online at https://investor.vanguard.com/financial-advisor/common-questions, checked on 9/27/2018.

The Vanguard Group Inc. (Ed.) (2020a): Fast facts about Vanguard. Available online at https://about.vanguard.com/who-we-are/fast-facts/, checked on 8/20/2020.

The Vanguard Group Inc. (Ed.) (2020b): Advisor Client Relationship Summary (Form CRS). Available online at https://personal.vanguard.com/pdf/vpabroc.pdf, updated on 6/30/2020, checked on 8/17/2020.

The World Bank (4/8/2019): Record High Remittances Sent Globally in 2018. Washington. Available online at https://www.worldbank.org/en/news/press-release/2019/04/08/record-high-remittances-sent-globally-in-2018, checked on 3/15/2020.

Thiele, Frank; Koslowski, Jano; Schmitt, Marc; Meißner, Sebastian (2017): Richtlinie über Zahlungsdienste (PSD2) – ein strategischer Wendepunkt? Available online at https://www2.deloitte.com/content/dam/Deloitte/de/Documents/financial-services/Deloitte_Richtlinie%20%C3%BCber%20Zahlungsdienste%20(PSD2).pdf, checked on 2/18/2019.

Thomas, Michael (2017): Why Kickstarter Decided to Radically Transform Its Business Model. Available online at https://www.fastcompany.com/3068547/why-kickstarter-decided-to-radically-transform-its-business-model, updated on 12/4/2017, checked on 10/30/2018.

Thomson Reuters (5/9/2016): Thomson Reuters 2016 Know Your Customer Surveys Reveal Escalating Costs and Complexity. London / New York. Available online at https://www.thomsonreuters.com/en/press-releases/2016/may/thomson-reuters-2016-know-your-customer-surveys.html, checked on 3/3/2018.

Thrasher, Michael (2018): A Primer on Artificial Intelligence for Financial Advisors. Available online at http://www.wealthmanagement.com/technology/primer-artificial-intelligence-financial-advisors, updated on 1/26/2018, checked on 12/16/2019.

Tracxn (2016): Tracxn Report December 2016. Available online at https://blog.tracxn.com/2016/12/08/robo-advisors-report-december-2016/, checked on 9/10/2019.

Types of Oracles (2019). Available online at https://blockchainhub.net/blockchain-oracles/, updated on July 2019, checked on 3/5/2019.

U.S. Securities and Exchange Commission (Ed.) (2011): Registration Under the Securities Act of 1933. Available online at https://www.sec.gov/fast-answers/answersregis33htm.html, updated on 9/2/2011, checked on 3/23/2020.

U.S. Securities and Exchange Commission (2017): Regulation Crowdfunding. Available online at https://www.sec.gov/smallbusiness/exemptofferings/regcrowdfunding, checked on 9/14/2018.

U.S. Securities and Exchange Commission (7/25/2017): Report of Investigation Pursuant to Section 21(a) of the Securities Exchange Act of 1934: The DAO. Available online at https://www.sec.gov/litigation/investreport/34-81207.pdf, checked on 3/23/2020.

U.S. Securities and Exchange Commission (2020): Avant Loans Funding Trust 2020-REV1 SEC Registration. Available online at https://sec.report/CIK/0001802260, updated on 2/24/2020, checked on 6/1/2020.

UnionPay International (Ed.) (2020): Partner Institutions. Available online at https://www.unionpayintl.com/en/aboutUs/partners/##, updated on 2/24/2020, checked on 2/24/2020.

Uzialo, Adam (2018): Google Pay vs. Apple Pay vs. Samsung Pay. Edited by Business.com. Available online at https://www.business.com/articles/google-pay-vs-apple-pay-vs-samsung-pay/, checked on 10/6/2018.

Verhage, Julie (2018): Credit Karma Missed 2017 Revenue Target, Documents Show. Edited by Bloomberg. Available online at https://www.bloomberg.com/news/articles/2018-04-16/credit-karma-missed-2017-revenue-target-documents-show, checked on 2/18/2019.

Vogel, John H. Jr.; Moll, Benjamin S. (2014): Crowdfunding for Real Estate. In *The Real Estate Finance Journal* (Summer/Fall 2014), pp. 5–16. Available online at https://www.google.com/url?sa%3Dt%26rct%3Dj%26q%3D%26esrc%3Ds%26source%3Dweb%26cd%3D1%26cad%3Drja%26uact%3D8%26ved%3D2ahUKEwiY9q2r6KHeAhXmlIsKHTkoA3wQFjAAegQICBAC%26url%3Dhttps//%3A%2F%2Fwww.researchgate.net%2Fprofile%2FAnna_Moisello%2Fpost%2FCrowdfunding_in_Real_Estate_Are_there_any_recommendable_publications%2Fattachment%2F59d64e8679197b80779a7d9c%2FAS%253A493141058744320%25401494585398022%2Fdownload%2Fcrowdfunding_real_estate.pdf%26usg%3DAOvVaw16UiSSOlDUgfQt7OFykLCXhttps://www.google.com/url?sa=t&rct=j&q=&esrc=s&source=web&cd=1&cad=rja&uact=8&ved=2ahUKEwiY9q2r6KHeAhXmlIsKHTkoA3wQFjAAegQICBAC&url=https://%3A%2F%2Fhttps://www.researchgate.net%2Fprofile%2FAnna_Moisello%2Fpost%2FCrowdfunding_in_Real_Estate_Are_there_any_recommendable_publications%2Fattachment%2F59d64e8679197b80779a7d9c%2FAS%253A493141058744320%25401494585398022%2Fdownload%2Fcrowdfunding_real_estate.pdf&usg=AOvVaw16UiSSOlDUgfQt7OFykLCX, checked on 10/25/2018.

Wagner, Kurt (2016): AngelList has acquired Product Hunt for around $20 million. Available online at https://www.recode.net/2016/12/1/13802154/angellist-product-hunt-acquisition/, checked on 10/29/2018.

Wang, Samantha (2011): How to Choose a Chinese Online Payment Solution. Available online at https://www.nanjingmarketinggroup.com/blog/china-internet/how-choose-chinese-online-payment-solution, checked on 10/10/2018.

we.trade (Ed.) (2020): Banking Partners. Available online at https://we-trade.com/banking-partners, updated on 3/10/2020, checked on 3/10/2020.

Wealthfront Inc. (2019a): Wealthfront Investment Methodology White Paper. Available online at https://research.wealthfront.com/whitepapers/investment-methodology/, checked on 12/16/2019.

Wealthfront Inc. (2019b): What is the minimum amount required to invest with Wealthfront? Available online at https://support.wealthfront.com/hc/en-us/articles/210994423-What-is-the-minimum-amount-required-to-invest-with-Wealthfront-, updated on 11/5/2019, checked on 12/16/2019.

Wealthfront Inc. (Ed.) (2019c): How much does Wealthfront charge for its service? Available online at https://support.wealthfront.com/hc/en-us/articles/211003683-How-much-does-Wealthfront-charge-for-its-service-, updated on 12/16/2019, checked on 12/16/2019.

Wei, Chen; Yu, Zhichen; Fong, Simon (2018): How to Build a Chatbot: Chatbot Framework and its Capabilities. In: Proceedings of 2018 10th International Conference on Machine Learning and Computing (ICMLC 2018). University of Macau, China, February 26–28, 2018. New York, New York: The Association for Computing Machinery (ICPS), pp. 369–373. Available online at https://dl.acm.org/citation.cfm?id=3195169, checked on 5/23/2019.

Weixin (2018): Frequently Asked Questions – WeChat Pay. Available online at https://pay.weixin.qq.com/wechatpay_guide/help_faq.shtml, checked on 10/17/2018.

WELT (2014): „Stromberg" zahlt Geld an seine Unterstützer. Available online at https://www.welt.de/wirtschaft/article133360379/Stromberg-zahlt-Geld-an-seine-Unterstuetzer.html, updated on 10/16/2014, checked on 11/29/2018.

Wenzlaff, Karsten; Philipps, Robert (2015): Crowdfunding. Bestandsaufnahme und Ausblick nach dem Kleinanlegerschutzgesetz. Bonn: Friedrich-Ebert-Stiftung Abt. Wirtschafts- und Sozialpolitik (WISO Direkt, 28).

Whitman, Meg (2006): Wall Street Folly: Ebay: Conference call transcript – 1/18/06. Available online at http://archive.is/vlMX, checked on 10/6/2018.

Wikifolio (2019a): In wikifolios investieren. Die wikifolio-Gebühren. Available online at https://www.wikifolio.com/de/de/hilfe/tutorials-anleger/zertifikat-investieren/wikifolio-gebuehren, checked on 12/23/2019.

Wikifolio (2019b): So wird Ihr wikifolio investierbar. Legitimierung des wikifolio.com Accounts. Available online at https://www.wikifolio.com/de/de/hilfe/tutorials-trader/handelsidee-inves tierbar/legitimierung, checked on 12/23/2019.

Wikifolio (2019c): So wird Ihr wikifolio investierbar: Das telefonische Emissionsgespräch. Available online at https://www.wikifolio.com/de/de/hilfe/tutorials-trader/handelsidee-investierbar/ emissionsgespraech, checked on 12/23/2019.

Wikifolio (2019d): Trader-Vergütung. Erfolgsprämie für wikifolio-Trader. Available online at https://www.wikifolio.com/de/de/hilfe/tutorials-trader/trader-verguetung/performancegebuehr, checked on 12/23/2019.

Wikifolio (2019e): Wer kann ein wikifolio erstellen? Wie wird ein wikifolio investierbar? Available online at https://www.wikifolio.com/de/de/hilfe/faq/social-trading/wikifolio-investierbar, checked on 12/23/2019.

Wikifolio (2019f): Wie alles begann. Available online at https://www.wikifolio.com/de/de/ueber-wi kifolio/firmengeschichte, checked on 12/23/2019.

Wikifolio (2019g): Wie sicher sind Invesitionen in wikifolio-Zeritifikate? Available online at https://www.wikifolio.com/de/de/hilfe/faq/geldanlage/sichere-investition, checked on 12/23/2019.

Wikifolio (2019h): wikifolio finden. Die Top-wikifolio-Rangliste. Available online at https://www.wi kifolio.com/de/de/hilfe/tutorials-anleger/wikifolio-finden/top-wikifolio-rangliste, checked on 9/4/2018.

Wikifolio (2019i): wikifolio-Arten. Die wikifolio-Kategorien. Available online at https://www.wikifo lio.com/de/de/hilfe/tutorials-anleger/wikifolio-arten/kategorien, checked on 12/23/2019.

Wildau, Gabriel; Jia, Yizhen (2019): Ant Financial's money market fund shrinks to 2-year low. Edited by Financial Times. Available online at https://www.ft.com/content/35bbbef6-20a8-11e9-b126-46fc3ad87c65, updated on 1/28/2019, checked on 7/29/2019.

WINHELLER Rechtsanwaltsgesellschaft mbH (Ed.) (2020a): Bitcoin und Steuer: Besteuerung von Kryptowährungen. Available online at https://www.winheller.com/bankrecht-finanzrecht/bit cointrading/bitcoinundsteuer.html, checked on 3/31/2020.

WINHELLER Rechtsanwaltsgesellschaft mbH (Ed.) (2020b): Blockchain, Bitcoin und Kryptowährungen. Available online at https://www.winheller.com/bankrecht-finanzrecht/bit cointrading.html, checked on 3/31/2020.

Wisniewski, Mary (2013): Intuit Finally Lets Banks White-Label Mint. Edited by American Banker. Available online at https://www.americanbanker.com/news/intuit-finally-lets-banks-white-label-mint, checked on 2/18/2019.

WorldPay (Ed.) (2017): Global Payment Report. Your definitive guide to the world of online payments. Available online at https://worldpay.globalpaymentsreport.com/wp-content/up loads/reports/GPR-English-2017.pdf, checked on 10/1/2018.

Wu, Kane; Zhu, Julie (2018): Explainer: Ant Financial's $150 billion valuation, and the big recent bump-up. Reuters. Available online at https://www.reuters.com/article/us-antfinancial-valua tion/explainer-ant-financials-150-billion-valuation-and-the-big-recent-bump-up-idUSKBN1HP1AA, checked on 10/10/2018.

Xiao, Eva (2017): Three months after launch, this unbanked crypto exchange made $7.5m in profit. Edited by Techinasia. Available online at https://www.techinasia.com/cryptocurrency-ex change-binance, updated on 12/1/2017, checked on 3/23/2020.

Yahoo Finance (Ed.) (2020a): ADYEN (ADYEN.AS) Stock Price, Quote, History & News. Available online at https://finance.yahoo.com/quote/ADYEN.AS/, updated on 7/30/2020, checked on 7/30/2020.

Yahoo Finance (Ed.) (2020b): Alibaba Group Holding Limited (BABA) Stock Price, Quote, History & News. Available online at https://finance.yahoo.com/quote/BABA?p=BABA&.tsrc=fin-srch, updated on 7/30/2020, checked on 7/30/2020.

Yahoo Finance (Ed.) (2020c): Amazon.com, Inc. (AMZN) Stock Price, Quote, History & News. Available online at https://finance.yahoo.com/quote/AMZN?p=AMZN&.tsrc=fin-srch, updated on 7/30/2020, checked on 7/30/2020.

Yahoo Finance (Ed.) (2020d): Apple Inc. (AAPL) Stock Price, Quote, History & News. Available online at https://finance.yahoo.com/quote/AAPL?p=AAPL&.tsrc=fin-srch, updated on 7/30/2020, checked on 7/30/2020.

Yahoo Finance (Ed.) (2020e): PayPal Holdings, Inc. (PYPL) Stock Price, Quote, History & News. Available online at https://finance.yahoo.com/quote/PYPL?p=PYPL&.tsrc=fin-srch, updated on 7/30/2020, checked on 7/30/2020.

Yahoo Finance (Ed.) (2020f): SamsungElectronics (005930.KS) Stock Price, Quote, History & News. Available online at https://finance.yahoo.com/quote/005930.KS?p=005930.KS&.tsrc=fin-srch, updated on 7/30/2020, checked on 7/30/2020.

Yahoo Finance (Ed.) (2020g): TENCENT HOLDINGS LIMITED (TCEHY) Valuation Measures & Financial Statistics. Available online at https://finance.yahoo.com/quote/TCEHY?p=TCEHY, updated on 7/30/2020, checked on 7/30/2020.

Yan, Jiaqi; Yu, Wayne; Zhao, J. Leon (2015): How signaling and search costs affect information asymmetry in P2P lending: the economics of big data. In *Financial Innovation* 1 (1). DOI: 10.1186/s40854-015-0018-1.

Young, Jamie (2019): Lending Club vs. Prosper: Which is Right for You? Edited by credible. Available online at https://www.credible.com/blog/personal-loan/how-lending-club-and-prosper-look-different/, updated on 12/16/2019, checked on 12/23/2019.

Yuen, Stacey (2017): MIT expert says robo-advisors lack an important ability: They can't create trust. CNBC. Available online at https://www.cnbc.com/2017/11/05/mit-expert-robert-merton-on-the-future-of-robo-advisors.html, checked on 9/27/2018.

Zaveri, Paayal (2017): Facebook Messenger users can now send money to each other with PayPal. Edited by CNBC. Available online at https://www.cnbc.com/2017/10/20/facebook-messenger-send-money-with-paypal.html, checked on 10/1/2018.

Zhang, Laney (2018): Regulation of Cryptocurrency in Selected Jurisdictions. China. In *The Law Library of Congress, Global Legal Research Center*, pp. 30–34. Available online at https://www.loc.gov/law/help/cryptocurrency/regulation-of-cryptocurrency.pdf, checked on 3/3/2019.

Zhang, Shu; Ruwitch, John (2018): Ant Financial is shifting its focus from finance to tech services: Sources. Edited by Reuters. Available online at https://www.reuters.com/article/us-china-ant-financial-regulation-exclus/exclusive-ant-financial-shifts-focus-from-finance-to-tech-services-sources-idUSKCN1J10WV, updated on 6/5/2018, checked on 12/9/2019.

Zhu, Feng; Zhang, Ying; Palepu, Krishna G.; Woo, Anthony K.; Hua Dai, Nancy (2019): Ant Financial. Edited by Harvard Business School Publishing. Harvard Business School. Available online at https://hbsp.harvard.edu/product/617060-PDF-ENG?Ntt=HBR+fintech+2020+fintech*&itemFindingMethod=Search, checked on 6/24/2020.

Ziegler, Tania; Shneor, Rotem; Garvey, Kieran; Wenzlaff, Karsten; Yerolemou, Nikos; Hao, Rui; Zhang, Bryan (2018): Expanding Horizons. The 3rd European Alternative Finance Industry

Report. Cambridge Centre for Alternative Finance. Available online at https://www.research
gate.net/publication/322642158_Expanding_Horizons_The_3rd_European_Alternative_
Finance_Industry_dReport, checked on 9/14/2018.

Ziegler, Tanja; Shneor, Rotem; Wenzlaff, Karsten; Wang, Wanxin Britney; Kim, Jaesik; Odorovic, Ana
et al. (2020): The Global Alternative Finance Market Benchmarking Report. Trends, Opportunities
and Challenges for Lending, Equity, and Non-Investment Alternative Finance Models. Edited by
Cambridge Centre for Alternative Finance. University of Cambridge Judge Business School.
Available online at https://jbs.cam.ac.uk/wp-content/uploads/2020/08/2020-04-22-ccaf-
global-alternative-finance-market-benchmarking-report.pdf, checked on 8/17/2020.

ZuluTrade (2014): FAQ. Available online at https://us.zulutrade.com/faq, checked on 8/20/2018.

ZuluTrade (2018): Trader Guide. Available online at https://us.zulutrade.com/trader-guide?Lang=
en, updated on 3/21/2018, checked on 12/23/2019.

ZuluTrade (2019a): Automatischer Handel nach Ihren Regeln! Available online at https://de.zulu
trade.com/automated-trading, checked on 12/23/2019.

ZuluTrade (2019b): Europäisches Forex-Handelshandbuch. Available online at https://de.zulu
trade.com/eu-guide, checked on 12/23/2019.

ZuluTrade (2019c): Geschäftszeiten des Kundendienst. Available online at https://de.zulutrade.
com/support, checked on 12/23/2019.

ZuluTrade (2019d): ZuluRanking-System. Available online at https://de.zulutrade.com/zuluranking,
checked on 12/23/2019.

ZuluTrade (2019e): ZuluTrade-Investor-Handbuch. Available online at https://de.zulutrade.com/
user-guide, checked on 12/23/2019.

ZuluTrade (Ed.) (2020): Forex-Handelsapps. Available online at https://de.zulutrade.com/plat
forms, checked on 8/20/2018.

Index

https://doi.org/10.1515/9783110704907-019

About the author

Matthias Fischer is professor of finance and banking at the Institute of Technology Nuremberg Georg-Simon-Ohm in Germany. His research has focused on strategy and M&A in the banking sector, value-based management, robo-advisory and fintechs. Dr. Fischer also serves as a member of the Groupe de Recherche en Management at the IAE Nice Graduate School of Management, Université Côte d'Azur in France. He is internationally active as a strategy and financial advisor. Matthias Fischer publishes on the impact of innovation in banking and finance, as well as strategy and value-based management in the banking sector. He regularly gives guest lectures at several European universities. He is also the founder of a strategy consulting company and of a fintech start-up in the field of robo advisory.

https://doi.org/10.1515/9783110704907-020

www.ingramcontent.com/pod-product-compliance
Lightning Source LLC
Chambersburg PA
CBHW081053220326
41598CB00038B/7081